CAMBRIDGE
COMPANION TO
THE AFRICAN
AMERICAN NOVEL

EDITED BY

MARYEMMA GRAHAM
University of Kansas

CAMBRIDGE
UNIVERSITY PRESS

CAMBRIDGE UNIVERSITY PRESS
Cambridge, New York, Melbourne, Madrid, Cape Town, Singapore,
São Paulo, Delhi, Dubai, Tokyo

Cambridge University Press
The Edinburgh Building, Cambridge CB2 8RU, UK

Published in the United States of America by Cambridge University Press, New York

www.cambridge.org
Information on this title: www.cambridge.org/9780521016377

First published 2004

A catalogue record for this publication is available from the British Library

Library of Congress Cataloguing in Publication data
The Cambridge Companion to the African American novel / edited by Maryemma Graham.
p. cm. – (Cambridge companions to literature)
Includes bibliographical references and index.
ISBN 0 521 81574 6 – ISBN 0 521 01637 1 (paperback)
1. American fiction – African American authors – History and criticism.
2. African Americans in literature.
I. Graham, Maryemma. II. Series.
PS374.N4C36 2003
813.009′896073 – dc21 2003046126

ISBN 978-0-521-81574-1 Hardback
ISBN 978-0-521-01637-7 Paperback

Transferred to digital printing 2009

The Cambridge Companion to the African American Novel

The Cambridge Companion to the African American Novel presents new essays covering the one hundred and fifty year history of the African American novel. Experts in the field from the US and Europe address some of the major issues in the genre: passing, the Protest novel, the Blues novel, and womanism among others. This *Companion* is full of fresh insights into the symbolic, aesthetic, and political function of canonical and non-canonical fiction. Chapters examine works by Ralph Ellison, Leon Forrest, Toni Morrison, Ishmael Reed, Alice Walker, John Edgar Wideman, and many others. They reflect a range of critical methods intended to prompt new and experienced readers to consider the African American novel as a cultural and literary act of extraordinary significance. This volume, including a chronology and guide to further reading, is an important resource for students and teachers alike.

CONTENTS

CONTRIBUTORS

The editor is most grateful to Patty Jasper-Zellner for her tireless efforts in assisting with the preparation of this text.

GISELLE LIZA ANATOL is Assistant Professor of English at the University of Kansas. She is currently completing a book-length manuscript on representations of motherhood in contemporary Caribbean women's literature and has published on the work of Lorene Cary, Edwidge Danticat, Jamaica Kincaid, Audre Lorde, and Paule Marshall. Her edited collection on J. K. Rowling's Harry Potter series, *Reading Harry Potter: Critical Essays*, was published by Greenwood Press (2003).

HERMAN BEAVERS is Associate Professor of English at the University of Pennsylvania. He is the author of two books, *A Neighborhood of Feeling* (1986), and *Wrestling Angels into Song: The Fictions of Ernest J. Gaines and James Alan McPherson* (1995). He has completed a collection of poems entitled *Still Life with Guitar* and is currently working on *And Bid Him Sing*, which examines representations of susceptibility and shame in twentieth-century African American writing by black male writers.

KEITH BYERMAN is Professor of English and Women's Studies at Indiana State University and Associate Editor of *African American Review*. He has taught courses in African American and Southern literature and culture at the University of Texas, University of Vienna, and Columbus College in Georgia. He is the author of several books and articles, including works on Alice Walker, W. E. B. Du Bois, John Edgar Wideman, and folklore in contemporary fiction.

SUSANNE B. DIETZEL is the Director of the Women's Resource Center at Loyola University, New Orleans. Her publications have appeared in *Feminist Teacher*, *Southern Quarterly*, *The History of Southern Women's Literature*, and *The Oxford Companion to African American Literature*.

M. GIULIA FABI is the author of *Passing and the Rise of the African American Novel* (2001) and the editor of a series of Italian translations of African American novels. She is tenured Assistant Professor of American Literature at the University of Ferrara, Italy.

MARYEMMA GRAHAM is Professor of English at the University of Kansas and founder/director of the Project on the History of Black Writing. She has published extensively on American and African American literature and culture and has directed numerous national and international workshops and institutes on literature, literary history, criticism, and pedagogy. Her most recent books include *Fields Watered with Blood: Critical Essays on Margaret Walker* (2001) and *Conversations with Margaret Walker* (2002). She is currently completing *The House Where My Soul Lives*, the authorized biography of Walker.

FRITZ GYSIN has just retired as Professor of English and American Literature at the University of Berne, Switzerland. Author of numerous articles and two books on American and African American literature, he most recently edited *Apocalypse* (2001) and (with Christopher Mulvey) *Black Liberation in the Americas* (2001).

GEORGE HUTCHINSON is the author of *The Ecstatic Whitman* (1986) and *The Harlem Renaissance in Black and White* (1995). He is the Booth M. Tarkington Professor of Literary Studies at Indiana University, Bloomington.

LOVALERIE KING is Assistant Professor of English at Pennsylvania State University and has published a number of critical essays, articles, and reviews on African American literature. She recently completed *A Students' Guide to African American Literature: Fiction* and is currently revising for publication *The African American Literary Countertext on Theft, Race, and Ethics*.

MARILYN MOBLEY McKENZIE is Associate Professor of English and African American Studies at George Mason University and is the author of *Folk Roots and Mythic Wings in Sarah Orne Jewett and Toni Morrison: The Cultural Function of Narrative* (1992) published under her former name, Marilyn Sanders Mobley. She is currently completing a book on Toni Morrison entitled *Spaces for Readers: Toni Morrison's Narrative Poetics and Cultural Politics*.

CHRISTOPHER MULVEY is Professor of English and American Studies at King Alfred's College, Winchester. He is author of *Anglo-American Landscapes* (1983) and *Transatlantic Manners* (1990). With John Simons he edited *New York: City as Text* (1990), and with Fritz Gysin, he edited *Black Liberation in the Americas* (2001).

PIERRE-DAMIEN MVUYEKURE is Associate Professor of English and African American Literature at the University of Northern Iowa and has published on Ishmael Reed, Alice Walker, Jewell Parker Rhodes, Paul Laurence Dunbar, Melvin Tolson, Patricia Grace, and Velma Pollard.

CLAUDINE RAYNAUD is Professor of English and American literature at the University of François-Rabelais, Tours, France where she heads the research program in English (GRAAT). She has published articles on African American autobiography in English and French and is author of *Toni Morrison: L'Esthétique de la Survie*. She is currently completing a manuscript on Hurston's autobiographical selves and on Morrison and memory.

ASHRAF H. A. RUSHDY is Professor of African American Studies and English at Wesleyan University. He is the author of *The Empty Garden: The Subject of Late Milton* (1992), *Neo-Slave Narratives: Studies in the Social Logic of a Literary Form* (1999), and *Remembering Generations: Race and Family in Contemporary African American Fiction* (2001).

STEVEN C. TRACY is the author of several books, including *Langston Hughes and the Blues*, and editor of *Write Me a Few of Your Lines: A Blues Reader* (1999) and the forthcoming *A Historical Guide to Langston Hughes* and *A Historical Guide to Ralph Ellison*. A blues singer and harmonica player, he is Professor of Afro-American Studies at the University of Massachusetts, Amherst.

JERRY W. WARD JR. is Professor of English and African World Studies at Dillard University. He is compiler and editor of *Trouble the Water: 250 Years of African American Poetry* (1997) and editor of *Redefining American Literary History* (1990) with A. LaVonne Ruoff and *Black Southern Voices* (1992). A poet and frequent contributor to journals and anthologies, he is currently completing *Delta Narratives: Memory, Testimony and Social Change* with Kim Lacy Rogers.

CHRONOLOGY OF MAJOR WORKS AND EVENTS,
1645–2000

1492   Columbus discovered the West Indies, opening markets for
        slave labor
1526   100 African slaves brought to the North American continent
1619   Jamestown, Virginia colony established with twenty Africans as
        indentured servants
1643   Sugar introduced into the West Indies, requiring slave labor
1645   Trade in African slaves begins in Boston, later to be known as
        the triangular trade between North/South America, Europe
        and Africa
1705   Slave code defines slave status: all Negro, mulatto and Indian
        non-Christians
1740   Comprehensive "Negro Act" denies slaves basic freedoms,
        including the right to read
1760   *Narrative of the Uncommon Sufferings and Surprizing
        Deliverance of Briton Hammon*, considered the first dictated
        slave narrative in America
1773   Phillis Wheatley's *Poems on Miscellaneous Subjects*, first book
        published by a black slave in America
1775   First anti-slavery society organized in Philadelphia
1776   Colonies declare independence from Britain; Continental
        Congress votes against the importation of slaves in all thirteen
        united colonies
1793   First Fugitive Slave Act
1808   African slave trade officially ended in Britain
1816   American Colonization Society founded in Washington, DC to
        return freed slaves to Africa
1822   Denmark Vesey organizes slave revolt in Charleston, SC
1829   George Moses Horton, slave poet, publishes poems to purchase
        freedom; Mexico abolishes slavery and welcomes US fugitives

1830	International slave trade officially ends; illegal traffic in slaves continues
1830–60	Slave narratives become the most popular form of American literature
1831	Nat Turner leads slave revolt in Southhampton County, VA; Underground Railroad begins operation
1833	Oberlin College founded as first coeducational, racially integrated US college
1839	The *Amistad* revolt with fifty-three Africans led by Joseph Cinque
1845	*Narrative of the Life of Frederick Douglass, an American Slave, Written by Himself*
1850s	Hannah Crafts, *The Bondwoman's Narrative*, first novel by an African American woman; Congress passes second Fugitive Slave Act mandating all fugitive slaves be returned to their masters; massive fugitive slave hunts begin
1852	Harriet Beecher Stowe's *Uncle Tom's Cabin; or, Life among the Lowly*
1853	William Wells Brown's *Clotel, or the President's Daughter*, first known African American novel
1857	*Dred Scott* decision; African Americans denied access to federal court system
1859	Harriet E. Wilson's *Our Nig*
1859–62	*Anglo-African Magazine* published
1861–65	American Civil War
1861	Harriet Jacobs's *Incidents in the Life of a Slave Girl*, originally thought to be a fictitious narrative
1862	Emancipation Proclamation abolishes slavery in states fighting the Civil War
1865	13th Amendment passed, granting freedom to former slaves; Freedmen's Bureau and Freedman's Bank established; Ku Klux Klan formed in Pulaski, Tennessee; President Lincoln assassinated
1866	Civil Rights Act guarantees citizenship for all Americans
1867	Howard University founded in Washington, DC for former slaves; Reconstruction begins
1868	14th Amendment passed by Congress, granting African American citizenship and civil rights
1870	15th Amendment passed, granting the right to vote to African American male citizens
1877	Reconstruction ends

1881   Booker T. Washington founds Tuskegee Institute in Alabama

1883   Supreme Court repeals Civil Rights Act of 1866

1892   Frances Ellen Watkins Harper's *Iola Leroy; or, Shadows Uplifted*

1895   Booker T. Washington's "Atlanta Exposition Address"

1896   *Plessy v. Ferguson Supreme Court* case upholds separate but equal doctrine

1897   Alexander Crummell founds the American Negro Academy in Washington

1898   Grandfather clause introduced as voting requirement

1900   Charles Chesnutt's *House Behind the Cedars*; *Colored American Magazine* begins publishing as outlet for African American literature

1901   Booker T. Washington's *Up from Slavery*

1903   W. E. B. Du Bois's *Souls of Black Folk*

1904   *Voice of the Negro* begins publication

1909   NAACP formed

1910–30   The Great Migration of African Americans from the South to the North

1910   National Urban League formed; *The Crisis*, journal of the NAACP, founded by Du Bois, begins continuous publication; anti-lynching campaign begins

1911   Arthur A. Schomburg, bibliophile, founds Negro Society for Historical Research (later the Schomburg Center for Research in Black Culture)

1912   James Weldon Johnson's *The Autobiography of an Ex-Colored Man*

1914–18   World War I

1915   Death of Booker T. Washington, considered the end of an era of black accommodation; Association for the Study of Negro Life and History founded by Carter G. Woodson

1916   *Journal of Negro History* begins continuous publication; *Opportunity* magazine founded by National Urban League

1917   *Messenger* magazine founded by A. Philip Randolph and Chandler Owen; Bolshevik Revolution in Russia

1919   Du Bois organizes first Pan African Congress; the "Red Summer," more than eighty lynchings and twenty-five race riots; Claude McKay, "If We Must Die"; Langston Hughes, "The Negro Speaks of Rivers"

1920   19th Amendment grants women the right to vote; Prohibition begins; Marcus Garvey's First International Convention of the Negro Peoples of the World leads to the founding of the

	Universal Negro Improvement Association (UNIA) to promote racial solidarity and return to Africa; The New Negro (Harlem) Renaissance begins
1922	*Shuffle Along*, black musical, brings African American culture to Broadway; T. S. Eliot's *The Waste Land*; James Joyce's *Ulysses*; Claude McKay's *Harlem Shadows*
1923	Jean Toomer's *Cane*
1924	Death of Lenin in Soviet Union; Jessie Fauset's *There Is Confusion*
1925–27	Literary contests sponsored by *Opportunity* and *Crisis* magazines
1925	Alain Locke's *The New Negro: An Interpretation*, official anthology of the Harlem Renaissance; Josephine Baker's *La Revue Negre* (Paris); Theodore Dreiser's *American Tragedy*; F. Scott Fitzgerald's *The Great Gatsby*; Countee Cullen's *Color*; 40,000 KKK parade in Washington, DC
1926	Langston Hughes's *The Weary Blues* and "The Negro Artist and the Racial Mountain," considered manifesto for younger artists; Wallace Thurman's *Fire!! Devoted to Younger Negro Artists*; Carl Van Vechten's *Nigger Heaven*; Nella Larsen's *Quicksand*; Negro History Week established
1927	Al Jolson appears in blackface in first talking movie, *The Jazz Singer*
1928	Claude McKay's *Home to Harlem*; Nella Larsen's *Passing*
1929	US stock market crash, Great Depression begins; Wallace Thurman's *The Blacker the Berry*, William Faulkner's *The Sound and the Fury*
1930	Langston Hughes's *Not Without Laughter*; Nine Scottsboro boys charged with raping two white girls; Black Muslims founded in Detroit
1931	George Schuyler's *Black No More*
1933	New Deal legislation; WPA (Works Progress Administration) begins, provides support for writers and artists
1934–37	*Challenge* and *New Challenge*, founded by Dorothy West and Richard Wright
1936	Arna Bontemps's *Black Thunder*
1937	Zora Neale Hurston's *Their Eyes Were Watching God*; Richard Wright's "Blueprint for Negro Literature," groundbreaking critical article represents break with African American writers of the 1920s; Sterling Brown's *The Negro in American Fiction*
1939–45	World War II

1939	J. Saunders Redding's *To Make a Poet Black*, first critical study of African American poetry
1940	Richard Wright's *Native Son*; bestselling novel and Book-of-the-Month Club selection; era of the "protest novel" begins
1941	Armed Forces and government are desegregated; A. Philip Randolph threatens mass protest march
1942–51	*Negro Digest* founded by John H. Johnson, devoted exclusively to African American literature, reprints African American novels (resumes publication 1961–70)
1942	Margaret Walker's *For My People*; first black poet to win National Award
1944–46	*Negro Story* founded by Alice C. Browning
1945	Richard Wright's *Black Boy*; Chester Himes's *If He Hollers, Let Him Go*; *Ebony* magazine founded by John H. Johnson
1946	Anne Petry's *The Street*; Frank Yerby's *Foxes of Harrow*; Cold War begins
1948	Dorothy West's *The Living Is Easy*; Hugh Gloster's *Negro Voices in American Fiction*
1950–53	Korean War
1950	Gwendolyn Brooks, first African American to win Pulitzer Prize, for *Annie Allen* (1949)
1952	Ralph Ellison's *Invisible Man*, represents major break with protest tradition; first African American novel to win National Book Award (1953)
1953	James Baldwin's *Go Tell It on the Mountain*
1954	*Brown v. Topeka Board of Education* decision declares segregated schools unconstitutional
1955	Rosa Parks arrested for refusing to go to the back of the bus; Emmett Till lynched in Mississippi
1956	Montgomery bus boycott; Martin Luther King Jr. emerges as civil rights leader
1957	Gold Coast becomes Ghana, first African state to become independent; Little Rock Nine challenged by Arkansas Governor Orville Faubus
1958	Robert Bone's *The Negro Novel in America*
1959	Paule Marshall's *Brown Girl, Brownstones*; Lorraine Hansberry's *A Raisin in the Sun* begins long Broadway run
1960	Four North Carolina A & T students' first sit-in at Woolworth's lunch counter in Greensboro; Student Nonviolent Coordinating Committee (SNCC) founded; death of Richard Wright

1961   *Freedomways* begins continuous publication
1962   John O. Killens's *And Then We Heard the Thunder*; James
        Baldwin's *Another Country*; James Meredith faces federal
        troops as he enrolls at University of Mississippi
1963   Civil Rights March on Washington, King's "I Have a Dream"
        speech; Civil Rights Movement in full swing; President John
        F. Kennedy assassinated; death of W. E. B. Du Bois
1964   Three civil rights workers murdered in Mississippi, kicking off
        Freedom Summer; Martin Luther King receives Nobel Peace
        Prize; Congress passes Civil Rights Act of 1964; Organization of
        Afro-American Unity founded by Malcolm X
1965–73 Vietnam War
1965   Malcolm X's *The Autobiography of Malcolm X*; Selma to
        Montgomery March; assassination of Malcolm X; Watts riots;
        Black Arts Movement begins; Zora Neale Hurston's *Their Eyes
        Were Watching God*, recovered and reprinted after thirty years
1966   Black Panther Party founded; "Black Power" slogan adopted by
        Student Nonviolent Coordinating Committee (SNCC) and
        Congress on Racial Equality (CORE); Edward W. Brooke of
        Massachusetts becomes first elected black senator since
        Reconstruction; Margaret Walker's *Jubilee*, first neo-slave
        narrative
1967   Race riots in Newark, Detroit, Chicago; Thurgood Marshall
        becomes first black US Supreme Court justice; death of Langston
        Hughes; Harold Cruse's *The Crisis of the Negro Intellectual*
1968   Martin Luther King Jr. assassinated; Senator Robert F. Kennedy
        assassinated; *Black Fire*, by Larry Neal and Leroi Jones (Amiri
        Baraka), principal anthology for Black Arts Movement
1969   Anti-Vietnam War demonstrations/peace movement in full
        swing; Sam Greenlee's *The Spook Who Sat by the Door*
1970–76 *Negro Digest* changes to *Black World*, under editor Hoyt Fuller,
        becomes a shaping force in the Black Arts/Black Aesthetic
        Movement
1970   Toni Morrison's *The Bluest Eye*; Alice Walker's *The Third Life
        of Grange Copeland*; Toni Cade's *The Black Woman*; African
        American women's literary renaissance begins; Angela Davis one
        of FBI's "most wanted"
1971   Addison Gayle's *The Black Aesthetic* presents a nationalist
        critical approach; Ernest J. Gaines's *The Autobiography of Miss
        Jane Pittman*, first African American slave story made into a

mini-series; Nathan Huggins's *The Harlem Renaissance*, first critical study of the period; Attica prison revolt

1972   Ishmael Reed's *Mumbo Jumbo* defines black modernist tradition in fiction; Congress passes Equal Rights Amendment; George Kent's *Blackness and the Adventure of Western Culture*

1973   Leon Forrest's *There Is a Tree More Ancient than Eden*

1974   Albert Murray's *Train Whistle Guitar*

1975   Ntozake Shange's *for colored girls who have considered suicide/when the rainbow is enuf* on Broadway; Gayl Jones's *Corregidora*

1976   Alex Haley's *Roots*, TV mini-series in 1977, attracts largest viewing audience in history

1977   Lawrence Levine's *Black Culture and Black Consciousness: Afro-American Folk Thought from Slavery to Freedom*

1978   James Alan McPherson awarded Pulitzer Prize for *Elbow Room* (1977)

1979   Barbara Chase-Riboud's *Sally Hemings*, kicks off controversy over Thomas Jefferson's mistress; Octavia Butler's *Kindred*

1980   Barbara Christian's *Black Women Novelists*, first major study of African American women's literary tradition

1981   David Bradley's *The Chaneysville Incident*

1982   Audre Lorde's *Zami: A New Spelling of My Name*; Gloria Hull and others, *All the Women Are White, All the Blacks Are Men, But Some of Us Are Brave: Black Women's Studies*

1983   Alice Walker awarded Pulitzer Prize for *The Color Purple* (1982); Gloria Naylor's *The Women of Brewster Place*

1984   Houston A. Baker's *Blues, Ideology, and Afro-American Literature: A Vernacular Theory*, groundbreaking study of a blues-based literary tradition; death of Chester Himes; Trudier Harris's *Exorcizing Blackness: Historical and Literary Lynching and Burning Rituals*, first major interdisciplinary study of African American fiction

1985   Barbara Christian's *Black Feminist Criticism*

1987   Rita Dove awarded Pulitzer Prize for *Thomas and Beulah* (1986); deaths of John Oliver Killens and James Baldwin; Bernard Bell's *The Afro-American Novel and Its Tradition*; Hazel Carby's *Reconstructing Black Womanhood: The Emergence of the Afro-American Woman Novelist*

1988   Toni Morrison awarded Pulitzer Prize for *Beloved* (1987); Henry Louis Gates Jr.'s *The Signifying Monkey: A Theory of*

Afro-American Literary Criticism, represents a major
contribution to literary theory and criticism

1989   Charles Johnson wins National Book Award for *Middle Passage*;
death of Sterling Brown; Robert Stepto's *From Behind the Veil*
proposes influential theory of African American narrative

1990   Walter Mosley's *Devil in a Blue Dress*; New Black Aesthetic era
begins

1991   Death of Frank Yerby, bestselling African American author
to date

1992   Terri McMillan's *Waiting to Exhale* is international bestseller
and blockbuster movie; death of Audre Lorde

1993   Yusef Komunyakaa wins Pulitzer Prize for *Neon Vernacular*;
Toni Morrison is first African American to win Nobel Prize for
Literature

1994   Death of Ralph Ellison

1995   Nation of Islam organizes Million Man March in Washington,
DC; death of Toni Cade Bambara

1997   Death of Leon Forrest

1998   Death of Margaret Walker; Claudia Tate's *Psychoanalysis and
Black Novels: Desire and the Protocols of Race*; death of
Kwame Toure (Stokeley Carmichael), who popularized the term
"Black Power"

1999   Ralph Ellison's *Juneteenth*, published posthumously;
Encyclopedia Africana, largest digital encyclopedia of
publications from the black world; Rosa Parks awarded
Congressional Medal of Honor

2000   Million Women March; death of Gwendolyn Brooks

MARYEMMA GRAHAM

Introduction

One hundred and fifty years ago the first known African American novel was published by the fugitive slave William Wells Brown. Brown was as uncertain about the audience for *Clotel*, a story about American miscegenation, as he was about the kind of text he was creating. He continued to experiment with the form and "test" his audience by publishing variations of the story for a decade. For a people prevented from reading and writing by law, it is not surprising that novel writing and novelists have since become highly valued within African American culture. The very idea of an "African American novel" then *and* now precipitates an intense debate about the form and function of any belletristic genre. Embedded in the term is a history of achievement and a cultural heritage that raises as many questions as it answers. These questions – most often about aesthetics and ideology as conflicting and compatible tendencies in the novel – have given African American authors a place of primary importance in contemporary critical discourse. As important as it is, therefore, to consider the novels written by people of African descent in America as thoroughly American, the cultural visibility and unique history of these novels demands they be read with closer scrutiny.

This kind of "segregation" has its roots in recent literary criticism as much as in the development of the genre. The earliest studies of novels by black writers, those by Sterling Brown (*The Negro in American Fiction,* 1937) and Hugh Gloster (*Negro Voices in American Fiction*, 1948), placed emphasis on the novel as historical and documentary evidence of black humanity. A second generation of critics, including Robert Bone, author of *The Negro Novel in America* (1958), evaluated the novel in terms of the prevailing formalist paradigms. Subsequent criticism, such as Addison Gayle's *The Way of the New World: The Black Novel in America* (1975), signified a shift, an ideological conversion, giving a new dynamism to discussions of African American expressive culture. In the last twenty years, studies such as Barbara Christian's *Black Women Novelists* (1980) and Bernard Bell's

The Afro-American Novel and Its Tradition (1987) trace a linear progression from the slave narrative to the heyday of the novel in the 1940s and 50s, symbolized by the work of Richard Wright and Ralph Ellison.

Mainstream literary criticism gave little attention to the African American novel until well after the middle of the twentieth century. Both Wright and Ellison represented the literary tastes of an age struggling with its moral, social, and political agendas deriving in part from two world wars accompanied by severe domestic strife. Critics of the African American novel before the Civil Rights Movement of the 1960s generally noted two directions: the social realist or "protest novel" exemplified by Wright; and the impressionism or "high modernism" of Ralph Ellison. The prevailing opinion was that Richard Wright's *Native Son* (1940) and the autobiographical *Black Boy* (1940) consolidated a tradition of social and political criticism, while Ellison's *Invisible Man* (1952) was more "appropriately" modernist because it privileged textual concerns over ideological ones. For some, the choice was between Wright's pathological sense of black life in America and Ellison's inventive, regenerative vision of black culture. In hindsight, as many later critics have pointed out, this debate was fueled as much by Ellison's statement that a novel is "a work of art" and should not be "a disguised piece of sociology"[1] as by the anti-communist and Cold War sentiments of the period. For all the differences between their conceptions of the African American novel, Wright and Ellison foreground the novel's discursive function within African American literary culture. In the wake of the Civil Rights Movement and its aftermath, the African American novel became a reminder that race was a political minefield and that a racialized culture found its origins in the interactions among Europe, Africa, and the two Americas. Thus, the novel became grounded within an apex of ideas about culture and cultural transmission and served up notions of human possibility. The African American novel was capable of representing the broadest human concerns, it could absorb multiple forms of expressive culture, and it could engage readers across economic and racial lines.

If the Civil Rights Movement provided a catalyst for the novel in the social and political realm, the demise of new criticism and the democratization of the academy midwived its rebirth. The New Critics had eschewed any kind of political intent in art, calling for the autonomy of art divorced from politics. These critics had countered what they saw as the decline of serious literary art in the 1930s, laying the basis for how subsequent generations would read and interpret literature. African American novelists would remain imprisoned by these paradigms just as they were imprisoned by the racial climate of America. Indeed, many black American novelists of the late 1940s and 50s expatriated to Europe, where they found greater acceptance.[2] The rise of

Black Studies, on the other hand, put an academic face on the Civil Rights and Black Power movements and forced reconsiderations of scholarship, bringing a new generation of black intellectuals to the fore. An increase in cultural production became one of the byproducts of the resurgence of interest in African American life and culture after the 1960s. African American novelists responded to these developments with a virtual explosion of literary talent. In 1970 alone, more than twenty-five African American novels appeared, including the first novels by Sharon Bell Mathis, Louise Meriweather, Toni Morrison, Alice Walker, and Al Young.

As the status of the African American novel as a genre has improved and the demand for it has increased, scholars have found a rich and complex area for investigation and research. Whether driven by the novel's previous history of critical neglect or by the need to reframe the current premises and redirect critical discourses, contemporary scholars of the African American novel have succeeded in exploding traditional interpretations of genre, periodization, and literary influence. The work of Houston Baker, Keith Byerman, Hazel Carby, Barbara Christian, Peter Bruck and Wolfgang Karrer, Ann duCille, Frances Smith Foster, Henry Louis Gates, Farah Griffin, Trudier Harris-Lopez, Robert Stepto, and Claudia Tate come quickly to mind. Because recovery and revision remain central concerns to any scholar in ethnic or feminist studies, new areas of inquiry about African American novels are continually emerging. We have yet, for example, to fully explore the history of those African American novels published outside of the US or the divergent novel-writing traditions in the pre- and post-Civil War eras.

To say that the study of the African American novel has become institutionalized with emphasis being placed upon the discovery and training of new talent today is not an overstatement. Not only are African American novelists widely recognized and revered, but they also claim a significant share of the world's highest literary prizes and awards. This recognition and the great achievement of African American literary critics, William Andrews convincingly argues, have "had a salutary effect on the black community's sense of its own literary resources and on the white literate community's sense of the importance of those resources."[3]

To read African American novels is, nevertheless, to be confronted with difference. And one of the fundamental differences between the earlier periods of African American novel writing and the present is not only the range of voices that we hear but also the intensity and creativity with which African American writers transform their own and other literary traditions. James Olney notes that a remarkable quality of the early slave narrative – the predecessor to the novel – was not its unqualified uniqueness, but its

3

sameness. Like the slave narrators, early African American novelists had to map a course for their fictional texts between an often hostile audience and a demanding sponsor or publisher. This "triangular relationship of narrator, audience, and sponsors"[4] continued to dictate the development of thematic and formal conventions in the novel well into the twentieth century. The burden of multiple allegiances evokes a Du Boisian "double consciousness" and has been reinterpreted by Bernard Bell as "socialized ambivalence . . . the network of understandings that defines black American culture and informs black American consciousness . . . resulting from systematic barriers of exclusions and discrimination . . . producing a residue of shared memories and frames of reference."[5] While the social mission of the novel bears a special relationship to the history of African Americans, its aesthetic significance lies in the rhetorical strategies and metaphorical language the author uses to reenact if not resolve the novel's inherent tensions. At times these tensions appear in the form of conflicting literary traditions: sentimentalism and realism in Frances Harper and Jessie Fauset; or gothicism and naturalism in Richard Wright and Gayle Jones, for example. At other times the novelist creates dramatic tension by borrowing from African-derived oral forms or traditional Western literary forms. Charles Chesnutt turns to the folktale; Alice Walker, the epistolary novel and the female *Bildungsroman*; Charles Johnson and Sherley Anne Williams, the slave narrative; Margaret Walker, the folk novel; James Baldwin and Leon Forrest, the African American sermon; and Ralph Ellison and Albert Murray, the blues. The value placed on narrative closure differs markedly from novel to novel as well. Ernest Gaines wants us to see the lessons learned by the men and women who people his narratives; Toni Morrison emphasizes the internalization of those conflicts that shatter our sense of reality, making narrative closure difficult.

The African American novel maintains its reputation for linguistic and rhetorical innovation, through reinvention as a narrative construct and the intensity of its social meaning. Informed historical criticism with close textual analysis has brought more clarity to our understanding of what is meant by the African American novel today. Those critical perspectives that assumed the novel to be a unified text emerging from a logo-centric or writing-centered tradition are continually being revised. Thus, while scholars consider "the shortcomings of imposing structuralist, post-structuralist, psychoanalytic and feminist theories on black texts,"[6] the motivation to find more relevant theories or to produce an African American literary theory from within the texts has created a dynamic, provocative, and anesthetically complex interplay between the African American novelist, the reader, and critic. In the African American novel, the world may be real or imagined, history can continue to haunt and anger, and the reader must confront the terrible silences that have made us a nation with a shared history from which no one can escape. Even in the more popular novels – by Octavia Butler, J. California Cooper, or Walter Mosley, for example – the lives of black people are presented through a veil of humor or satiric displacement that defies simplistic analysis. The African American novelist is aware of a new relationship to the reader and critic, one that pleases and challenges, always testing the limits of our current critical understanding.

With the boundaries of critical theory still expanding and the recovery of history and texts an ongoing process for scholars and students, our best reading of the African American novel is an open one, which questions both the objective and subjective reality, recognizes both the discontinuities and continuities in traditions, and considers the relationships between oral and written forms of discourse. While these elements may be true of many novels, they apply with greater consistency to the novels written by African Americans who write against the very same establishment from which they need approval.

Of particular significance is the autobiographical impulse in the African American novel. The continuous need to explain and "inscribe the self" in a world which has historically denied the existence of that self gives both focus and intensity to the act of writing a story about black life. To examine the African American novel, then, is to understand its paradoxical nature: it grants the African American author the freedom to create a sustained vision in a world characterized by a series of counter-freedoms and conflicting visions; it allows for the humanistic formation of cultural memory, and it gives particularity to something that is often a fluctuating collection of perceptions and abstractions.

For many an African American author, the act of writing is part of a larger process of cultural revisionism, of redefining history and historical memory, and of confronting the past in innovative and provocative ways that are intentionally self-reflexive. To change the future is to to give meaning to a common past in new ways. The common part of America lies in the experience of slavery, an experience that has much to teach us when treated narratively. As the only indigenous form of American writing, the slave narrative "belongs" to African American novelists as no other literary form does. Remembering that the African American novel, like the novel generally, has the capacity to alter the world by putting it into words, African American writers have reappropriated the slave narrative as a principal means for looking more deeply into human consciousness as they alter that world for us. In the novels of Octavia Butler, Charles Johnson, Sherley Anne Williams, Ishmael Reed, and Toni Morrison, reclaiming and returning to slavery allows us to locate in that psychic wound those aspects of human identity which are part of all

Americans, that cannot be forgotten, the site of America's most important triumph and failure.

Although this companion covers a wide range of novels written by African Americans, it does not claim to be comprehensive. Rather it is intended to be a conversation between the reader and a group of scholars currently working in the field of African American fiction studies. Of major importance to the writers of these essays is the need to rethink African American cultural paradigms and traditions by broadening the general readership and making connections to the work in related disciplines. While the slave narrative is featured in many graduate and undergraduate classes, few courses cover the nineteenth-century beginnings of the novel. The majority of courses focus on novels written after Richard Wright. Still more concentrate on a select group of contemporary writers, and an increasing number of courses treat novels by African American women.

The rise of the African American novel in the nineteenth century is both a social and a literary phenomenon, important for understanding the boundaries that novelists have confronted and the ways in which these boundaries have been crossed. The nineteenth century is important also for understanding the current focus upon the history of slavery and the slave heritage. Since the early twentieth century, the African American novel has paid frequent attention to themes of migration, racial confrontation and adjustment, and the struggle for human, civil, and equal rights. Generally, novel writing increased during periods of radical social change and major demographic shifts. Peak periods include the 1920s when America's cities absorbed large numbers of black migrants and the publishing industry supported "race writing"; the 1930s when the Works Progress Administration (WPA) employed a large number of writers; and the 1970s when the call for a new literary politics became consolidated as the Black Arts Movement. Emphasis here is placed on the ways in which the African American novel has participated in an ongoing dialogue about race and identity while offering challenges to novelistic form and technique. Critics such as Houston Baker, Kimberly Benston, Philip Brian Harper, and Craig Werner, for example, have questioned the exclusionary tendencies of modernism, preferring instead to revisit the meaning of modernism and modernity in relation to post-Reconstruction African American life and its various cultural and ideological registers.

The rise of theory – in contrast to the rise of criticism – has been useful to the study of the African American novel generally because it has enabled new areas of investigation and validated others. What was once considered marginal to the study of black writing, political and social interpretations, for example, are now widely accepted as standard. Likewise, the African American novel readily lends itself to close textual examination and

deconstructive readings. Many recent scholars see African American literature as having been engaged in a specific productive process that transforms
conventional language. These critics interpret the novel as a textual system
complete with gaps and silences, one that assumes the reader to be more
actively engaged in the making of meaning. At the same time, the study
of African American literature and the novel has invigorated the study of
the Anglo-American and European tradition, especially in relationship to
concepts of the Other.

With more than 1,500 novels published between 1853 and 1980, and an
untold number published since,[7] the value of reading canonical and non-
canonical texts becomes apparent. In addition, the contemporary African
American novel, such as Alice Walker's *The Color Purple*, Toni Morrison's
Beloved, and Terry McMillan's *Waiting to Exhale*, has become a cultural
phenomenon of considerable importance. The proliferation of black book
clubs is just one of the signs of the tenuous boundary separating the academic
and nonacademic worlds where reading novels is central to both.

It is no small matter that more than a few young people aspire to be African
American novelists today when a new black novel is appearing almost daily.
For a people who have had to argue the case for their humanity, who live
in constant fear of losing their civil and equal rights, this might appear as
an anomaly. But it is very much related to the growth and popularity of the
African American novel in our time. The novel continues to serve both an
ideological and a social purpose, affirming the need to reflect lived reality
across class and gender lines, attending to its own improvisational nature,
embracing and resisting the past, deepening our sense of who and what it
means to be black in a postmodern, postcolonial world, and demanding all
the while to be seen as art. While earlier authors may have felt that to be
political would somehow diminish the status of their art, contemporary black
novelists see this dual mission in complementary rather than oppositional
terms. The threatening nature of double consciousness that W.E.B. Du Bois
saw as the inevitable fate of African Americans has been reconfigured as an
extraordinary gift for the novelists whose mastery of the languages of culture
and craft have expanded their vision and enriched their creative imagination.

For the more advanced student of literature, this book is an attempt to
chart the interaction of distinct but different traditions – rather than a unitary
phenomenon – that have characterized the African American novel. The
focus on both canonical and noncanonical texts will suggest the rhetorics
and strategies that have come out of a particular cultural discourse and
found their way into the novel. The intention in the essays is to pay as much
attention to the novel as part of a process and a performance as well as the
product or result of specific developments.

The categories devised here – three parts and fifteen chapters – represent the way studies of the African American novel today are configured. Part I, "The long journey: the African American novel and history," follows the emphasis placed upon historical reconstruction, still a major focus for the field. The "journey" implies both the path from slavery to freedom and the journey to establish and document a novelistic tradition among black people in America. In "Freeing the voice, creating the self: the novel and slavery," Christopher Mulvey considers the importance of the originary moment, when "the writers were giving up the authenticity of life for the authenticity of imagination." Studying the novel of slavery sheds light on the relationship between slavery and freedom, but also between abolitionism and African American cultural production. It was the struggle against stereotypes and prejudices that opened up the literary space for black representation, M. Giulia Fabi suggests in "Reconstructing the race," providing an overview of the fictional legacy of post-slavery novels. This is a period of considerable growth and experimentation for the novel, which benefited from expanded educational opportunities for former slaves, the rise of a black middle class, and a powerful independent press. Fabi revisits the "passing" theme, going beyond conventional readings of the nineteenth-century African American novel to present a much broader literary landscape.

By the 1920s, the term "Negro novel" had entered the lexicon. Moving from novels with "Negro subject matter" to "Negro novel" meant a growing acceptance of the literary representations *of* blacks *by* blacks, according to George Hutchinson in his review essay "The novel of the Negro Renaissance." While he looks at the achievements of the renaissance in fiction writing, Hutchinson identifies the period more with a "sense of collective identity [that] produced a field of discourse" rather than an individual school. Nevertheless, the "Harlem Renaissance" became important as a modernist strategy for staking new ground. As the popularity of literary representations of blacks expanded beyond the US borders, it also introduced a new set of contradictions. Giselle Anatol's "Caribbean migration, ex-isles, and the New World novel" addresses some of these contradictions and analyzes literary representations from the standpoint of African diasporic populations in the US. By paying literary-critical attention to the history of various novelists' engagement with the politics of cultural pluralism, Anatol highlights the importance of the Caribbean American novel. Aware of the paradox of double invisibility, writers such as Paule Marshall, Jamaica Kincaid, and Edwidge Danticat produce fictions with a strong sense of national and ethnic identity.

Part II, "Search for a form: the New American novel," is less concerned about the progressive development of the novel than it is about the way the narrative and linguistic enactments of individual texts are organized by genres. That the African American novel has developed its own aesthetics of storytelling art is clear from Ashraf Rushdy's "The neo-slave narrative." Because of its relationship to the novel and to American history, the slave narrative offers an endless range of possibilities. As the arbiter of memory, it allows history, autobiography, and folklore to claim space in a single text. Looking at the poetics and politics of race and historical representation becomes primary to the novelistic imagination. Which aspects of America's shared cultural memory are to be shared, which discarded, and how we create a usable past are key questions raised by Claudine Raynaud in "Coming of age in the African American novel." The chapter reexamines the traditional *Bildungsroman*, another form that suggests the generic continuity within African American fiction as well as its symbiotic relationship to world literature. Novelists use the coming of age trope to map the discourses on racism, maturation, and manhood/womanhood. Steven Tracy extends the discussion of generic continuity and evolution in his chapter "The blues novel." African American novelists force open an even wider linguistic and cultural space, sharpen our sensitivities and broaden our vision when they utilize the blues, which "provide a basic structure which is yet free enough to accommodate individual temperament, abilities, and creativity," according to Tracy.

Although many scholars have questioned the relevance of the debates between modernism and postmodernism to African American literature, the blues novel is certainly one place where the postmodern is acted out. Storytelling and orality engender new aesthetic possibilities, new forms of consciousness. If these are endemic to African American literature, so, too, is a postmodern consciousness. And yet it is necessary to distinguish between the postmodern as a *condition* and as a *mode of writing*, as Fritz Gysin does in his chapter, "From modernism to postmodernism: black literature at the crossroads." This necessary dialogue situates African American novel writing in the broader philosophical and cultural debates, debates which it has reshaped in significant ways. African American novelists shift narratives and juxtapose discourses, responding to the mediating effects of jazz and blues, myths and legends, assorted documentary material, popular narrative forms, poetry, the visual arts, film, humor, and the black verbal arts. Gysin explores this engagement with the postmodern as an "age-old condition of marginalized groups," paying particular attention to the work of Ishmael Reed, Clarence Major, and William Melvin Kelley, novelists whose fictions have met with a very divided critical audience. Susanne Dietzel turns the question of audience and critical response in another direction in her chapter "The African American novel and popular culture." The shift toward theory has made the "literary" novel a high priority, but Dietzel argues for

increased attention to the popular novel. By looking at contemporary reading practices that foreground the production, distribution, and reception of
black novels, her work follows a trend initiated by Nina Baym in her study
of nineteenth-century women's popular fiction. Exposing the literary-critical
biases and prevailing hierarchies raises important questions about the relationship between reader and writer and about how value is determined and
negotiated. The field of popular fiction is, nevertheless, unstable, as Dietzel
suggests, since many novelists not only cross over into mainstream literary genres as Octavia Butler did with *Kindred*, but also can earn respect
as a critic, as is the case with Samuel Delany. The popular novelist is ever
mindful of breaking racial barriers and some, like Terry McMillan, achieve
extraordinary commercial success.

The theoretical shifts, aesthetic concerns, and generic developments are
given more explicit expression in Part III, "African American voices: from
margin to center," where six case studies are considered. Jerry Ward revisits the protest tradition in "Everybody's protest novel: the era of Richard
Wright," insisting that Wright's pioneering work was a "weapon against
culturally sponsored ignorance as well as a medium for expressing his intellectual vision." Ward deconstructs the term "protest novel," seeing its
racial coding as a peculiarly American phenomenon, and questions whether
the term is an accurate definition of the kind of fiction Wright actually produced. Yet it was to the term "protest novel" that both Ralph Ellison and
James Baldwin objected, as Herman Beavers explains in "Finding common
ground." Writing in the decade that saw the dismantling of legal segregation
and a radical social movement, each author claimed for himself a different
kind of literary space. Ellison and Baldwin's shift to what Beavers calls a
"narrative of injury" depicts suffering as inevitable and instructive; it was
necessary to effect change, especially the sort prefigured by civil rights activism. Ellison's belief in the mythopoetic chaos and in the idea of death and
rebirth is not unlike Baldwin's call for testimony and the search for moral
legibility as the path toward wholeness.

The contemporary African American novel – by which we mean the novel
written after about 1970 – is clear in its rejection of the traditional opposition between literature and politics. It functions as a cultural object in
designing its own system for interpretation, often challenging the reader's
understanding, and shows a high degree of technical proficiency. Partly, this
is a function of the subject matter that novelists seem more willing to explore. Partly, it is a function of our current preoccupation with subjectivity,
identity, and consciousness. The migration of blacks to America that began
with the transatlantic slave trade, a forced journey of savage horrors, is being
understood in new ways. If it brought an unwilling people to a strange land,

it also initiated the transformation of an African cultural consciousness into an African American one. This forced migration created a contradictory experience of neither being in one world nor welcomed in another. Migration and exile, crossing and even transgressing boundaries, therefore, become a natural arena for exploration by the novelist. Earlier novelists found unique ways to dramatize the relationship to physical and psychological boundaries: McKay, Wright, Baldwin, Himes, and Yerby wrote as expatriates; Larsen and Fauset wrote about racial passing. Contemporary novelists are more aware of and represent various forms of transculturalism and transnationalism, exploring what it means to be part of a "diasporic" and "creolized" or "postcolonial" world, where boundaries and borders are always being redefined. They acknowledge an African-based culture, one impacted by the historical legacies of racism and colonialism as well as sexism and homophobia. New themes emerging from identity struggles in the post-Civil Rights and Black Power eras, the sexual revolution, the decolonization of Africa and the third world get reflected in a greater focus on intragroup relations, gender and class identity, including lesbian and gay themes. The contemporary black novel creates a narrative space for exploring the politics of race and identity on the one hand, while maintaining a primary focus on historical subjects and themes on the other. Ishmael Reed, Toni Morrison, and Alice Walker are specific examples of novelists who plumb the depths of a vast novelistic universe, creating new demands on the reader and the text. Reed's multicultural poetics are given careful attention by Pierre-Damien Mvuyekure in "American Neo-HooDooism." The title and the term have become Reed's signature, and his genre-crossing makes him the most experimental of contemporary novelists.

A less-talked-about theme in Morrison is the subject of Marilyn Mobley McKenzie's chapter, "Spaces for readers." Toni Morrison is not only the most widely discussed African American novelist, but she is also singled out for returning African American literature to its "village" origins. The concept refers to a definable culture and physical space within which her characters live, from which they are ostracized, and to which they return. McKenzie reminds us, however, that the most important part of Morrison's village is the space it affords the reader, who must work with the author in constructing the book's meaning. For Alice Walker, the parochialism of the village must be exchanged for the unity of a broader world. Emphasizing the importance of a gendered vision of that world, Walker coined the term which serves as the title for Lovalerie King's chapter, "African American womanism." Although King traces the woman-centered narrative back to Zora Neale Hurston, it is Alice Walker who has been most identified with the theory and literary practices of a black woman's renaissance.

Much less recognized but no less important are the novels of John Edgar Wideman and Leon Forrest, discussed here by Keith Byerman in "Vernacular modernism." These authors have brought a different kind of awareness to a still bothersome term by showing the ways in which African American expressive culture restores a lost vitality to civilization through its most suppressed elements. These writers are enacting what some call a "blues aesthetic" or "Afromodernism," both of which are subsumed under Byerman's preferred term "vernacular modernism."

Many contemporary scholars credit the positive impact of the postmodern turn, agreeing with bell hooks that "many other groups now share with black folks a sense of deep alienation, despair, uncertainty, loss of a sense of grounding even if not informed by shared circumstance."[8] Still others argue that this is not simply a correlation between African American writing and contemporary critical trends. African American novelists are extremely deliberate as they recreate and revise conventional structures, "speak the unspeakable," and invite each reader to ponder the world created within the text. In order to do so, they must necessarily move beyond the confines of any one construct or ideology. In this sense, modernism and postmodernism are themselves limiting since they traditionally privilege disintegration and fragmentation. Even when African American novels resist normative closure, they consistently point to a mythic, fantastic, or functional return to order, the importance of cultural continuity, innovation, and radical change. The socio-political and literary-critical agendas are enunciated with full disclosure. In this way, the African American novel continually renews itself passionately and discursively, reminding us all just how important telling a free story is.

NOTES

1. Ralph Ellison, *Going to the Territory* (New York: Vintage-Random, 1987), p. 293.
2. Richard Wright (1908–1960), William Gardner Smith (1926–1974), Frank Yerby (1916–1991), Chester Himes (1909–1984), Willard Savoy (b. 1912), James Baldwin (1924–1987), William Demby (b. 1922), Hal Bennett (b. 1930), Ronald Fair (b. 1932), Barbara Chase-Riboud (b. 1939) William Melvin Kelley (b. 1937), and Carlene Hatcher Polite (b. 1932) are among the novelists who have spent a significant part or all of their professional lives in Europe or Mexico.
3. William Andrews, "Toward a Poetics of Afro-American Autobiography," *Afro-American Literature Study in the 1990s*, ed. Houston A. Baker Jr. and Patricia Redmond (Chicago: University of Chicago Press, 1989), p. 79.
4. James Olney, "'I was Born': Slave Narratives, Their Status as Autobiography and as Literature," *The Slavis Narrative*, ed. Charles Davis and Henry Louis Gates Jr. (New York: Oxford University Press, 1985), p. 154.

5. Bernard W. Bell, *The Afro-American Novel and Its Tradition* (Amherst: University of Massachusetts Press, 1987), p. 5.
6. Madelyn Jablon, *Black Metafiction* (Iowa City: University of Iowa Press, 1997), p. 1.
7. The best source of information about the publication history of the African American novel is the Project on the History of Black Writing, University of Kansas.
8. bell hooks, "Postmodern Blackness," *Yearning: Race, Gender, and Cultural Politics* (Boston: South End Press, 1990), p. 27.

PART I

THE LONG JOURNEY
THE AFRICAN AMERICAN
NOVEL AND HISTORY

I

CHRISTOPHER MULVEY

Freeing the voice, creating the self: the novel and slavery

The list of early African American fictions is unexpectedly provisional. Presently it includes "The Heroic Slave" (1853) by Frederick Douglass, *Clotel, or the President's Daughter* (1853) by William Wells Brown, *The Garies and Their Friends* (1857) by Frank J. Webb, *The Bondwoman's Narrative* (1857?) by Hannah Crafts, *Our Nig or, Sketches from the Life of a Free Black* (1859) by Harriet E. Wilson, *Blake, Or the Huts of America* (1859–62) by Martin R. Delany, and "The Two Offers" (1859) by Frances Ellen Watkins Harper. But the list has been evolving. The full text of *Blake* was not made available until 1969.[1] *Our Nig* was not identified as an African American novel until 1982; *The Bondwoman's Narrative* was not discovered to be an African American fiction until 2001. It has been identified by several kinds of forensic and scholarly tests as a manuscript written by an escaped slave woman.[2] On the authority of its finder, Henry Louis Gates Jr., it is proper to treat that manuscript as authentic, but it is so newly found that it is also proper to retain the possibility that it might prove to be otherwise.

Early African American fiction is a decidedly unstable field. *Our Nig* had been thought to be a novel by a white woman. Another title which had been thought to be a novel by a white woman was shown in 1981[3] to be a genuine slave narrative written by an African American woman whose name is now on its cover: Harriet Ann Jacobs's *Incidents in the Life of a Slave Girl*.[4] The border between fact and fiction is a broad territory, not a dividing line, and an item in the September 1859 issue of the New York *Anglo-African Magazine* illustrates the vagueness of the border. "Patrick Brown's First Love" reports the story of a slave who has become free by default.[5] So many of his masters have met violent deaths that nobody wants to buy him. Patrick Brown tells the reporter that he has secretly killed all the white men who mistreated him. It is remarkable that a slave should spend a lifetime concealing the fact that he is a murderer and then allow his story to be told in a newspaper. "Patrick Brown's First Love" may in fact be the first African American short story, but it is only one of many items purporting to be true stories which appeared in anti-slavery newspapers and magazines. In the London *Anti-Slavery Advocate* in 1852, William Wells Brown wrote an article he called "A True Story of Slave Life." It is an account of the sale of a beautiful mulatto woman on the auction block in Richmond, Virginia.[6] The details are reproduced the following year as chapter 1 of *Clotel*, "The Negro Sale."[7] Fiction was emerging everywhere in African American writing in the decades before the Civil War, and there may be no definitively first story.

When African Americans made the move from the writing of narratives to the writing of novels, they were stepping across a void no matter how close the last narratives were to the first novels. At that moment the writers were giving up the authenticity of life for the authenticity of imagination, and the guarantee to the reader had to be of a different order. For Addison Gayle, that moment was one of failure because "ignoring their own history and culture, the early black writers attempted to create a literature patterned upon that of whites."[8] In the 1970s, Gayle was voicing an anger provoked by the ambiguities of early African American fiction: Was it black or was it white? Was it African or American? Was it a proud development of an authentic slave tradition or a poor imitation of the Victorian novel of manners? Did it help or did it hinder the African American cause? Answers depend on what you read as well as how you read. Gayle was reading a list of titles different from the titles now available, and the first answers come in response to another question: Where did early African American fiction come from?

Texts come from texts, and two answers have been given for the starting point of these texts: the black slave narrative and the white popular novel. The fact is that the African American fiction is rooted in both, but it owes its distinctiveness to the slave narrative. The greatest slave narrative is the eighteenth-century masterpiece, *The Interesting Narrative of the Life of Olaudah Equiano*,[9] but it is not this treasure that was the direct model for the fictions being written in the 1850s. Equiano's voice – aristocratic, genteel, Augustan, and deferential, more English than American – was not the voice being heard in the thirty years before the Civil War. The classic American slave narrative is democratic, businesslike, plainspoken, and self-assertive.

The *Narrative of the Life of Frederick Douglass, An American Slave* (Boston, 1845)[10] and the *Narrative of William W. Brown, A Fugitive Slave* (Boston, 1847)[11] work through a pattern of realization, resistance, flight, survival, and deliverance focusing on actions and themes that were not the commonplaces of the Victorian novel.[12] They spoke of the human body with a directness which gave them an unrivaled impact in the nineteenth century. Frederick Douglass's "The Heroic Slave" takes off from his *Narrative* to work though the story of a fellow fugitive whose acts of liberation bring death to his wife and freedom to his people. William Wells Brown's *Clotel* has as part of its subtitle *A Narrative of Slave Life in the United States*. Its introduction, "Narrative of the Life and Escape of William Wells Brown," is a version of his 1847 narrative, and it stands as a guarantee of the authenticity of the fiction that is to follow. Frank Webb was a Free Colored man living in the North, but he begins *The Garies* with the flight of two families, and he goes on to show that fugitives from the South must keep running in the North. Hannah Crafts might have provided a classic slave narrative, one to stand alongside Harriet Ann Jacobs's *Incidents in the Life of a Slave Girl*, but she chose not to tell her story in that form. Instead Hannah Crafts's *The Bondwoman's Narrative* makes fiction out of three escape attempts in ways which contradict as well as confirm the slave narrative pattern. Harriet Wilson was a Free Colored woman living in the North, and there are no slave codes where the heroine of *Our Nig* lives, but "she was indeed a slave, in every sense of the word; and a lonely one, too."[13] Wilson's novel presents another evolution of the slave narrative by universalizing the virtual slavery of so many caught in segregation's trap and from which escape was less easy than from the plantation. Martin Delany develops the patterns of the slave narrative in *Blake* so that the escape from the plantation becomes a mission to "establish a Negro government."[14] Of the early stories and novels, only Frances Harper's "The Two Offers" shows no link with the slave narrative.

Self-liberating African Americans produced first their own factual accounts of slave life and second, their own fictionalized versions of that life. But when Douglass and Brown impelled themselves into print in 1853, they did so because the most successful of all New England novels had appropriated their narratives and outstripped their sales. In 1851, Harriet Beecher Stowe began publishing *Uncle Tom's Cabin: or, Life among the Lowly* in serial form in the abolitionist *National Era*. At the end of 1852, she published it in book form,[15] and over 300,000 copies were sold.[16] *Uncle Tom's Cabin* was an anti-slavery novel and not the first example of its kind. That had appeared in 1836 with the publishing of Richard Hildreth's *The Slave; or, Memoirs of Archy Moore*.[17] It described the experiences of a free black man kidnapped into Southern slavery. At first readers believed they were reading an authentic slave narrative, but the author was a white abolitionist.

The Slave was the most successful of fourteen anti-slavery novels published before *Uncle Tom's Cabin*,[18] and Stowe's novel was remarkable not for its invention but for its success. She brought the anti-slavery novel to the attention of the whole world and at the same time exposed the limits of the genre. Part of her success arose from the fact that *Uncle Tom* was ambiguously placed between the anti-slavery novel and the plantation novel – celebrations of slavery which, beginning in the 1830s, constituted the first white Southern fiction. Despite Stowe's support of the abolitionist cause, it was not clear to all her readers which kind of novel she was writing. In 1852, Lydia Maria Child wrote to a friend: "It is really droll to see in what different states of mind people read *Uncle Tom*. Mr. Pierce, Senator from Maryland, read it lately, and when he came to the sale of Uncle Tom, he exclaimed with great emotion, 'Here's a writer that knows how to sympathize with the South! I could fall down at the feet of that woman! She knows how to feel for a man when he is obliged to sell a good honest slave!' In his view the book was intended as a balsam for bereaved slave-holders."[19]

Contemporary African Americans saw Stowe as the strongest white fighter in their cause, and responses to her are everywhere evident in their fiction. Douglass's master-murdering slave in his 1853 short story is the antithesis of Stowe's master-submissive slave of 1852, and it is too easy to presume on the exact nature of contemporary African American responses to Stowe. Martin Delany headed the two parts of his novel, *Blake*, with epigraphs from Stowe's poem "Caste and Christ,"[20] and in the 1930s, Vernon Loggins, with only half the novel in front of him, presumed it was "among the numerous analogues of *Uncle Tom's Cabin*."[21] But the full text of *Blake* shows that any initial likenesses between *Uncle Tom's Cabin* and *Blake* were superficial. Frank Webb took advantage of Stowe's name to have her write an encouraging preface to *The Garies*, but his novel is not anti-slavery; it is anti-segregation. Stowe was generous with her support, and African American writers were keen to take advantage of her name. At the same time, the source of Stowe's success was the genre that had come to perfection in the *Narrative of the Life of Frederick Douglass, An American Slave* and the *Narrative of William W. Brown, A Fugitive Slave*.

Questions raised by the conflict between narrative and novel, between support and subversion of slavery, between collaboration and appropriation, entangle African American texts as much as they entangle Stowe's text. Issues of authenticity have been central to the critical debate from the beginning: Have the texts been written by persons who are authentically African American? Have the texts been misrepresented by the mediation of white helpers and editors? Have the African American writers been true to black thinking and black values? These questions mix racial and literary issues in ways that obstruct theoretical rationalization. They were not resolved in the 1850s; they cannot be resolved now. The fictions and the questions require readers to negotiate, mediate, and judge. And when readers make their decisions, they will find they have had to compromise.

The first question – have the texts been written by persons who are authentically African American? – provides simple answers if the term

"African American" is taken to mean an American with some degree of descent from a person of black African origin. It is in these terms that *Our Nig* and *The Bondwoman's Narrative* have been declared African American texts. The second question – have the texts been misrepresented by the mediation of white helpers and editors? – raises questions that require a different kind of answer. Henry Louis Gates says of *The Bondwoman's Narrative*: "never before have we been absolutely certain that we have enjoyed the pleasure of reading a text in the exact order of wording in which a fugitive slave constructed it."[22] The authenticity of Crafts's voice seems to promise a great deal, but there are two important qualifications to be made. The first is that no one in the nineteenth century was writing in a literary vacuum. As Gates points out, "Dickens – and *Bleak House* in particular – was a fertile source for Hannah Crafts."[23] Literary and classical allusions are frequent, and her novel shows a full awareness of the contemporary white novel. Crafts trained in the same school of self-education as Douglass and Brown and was influenced by what she read, as they were.

The second qualification to any special claims for *The Bondwoman's* unmediated condition is that there were a number of African American printers and editors in the 1850s. They set up business to trade for themselves and to be independent of white influence. Frederick Douglass's *Frederick Douglass' Paper* depended on some white financial support, but independence was his aim. Thomas Hamilton's New York *Anglo-African Magazine* had no white support, and he told the readers of the January 1859 first issue that African Americans "must speak for themselves; no outside tongue, however gifted with eloquence, can tell their story."[24] Hamilton was an African American who encouraged other African Americans. He published a revised version of *Clotel* under the title of *Miralda*, he published *Blake*, and he published Harper's "The Two Offers."

Douglass and Hamilton failed commercially, but the fictions embedded in *Frederick Douglass' Paper* or *The Anglo-African Magazine* took on the color of their papers. It was in the September 1859 issue of *The Anglo-African* that Hamilton published "Patrick Brown's First Love." The last sentence reads: "It was a strange feeling of horrid pity that reached back through my fingers, as I drove my sheath-knife through and through that man's bowels." Then the words "What is the matter with you, Laura, this morning?"[25] as the reader is beginning "The Two Offers." Hamilton radicalized its reading by linking Harper's discussion of white women's lives to Brown's discussion of white men's deaths. The bleaching power of Anglo-American culture takes effect when the Anglo-African frame is removed, and only Martin R. Delany's *Blake* maintains its radical tone undiminished when read in isolation from the anti-slavery journal in which it was published.

The third question raised in relation to the authenticity of early African American fiction – have the African American writers been true to black thinking and black values? – implicates the most complex ideas, mainly relating to race. It is not a question that can be given any one answer at any one time. In 1854, in *The Claims of the Negro, Ethnologically Considered*, Frederick Douglass wrote: "The relationship subsisting between the white and the black people of this country is the vital question of the age."[26] Early African American fiction, recognizing that fact, is fundamentally about race, and race generates the oppositions on which the form is constructed. In the introduction to *Clotel*, William Wells Brown said, "there appears to exist a deadly antagonism between the white and coloured races" (22), and his use of the word "appears" is a signal to difficulties of meaning. Like Douglass, Brown believed that the human race was a single entity and that it was only in their own time that men had begun to argue otherwise. "I say it is remarkable," said Douglass, "– nay, it is strange that there should arise a phalanx of learned men – speaking in the name of *science* – to forbid the magnificent reunion of mankind in one brotherhood." His conclusion, one that Brown shared, was that the men who needed to deny the unity of the human race were slaveholders who wished to maintain a belief in the Declaration of Independence (*Claims* 10–11). The unexpected effect of the Declaration was the theme of *Clotel; or the President's Daughter*, provocative not because it pointed to the promiscuity of a president but because it pointed to the lie on which the American Republic was founded.

In *Our Nig* and *Blake*, slavery is presented as the white appropriation of black labor, but in *Clotel*, *The Garies*, and *The Bondwoman*, slavery is presented as the white ownership of the black body. It is an emphasis that leads repeatedly to the subjects of black–white sexual relationships, the mulatto, and passing. Those were radical subjects in the 1850s. Paradoxically, the preoccupation with plantation sexuality over plantation economics meant that in the twentieth century what had once appeared radical was seen to be reactionary. The action of *Clotel* focuses on five mulatto heroines: daughters and granddaughters of Thomas Jefferson. For constructing such a plot, Addison Gayle accused William Wells Brown of surrendering "his racial identity to the American Mephistopheles for a pittance that Faust would have labeled demeaning."[27] But when Brown chose to write about mulattoes, he was not turning away from his condition but towards it, and it is only by the standards of an absolute black nationalism that he can be accused of denying his people. Like Frederick Douglass, Brown hated what his white father had done to his black mother, but the mulatto's repudiation of whiteness was not an option offered in *Clotel*. Brown's "racial identity" was not a single matter. In 1853 and living in England, he was rejecting a world divided into black and white. By 1860 and living in the United States, he had begun to abandon the hope that his selves – white and black – could be accepted by both black and white. The introduction in *Miralda* of a "perfectly black" hero[28] in place of the hero of *Clotel* (222) "as white as most white persons," represents Brown's reactions to a renewed experience of American racism. The hero and heroine of *Clotel* live happily in England as white; the hero and heroine of *Miralda* live happily in France as black. So do the hero and heroine of the third version of the novel – *Clotelle,* 1864. The hero and heroine of the fourth version of the novel – *Clotelle,* 1867[29] – return to take part in the Civil War during which the hero is killed. In none of the versions does Brown imagine his couple living peacefully in the United States.

Four of the five white-skinned heroines of the 1853 *Clotel* die unhappily, and the type came to be called "the Tragic Mulatto," but William Wells Brown did not invent the type. He took his model directly from Lydia Maria Child's story, "The Quadroons."[30] In *Neither Black Nor White Yet Both,* Werner Sollors shows that Child in turn took her model from a tradition that traced its origins to a story published in London in 1711.[31] Sollors believes that Sterling Brown was the first critic to identify the tragic mulatto as a literary stereotype, and Brown thought it was more attractive to white writers than to black. As Sollors says, that is not the case.[32] The mulatto character appeared in African American fiction from the beginning, and William Wells Brown was followed by Webb, Crafts, and Wilson in making the mulatto the focus of attention.

Unlike Brown, Webb makes no attempt to create a space in which the mulatto might exist between the black and white races. *The Garies* explores the question through the stories of a brother and sister. The boy accepts the advice of white friends to repudiate all black links, is exposed before marriage to a white woman, and dies of symbolic fever. The girl accepts the advice of black friends, marries a black man, and lives out a useful life. The novel's reiterated advice is: "'You'll have to be either one thing or other – white or coloured. Either you must live exclusively amongst coloured people, or go to the whites and remain with them.'"[33] Webb denies the existence of the space that Brown failed to find, but that space is where the action of Crafts's novel takes place. She describes seven versions of a type that she calls the "beautiful quadroon"[34] – women who can pass for white. Some of them end their lives tragically but not all, and the heroine achieves freedom and happiness. The quadroons contrast with a character who "was a dark mulatto, very quick motioned with black snaky eyes, and hair of the same color" (203). This woman tries to destroy the heroine, and her coloring is emphasized to reduce the reader's sympathy. The complex of meanings

Crafts generates around black and white is deeply conflicted and worth a study in itself, but Crafts seems to have believed that a happy life between black and white was possible in the North.

The possibility of there being any such space is not debated by Harriet Wilson's study of the mulatto. Her orphaned heroine comes to cultural consciousness in a white world which tells her she is black. She is set going on a process of slow destruction in a casually brutal community which can hardly bring her into focus. *Our Nig* owes nothing to the stereotyping of either Crafts's "beautiful quadroon" or her "dark mulatto," and Wilson rejects sentimental reverberations, romantic auras, and Gothic mysteries. It is the two Northern novels which hold out least hope for the mulatto. They are also the novels at a greater remove from the slave narrative. The fugitive's formula for happiness – escape to the North – did not work in Pennsylvania and Massachusetts.

Wilson makes little of many issues that might be raised by the sexual union of black and white as she plausibly describes how a destitute white woman (the heroine's mother) takes up with a less destitute black man (the heroine's father). But though the focus of Wilson's attention is on the destructive social and economic effects of white exploitation of black labor, still *Our Nig* is a novel about the mulatto. And even Delany, who does not focus on the mulatto and who expressed a dislike for "the lighter refusing to associate with the darker,"[35] weds his black hero to "a dark mulatto of a rich, yellow, autumn-like complexion, with a matchless cushion-like head of hair, neither straight nor curly, but handsomer than either" (5). Why was there such a preoccupation with a group that made up little more than 10 percent[36] of the African American population in the 1850s?

"The trope of appearance – the metaphor of the mulatta – was an awkward artifice that in some instances inadvertently constructed slavery as the greater tragedy of the nearly white," says Ann duCille in *The Coupling Convention*.[37] In *The Foremother Figure in Early Black Women's Literature*, Jacqueline K. Bryant questions William Wells Brown's attitudes to both race and gender, coming to the conclusion that Brown's characterization of his heroines has "more to do with the way white men chose to perceive black women than the way black men perceived them or black women perceived themselves."[38] Jane Campbell attempts to save Brown (and by association Webb and Crafts, too): "The modern reader may react with anger and dismay at Brown's dependence on the tragic mulatto motif, and rightly so. But for Brown, mythmaking was impossible without this motif."[39] It was not immaterial that five out of the seven writers of early African American fiction might have been counted "mulatto" in the census of 1850, but beyond that is the argument that Sollors develops in *Neither Black Nor White Yet*

Both: "the literary representation of biracial characters, whatever their statistical relevance may have been, does not constitute an avoidance of more serious issues, but the most direct and head-on engagement with 'race,' perhaps the most troubling issue in the period from the French Revolution to World War II."[40] In support of this, Sollors quotes Alain Locke's argument that, by focusing on the mulatto in the pre-Civil War period, African American writers were exposing the myth of the South and striking where they considered the moral and political claims of the American South were weakest.

Those claims made the sexual politics of the plantation a shaping force in the plots of *Clotel*, *The Garies*, *The Bondwoman's Narrative*, and *Blake*. With variation those politics shape *Our Nig* since its plot equates the Northern home with the Southern plantation, and its story is put in motion by the liaison most denied on the plantation: the love of white woman and black man. Jim in *Our Nig* is the equal of President Jefferson in *Clotel*, Mr. Garie in *The Garies*, Mr. Vincent and Mr. Cosgrove in *The Bondwoman* and Colonel Franks in *Blake*. A restraining romance structure was trying to contain an uncontainable politics, and African American writers needed to amplify a repertoire of inherited characters to reflect actualities and ambitions not accommodated in the white novel and only hinted at in the slave narrative. In order to do this and to make a match for the tragic mulatto, early African American fiction introduced the character type of the noble African. This too was a creation of the English novel. In 1688, Aphra Behn fixed the type with her verbal portrait of the African prince Oroonoko: "He was pretty tall, but of a shape the most exact that can be fancied: the most famous statuary could not form the figure of a man more admirably turned from head to foot. His face was not of that brown rusty black which most of that nation are, but of perfect ebony, or polished jet."[41] Behn's model was adapted to become the type of the heroic slave: reluctantly violent, uneasily Christian, magnificently male, and very black.

Crafts, Wilson, and Harper seem not to have met him, but the male African American writers celebrated the type: "Madison was of manly form . . . His face was 'black, but comely.' His eye, lit with emotion, kept guard under a brow as dark and as glossy as the raven's wing" – Douglass in "The Heroic Slave"[42]; Jerome "was of pure African origin, was perfectly black, very fine-looking, tall, slim, and erect as any one could possibly be" – Brown in the *Clotelle* of 1864[43]; "Mr. Walters was above six feet in height, and exceedingly well-proportioned; of jet-black complexion, and smooth glossy skin" – Webb in *The Garies* (121–122); "Henry was a black – a pure Negro – handsome, manly and intelligent" – Delany in *Blake* (16). The heroic slave as the violent slave was not a type found in either anti-slavery or plantation novels.

It represented an innovation when imported and adapted from English literature by Douglass in 1853. Madison, Jerome, Mr. Walters, and Henry were African American answers to Uncle Tom, men who refused to be beaten, and some of them ready to kill.

The heroic slave was not the only figure in this literature to stand in contrast to the tragic mulatto. The field woman provided another opposition. Black-skinned women are infrequently developed as characters, infrequently given a name, and are infrequently made to speak. There are so many bit-part characters in the four versions of *Clotel* that Brown does have black women break the general silence in a way which reflects well on them, but more commonly he offers a character such as Dinah, a black cook, who appears briefly to make a cruel remark about the mulatto heroine (153). Webb has Aunt Rachel, another black cook, act the role of the mean and lazy servant on the watch for her stealthy mistress (74). Crafts does not give names to black female characters unless they are mulatto, and the black-skinned women only come into focus in ways which amuse the heroine – "fat portly dames whose ebony complexions were set off by turbans of flaming red" (119) – or distress her – "promiscuous crowds of dirty, obscene and degraded objects" (207). Wilson has no black women characters in *Our Nig* other than the mulatto Frado, and Harper has no black women in "The Two Offers."

Only Delany breaks out of the conventional model to permit his hero to treat field women as his equals: "'They allow you Sundays, I suppose.' 'No sir, we work all day ev'ry Sunday.' 'How late do you work?' 'Till we can' see to pick no mo' cotton; but w'en its moon light, we pick till ten o'clock at night'" (*Blake* 74–75). Although Delany treats his field women with respect, he has them speak in a dialect different from the hero, who speaks like a gentleman. The conventions of the nineteenth-century novel required that refined characters talk in a refined English and that common characters talk in common English. Refinement could be a matter of the soul as well as of rank, but the rule was observed in all English and American literary productions in the 1850s. Not to follow the rule was to show a lack of education. Robert Bone says that "dialect distinguishes the comic (folk) characters from the serious (middle-class) characters, who of course speak only the white man's English,"[44] but he overlooks the difficulties faced by writers breaking into the literary world of the 1850s.

Black English[45] is used extensively for the speech of field blacks in early African American fictions though it is not used in all of them. Douglass does not use it for his non-heroic black characters, but he does give his low white characters dialect speech; Wilson hardly uses it; Harper has no call for it. Frank J. Webb alternates speech registrations so well in *The Garies* that he begins to show the way in which African American writers could solve a problem caused by a literary convention designed to express English class prejudice. But Brown and Crafts use Black English in a different way. Brown relishes the opportunities it gives him for comic writing. Some of his characters speak in a language so exaggerated that they become caricatures. Sam, the slave valet, and Pompey, the slave assistant, are examples. Brown has strangely purposive variations on the dialogue convention so that he makes the heroine's mother speak Standard English when she lives independently with her daughters but makes her speak Black English when she becomes a kitchen slave. In *The Bondwoman* white-skinned characters speak in Standard English; black-skinned characters speak in Black English. There is one exception. A character, described as a "black man" (215), speaks Standard English. His exceptional language is matched by his exceptional character, and he is instrumental in helping the heroine in her final escape. Like Brown and Delany, Crafts was following English literary convention as they all would have found it in Dickens and the Brontës.

The earliest African American fiction is a literature of fusion. It fused slave narrative, Gothic mystery, satire, pastoral, novel of manners, document, and polemic. It fused black and white character, speech, and behavior, and it fused the African and the American in religion and belief. The Christian religion was one shared with slave-owners – a bond and a barrier. A solution was to contrast true religion with deformed religion, and Brown makes the hypocrisy of the slave-owning Christianity of the United States a theme parallel to the hypocrisy of the slave-owning democracy of the Constitution. He devotes nine chapters of *Clotel* to describing the world of a slave-owning minister who hires an even-more-degraded minister to preach pro-slavery Christianity to his slaves. The slaves fall asleep during a long sermon (93–98). Delany took the theme of deformed religion further. Asked by two pious old slaves to put his trust in religion, Blake answers: "'Don't tell me about religion! What's religion to me? My wife is sold away from me by a man who is one of the leading members of the very church to which both she and I belong! Put my trust in the Lord! I have done so all my life nearly, and of what use is it to me?'" (16). Blake does not only speak religious defiance; he also acts it. In the Red River Country he meets slaves whose driver makes them work Sundays. "The next day Jesse the driver was missed, and never after heard of" (79). Murder becomes a religious duty in an ironic reinforcement of the Sabbath commandment. Rennie Simson argues that in early African American novels "neither the authors nor their black characters rejected the Christian religion; in fact, they displayed a deep faith in the principles of Christianity."[46] But Douglass, Brown, Webb, Wilson, and Delany display a formal Christianity with little warmth or religious feeling. *The Bondwoman's*

Narrative is an exception. Christianity pervades the work, and in the middle of the novel the focal point of the heroine's world is a slave-owning minister, of whom she writes: "what language could portray the ineffable expression of a countenance beaming with soul and intelligence?" (124). The difference between her Christian slave plantation and Brown's is striking. Ironic readings do not seem to be invited because signifying on Crafts's minister involves signifying on Crafts's Christianity.

For Brown religion functioned as a cultural as well as a spiritual resource – one that worked most effectively in the absence of white clergy and white people. Religion could then become a manifestation of the world which the slaves reserved to themselves. After the slaver's sermon, the slaves hold their own more meaningful service (*Clotel* 99–100). Brown and Delany give the best access to this enclosed world, and *Clotel* and *Blake* are rich resources for black folkways, providing details of slave entertainments, dress codes, hierarchies, songs, and rhymes. There is a song to celebrate the master's death – "He no more will hang our children on the tree" (*Clotel* 150). There is a rhyme to mock the master's greed – "The big bee flies high" (*Clotel* 138) – possibly the first reference to this slave satire.[47] Like Brown, Delany recorded African American song, and perhaps the most important recording of all is Delany's rendition of the "men of sorrows" singing "Way down upon the Mobile river" (100) – possibly the first reference to sorrow songs.[48]

These fictions enter worlds so remote that in them slave hunters abandoned pursuit. Brown imagines a figure called Picquilo, who "had been two years in the swamps, and considered it his future home. He had met a Negro woman who was also a runaway; and, after the fashion of his native land, had gone through the process of oiling her as the marriage ceremony" (212–213). Brown gives the swamps a mysterious quality, a quality that Delany makes at once more exotic and more concrete. As Blake travels through North Carolina recruiting rebel slaves, Delany has him meet "some bold, courageous, and fearless adventurers, denizens of the mystical, antiquated, and almost fabulous Dismal Swamp, where for many years they have defied the approach of their pursuers" (112). These figures are High Conjurers, who "were regularly sent out to create new conjurers, lay charms, take off 'spells' that could not be reached by Low Conjurers, and renew the art of all conjurors of seven years existence" (114). Blake agrees to be anointed by the Swamp's "ambassadors," and his encounter with the "goombah" religion is as close to Africa as he comes before his actual voyage to the Gulf of Guinea. Chapter 52, "The Middle Passage," starts Blake on his return to the New World as a crew member on a slave ship, and Delany has his hero listen to "the wailing and cries, groaning and moaning of the thirsty, hungry, sick, and dying, in tones of agony, such to rend the soul with anguish" (228). *Blake* is the first title in the great tradition of African American fiction which reenacts the ancestral tragedy, but before the Civil War it was being reenacted as a thing of the present, not of the past. Delany's combined themes of the African American holocaust, the African homeland, and the black nation resonated powerfully in the 1970s at the time of the rediscovery of *Blake*, but they had helped to bury the novel in the 1860s when they timed out in the new political context created by the Civil War. Readings of these early novels and stories have been sensitive from the beginning to attendant conditions.

Their reception has been further affected by critical silence, title loss, and the late development of scholarly interest. As a result, it is only now that the title list is being rebuilt. The process cannot be presumed to be over, but it does mean that modern readers have a fuller knowledge and a fuller list than any previous generation. At the same time it implies that the inherited tradition of the African American novel has been damaged. Critical silence meant that William Wells Brown and Martin Delany were not reviewed in the white press. Racial isolation meant that Frank Webb in London, Harriet E. Wilson in New England, and Hannah Crafts in New Jersey could have no impact on their contemporaries. Silence and isolation prevented normal writerly exchanges of example, inspiration, and competition. Modern readers can bring the titles together and see patterns and influences, but there is a sense in which all of these titles stand apart. Each one represents a fresh start. The only title which has generated an uninterrupted pattern of creative action and critical reaction is the *Clotelle* of 1864.

Even so, in the long years from the end of the Civil War to the end of the Depression, *Clotelle* effectively dropped below the critical horizon. In a review of African American culture which W. E. B. Du Bois wrote in 1913, William Wells Brown is treated as a historian. No mention is made of his work as a novelist.[49] When commentary begins to focus on early African American fiction in the survey work of the 1930s, it is negative. Vernon Loggins dismissed all African American novels with the remark: "When a really noteworthy American Negro novel is written, it will probably be on the theme which Webb attempted."[50] Sterling Brown followed suit: "*Clotel* is not well written or well constructed, but these failings are common to its type."[51] In the 1940s, Hugh M. Gloster passed over early African American fiction because "William Wells Brown, Frank J. Webb, Martin Delany, and Frances E. W. Harper . . . generally exhibit the methods and materials of Abolitionist propaganda."[52] In the 1950s, Robert Bone presumed that there were only three full-length novels published before 1890 – in fact the number is thirteen – and judging by what he read, he came to the conclusion that

"The early novel was an aesthetic failure largely because it never solved [the] problem of rounded characterization."[53]

Serious study of early African American fiction, or study that took it seriously, did not begin until the 1960s and 1970s with the impact of the Civil Rights and Black Power Movements. It needed the appearance of the full edition of Delany's *Blake* in 1969 to fire critical reaction, and it came most powerfully with Addison Gayle's *The Black Aesthetic* (1971), and *The Way Of The New World: The Black Novel in America* (1975). The new *Blake* was the book that Black Power critics were looking for: "Had Henry Blake become the symbol of black men instead of Mr. Walters, Bigger Thomas and his cousins would not have been necessary."[54]

The 1980s saw an increasing development of scholarly resources; more and better edited texts were available. At the same time the expansion of the 1970s Black Studies programs into a network of African American departments throughout North America meant that there was an ever-growing body of studies of all kinds, but particularly historical, which gave the field breadth and depth. John W. Blassingame's study *The Slave Community: Plantation Life in the AnteBellum South* (1972)[55] not only revised the way that the plantation was to be treated by historians, but it also led to a recognition of the value of the slave narrative, first as a historical source and then as a literary genre. The rehabilitation, identification, editing, and publication of slave narratives have been instrumental in redirecting attention to early African Americans as writers of genius. One important effect has been the development of more inclusive and more sympathetic ways of reading texts. Nina Baym's *Woman's Fiction* (1978)[56] not only gave a new impetus to the reading of the popular fiction that she treated but also showed a new way of reading *Clotel* and *The Garies*. With Henry Louis Gates's recovery in 1982 of *Our Nig* as an African American text and his use of Baym to interpret the "new" novel, the strength of the feminist's readings became apparent.[57] Gates did more. *The Signifying Monkey* (1989) provided a new tool for reading early African American fiction. "Signifyin(g) is so fundamentally black," he argued, that the potentiality for ironic reading must be held open for any black text of any period.[58]

Early African American fiction has profited from new scholarship that has seen the subject finally supported by the research tools with which other literatures have been supplied for the past fifty years. It has profited from newly generous readers willing to accept the fictions in the terms they set themselves. It has profited from a new appreciation of a literature of crossing, passing, and mixing.[59] In its own language, it is a "mulatto" literature. It is a literature that does not wish to make clear distinctions between black and white, between African and American, between authentic and fictitious. Instead, it offers a complex view of life that speaks directly to the twenty-first century, a century in which we are all mulatto.

NOTES

1. Floyd J. Miller, "Introduction," *Blake; or the Huts of America* by Martin R. Delany (Boston: Beacon Press, 1970), p. viii.
2. Henry Louis Gates Jr., "Introduction," *The Bondwoman's Narrative* by Hannah Crafts (New York: Warner Books, 2002), p. xiii.
3. Jean Fagan Yellin, "Written by Herself: Harriet Jacobs's Slave Narrative," *American Literature* 53 (1981): 479–486.
4. Harriet A. Jacobs [as Linda Brent], *Incidents in the Life of a Slave Girl: Written by Herself* (Boston: Published for the Author, 1861).
5. Anon, "Patrick Brown's First Love," *The Anglo-African Magazine* (Sept. 1859): 286–287, rpt. in *The Anglo-African Magazine. Volume 1–1859* (New York: Arno Press and the New York Times, 1968).
6. William Wells Brown, "A True Story of Slave Life," London *Anti-Slavery Advocate* 1.3 (1852): 23.
7. William Wells Brown, *Clotel; or the President's Daughter: A Narrative of Slave Life in the United States* (London: Partridge & Oakey, 1853), p. 62.
8. Addison Gayle, *The Way of the New World: The Black Novel in America* (New York: Doubleday, 1975), p. xii.
9. Olaudah Equiano, *The Life of Olaudah Equiano, or Gustavus Vassa, the African*, ed. Joslyn T. Pine (New York: Dover, 1999).
10. Frederick Douglass, *Narrative of the Life of Frederick Douglass, An American Slave. Written by Himself* (Boston: Published by the Anti-Slavery Office, 1845).
11. William Wells Brown, *Narrative of William W. Brown, A Fugitive Slave. Written by Himself* (Boston: Published by the Anti-Slavery Office, 1847).
12. See Bernard W. Bell's discussion of the narrative pattern in *The Afro-American Novel and Its Tradition* (Amherst: University Of Massachusetts Press, 1987), p. 28. The best study of the narratives is William L. Andrews, *To Tell a Free Story: The First Century of Afro-American Autobiography, 1760–1865* (Urbana: University of Illinois Press, 1986).
13. Harriet E. Wilson, *Our Nig or, Sketches from the Life of a Free Black, In a Two-Story White House, North. Showing that Slavery's Shadows Fall Even There. By "Our Nig,"* ed. R. J. Ellis (Nottingham: Trent, 1998), p. 77.
14. Martin R. Delany, *Blake; or the Huts of America*, Introduction by Floyd J. Miller (Boston: Beacon Press, 1970), p. 270.
15. Harriet Beecher Stowe, *Uncle Tom's Cabin; or, Life among the Lowly* (Boston: John P. Jewett and Company, 1852).
16. Peter M. Bergman, *The Chronological History of the Negro in America* (New York: Harper & Row, 1969), p. 200.
17. Richard Hildreth, *The Slave; or, Memoirs of Archy Moore* (Boston: John H. Eastburn, 1836).

18. Nicholas Canaday, "The Antislavery Novel Prior to 1852 and Hildreth's *The Slave* (1836)," *CLA Journal* 17 (1973): 177.

19. Lydia Maria Child, *Letters of Lydia Maria Child* (Boston: Houghton, Mifflin and Company, 1883), pp. 69–70.

20. See Julia Griffiths, ed., *Autographs For Freedom* (Boston: John P. Jewett and Company, 1853), p. 4.

21. Vernon Loggins, *The Negro Author: His Development in America* (New York: Columbia University Press, 1931), p. 186.

22. Gates, "Introduction" to Crafts, *Bondwoman*, p. xxxiii.

23. Gates, Notes to Crafts, *Bondwoman*, p. 331.

24. Thomas Hamilton, "Apology," *Anglo-African Magazine. Volume 1–1859* (New York: Arno Press and the New York Times, 1968), p. 1.

25. Frances Ellen Watkins [Harper], "The Two Offers," New York *Anglo-African Magazine* (September, 1859): 288–291; (October 1859): 311–313.

26. Frederick Douglass, *The Claims of the Negro, Ethnologically Considered* (Rochester: Lee, Mann & Co., 1854), p. 5.

27. Addison Gayle Jr., "Introduction," in Gayle Jr., ed., *The Black Aesthetic* (Garden City: Doubleday, 1971), p. 412.

28. William Wells Brown, *Miralda*, New York *Weekly Anglo African* (Jan. 19, 1861): 1.

29. William Wells Brown, *Clotelle; or the Colored Heroine, A Tale of the Southern States* (Boston: Lee & Shepard, 1867).

30. Lydia Maria Child, "The Quadroons," *Fact and Fiction: A Collection of Short Stories* (London: William Smith, 1847).

31. Werner Sollors, *Neither Black Nor White Yet Both: Thematic Explorations of Interracial Literature* (New York: Oxford University Press, 1997), p. 193.

32. *Ibid.*, pp. 223–225.

33. Frank J. Webb, *The Garies and Their Friends* (London: Routledge, 1857), p. 41.

34. Hannah Crafts, *The Bondwoman's Narrative* (1857?), ed. Henry Louis Gates Jr. (New York: Warner Books, 2002), p. 119.

35. Nell Irvin Painter, "Martin R. Delany: Elitism and Black Nationalism," *Black Leaders of the Nineteenth Century*, eds. Leon Litwack and August Meier (Urbana: University of Illinois Press, 1988), p. 165.

36. Bergman, *Chronological History*, p. 194.

37. Ann duCille, *The Coupling Convention: Sex, Text, and Tradition in Black Women's Fiction* (New York: Oxford University Press, 1993), p. 18.

38. Jacqueline K. Bryant, *The Foremother Figure in Early Black Women's Literature: Clothed in My Right Mind* (New York: Arland Publishing, 1999), p. 17.

39. Jane Campbell, *Mythic Black Fiction: The Transformation of History* (Knoxville: University of Tennessee Press, 1986), p. 4.

40. Sollors, *Neither Black Nor White*, p. 235.

41. Aphra Behn, *Oroonoko, or, the History of the Royal Slave. A True History* (1688), rpt. in Aphra Behn, *Oroonoko, Rover, and Other Works*, ed. Janet Todd (London: Penguin, 1992), p. 108.

42. Frederick Douglass, "The Heroic Slave," *Frederick Douglass' Paper* (Mar. 4, 1853): 1.

43. William Wells Brown, *Clotelle: A Tale of the Southern States* (Boston: J. Redpath, 1864), p. 54.

44. Robert A. Bone, *The Negro Novel in America* (New Haven: Yale University Press, 1965), p. 26.
45. Guy Bailey, "Speech, Black," *Encyclopedia of Southern Culture*, ed. Charles Reagan Witson and William Ferris (Chapel Hill: University of North Carolina Press, 1989), p. 194.
46. Rennie Simson, "Christianity: Hypocrisy and Honesty in the Afro-American Novel of the Mid-19th Century," *University of Dayton Review* 15.3 (1982): 15.
47. William Barlow, *Looking Up at Down: The Emergence of Blues Culture* (Philadelphia: Temple University Press, 1989), p. 12.
48. Note to *Blake*, p. 100.
49. W. E. B. Du Bois, "The Negro in Literature and Art," *Annals of the American Academy of Political and Social Science* (September 1913) reprinted in *Writings*, ed. Nathan Huggins (New York: The Library of America, 1986), pp. 864–865.
50. Loggins, *Negro Authors*, p. 251.
51. Sterling A. Brown, *The Negro in American Fiction* (Washington: Associates in Negro Folk Education, 1937), p. 39.
52. Hugh M. Gloster, *Negro Voices in American Fiction* (Chapel Hill: University of North Carolina Press, 1948), p. 25.
53. Bone, *The Negro Novel*, p. 27.
54. Gayle, *Black Novel*, p. 24.
55. John W. Blassingame, *The Slave Community: Plantation Life in the AnteBellum South* (New York: Oxford University Press, 1979).
56. Nina Baym, *Woman's Fiction: A Guide to Novels by and about Women in America, 1820–1870* (Ithaca: Cornell University Press, 1978).
57. Henry Louis Gates Jr., "Introduction," *Our Nig: or, Sketches from the Life of a Free Black, in a Two-Story White House, North* by Harriet E. Wilson (New York: Random House, 1983), pp. xi–lix.
58. Henry Louis Gates Jr., *The Signifying Monkey* (New York: Oxford University Press, 1989), p. 64.
59. A model of the new work is M. Giulia Fabi's *Passing and the Rise of the African American Novel* (Urbana: University of Illinois Press, 2001).

2

M. GIULIA FABI

Reconstructing the race: the novel after slavery

The republication, starting in the 1960s, of many long-unavailable nineteenth-century African American novels, and the wealth of critical discourses on those recovered texts that have flourished since the 1970s, have led to a profound rethinking of traditional critical evaluations of the fiction written by African Americans after slavery. Rather than as a historically valuable but artistically less significant bridge between the antebellum origins of the African American novel and the celebrated explosion of literary creativity during the New Negro Renaissance, postbellum African American fiction is now being reevaluated as important in its own right for its formal experimentation with, and revision of, a large variety of novelistic genres.

African American authors wrote historical, utopian, political, and religious novels, juvenile and detective fiction, and *Bildungsromane*. They explored international themes, expanding their focus to include not only Europe but also Africa and the Caribbean, and they were actively engaged with contemporary literary movements such as local color fiction, realism, naturalism, and, in the early twentieth century, modernism. Actively opposing the stereotypes and prejudices prevalent in contemporary mainstream American literature and determined to intervene as writers in the culture wars raging at the time, they forcefully opened a new literary space for the representation of blacks in fiction. They challenged restrictive definitions of American literature, and of American culture as a whole, through a radical revision of prevalent literary modes and the use of metanarrative clues that call attention to those revisionary practices, as well as through the elaboration of innovative strategies of representation, including the transgressive blending of different genres. In the novels of Charles W. Chesnutt, Frances E. W. Harper, Pauline E. Hopkins, Sutton E. Griggs, Katherine Davis Chapman Tillman, J. McHenry Jones, Paul Laurence Dunbar, and W. E. B. Du Bois, for instance, realism is cross-fertilized by romance and the oral folk tradition, as well as by intricate family sagas and utopian longings that bring the weight of the past or the politically charged hopes for a better future to bear upon the representation and interpretation of the present.

The decades that followed the end of the Civil War in 1865 and the abolition of slavery witnessed both the opening up of new opportunities for former slaves and the continuation of old racial hierarchies and prejudices under new forms. Since there was no redistribution of land in the South and the promise of "40 acres and a mule" remained unfulfilled, freedom for millions of ex-slaves came without any structural improvement in their condition of economic dispossession and subordination. Nevertheless, against overwhelming odds, African Americans fought actively to change that situation, pursuing the goals of social, political, and economic advancement. Education was deemed central to the uplift of the race. Postbellum decades saw a proliferation of freedmen's schools, black colleges, literary societies and clubs, journals, and independent black presses.

At the national level, however, the increasing disinterest in the plight of former slaves and the end of Reconstruction in 1877 led to a rapid reorganization of the old racialized power structure in the South and to an increase of racial tension and discrimination also in the North. The economic neo-slavery of tenancy and sharecropping, the violence and intimidation of terroristic white-supremacist groups like the Ku Klux Klan, and the systematic political disenfranchisement of African Americans, with the proliferation of "Jim Crow" laws which eroded the civil rights supposedly guaranteed by the 14th and 15th Amendments, were accompanied by an increase in racial violence that saw the outbreak of major anti-black riots both North and South and a dramatic rise in the number of lynchings, which reached a peak in the 1890s. Lynchings, ritualized and publicized spectacles of mutilation and murder that drew large crowds of men, women, and also children, emerged as tools of social control and repression of blacks considered "too" determined or enterprising, as African American journalist Ida B. Wells documented at the time.

The epitome and the emblem of the virulent racism of the times, racial violence and lynchings, are themes present in most of the major novels discussed in this chapter. They are also featured prominently in lesser-known African American works of fiction such as Walter H. Stowers and William H. Anderson's *Appointed: An American Novel* (published under the pseudonym "Sanda" in 1894), G. Langhorne Pryor's *Neither Bond nor Free: A Plea* (1902), Charles H. Fowler's *Historical Romance of the American Negro* (1902), Edward A. Johnson's *Light Ahead for the Negro* (1904), J. W. Grant's *Out of the Darkness: or Diabolism and Destiny* (1909), Robert Lewis Waring's *As We See It* (1910), Charles Henry Holmes's *Ethiopia: The Land of Promise (A Book with a Purpose)* (1917), J. A. Rogers's *From*

Superman to Man (1917), and Sarah Lee Brown Fleming's *Hope's Highway* (1918). Novels like J. McHenry Jones's *Hearts of Gold* (1896) featured also other kinds of violence, such as that directed against black prison inmates in labor camps in the South. As had happened during slavery, "Jim Crow" segregationist practices, which were institutionalized in 1896 with the infamous "separate but equal" Supreme Court decision in *Plessy v. Ferguson*, enforced two dramatically different experiences of American life for blacks and whites. Significantly, the years at the end of the nineteenth and at the beginning of the twentieth century, which American historians call respectively the "Gilded Age" and the "Progressive period," have been defined the "nadir" of African American history.[1]

Segregation, of course, had a devastating impact not only at a social, but also at a cultural level. Societal inequalities and discriminatory practices were in fact actively rationalized and legitimized by pseudo-biological theories on the inferiority of blacks, alternatively portrayed as "naturally" docile Sambos or violent brutes. The numerous pseudo-scholarly treatises on the topic were compounded and reinforced at a more capillary level by the prevailing demeaning stereotypes of African Americans in popular culture. The success of blackface minstrel shows, with their caricatural portrayals of blacks, is but an example of the mainstream cultural consensus on the inferiority of blacks which also found more "highbrow" expression in literature: from the violent racism of Thomas Dixon's Ku Klux Klan novels to the insidious condescension of bestselling plantation fiction à la Thomas Nelson Page (which reinterpreted slavery as a benign institution that took care of a supposedly defenseless and naturally servile race).

In response to this extremely hostile cultural terrain, the second half of the nineteenth century witnessed a veritable flowering of African American fiction, stimulated by the growth of a black readership, by the multiplication of African American journals and publishing houses, and by the conviction, prevalent among black intellectuals and activists, that literature was a powerful tool to combat prevalent racial stereotypes, to reinforce the cultural pride and self-awareness of African Americans, and to foster the process of racial uplift. In combating the "battle of images" that raged in this period, the strategy of African American novelists was not simply to produce propagandistic work that reversed popular stereotypes.[2] Rather, they proposed complex and literarily innovative representations of the rich cultural heritage, the complex humanity, and the history of resistance of African Americans. Indeed, it is one of the ironies of literary history that the extremely oppressive historical circumstances in which African American writers produced their fictions have for a long time been invoked more as a benign excuse for the supposedly poor quality of their craft (and therefore as a reason for the

critical neglect of their work), rather than as proof of the irrepressible determination and artistic self-awareness with which African American authors
defied contemporary dicta of race and gender, devising transgressive and
original literary means for the counter-hegemonic representation of blacks.
Their proclaimed faith in the power of the pen notwithstanding, African
American authors could not, of course, magically rectify contemporary injustices, but they did actively intervene as writers in the battle to shape the
cultural imagery of their time in less racially oppressive ways. Their strategies
of literary intervention had a crucial, albeit not yet fully recognized, impact
on the development of subsequent African American and American fiction
as a whole.

The challenges that African American novelists faced in their determination to represent a segregated, racially "bifurcated American world" from
their subaltern and socially marginalized point of view were many and
serious.[3] In the first place, they faced a double and profoundly divided audience of black and white readers with often diametrically opposed perspectives, histories, and experiences of American society, as well as with
very disparate degrees of knowledge of black culture and evaluations of its
significance.

Recently, scholars like Claudia Tate and Frances Smith Foster have questioned traditional critical assumptions that post-slavery fiction was aimed
primarily at a white audience. The above-mentioned growth of a black readership, the multiplication and cultural impact of literary societies, and the
rise of a strong independent black press, meant that African American writers could count also on a black audience. *Minnie's Sacrifice* (1869), *Sowing
and Reaping* (1876–1877), and *Trial and Triumph* (1888–1889), the first
three novels written by Frances E. W. Harper (all recently rediscovered by
Foster), were serialized in the newspaper of the African Methodist Episcopal
Church, *The Christian Recorder*, and they were primarily aimed at a black
audience. Similarly, Pauline E. Hopkins serialized in *Colored American
Magazine* three of her four novels (*Hagar's Daughter: A Story of Southern
Caste Prejudice*, 1901–1902; *Winona: A Tale of Negro Life in the South
and Southwest*, 1902; *Of One Blood; or, The Hidden Self*, 1902–1903).
Katherine Davis Chapman Tillman's, *Beryl Weston's Ambition: The Story
of an Afro-American Girl's Life* (1893) and *Clancy Street* (1898–1899) first
appeared in *The A.M.E. Church Review*. Sutton E. Griggs published his own
novels and distributed them in black communities in the South.

However, since one of the aims of the African American novel was not only,
so to speak, to preach to the converted, but also to promote intercultural
understanding and undermine the prevailing stereotypes of blacks in white
minds, typically the novel after slavery is a multilayered, multiple-voiced

text, aimed at a dual audience and readable at a variety of levels depending on the kinds of cultural knowledge the reader brings to the text. The interpretation of any novel is always contingent upon the reader's degree of knowledge, but the specificity of these African American texts rests in their deliberate multiple-voicedness, in their use of strategies of signifying, of coded communication, and in the systematic metanarrative ways in which the authors draw the readers' attention to the process of interpretation, pointing to the treacherousness of the act of reading, foregrounding the unreliability of appearances, underlining the superficiality of traditional cultural scripts, and questioning the politics of production and transmission of knowledge. Explicit comments on the revisionary goals and the dual audience of African American fiction are made in the forewords, openings, or closures of such different novels as Harper's *Minnie's Sacrifice* and *Iola Leroy; or, Shadows Uplifted* (1892), Hopkins's *Contending Forces: A Romance Illustrative of Negro Life North and South* (1900), Dunbar's *The Sport of the Gods* (1902), Fowler's *Historical Romance of the American Negro* (1902), Johnson's *Light Ahead for the Negro* (1904), or Griggs's *The Hindered Hand; or, The Reign of the Repressionist* (1905), which explicitly critiques Dixon's Ku Klux Klan novels. Along similar lines, the deferred happy endings that characterize many African American domestic novels of this period (e.g. Hopkins's *Contending Forces* or Johnson's 1890 *Clarence and Corinne*), and the predominance of the theme of passing-for-white, or passing as it is generally known, are narrative devices that unsettle, respectively, the readers' expectations and their sense of the legibility of reality in ways that foreground the process of interpretation itself.

The African American novel after slavery is characteristically also dominated by a deconstructive approach to the past which prefigures late twentieth-century literary concerns. It re-told and reinterpreted the past, reading the black experience as an inextricable part of the nation's past and as an indispensable vantage point to interpret American culture and society as a whole. This reflexive attitude toward the past dominates not only those works that are set in the slavery period, like James H. W. Howard's antiplantation *Bond and Free: A True Tale of Slave Times* (1886), Thomas Detter's *Nellie Brown; or, The Jealous Wife* (1871), or Hopkins's *Winona* (1902). The emphasis on the continued impact of the slave past on the social and cultural hierarchies of the present, as well as on the most personal choices of the protagonists (including the choice of a marriage partner) characterizes also those African American novels that focus mostly on the decades that followed the end of the Civil War. In both cases, the emphasis on the past serves a dual goal. On the one hand, the reinterpretation of slavery and the focus on the culture of resistance of the slaves – issues which African American novelists knew to be absent from traditional history books – revised the history of African America, stimulated cultural pride, and functioned as a means of community building. On the other, they represented a way to anticipate objections and to help suspend the white readers' disbelief when presented with a black-centered view of American society that questioned dominant historical accounts and ran against white readers' own experiences and self-interest.

In response to these complex and conflictual representational needs, mulatto heroes and heroines feature prominently in the African American novel after slavery. In white fiction, the mulatto was a stock literary figure that had enjoyed great popularity in the antebellum period, and had prospered also in postbellum decades. Several ideological issues coalesced in the white stereotype of the tragic mulatto. What spelled the tragic fate of these in-between figures, in fact, was the supposedly clear differentiation and incompatibility of the races, which fed the reassuring conviction that racial difference was ultimately always legible and easy to regulate, since "blood will tell." Precisely because of its popularity and stereotyped qualities, the mulatto had been profoundly revised in the works of the founding authors of African American fiction, as noted in chapter 1. Also in the hands of postbellum African American authors, the mulatto could be profoundly subversive, emerging as the living symbol of the historical reality of racial interconnectedness and as proof that, contrary to racist mythology, blacks and whites were "of one blood." While the option to pass for white is characteristically rejected in favor of belonging to the black community, mulattoes more often than not enjoy a far from tragic fate in black fiction. In fact, the mulatto hero's or heroine's survival against all stereotypes, discriminations, and societal odds parallels and highlights that of the black community as a whole.

Long indicted as a symptom of middle-class bias, racial self-hatred, and internalization of white values, in African American fiction before the New Negro Renaissance, the trope of passing functions instead as an aggressive strategy to reinterpret race as a sociocultural construct, rather than a biological destiny, and to appropriate and deconstruct the oppressive, albeit elusive, notion of whiteness that served as the normative standard to identify and evaluate blackness. African American novelists explored explicitly this transgressive potential of passing as a theme, using it as a literary device to cross the color line, to bridge fictionally the social separation between blacks and whites that was systematically enforced by segregation, to undermine pseudo-biological arguments on the naturalness of racial hierarchies, as well as to show, through the increased social mobility and success of the white-looking passer, the systematic discriminatory practices that enforced separate social destinies for blacks and whites. The dislike of white readers for and the interest of black audiences in this literary transgression of the societal norms of racial segregation emerge clearly from Hopkins's scathing 1903 reply to the letter of complaint of a white reader of the *Colored American Magazine*.[4]

Through their use of the trope of passing and the foregrounding of seemingly more conventional all-but-white protagonists, African American writers also opened a space for the non-caricatural representation of visibly black characters and for a reevaluation of the distinctiveness of African American culture. The black characters who surround the all-but-white protagonist in Harper's, Chesnutt's, or Hopkins's fiction do not provide stereotypical comic relief. On the contrary, they are the spokespersons of those historic and cultural values of black America that lead Iola Leroy, for instance, to relinquish the possibility of passing and instead to cast her lot with her mother's people. In turn, the passer's preference for the black community reinterprets African Americanness as the consciousness of a distinctive historical, social, and cultural heritage, rather than as an intrinsic condition of dispossession. To avoid stereotyped misinterpretations, the aforementioned authors significantly insert in their novels also visibly black major characters who vie with the all-but-white protagonist for predominance. In Harper's *Iola Leroy* (1892), the character of Lucille Delany represents the truly new professional black woman Harper celebrates; in Hopkins's *Hagar's Daughter* (1901), Venus Johnson emerges as detective heroine of the novel; and in Chesnutt's *The House Behind the Cedars* (1900), dark-skinned and working-class Frank Fowler proves himself to be the only truly noble-hearted Southern gentleman, whose selflessness and generosity will give way, in Chesnutt's second published novel, *The Marrow of Tradition* (1901), to the more overtly confrontational heroism and courage of the folk character Josh Green. Dark-skinned folk characters emerge not only as major supporting actors, but as the unquestioned protagonists of several novels of this period, such as Tillman's *Clancy Street* (1898–1899), Griggs's *Imperium in Imperio* (1899), and Du Bois's *The Quest of the Silver Fleece* (1911).

The conflicting representational needs that led many African American authors to deploy the mulatto as a "narrative device of mediation" also led them to adopt and adapt the conventions of utopian fiction.[5] Utopian fiction, which centers on the imaginative construction of an ideal society, had become extremely popular at the turn of the century. In their enormously influential works, white bestselling authors like Edward Bellamy projected into the future the racist and eugenist tendencies of their times, imagining in *Looking Backward, 2000–1887* (1888) a perfect future from which blacks have disappeared or where they enjoy separate and unequal status, as in the sequel *Equality* (1897). Building on a little-known early antecedent like

Lorenzo D. Blackson's Christian utopia, *The Rise and Progress of the Kingdoms of Light and Darkness; or, The Reigns of Kings Alpha and Abandon* (1867), turn-of-the-century African American writers profoundly revised the formal conventions and thematic concerns of utopian fiction. Blending utopia with the *Bildungsroman*, the romance, and intricate family sagas to emphasize the continued impact of the past on the future, African American writers focused less on the description of a perfect future social order than on the process of personal and social change that could make such a perfect society possible by preparing individuals worthy of inhabiting it. A case in point is Sutton E. Griggs's first novel, *Imperium in Imperio* (1899), where the author details the birth of a "new Negro, self-respecting, fearless, and determined in the assertion of his rights."[6] Griggs foregrounds the meaning of the black experience in dystopian, segregated, and racist turn-of-the-century American society, by focusing on the *Bildung* of two exceptionally talented black youths: Belton Piedmont, the son of a poor but caring mother, and Bernard Belgrave, the unacknowledged mulatto son of a powerful white senator who uses his power to secretly promote his son's career. It is Belton's life especially that reveals the absurd, wildly oppressive workings of segregation that haunt and hamper the lives of Griggs's protagonists in this and in his other four novels (*Overshadowed*, 1901; *Unfettered*, 1902; *The Hindered Hand*, 1905; and *Pointing the Way*, 1908).

Imperium in Imperio celebrates Belton's resilience and self-respect in the face of unbelievable oppression. Griggs uses "race travel," as opposed to the more traditional utopian devices of space or time travel, to foreground the parallel, but dramatically different realities blacks and whites live in because of segregation. Within the economy of utopian conventions, the presence of segregation is defamiliarized as a world turned upside down, dominated by perverted values that punish (black) intelligence and reward (white) violence and cowardice. In the novel, black resilience and self-determination take political reality in the Imperium, a secret black society that has military and institutional powers and that, to fulfill its mission to protect the life and property of black Americans, contemplates the possibility of secession and war against the United States. While the disruptive potential of the Imperium is ultimately exorcized by its dismantlement, the closure of the novel sees Griggs's fictional narrator threaten white America with the possibility of the Imperium's rebirth, unless racial equality is achieved.

With a similarly innovative use of utopian conventions, in *Of One Blood* Pauline E. Hopkins blends the utopian element connected with the splendid secret African civilization of Telassar, where the ex-passer Ruel Briggs will eventually rule as king, with an intricate family saga rooted in United States slavery. This interracial family saga, a theme which also characterizes her other three novels, foregrounds the long-term evil consequences of the peculiar institution, the moral bankruptcy of segregation, and its disruptive consequences on the entire American social fabric. In another important novel of this period, *Iola Leroy* (1892), Frances E. W. Harper writes a historical novel of slavery and reconstruction that, like Hopkins's, goes against plantation nostalgia. In *Iola Leroy*, Harper depicts realistically the difficulties and violence of the Reconstruction period, and finally articulates an inspirational utopian vision of a future South that will be a land of freedom for all. With her emphasis on the *Bildung* of the title character and on the qualities of the truly "new," professional black woman, Lucille Delany, Harper adds a specifically feminist dimension to her utopia.

The focus on the plight of the black woman, as paradigmatic of the condition of oppression and also of the ethos of resistance of the black community as a whole, dominates the fiction written by Harper, Hopkins, and other literary exponents of the Black Woman's Era at the turn of the century, including Amelia E. Johnson, Emma Dunham Kelley-Hawkins, and Katherine Davis Chapman Tillman. As critic Claudia Tate has argued, these domestic novels foreground female-centered environments, marginalizing and subverting patriarchal power relations, and centering on new models of more independent women who are able to reconcile familial duties with a satisfying professional career, as in the case of Lucille Delany in *Iola Leroy* or of the title character of Tillman's *Beryl Weston's Ambition*.

The work of Amelia E. Johnson reveals a different strategy to deal with the dilemmas of representing race in a segregated society. Johnson was the first black woman to write Sunday School fiction for the American Baptist Publication Society, one of the largest white publishing houses of the time, and her fiction represents an important and long-neglected early moment in the tradition of African American juvenile fiction. Amelia E. Johnson was an activist in the African American community, and in her essays for such journals as T. Thomas Fortune's *The New York Age* she was outspoken on racial issues, including, for instance, the need for "race publishing houses" to enable African American authors to write without incurring white censorship.[7] However, her three Sunday School novels (*Clarence and Corinne; or, God's Way*, 1890; *The Hazeley Family*, 1894; *Martina Meriden; or, What Is My Motive?*, 1901) feature racially indeterminate characters, that is, characters who are not explicitly described as black and could therefore be assumed to be white by white readers. This choice was not unique, nor was it only a defensive strategy to circumvent white readers's disinterest in black matters. Several other African American writers opted for racially indeterminate or even white protagonists, including Emma Dunham Kelley-Hawkins, author of *Megda* (1891) and *Four Girls at Cottage City*

(1895), Charles Chesnutt in *The Colonel's Dream* (1905), Edward A. Johnson in his utopian novel *Light Ahead for the Negro* (1904), as well as Paul Laurence Dunbar, the celebrated poet and short story writer, in his first three novels (*The Uncalled*, 1898; *The Love of Landry*, 1900; *The Fanatics*, 1901). In these novels that engaged in passing for white, the choice of racially indeterminate or white characters afforded a way to address problematic issues (such as the need for self-realization in the face of societal constraints or prejudices, as in Dunbar's *The Uncalled*, or the pressing contemporary realities of urban poverty, alcoholism, and family disruption, in the case of Amelia Johnson's novels), without presenting them as specifically racialized problems linked with the supposed social pathology of blacks.

In Amelia E. Johnson's juvenile fiction, her young, racially indeterminate heroines, who are typically isolated in a hostile environment dominated by poverty and family disruption, are prized for their determination and resilience in the face of such unfortunate circumstances. They triumph spiritually, in the first place, by strengthening their faith in "God's way," but also, more practically, by enforcing those values of domesticity, orderliness, and self-discipline that eventually enable them to overcome the adverse circumstances they happen to live in. Both Amelia E. Johnson and Emma Dunham Kelley-Hawkins do include racial signifiers that make it possible to decode their protagonists' racial indeterminacy not necessarily as whiteness but also as blackness (e.g. the color-coded title of Johnson's second novel and her emphasis on her female protagonists' dark, black, or brown eyes, or Kelley-Hawkins's references to a well-known black resort town in *Megda*), thereby restoring the multilayered, signifying qualities of their novels. Nevertheless, the novels that engage in passing reveal a diminished, or at least more covert, oppositional value. They emerge as less transgressive and innovative in terms not only of their social critique, but also of their literary qualities. For instance, the spiritual and religious emphasis of Johnson's and Kelley-Hawkins's new women translates into their greater adherence to the standards of true womanhood, which are less problematized than in Harper's or Hopkins's novels, while E. A. Johnson's *Light Ahead for the Negro* follows more closely the literary conventions of utopian fiction and advances a less radical vision of racial equality than Griggs projected in *Imperium*. To make this same point from a different angle, Dunbar's only novel with explicitly black protagonists moves more radically than his previous ones toward naturalism and anticipates concerns of the New Negro Renaissance.

In the first novel published by the most widely nationally acclaimed African American prose writer of the pre-Harlem Renaissance period, Charles W. Chesnutt, passing is central both as theme and as narrative device, a dual use that enables the author to articulate a sharp and literarily sophisticated critique of traditional narrative representations of blackness. Chesnutt had theorized a strategy of oblique literary intervention early on. In 1880, when he was 21 years old, he wrote in his journal: "The subtle, almost indefinable feeling of repulsion toward the negro, which is common to most Americans . . . cannot be stormed and taken by assault . . . It is the province of literature . . . to accustom the public mind to the idea; and . . . while amusing them to . . . lead them on imperceptibly, unconsciously step by step to the desired state of feeling."[8] Chesnutt first practiced this strategy in short stories that he succeeded in having published in the prestigious white literary magazine *The Atlantic Monthly* and which were later collected in *The Conjure Woman* (1899), published by Houghton Mifflin. Superficially evocative of plantation nostalgia, these stories juxtapose a first-person, racially indeterminate narrator and an ex-slave, whose stories of the old times before the war bring to life the greed and inhumanity of the masters, as well as the spiritual and physical world of the slaves. The storyteller's eloquence and verbal inventiveness strengthen, in the very process of telling, the revisionary portrayal of blacks as complex figures that emerges also from the content of the stories. In the longer fiction Chesnutt wrote after the success of *The Conjure Woman*, such literary sophistication and revisionary strategies became even more subtle and oblique, both because his identity as a black writer had become known to the public (a fact that heavily influenced the reception of his subsequent work) and because of the more overtly controversial topics he dealt with, such as miscegenation in *The House Behind the Cedars*, a race riot in *The Marrow of Tradition*, and post-Reconstruction politics in *The Colonel's Dream*.

The censorship white editors exercised on innovative, realistic representations of blackness emerges clearly from the repeated rejections of earlier versions of Chesnutt's first novel, such as "Rena Walden" and *Mandy Oxendine*. The version of *The House Behind the Cedars* that was finally accepted for publication by the prestigious white publishing house Houghton Mifflin features a story of miscegenation that seems to evoke rather straightforwardly the traditional white script of the tragic mulatto, while instead involving the reader in a complex metanarrative and intertextual questioning of traditional modes of representation and reception of blackness. This process occurs at several levels. In telling the story of the two siblings John and Rena Walden, who decide to pass for white to take advantage of the opportunities that segregation denies to African Americans, Chesnutt masterfully manipulates the Jamesian narrative strategy of the limited point of view. He introduces the readers to the opinions of a character, John Walden, who is only later revealed to be black. By the time that discovery occurs, however, readers have already learned to sympathize with and appreciate the intelligence, irony, and business sense of this self-made man, a fact which later makes it difficult even for potentially biased readers to see him as a stereotypically simple-minded and thriftless black character. At the same time, Chesnutt plays with intertextual references to such popular texts as Sir Walter Scott's *Ivanhoe* (1819) in order to ridicule the chivalric pretenses of an unregenerate post-Reconstruction South. He also constructs his all-but-white heroine as a composite of such opposite female characters as Scott's Rowena and Rebecca, unsettling the readerly expectations elicited by his references to these popular characters. Chesnutt thus succeeds in making the reader experience as problematic the tragic fate of his female protagonist and, by extension, the politics of representation of race in American (as well as in European) fiction. Similarly, the contrast between the realism of the first half of the novel and the exasperated melodrama of the second half is so extreme as to call attention to itself and become parodic of traditional tragic mulatto fictions. The traditional tragic fate of the mulatto in white-authored novels is also transgressed through the final survival of the greatest trickster of the novel, John Walden, who at the end resumes his life as successful passer.

Chesnutt's critique of romanticized portrayals of the segregated South becomes even more explicit in *The Marrow of Tradition*, a historical novel that focuses on the racist terrorism that led to the 1898 anti-black riot in Wilmington, North Carolina, an infamous historical event that also inspired David Bryant Fulton's 1900 novel, *Hanover, or the Persecution of the Lowly*. The negative reception that greeted *The Marrow of Tradition* confirmed that realistic portrayals of race in American society were not welcomed by mainstream critics (including Chesnutt's long-time supporter William Dean Howells) and led the author to conclude: "I am beginning to suspect that the public as a rule does not care for books in which the principal characters are colored people, or written with a striking sympathy with that race as contrasted to the white race."[9]

At the beginning of the twentieth century, however, Chesnutt was not the only African American novelist to respond with increased narrative direct-ness and realism to the worsening conditions African Americans faced, as racial violence was rampant and segregation was an institutionalized fact of American society that severely restricted the life opportunities of black Amer-icans. Building on the militancy and readiness for armed self-defense that Griggs had voiced explicitly in *Imperium in Imperio*, Chesnutt introduces in *The Marrow of Tradition* the character of Josh Green, a "black giant" who fights back against rioting whites and also avenges his father's death at the hands of a white mob.[10] While in *The Marrow of Tradition* Josh Green dies after having killed the white villain, other novels of this period sanction the legitimacy of self-defense against wanton white racial violence through their protagonists' survival. In Robert Lewis Waring's *As We See It* (1910), for instance, the protagonist Abe Overlay moves North after killing the murderers of his mother and sister, while in Pauline Hopkins's *Winona*, the enslaved Judah fights bravely with John Brown and then expatriates to England where he enters the service of the Queen and is eventually knighted.

Focusing on a Southern black family in his fourth novel, his only one featuring black protagonists, Dunbar also responded to worsening social conditions. In *The Sport of the Gods*, which opens with an ironic comment on the great quantity of novels monotonously reiterating "regret of the old days" of slavery, Dunbar gives a naturalistic portrayal of the devastating and inescapable effects of racism not only in the South but also in the North.[11] The Hamiltons' move to New York, in fact, does not open up real alternatives for them. In his stark description of the superficial glitter and tough realities of the city, Dunbar builds on the realistic portrayal of working-class urban poverty in Tillman's *Clancy Street* and Johnson's *Clarence and Corinne*, and also anticipates the Harlem novels of the New Negro Renaissance. In his first novel, *The Quest of the Silver Fleece* (1911), the famous African American intellectual Du Bois focused both on the South and the North to give voice, like Dunbar, to the changing realities of African America, including the early stages of the Great Migration that in the years around World War I would bring millions of black Southerners to the major Northern cities. Du Bois, however, eschewed Dunbar's naturalistic sense of inescapability and doom. He blended his analysis of the economics of racism and the exploitation of blacks in the cotton industry with a romance, unsettling the literary conventions of naturalism (with its problematic emphasis on racial destiny) and opening instead a narrative space for the celebration of the culture and the spirituality of black folk.

Published a year after *The Quest of the Silver Fleece*, James Weldon Johnson's *The Autobiography of an Ex-Coloured Man* (1912) also reflects the cultural and social impact of the changing demographics of African America, while celebrating the rich expressive culture of black folk. In this novel, Johnson deliberately builds on the previous tradition of African American prose. He puts classic tropes to new modernist literary uses, but also shows the continuity and distinctiveness of black American culture. Like Chesnutt, Johnson engages in an innovative and experimental play with the limited point of view and with parodic intertextuality to construct a fictional first-person narrator who is profoundly unreliable. The Ex-Coloured Man reveals his unreliability in the very process of recounting his life. His ambition to present himself as a race hero is constantly undercut by his egotistic self-pity, by superficial evaluations that bespeak his alienation from African American culture, and by a deep-seated materialism that leads him to admire uncritically the white American world he will eventually join permanently by passing. Significantly, the narrator remains nameless throughout the novel because, having passed into white society and, unhampered by discrimination, having prospered as a businessman, he does not want to jeopardize his social standing and economic success by making his racial heritage known.

The peregrinations of the fictional narrator follow classic trajectories in African American history and fiction, foregrounding also tropes and environments that will become characteristic of New Negro fiction: the migration from the rural South to the urban North, the expatriation to Europe, the return to the South, where the Ex-Coloured Man, who at one point decides to make a career as a musician, looks for sources of inspiration in the folk traditions of music and oratory. Johnson filters reality through the eyes of his protagonist, whose unreliability emerges obliquely and ironically through his self-aggrandizing attempt to compare himself to such heroic protagonists of African American history and culture as Frederick Douglass and William E. B. Du Bois, while misinterpreting in unwittingly parodic ways their life and work. Similarly revealing are the intertextual references to classic dramatic situations in nineteenth-century African American fiction, like lynching. While in previous African American novels the reality of racial violence motivated the protagonists to commit themselves even more fully to the cause of racial justice, in the case of the Ex-Coloured Man, on the contrary, the lynching he witnesses leads him to praise the murderers as belonging to "a great people," to express contempt for the victim, as well as to finalize his decision to pass.[12]

While parody is unwitting in the case of the fictional narrator, it is deliberately and finely tuned by the author. The selfishness and racial alienation of the Ex-Coloured Man emerge by contrast to the heroic models he misinterprets, and serve a dual narrative function. On the one hand, the Ex-Coloured Man becomes a ridiculing parody of the racial prejudices of the white society he so deeply admires. On the other, that same parody celebrates, indirectly but powerfully, the values of race solidarity, loyalty, and pride the protagonist cannot live up to. As critic Robert Stepto has argued, within the parodic economy of the novel, the Ex-Coloured Man functions as a "negative example" of blackness, and his condescending evaluations of black culture and constant surprise at black excellence turn into a celebration of that culture and a critique of white stereotypes.[13] James Weldon Johnson thus reelaborates within a modernist aesthetic those strategies of signifying, of coded communication that characterize African American fiction from its inception. He creates a multilayered text that, like its African American fictional antecedents, is readable at a variety of levels and addresses a double and divided audience.

Ironically, Johnson's sophisticated modernist parodic novel has for a long time been taken at face value. First published anonymously in 1912, it was largely read as a real autobiography, and it did not elicit much interest. Republished explicitly as a novel in 1927, with the author's name appended to it, at the height of the New Negro Renaissance, at a time when Johnson was famous as the curator of important anthologies and as NAACP secretary, *The Autobiography of an Ex-Coloured Man* was received triumphantly, though it was still praised for its documentary value. Six years later, in 1933, Johnson would publish his real autobiography, *Along This Way*, also in the attempt to dispel misconceptions about his novel. Today, the critical work of Robert B. Stepto, Valerie Smith, and Lucinda MacKethan has conclusively established the generic status and literary sophistication of Johnson's novel.

The history of the reception of *The Autobiography of an Ex-Coloured Man*, however, remains revealing and paradigmatic of the underestimation from which African American fiction, and especially pre-Harlem Renaissance fiction, has suffered and, to some extent, continues to suffer. The process of recovery and reinterpretation of the early texts that is currently under way is slowly changing and expanding our perception of the African American, as well as of the American literary canon. Much critical work still needs to be done, however, to restore a more historically and critically sensitive appreciation for the literary craft of early African American novelists, for the depth and originality of their revision of contemporary genres, as well as for the intra- and interracial intertextual relationships they established with other contemporaneous American writers. Most importantly, recovering a fuller sense of the power of their vision and their innovative contributions to the development of the art of fiction will open up the possibility of revising traditional literary genealogies, moving beyond long-standing assumptions of a one-way influence of white on black writers, and enriching in new and complex ways our reading of American literary history and culture as a whole.

NOTES

1. Rayford W. Logan, *The Negro in American Life and Thought: The Nadir, 1877–1901* (New York: Dial, 1954).
2. Barbara Christian, *Black Women Novelists: The Development of a Tradition, 1892–1976* (Westport, CT: Greenwood, 1980), p. 25.
3. Dickson D. Bruce, *Black American Writing from the Nadir: The Evolution of a Literary Tradition, 1877–1915* (Baton Rouge: Louisiana State University Press, 1989), p. 10.

4. Pauline E. Hopkins, "Reply to Cordelia A. Condict," March 1903, in *The Norton Anthology of African American Fiction*, ed. H. L. Gates and N. Y. McKay (New York: W. W. Norton, 1997), pp. 594–595.

5. Hazel V. Carby, *Reconstructing Womanhood: The Emergence of the Afro-American Woman Novelist* (New York: Oxford University Press, 1987), p. 89.

6. Sutton E. Griggs, *Imperium in Imperio* (1899; rpt. New York: Arno, 1969), p. 62.

7. Amelie E. Johnson, "Afro-American Literature," *The New York Age*, 30 January 1892: n.p.

8. Charles W. Chesnutt, *The Journals of Charles W. Chesnutt*, ed. R. Brodhead (Durham: Duke University Press, 1993), pp. 139–140.

9. Charles W. Chesnutt, qtd. in W. L. Andrews, *The Literary Career of Charles W. Chesnutt* (Baton Rouge: Louisiana State University Press, 1980), p. 127.

10. Charles W. Chesnutt, *The Marrow of Tradition* (1901; rpt. Ann Arbor: University of Michigan Press, 1969), p. 309.

11. Paul Laurence Dunbar, *The Sport of the Gods* (1902; rpt. New York: Dodd, Mead, 1981), p. 23.

12. James Weldon Johnson, *The Autobiography of an Ex-Coloured Man* (1912; rpt. New York: Hill & Wang, 1960), p. 189.

13. Robert B. Stepto, *From Behind the Veil: A Study of Afro-American Narrative* (Urbana: University of Illinois Press, 1979), p. 104.

3

GEORGE HUTCHINSON

The novel of the Negro Renaissance

While the location and duration of the movement popularly known as the Harlem Renaissance remain highly contested, its importance in the development of African American literature – and "modernism" in general – is more widely accepted today than ever. Central to the movement then known as the "Negro Renaissance" was the effort of black writers and artists after World War I to re-conceptualize "the Negro" independent of white myths and stereotypes that had affected African Americans' own relationship to their heritage and each other – independent, too, of Victorian moral values and bourgeois shame about those features of African American life that whites might take to confirm racist beliefs. The struggle with one-dimensional mainstream stereotypes was, of course, far from over, and it was hardly new; a central feature of the work of Frances E. W. Harper and Charles Chesnutt in the 1890s, it played a major role in such novelistic "forerunners" to "renaissance" fiction as James Weldon Johnson's *Autobiography of an Ex-Coloured Man* and W. E. B. Du Bois's *The Quest of the Silver Fleece*. But in the 1920s and 1930s a burst of black-authored fiction published by new and prestigious New York houses helped transform the landscape of African American, and by extension American, fiction. At the same time, it had an immense quickening effect on black literature internationally.

The sudden expansion can be attributed to many causes, but perhaps the four crucial factors were the Great Migration from the rural South and the Caribbean to Northern cities, new intellectual currents concerned with cultural pluralism and anti-racism, the dramatic growth of the black middle class and of literacy from Reconstruction forward, and the transformation of the American culture industry after 1915. These developments also form basic integuments of most of the black novels published in the 1920s and 1930s, despite great variations in theme, cultural politics, and aesthetic approach. Collectively, the novels are notable for their concentration on contemporary life and its social and cultural instability – its "modernity." But equally striking are intense contrasts in cultural politics, strong disagreements about such essential issues as the meaning and value of racial identity as such, and deeply conflicting approaches to novelistic form and technique.

The widespread belief that patrons and publishers turned away from black fiction (supposedly a 1920s fad) in the 1930s is belied by the fact that more novels by black authors appeared from more presses in the 1930s than in the 1920s – and this happened during a major contraction in the publication of American fiction generally. The number of black authors supported by patrons in the 1920s was actually very small in comparison to the number supported by federal programs in the 1930s, and these programs developed from the intellectual networks of the 1920s. Several authors identified with the 1920s published their first novels in the 1930s – most notably Langston Hughes, Zora Neale Hurston, George Schuyler, and Countee Cullen. The Negro Renaissance, notably, changed the very meaning of the term "Negro novel." Before and during the 1920s, both black and white authors and critics routinely used the phrase to designate novels by either whites or blacks focusing on "Negro" subject matter. By the mid- to late 1930s, this was no longer true: "Negro fiction" had come to designate, by and large, fiction by Negroes. The semantic shift marks the emergence of a semi-autonomous, highly diversified field of artistic expression, and a growing acknowledgment of black writers' authority over the literary representation of African American experience.

One of the first novels of the "Harlem Renaissance" proper (that is, the phase of the Negro Renaissance centered in Harlem following World War I), Jessie Fauset's *There Is Confusion* (1924) meditated on the significance of the rise of the black middle class, New Negro race consciousness, and the transformation of the culture industry as black music and performance art began making inroads into the "legitimate" theater. Within the form of the novel of manners and the thematic frame of racial "uplift," Fauset advocated, in the clear moral terms of an essentially liberal ideology, American patriotism, hope for the future, and African American solidarity across class, gender, and generational lines. In this novel, the "American" future belongs to the descendants of Negroes, whose moral superiority and generations of servitude make them the appropriate inheritors of the "best" of American traditions. Yet to come into their own, they must overcome the various forms of "confusion" white supremacy has brought about within the race – intraracial "colorism," class snobbishness, internalized racism, self-defeating bitterness bred by white prejudice, lack of race pride, even excessive moral earnestness among talented idealists of the race. On the other hand, white Americans in this novel have mortgaged their future to racism and shallow materialism. Essentially a romantic novel of manners with a classic comic resolution, *There Is Confusion* showcases some of the core beliefs, anxieties, and weaknesses of the New Negro elite in order to finally justify their intellectual and moral leadership.[1]

The same point can be made about Walter White's *The Fire in the Flint* (1924), focused on the career and ultimate lynching of Kenneth Harper, MD – a brilliant graduate of Atlanta University and medical school in the North, a veteran of World War I and, as the novel opens, a proud young physician starting his career in his South Georgia hometown. Clearly a "message novel" on the necessity of civil rights activism, *The Fire in the Flint* informs white readers about the existence of a distinguished black professional class held back by irrational prejudice, and castigates the nation for its racial barbarism. Accommodation to the mores of Southern segregation, the book reveals, can no longer keep any Negro safe. While neither Fauset's nor White's first novels departed dramatically from earlier models produced by Frances E. W. Harper and Charles Chesnutt, and while neither made major innovations in novelistic form, they demonstrated the potential for black-authored fiction to make a mark in the literary field as a new set of "modernist" publishers took interest in American cultural diversity and radical critique. The work that really broke the mold and helped inspire new forms of African American fiction was published a year before Fauset's and White's – Jean Toomer's multi-generic tour de force, *Cane* (1923).

While not exactly a novel, *Cane* explored many of the different possibilities for black fiction that would be taken up by others and worked out in novelistic form. Toomer borrowed techniques and structural innovations eclectically from such literary models as the "lyric novels" of Sherwood Anderson and Waldo Frank and the drama of Eugene O'Neill, while infusing these with the improvisatory qualities and the rhythms of African American spirituals and jazz, the latter of which, to Toomer, epitomized American modernism in the field of music. This merging of forms associated with different racial backgrounds of avant-garde art suited his belief in the birth of a new "American race" – an idea one can find in his predecessor Charles Chesnutt and that remained a minor yet significant thread in Negro Renaissance thought and art. Toomer's creation of a hybrid literary form consonant with new types of popular culture suggested exciting possibilities for black literary experimentation and implied the need to improvise new idioms and new formal and technical strategies for an adequate expression of African American responses to human experience.

By 1926, following the publication of White's and Fauset's first novels; of books of poetry by Claude McKay, Countee Cullen, and Langston Hughes; and of the landmark anthology *The New Negro*, black literary circles around the country – but especially in New York – debated the new possibilities for black writing and different positions on what forms "the literature of the Negro" should take. Was there, or should there be, such a thing as "Negro art"? Was there anything so distinctive about black culture and experience that it called for special methods of poetic or fictional representation? What relationship should there be between African American culture and African art? Were there aspects of black experience that, in the context of the struggle to overcome centuries of demeaning caricature in European and American art, and in the context of a current vogue for the "primitive," ought to be left alone? Would black authors allow the expectations of white audiences and institutions to corrupt and co-opt their talent? Whereas in the early 1920s W. E. B. Du Bois had castigated black readers for insisting on melodramatic plots, fantastically good heroes and heroines, and racial propaganda generally – all potentially inimical to artistic achievement – by 1926 he feared the Negro Renaissance was becoming apolitical, that white editors and audiences had seduced black artists into a hollow aestheticism – or worse. "All art is propaganda and ever must be, despite the wailing of the purists," he announced in "Criteria of Negro Art." The abandonment of propaganda that the philosopher Alain Locke had called for in his essays for *The New Negro*, Du Bois feared, would "turn the Negro Renaissance into decadence."[2] Writers, theorists, and literary historians have long commented on the black novelist's problem of a "divided audience" (that is, an audience divided between blacks and whites); in the 1920s, divisions within the African American readership were just as significant.

The white novelist and music critic Carl Van Vechten's *Nigger Heaven* dropped into the midst of this debate with incendiary éclat and made vividly evident wide divergences of opinion on the directions black fiction should take.[3] By placing the abortive relationship between an aspiring black novelist and a frustrated black librarian (named Mary Love) at the center of the novel, Van Vechten tried to suggest the potential of a black literary universe begging to be born – comprising novels of the black underworld, of the glamorous as well as "low-down" cabarets, of the striving middle class and struggling young professionals, of those who "pass," of Harlem's everyday working people, of the white interlopers and "friends of the Negro," as well as slummers and mediocre writers looking for "material," of the black vamps and "sweetmen," and of blues women and jazz men. Attempting (unsuccessfully) to patch together examples of all these different types of fiction around the central romantic tragedy, spiced up with sensational scenes of sadomasochism and a title guaranteed to shock, *Nigger Heaven* became a kind of Rorschach test of literary taste – and a bestseller. Many black readers found the novel a vicious slander on their race, but Van Vechten's friends in Harlem – including several of the most important novelists of the renaissance – warmly praised the novel, were reviled by its critics, and kept writing. Two of them were Nella Larsen and Rudolph Fisher, whom Van Vechten and Walter White steered to their own publisher, Alfred A. Knopf.

Larsen's semi-autobiographical *Quicksand* (1928) followed the labyrinthine search for "home" of a young woman born in a Chicago slum to a Danish immigrant woman and a black man. In a radical subversion of earlier patterns of tragic mulatto fiction and romances of racial uplift, Larsen explores the subordination of family to race, the articulation of race with male dominance, and the enslavement of women's bodies to procreation of racial subjects alienated from themselves and their mothers by national ideologies of racial and class identity.[4] As Hazel Carby has argued, it would be some twenty years before black women's fiction returned to such a complex, comprehensive confrontation of race, class, and sexuality within an urban setting.[5] Larsen, whose feminism derived in part from her nursing career and the experience of being torn from her white mother by racial segregation, reveals black feminist consciousness not as an "inheritance" from Southern folk or the creation of college-trained intellectuals but as a critical and highly diversified feature of modernity, responding to historically specific modes of women's oppression and subordination, always articulated with racial power.

In contrast to Larsen, Jessie Fauset remained wedded to the traditional romance format and to the ideology of racial uplift, believing in the essential moral superiority of African Americans and the ideal of race as a focus of personal identity. In Fauset's "passing" novel, *Plum Bun*, Angela Murray decides to "pass" as white, only to discover the shallowness and corrupt nature of white society. She learns that she is much better off within the fold of her own race and family. After a series of plot twists generated in the first instance by Angela's racial confusion and moral weakness, eventually all ends well with the leading women characters reconciled, properly matched to men of their own race, and devoted to the cause of racial advance. Subtitled "A Novel Without a Moral" in a direct slap, apparently, at Carl Van Vechten's recently published *Nigger Heaven* (which had been reviewed positively in the black-owned *New York Age* under the heading "A Novel With a Moral") and possibly Claude McKay's *Banjo* (subtitled "A Story Without a Plot"), *Plum Bun* exemplified the sort of idealism, optimism, and pride of race that many African Americans believed the white publishing industry would not accept in "Negro fiction."[6]

Only a few weeks after *Plum Bun*'s appearance, Alfred A. Knopf brought out Nella Larsen's *Passing* novel, dedicated to Carl Van Vechten and his wife, Fania Marinoff, in a clear statement of where Larsen stood in the contemporary debates over black fiction. Again shredding the seams of the conventional romance – and, for that matter, earlier passing fiction – Larsen almost exactly inverts *Plum Bun*'s narrative logic and structural resolutions. While in most earlier black-authored "passing" novels the goal of passing is to get what white people have, and to be "free," in Larsen's novel Clare Kendry passes in order to get what her better-off black friends have, for her family background precludes her moving into their class position within the carefully policed boundaries of respectable black society. Ultimately feeling trapped and lonely in the white world, she seeks to return to the black world, fearless about whether she will be "found out" by her racist husband. Whereas "Angele Mory" ("Dead Angel") is reborn as Angela Murray after happily rejoining the race at the end of *Plum Bun*, in Larsen's novel, Clare's closest black friend, Irene Redfield, is determined to prevent her return to the "race." In a striking reversal of the usual tropes connecting whiteness with freedom and blackness with unfreedom, Irene decides she cannot "have [Clare] free" – that is, free of her white identity, or her husband – and kills her just as her identity as a black white woman is exposed.[7] The novel ingeniously develops Irene's feelings of attraction to and repulsion from the transgressive subjectivity of a woman both black and white – whose brazen border-crossings threaten the boundaries on which Irene's secure life has been carefully built. Daring in her address to issues of homoeroticism, Larsen at the same time spotlights the threat (and fetishistic appeal) of interraciality to racial order.[8] Even structurally, *Passing* practically inverts the patterns of the classic romance that emerged in the context of legitimating European "races" and nations.

The intersection of race, class, gender, and sexuality in the urban black context also defines the geography of Rudolph Fisher's first novel, *The Walls of Jericho* (1928), but with the focus on black men. Fisher sets his narrative in the midst of black Harlem's expansion and attempts to comprehend all classes of black society. In particular, the novel addresses the class division between "dickties" and "rats" – professional and working-class men – with an understated theme that African Americans in the city need a "business class, an economic backbone" that would bind the "dickties" and "rats" together.[9] The hopeful vision of the future with which the novel ends derives from a conviction that blacks can make capitalism work for them if they can join together and overcome barriers to self-knowledge – the "walls of Jericho" named in the title. The core of the novel, however, focuses on those barriers to self-knowledge as conditioned by historical trauma and white racism; and these barriers are highly gendered. Men turn the anger born of that trauma toward each other, or remain imprisoned by an obsessive hatred that isolates them and prevents self-knowledge, even in those most dedicated to the common cause of the "race." Fisher analyzes the hard shell that black men wear to keep from exposing weakness or fear, a shell that affects their relationships with each other as well as with women – preventing them from expressing tenderness or friendship openly. He presents glimpses, nonetheless, of a deep fraternal bond black men too rarely acknowledge openly. A greater self-knowledge, he implies, would allow black men to renegotiate all their human relationships in more productive ways – relationships, particularly, with each other and with black women. This would become a classic theme in twentieth-century black fiction.

Fisher's second novel, *The Conjure-Man Dies* (1932), apparently only the second black-authored mystery novel, also essentially circles around issues of black masculinity in American society, but in an even more obsessive and perhaps psychologically revealing way. The Harlem detective, Perry Dart, and the physician who assists him, Dr. John Archer, must solve the mystery of who murdered an African "psychist" named N. Frimbo during a psychic session. It turns out that Frimbo was not murdered (although he will be in the end), and the conventional "murder mystery" pattern is soon overshadowed by a series of mysterious motifs concerning male sexuality, beginning with questions about an "over-absence of the feminine" in Frimbo's apartment. In the early chapters of the novel, Dart and Archer discover in the rear room of Frimbo's flat a chemical workbench and cabinets, one of which contains a specimen jar containing two male "sex glands." The real mystery, from this point on, centers around the meaning and origin of the pair of testicles. Near the novel's close, Frimbo reveals to Archer the African rite that has been a secret of his family for hundreds of years, "the rite of the gonad" that maintains "the unbroken heritage of the past." The protoplasm within the gonad, "continuously maintained throughout thousands of generations," turns out to be the very key to freedom, for "[H]e who can master his past – that man is free."[10] This emphasis on mastery of the past as the key to freedom, and specifically of male freedom and masculine potency, responds to the emasculation of black American men, the loss of African cultural foundations, and the continuous erasure of or assault on father–son ties – a theme in later black fiction, notably by Alex Haley and Toni Morrison. Yet the apparent equation of racial self-possession and "freedom" with recovery of hereditary male authority and sexual dominance stands in powerful tension with, for example, the feminist aspects of Larsen's and Zora Neale Hurston's fiction.

Toomer's turn to "folk" sources in the first section of *Cane* connected with contemporary interest in "authentic" experience and/or expression in the modern wasteland, as understood by transatlantic modernists. This strain of modernist thinking and art tended toward primitivism and romanticism, as well as toward the belief, going back to the eighteenth century, that all cultures develop from a distinctive "folk" background. The success of the Irish Renaissance and of new Russian drama based on peasant life helped stimulate artistic interest in the "black folk" of the South and their cultural expressions. Moreover, critically acclaimed "Negro folk novels" by whites such as DuBose Heyward and Julia Peterkin created a stir in black intellectual circles and encouraged the move toward a fiction based on the lives of the people "farthest down." Authors such as Claude McKay, Langston Hughes, Arna Bontemps, and Zora Neale Hurston began not just incorporating folk forms into fiction, but bending generic conventions to create novelistic equivalents to popular black musical and narrative forms – specifically blues, ballads, and folktales.

Claude McKay's *Home to Harlem* (1928) takes its readers on a detailed tour of what McKay termed the "semi-underworld" of black working-class life, among the buffet flats and speakeasies frequented by single black men. McKay deliberately defied the critics who insisted black art should serve racial uplift, partly because he thought they knew nothing about art, and partly because their point of view was too conservatively bourgeois. McKay, a radical socialist at the time, no doubt felt he was writing a type of proletarian novel. His very choice of the picaresque tale as opposed to the more complex plotting of the classic novel constitutes a gesture of independence from bourgeois conventions.

The novel centers on the adventures of Jake, a longshoreman who deserted from the US Army during World War I. On his first night back in Harlem, he picks up a charming occasional prostitute who likes him so much she returns his payment for her services. Jake spends much of the rest of the novel hoping to find his beautiful "brownskin" again, while McKay introduces us to a considerable range of black male working-class "types," first in Harlem, then on the railroad and in a variety of cities where black railroad employees stop over between runs. Throughout, blues music provides a kind of steady backbeat and refrain, distilling the rhythms and "melancholy-comic" quality of the black workingman's response to existence. Most important of the characters other than Jake is the Haitian intellectual and aspiring novelist, Ray, who generally enunciates McKay's intellectual and aesthetic principles. Like McKay, Ray aspires to make art out of the "fertile reality around him," signifying McKay's belief in the proletarian or peasant black's "primitive birthright," the most valuable weapon for human self-preservation in the modern world and a central component of McKay's black cultural nationalism.[11] Believing that the future of the race depends on those (mostly dark-skinned and lower-class) still in touch with their "primitive" selves, McKay depicts their lives unapologetically, and yet in a romantic way that betrays his own sense of intellectual superiority to their authentic yet rather unreflective lives.[12]

When *Home to Harlem* became a bestseller – the only black-authored novel of the period to so succeed commercially – its critics felt vindicated in their judgment that this was the sort of black fiction white readers wanted; conversely, they reasoned, it was exactly what the black community did not need, and McKay shared in the obloquy showered upon Van Vechten for *Nigger Heaven*, which many (wrongly) thought McKay had tried to emulate. W. E. B. Du Bois fumed, "After the dirtier parts of its filth, I feel distinctly like taking a bath." McKay, he charged, had prostituted his talent to the "prurient demand" of a "certain decadent section of the white American world."[13] Rejecting the criticism of black periodicals, McKay wrote Langston Hughes, "We must leave the appreciation of what we are doing to the emancipated Negro intelligentsia of the future, while we are sardonically aware now that only the intelligentsia of the superior race is developed enough to afford artistic truth."[14]

Significantly, Langston Hughes considered *Home to Harlem* "undoubtedly the best thing we've done yet."[15] In *Not Without Laughter* (1930), following in important respects the lead of McKay but in a more middle-American cultural geography, Hughes strove to depict "more or less typical small-town life in any town outside of the South . . . the average, small Main Street town."[16] The texture of black working-class life had never been rendered with such unapologetic tenderness and fidelity as in this novel centering on the life of young James "Sandy" Rodgers. Hughes exposed, with searing authority, the everyday wounds of racism on blacks in the South and Midwest between the turn of the twentieth century and World War I, and the long prehistory of white terror. In the context of this inescapable reality, popular music (particularly the blues) and black religion provide competing forms of saving grace. The conflict between the "sinners" and the "saved" within Sandy's family provides the chief source of rising tension in the novel and its thematic focus. The conflict is finally resolved when Aunt Harriett, the "Princess of the Blues," insists on Sandy's continuing his education; he must, as his "dicty" Aunt Tempy might have said, "get ahead – all of us niggers are too far back in this white man's country to let any brains go to waste!"[17] In the closing passages of the novel, as Sandy walks home with his mother from a Chicago restaurant (having migrated to that city in the final chapters), they hear the congregation of a "Southern" church in a back street singing: *"By an' by when de mawnin' comes, / Saints an' sinners all are gathered home"* (p. 298). Sandy speaks for the young Langston Hughes, on whose youth the story is partially based, in finding here a model for black aesthetic achievement. No novel had yet portrayed so successfully an "ordinary" black working-class family, revealing the extraordinary tensions and complexity of their lives, and their essential, sustaining spirituality, whether "sacred" or "profane." And no novel had woven black popular music and dance so effectively into its story-line to help carry the major leitmotifs and themes of the novel. The result was not merely to show the origins and function of the music in small black communities across the country, but to suggest the possibility of a reading experience vaguely akin to that of listening to "folk" blues, spirituals, and early jazz.

Only a year after Hughes's novel, another novel working in the "folk" style and liberally seasoned with blues lyrics and roustabouts appeared in the form of Arna Bontemps's *God Sends Sunday* (1931), focusing on the up-and-down career of "Little Augie," a black jockey from the South. Not surprisingly, however, Bontemps's focus on the "disorganized" life of black vice districts and sporting circles (which he may have justified as true to his "folk" models) provoked the wrath of African American critics who considered it a confirmation of white stereotyping, a form of literary pandering. Filled with bad men and loose women, sports and prostitutes, *God Sends Sunday* received the same sort of criticism that McKay's *Home to Harlem* had. Yet in this case, the use of primitivism and "folk types," as Amritjit Singh has argued, does not serve to define racial identity or a basis of black nationalism as overtly as in McKay's novel.[18] What made the novel a contribution in its time was a skillful handling of dialogue and "folk humor" (as it was called at the time) presented in a straightforward and nonjudgmental style. In his review of the book for *Opportunity*, Sterling Brown astutely affiliated the novel with the folk ballad tradition and termed its protagonist "a genuine creation in our gallery of folk portraits."[19] The simple storytelling style and episodic development indicate that Bontemps was attempting a novelistic equivalent of folk ballads such as "Frankie and Johnny" – echoes of which Brown immediately recognized – and "low-down blues" of the sort the novelist liberally reproduces throughout the narrative.

A rarely discussed novel of the "folk," George Wylie Henderson's *Ollie Miss* (1935), attests to the continuing hold of Booker T. Washington's gospel of work and rural self-sufficiency.[20] This *Bildungsroman* follows the life of the poverty-stricken title character as she struggles through various forms of alienation and romantic crisis to finally acquire her own farm, on which she raises a child without the support of a man. Sexually autonomous, "masculine" in physical strength and manners, Ollie Miss achieves self-fulfillment in harmony with a collective "folk" rhythm of dignified rural labor and natural cycles that Henderson renders with a high degree of technical skill. Yet the real socio-economic structures and historical trajectory of his native region challenge Henderson's lyric idyll, as Ollie's "own" farm is actually a piece of her uncle's tenant farm. Thus, an aesthetic that dignifies black "folk life" and the putative autonomy of a female heroine need not have progressive political implications – as some black authors of the 1930s themselves understood.

This understanding helps explain why some left-wing critics reacted negatively to Zora Neale Hurston's fiction, finding in it a romantic nostalgia ignoring economic and racial exploitation. The "protest" aspects of Hurston's fiction were perhaps too indirect and subtle for readers of the 1930s to detect, but when all is said and done, Hurston's greatest accomplishment remains her extraordinary command of language, her success in dramatically transforming the uses of literary "dialect" and its relation to narrative voice. Hurston came up with the sort of "speakerly text," as Henry Louis Gates Jr. has called it, that moves easily between "authentic" Southern black dialogue and the "free indirect discourse" of the narrative voice.[21] For African American prose narrative, her achievement was the literary equivalent of the Great Migration, dependent not only on her rural Southern background but on the opportunities she seized in the intellectual phantasmagoria of Manhattan.

In view of the common belief that publishers had lost interest in black authors with the onset of the Depression, it is worth pointing out that Hurston wrote her first novel only after an editor at J. B. Lippincott, impressed by one of her short stories, asked if she was working on a novel. The query prompted her to go back to her native Florida and start writing one. *Jonah's Gourd Vine* was accepted for publication four months later, in October 1933. In this *Bildungsroman* centered on the life of John Pearson, a poor and fatherless "yellow" boy become preacher and philanderer, Hurston the anthropologist and folklore collector is not yet thoroughly fused with the storyteller and modern novelist, but all the basic ingredients are laid out for one of the major developments in black fiction. Frequently suggesting African origins for the spirituality, music, and preacher's role she features throughout the book, Hurston's overriding purpose, as John Lowe identifies it, is "to show the world the glory of African American folklore and language and the central role it plays in sustaining the community."[22] Notably, for Hurston this function has almost completely displaced that of rescuing the "image of the Negro" from stereotypes or *directly* protesting racial oppression.

Another *Bildungsroman*, this time of a black woman, Hurston's *Their Eyes Were Watching God* (1937) shows the complete fusion of the competing strains (of voice, narrative strategy, and point of view) so noticeably unreconciled in the first novel. Hurston's personal background and infallible ear, her training in anthropology, her fearlessness, her belief in the power of African American expressive culture, all combined to produce voices previously unheard in American literature. Those voices saturate the "free indirect style" of her narrative voice and, simultaneously, provide one of her greatest themes:

> It was the time to hear things and talk. These sitters had been tongueless, earless, eyeless conveniences all day long. Mules and other brutes had occupied their skins. But now, the sun and the bossman were gone, so the skins felt powerful and human. They became lords of sounds and lesser things. They passed nations through their mouths. They sat in judgment.[23]

Never mind that at the moment, the talkers were casting aspersions on – indeed, deliberately scapegoating – Hurston's heroine. Hurston, an individualist to the core, was not one to sweep away contradictory aspects of "the black community"; communities are, by nature, double-edged necessities, and Hurston herself, it seems, always lived between them. Critics will long debate Hurston's politics and the nature of her feminism. Her ability to hear the unheard and "inappropriate," her view of self-revelation as the "oldest human longing" – a belief only available to an author of the broadest sympathies – makes her the most unruly novelist of the Negro Renaissance. It is not surprising that, of all the black novelists of the "renaissance" generation who aspired to write a "white novel," Hurston was the first to complete and publish one: *Seraph on the Suwanee* (1948).

While several writers thought of the "folk" as the authentic origin of a black modernist aesthetic, as David G. Nicholls has argued, the "folk" concept is as much a *product* of modern race consciousness as its historical origin.[24] It thus serves as a kind of medium or metaphor through which authors coming from different ideological, geographical, social, and aesthetic positions compete in the struggle to define a modern collective project for racial advance. The tension between black authors' approaches to the "folk," then, attests to the emergence of a field of literary discourse that had been, before 1923, comparatively one-dimensional and confining – and overwhelmingly circumscribed by conventions developed in white-authored novels. Richard Wright would dismiss Hurston as a romantic of backward political orientation, but both the quality of his own early fiction and its favorable reception would have been inconceivable without her example, and that of Langston Hughes and Claude McKay. One thinks especially of Wright's novellas collected in *Uncle Tom's Children* (1938), the pivot between the Negro Renaissance and what was to come.

An important strain in several novels of the Negro Renaissance is a self-conscious critique of the "Negro vogue." One main character in *Nigger Heaven* complains, "Now the white editors are beginning to regard Negroes as interesting novelties, like white elephants or black roses"; other characters deride the white vogue for Harlem nightclubs that has even led some clubs to exclude black patrons. Major characters mock the idea of Harlem as a "mecca" of the New Negro and the notion that artists and writers can break the bars of racial exclusion: "Of course, Paul Robeson and Roland Hayes and Countee Cullen can go anywhere within reason. They will be invited to white dinner parties, but I don't see how that's going to affect the rest of us."[25] Fisher, similarly, satirizes the notion that "social mixing" will overcome racism, aims bitter sarcasm toward notions of black "primitivism," and makes fun of white editors who enthuse about "the 'wealth of material' to be found in Negro Harlem," or who jump to praise anything written by a Negro, as long as it has some element of the "African" in it.[26] Such critiques also play an important role in Claude McKay's *Banjo*, Nella Larsen's *Passing*, George Schuyler's *Black No More*, and Wallace Thurman's *The Blacker the Berry*. . . . Satire on the "vogue of the Negro" was not merely a retrospective phenomenon but an essential feature of the "renaissance" itself.

Wallace Thurman's *The Blacker the Berry* . . . (1929), centering on the experiences of lonely, dark-skinned Emma Lou Morgan, mercilessly attacks intraracial "colorism" and classism, and in the process realistically exposes the deteriorating conditions in "renaissance" Harlem, where the latter half of the novel takes place. Here, outside the comfortable homes of the elite, the mass of people struggle to find and keep work in order to pay for miserable tenement rooms and to divert themselves in cheap theaters or public dance halls where, it seems, everyone is "on the make" and no one, including Emma Lou, finds black to be beautiful – Negro vogue or not. The only people who rise above such prejudices – the young "New Negro" writers and artists to whom she is introduced – are themselves crippled by self-doubt and detached by temperament and training from the "common people" they admire.

Capping the cynicism of Thurman's novel, in *Black No More* (1931) George Schuyler, the most skeptical of all black authors about the notion of a "Negro renaissance," takes broad aim at the multifaceted American racial discourse of the era and all the "scams" dependent on it (in Schuyler's view), including white supremacy and "Negro uplift" as well as the literary Renaissance itself. The two great driving forces of American culture (and perhaps all culture), in Schuyler's novel, are greed and sexual desire – and they are deeply intertwined at the racial border. The origin of American racial institutions, according to Schuyler, lay in economic history going back to the early years of American settlement, when "race-mixing" had to be repressed – or, where it could not be repressed, disavowed – to preserve a slave system dependent on racial distinction. Thus race became one of the major integuments of the capitalist system in the United States, and the sites of the disavowed yet pervasive racial "mixture" that characterized the nation displayed all the characteristics of both commodity fetishism, in the Marxian sense, and sexual fetishism, in the Freudian sense. Racial distinction became a source of economic gain and erotic fantasy while the actual extent of "miscegenation" was hidden behind the luster of racial purity.

The novel's dual plot structure follows, on the one hand, the attempts of Max Disher (an "ex-colored man") to connect with the white Helen Givens (daughter of the head of the Knights of Nordica) and, on the other, the social and political effects of Dr. Junius Crookman's invention, "Black No More." The first story is a classic comic romance, with the romantic couple blocked by hereditary institutions but finally united as the nucleus of a new configuration. The second has no true resolution but, in the mode of political satire, stresses the abstract design of incidents to achieve a concentration of irony and sarcasm. At the end of the novel Crookman becomes Surgeon General of the United States – a particularly ironic denouement in view of the era's concerns about "race hygiene" – and the American social and political landscape have been transformed, but not necessarily for the better. A satirist to the end, Schuyler does not offer a successful antidote to the absurdities of American race-thinking but rather revels in them while exploding the genealogical narratives that undergird notions of "tradition" and "purity."

In his *roman-à-clef*, *Infants of the Spring* (1932), Wallace Thurman revived several figures from his first novel and thrashed out many of the cultural debates that exercised the "Harlem school" of New Negro authors while coming to a bleak conclusion about the nature of the "renaissance" and, more broadly, the future of black culture. Debilitating black self-doubt, condescending white patronage, self-destructive Bohemianism, gay sexual ambivalence, interracial misunderstanding, and class conflict all combine to nip the hopes of cultural rebirth in the bud, as the title borrowed from *Hamlet* suggests. *Infants of the Spring* is a painful novel to read, not so much because of its satirical treatment of the Negro Renaissance as because of its own failure to rise above the kind of adolescent self-consciousness it projects onto a movement far broader and more firmly grounded than what it portrays. Thurman's self-consciousness, that is, about being one of the "avant-garde" – along with his purported disdain for all things held sacred by both the bourgeoisie and the rabble (an attitude much beholden to the model of H. L. Mencken) – causes him to generalize the dysfunctions of a small clique housed in "Niggerati manor" to the fate of African American literature and art generally. The strongest passage in all Thurman's fiction can be found in the novel's conclusion, in which he describes a drawing by Paul Arbian of

> an inky black skyscraper, modeled after Niggerati Manor, . . . on which were focused an array of blindingly white beams of light. The foundation of this building was composed of crumbling stone. At first glance it could be ascertained that the skyscraper would soon crumble and fall, leaving the dominating white lights in full possession of the sky.

This passage is most often interpreted as an epitaph to the Negro Renaissance. Thurman may have so intended it, but in reality it was the exemplary gesture of a broader movement toward the somewhat limited phenomenon better termed "the Negro vogue."

Probably the most important novel of the 1920s in connecting the "American" dimensions of the Negro Renaissance with black culture globally was Claude McKay's *Banjo: A Story Without a Plot* (1929).[27] Forming a kind of "pendant" with *Home to Harlem*, this picaresque tale brings many of the thematic concerns and techniques of the former novel to bear on the more international black context of "the Ditch" in Marseilles, the squalid quarter inhabited by itinerant working-class men of all races, and, more notably for the Jamaican McKay, black working-class men of all nations. The novel showcases debates about various forms of pan-Africanism by a broad array of workingmen and drifters, but also reintroduces Ray of *Home to Harlem* as the self-conscious "intellectual" who allows McKay to enunciate his own positions on black art, as in the earlier novel. Through Ray, too, McKay answers the critics of that work and deliberately rejects any concern about a racially "dual" audience:

> I think about my race as much as you . . . but if I am writing a story – well, it's like all of us in this place here, black and brown and white, and I telling a story for the love of it. Some of you will listen, and some won't. If I am a real story-teller, I won't worry about the differences in complexion of those who listen and those who don't, I'll just identify myself with those who are really listening and tell my story.[28]

The novel places its hopes for the future of the race in the "primitive" blacks of all nations who remain in touch with their "native roots." Lacking any sort of social or economic power, these men perform political resistance unself-consciously through everyday cultural practices, descended from African traditions, in the interstices of national formations. Several setpieces render storytelling, music, and dance performed by men from Africa, the Caribbean, and the United States to reveal continuities in black diasporic cultures, adapted to the specific circumstances of life in different geographies.

A "biological kinship to the swell of primitive earth life" saves lower-class blacks from being completely deadened and integrated into the machine civilization that has enervated the white proletariat. Here the "primitive" is not the antithesis of the "modern" but a kind of participation in the rhythms of life that grounds what McKay regards as true "culture." By the same token, the language of the men of "the Ditch" retains a vitality and artistic edge that keeps up with the real conditions of modern life. *Banjo* offers a striking argument about who constitutes the linguistic vanguard in the era of high modernist poetics. Similarly, doubting the Leninist model of proletarian revolution, Ray has come to place his hope in the race's ability to remain spiritually impervious to "the machine" until, perhaps, the machine "stopped of its own exhaustion." The great question McKay leaves us with is whether the uncommon common people of the black diaspora can preserve their "primitive birthright" in future generations.

It should not be surprising to find an almost diametrically opposed notion of third-world race-based politics in W. E. B. Du Bois's *Dark Princess* (1929). Du Bois's long-standing belief in the need for an intellectual–political vanguard composed of the "Talented Tenth" of subaltern peoples here combines with his belief in the world-historical role of African Americans. Weakening the international anti-imperialist movement of colored peoples at the beginning of the novel is the assumption that the movement must be led by hereditary elites, members of the traditional nobility; and this ideological weakness connects with their conviction that American blacks (descendants of slaves) are cowardly, intellectually inferior, and politically docile. Matthew Towns, however, inspires them, with the help of the Indian Princess Kautilya, to recognize the virtue of democratic idealism (the one thing of value that "America" has given the world), of building the revolutionary vanguard out of an aristocracy of merit rather than birth – in short, what Du Bois had years earlier termed a "Talented Tenth."

Dedicated to "Titania XXVII" by the "Queen of Faerie," and subtitled *A Romance*, the book frankly announces its fantastic quality and its generic debts.[29] It is no coincidence that a form identified with feudal social structures and genteel aesthetics should serve as Du Bois's vehicle for a political novel, as opposed to McKay's choice of the picaresque. If McKay finds the most valid internationalism and the most salvific cultural politics for blacks in the vulgar and the "low," Du Bois finds them in the "High Command" of the "Great Central Committee of Yellow, Brown, and Black" of the "Great Council of Darker Peoples" – something in the order of a modern Round Table, which has deliberately planned the liberation of the "darker races" to begin in 1952. Du Bois's romance plot, after putting its two main characters – Princess Kautilya of Bwodpur, India, and Matthew Towns of rural

Prince James County, Virginia – through the trials and tribulations necessary for full political enlightenment and indestructible moral resolve, ecstatically unites the darker races of the world through them, and more particularly through the birth of their son, the "Messenger and Messiah to all the Darker Worlds." Nothing could be further from McKay's tendencies to paganism, unconcern for long-term romantic heterosexual commitment, and locating the most authentic expressions of black political resistance in "low" aesthetic forms – the expressions of what Kautilya refers to as the "dead, sluggish, brutalized masses of men" (p. 225). While the picaresque plot of McKay's novel ends without any true resolution, on a "realistic" note of wondering whether blacks will be able to resist the soul-deadening rationality of the "machine" civilization, "the providential nature of the romance," as Claudia Tate points out, "facilitates Du Bois's conscious endeavor to preserve his faith in the inevitability of racial justice."[30]

The next deliberately "radical" black novel to put African American rebellion in the context of revolutionary movements of the world's "darker races" would be Arna Bontemps's *Black Thunder* (1936), partly inspired by the Scottsboro trial in Alabama and by the Indian independence movement led by Gandhi. Bontemps took for the subject of this important historical novel an aborted uprising of the "brutalized masses" – black Southern slaves – led by Gabriel Prosser in 1800. What most distinguishes *Black Thunder* from the African American novels of the 1920s is the turn to historical reflection on slavery and emphasis on revolutionary violence as a necessary aspect of proletarian upheaval. The thoughts of a sailor from San Domingo who looks on as the hero of the novel is taken from jail might be those of Bontemps in the era of Scottsboro and Gandhi's rebellion: "He understood now that words like *freedom* and *liberty* drip blood – always, everywhere, there was blood on such words" (p. 196). Set in the period just after the revolution led by Toussaint L'Ouverture in San Domingo, the novel implies clear parallels between the worldwide revolutionary currents of that era and those of the 1930s, to the extent that Bontemps's French radicals (immigrants to the United States) speak in terms drawn straight from the left-wing lexicon of Depression-era America. But while associating the uprising with other revolutionary movements (in Ireland, France, and the Caribbean), in a clear parallel to the communist movements of his own time, Bontemps stresses that it is self-motivated and autonomous, inspired by a will to freedom and not by "white" intellectual concepts – even though Bontemps articulates the uprising's connections to a broader radical intellectual tradition and the contemporary discourse of the "Rights of Man." If earlier novels had begun exploring the possibilities of fiction rooted in the contemporary experiences and expression of "the folk," Bontemps re-imagined those possibilities in the context of re-imagining black history. As Eric Sundquist has pointed out, "No one, no historian and novelist, had written so completely of the motives and barriers to revolt as though from within slave culture."[31] Bontemps's work is an attempt to imagine a broad cross-section of African American slave culture as a potentially revolutionary proletariat, and to examine the many forces that made its potential, as well as its possible conjunction with white working-class radicalism, historically unrealizable – and thus tragically heroic.

Looking back in 1968, Bontemps considered this, his second novel, a work not of the Harlem Renaissance but rather of a succeeding period of dispersion when various Harlem Renaissance writers and leaders moved away from New York in the wake of the stock market crash. Nonetheless, many of the fundamental strategies, motifs, and patterns of African American achievement in the novel developed during the "renaissance," even if they were not all brought to full fruition at that time. Crucial to this phenomenon and its enduring significance in African American literary history was the diversity of aims and aesthetics, of social and cultural assumptions, and of political positions adopted by the authors. Their implicit and explicit critiques of each other combined with their sense of collective identity to produce a field of discourse rather than a singular "school" or tradition. If the next generation of black novelists defined themselves against what they often called "the Harlem School," we should remember that this is a typical modernist strategy for staking new ground; the fact remains that their work would have been inconceivable without that of their predecessors. The legacy of the Negro Renaissance is still very much alive, legible in the vast majority of black novels published in the seven decades that have followed.

NOTES

1. Hazel V. Carby, *Reconstructing Womanhood: The Emergence of the Afro-American Woman Novelist* (New York: Oxford University Press, 1987), pp. 168, 171. Important scholarship that has helped resurrect Fauset's reputation includes Carolyn Wedin Sylvander's *Jessie Redmon Fauset, Black American Writer* (Troy, NY: Whitston, 1981); Deborah E. McDowell's introduction to *Plum Bun* (Boston: Pandora, 1985); Thadious Davis's Foreword to *There is Confusion* (Boston: Beacon Press, 1989); Ann DuCille, *The Coupling Convention: Sex, Text, and Tradition in Black Women's Fiction* (New York: Oxford University Press, 1993), pp. 86–105; and Jacquelyn Y. McLendon, *The Politics of Color in the Fiction of Jessie Fauset and Nella Larsen* (Charlottesville: University Press of Virginia, 1995). See also Jane Kuenz, "The Face of America: Performing Race and Nation in Jessie Fauset's *There is Confusion*," *Yale Journal of Criticism* 12 (1999): 89–111.
2. Du Bois, review of *The New Negro*, rpt. in Herbert Aptheker, ed., *Book Reviews by W. E. B. Du Bois* (Millwood, NY: Kraus-Thompson, 1977), pp. 78–79.

3. For discussions of responses to the novel, see Emily Bernard, "What He Did for the Race: Carl Van Vechten and the Harlem Renaissance," *Soundings* 80 (1997): 531–542; and Kathleen Pfeiffer's recent introduction to the novel, in Carl Van Vechten, *Nigger Heaven* (Urbana: University of Illinois Press, 2000), pp. ix–xxxix. I am particularly indebted to Bernard's argument that the novel served as a catalyst of literary debate between different factions.

4. I make this argument at length in "Subject to Disappearance: Interracial Identity in Nella Larsen's *Quicksand*," *Temples for Tomorrow: Looking Back at the Harlem Renaissance*, eds. Geneviève Fabre and Michel Feith (Bloomington: Indiana University Press, 2001), pp. 177–192.

5. Carby, *Reconstructing Womanhood*, p. 175.

6. "A Novel With a Moral," *New York Age*, September 4, 1926.

7. *Passing*, in *"Quicksand" and "Passing"*, ed. Deborah E. McDowell (New Brunswick: Rutgers University Press, 1986), p. 239.

8. For a similar position, see Carby, *Reconstructing Womanhood*, p. 168.

9. Rudolph Fisher, *The Walls of Jericho* (New York: Knopf, 1928), p. 282.

10. Rudolph Fisher, *The Conjure-Man Dies: A Mystery Tale of Dark Harlem* (1932; rpt. Ann Arbor: University of Michigan Press, 1992), p. 269.

11. Claude McKay, *Home to Harlem* (1928; rpt. Boston: Northeastern University Press, 1987), p. 228. On the connection between McKay's cultural nationalism and primitivism, see especially Tracy McCabe, "The Multifaceted Politics of Primitivism in Harlem Renaissance Writing," *Soundings* 80 (1997): 475–497.

12. McKay's primitivism, as Tracy McCabe has pointed out, is politically radical but "inflected by traditional class and gender hierarchies." Tracy McCabe, "Multifaceted Politics," p. 492. For a critique of McKay's sexism and classism, see also Hazel V. Carby, "Policing the Black Woman's Body in an Urban Context," *Critical Inquiry* 18 (Summer 1992): 738–755.

13. Du Bois, review of Nella Larsen's *Quicksand*, Claude McKay's *Home to Harlem*, and Melville Herskovits's, *The American Negro*, *Crisis* (June 1928), rpt. in Aptheker, ed., *Book Reviews*, pp. 113–115.

14. Qtd. in Wayne F. Cooper, *Claude McKay: Rebel Sojourner in the Harlem Renaissance* (Baton Rouge: Louisiana State University Press, 1987), p. 247.

15. Langston Hughes to Claude McKay, qtd. in Cooper, *Claude McKay*, p. 243.

16. Qtd. in Hugh Gloster, *Negro Voices in American Fiction* (1948; rpt. New York: Russell & Russell, 1965), p. 185.

17. Langston Hughes, *Not Without Laughter* (1930; rpt. New York: Simon & Schuster, 1995), p. 298.

18. Amritjit Singh, *The Novels of the Harlem Renaissance: Twelve Black Writers, 1923–1933* (University Park: Pennsylvania State University Press, 1976), p. 56.

19. Sterling Brown, review of *God Sends Sunday*, *Opportunity* 9 (June 1931): 181.

20. See David G. Nicholls's discussion of *Ollie Miss*, to which I am much indebted, in *Conjuring the Folk: Forms of Modernity in African America* (Ann Arbor: University of Michigan Press, 2000), pp. 85–101.

21. See Henry Louis Gates Jr., *The Signifying Monkey: A Theory of African-American Literary Criticism* (New York: Oxford University Press, 1988), pp. 170–216.

22. John Lowe, *Jump At The Sun: Zora Neale Hurston's Cosmic Comedy* (Urbana: University of Illinois Press, 1994), p. 146.

23. Zora Neale Hurston, *Their Eyes Were Watching God* (1937; rpt. New York: Harper & Row, 1990), pp. 1–2.
24. *Conjuring the Folk*, especially pp. 1–7. See also Hazel V. Carby, "Ideologies of Black Folk: The Historical Novel of Slavery," *Slavery and the Literary Imagination*, ed. Deborah E. McDowell and Arnold Rampersad (Baltimore: Johns Hopkins University Press, 1989); and Carby, "The Politics of Fiction, Anthropology, and the Folk: Zora Neale Hurston," in Michael Awkward, ed., *New Essays on Their Eyes Were Watching God* (Cambridge: Cambridge University Press, 1990), pp. 71–93.
25. Van Vechten, *Nigger Heaven*, p. 48.
26. Rudolph Fisher, *The Walls of Jericho* (New York: Alfred A. Knopf, 1928), p. 100.
27. Brent Hayes Edwards, "Three Ways to Translate the Harlem Renaissance," *Temples for Tomorrow*, eds. Fabre and Feith (Bloomington: Indiana University Press, 2001), pp. 304–305.
28. Claude McKay, *Banjo: A Story Without a Plot* (1929; rpt. New York: Harcourt Brace Jovanovich, 1957), p. 115.
29. In *Psychoanalysis and Black Novels: Desire and the Protocols of Race* (New York: Oxford University Press, 1998), p. 61, Claudia Tate makes good use of M. H. Abrams's scholarship on the romance form with reference to *Dark Princess*.
30. Tate, *Psychoanalysis*, p. 61.
31. Eric J. Sundquist, *The Hammers of Creation: Folk Culture in Modern African-American Fiction* (Athens: University of Georgia Press, 1992), p. 99.

4

GISELLE LIZA ANATOL

Caribbean migration, ex-isles, and the New World novel

The African-Caribbean presence in the United States can be read as a paradox of discrimination: "first, an invisibility (in Ellisonian terms) because
the blackness of their skin color, which relegates them to classification as
Afro-Americans, which leaves their special needs as immigrants relatively
unattended; and second, a double visibility – as blacks to whites, and as foreigners to native blacks."[1] Literary representations of the dynamics between
African diasporic populations in the US – from the erasure and/or collapsing
of all cultural differences, to contention between US-born African Americans
and Caribbean immigrants, to calls for social and political allegiances –
will be the focus of this chapter. Particular attention will be paid to the
works of Caribbean-American writers, such as Paule Marshall and Edwidge
Danticat.

Within the black community, desires to fully participate in a supposedly
superior US society while simultaneously battling against its ideology of
white American superiority can significantly contribute to the erasure of a
Caribbean discourse from the US African American one.[2] Cultural elitism
(on both sides of the ethnic fence) – outweighing the pull of potential allegiances between different cultural groups – can be witnessed in the historical antagonisms between migrant groups (Jamaicans and Trinidadians, for
example), and US-born black subjects and the Caribbean immigrants who
were believed to be, alternately: (1) economically grasping, cold-hearted people, intent upon viciously undermining black Americans by accepting lower
wages; (2) primitive "monkey-chasers"; and (3) snobs who thought themselves intellectually and socially superior to African Americans.

This attitude is represented in Claude McKay's *Home to Harlem* (1928), as
one of the minor characters exclaims "Scotch! That's an ofay drink . . . And
I've seen the monkey chasers order it when they want to put on style" (38).
The Jamaican-born McKay, however, reveals the danger of such general-
izations: Jake, the African American hero of the novel, whom "everybody
liked and desired" (103), drinks scotch. Jake initially possesses a xenophobic

prejudice against Caribbean people: he "was very American in spirit and shared a little of that comfortable Yankee contempt for poor foreigners. And as an American Negro he looked askew at foreign niggers. Africa was jungle, and Africans bush niggers, cannibals. And West Indians were monkey chasers" (134). However, these views begin to be abraded by his friendship with Ray, a Haitian immigrant who educates Jake about black Haiti's independence movement, the false myth of the savage African jungle, and the destroyed ancient cultures and royalty of the Ashanti, Dahomey, Benin, Zulu, and Abyssinian kingdoms.

During much of the twentieth century, many Caribbean migrants did cling tightly to their national and ethnic identities in order to avoid identification with African Americans, whom they were socialized by US mainstream culture and European colonialism to see as lower-class and less ambitious.[3] This separatism obviously increased intraracial resentment. The myth of "West Indian exceptionalism" in the United States – the so-called model minority willfully holding itself apart from and above African Americans – was more often perpetuated by the fact that African Caribbeans did not usually become citizens, as they recognized that they had greater rights as foreigners than African Americans had as citizens.[4]

Caribbean-American novelist Paule Marshall highlights the diversity of Barbadian immigrant opinion regarding the native African American population in her 1959 novel *Brown Girl, Brownstones*. One of the members of the World War II era Brooklyn Barbadian Association urges his audience to earn enough money to make their group's voice heard at City Hall; he associates whiteness with power and luxury: "[T]hose big-shot white executives does play in their exclusive clubs – all the while drinking the best of scotch and smoking the finest cigars. No, we don have none of that. We ain white yet" (221). His proclamation of "we ain white *yet*" clearly sets forth his goals for joining the white American, and not the black American, community. Likewise, the protagonist's mother, Silla, confesses that she has resolved to succumb to US individualism and the capitalist ethos: to "make your way in this Christ world you got to be hard and sometimes misuse others, even your own" (224). For her, racial allegiance is to be jettisoned in favor of rising in socio-economic status. Significantly, she suggests that even ties of national and cultural origin will be abandoned for success. In other words her struggle is not specifically with US African Americans; it is with everyone (including Deighton, her own husband) who stands in the way of her progress. In striking contrast, another member of the Association counters that the group needs "to strike out that word *Barbadian* and put *Negro* . . . We got to stop thinking about just Bajan. We ain't home no more" (222). At the time in which the action takes place, however, his call for a diasporic community is shunned in favor of the individualism of the American Dream.

Unbeknownst to the African-Caribbean subjects who pursued this Dream, however, throughout much of the twentieth century they were faced with the racial hierarchies usually hidden by notions of immigrant mobility. As they entered the States, they were supposed to be the "new ethnics" who could bring cultural "flavor" to the American melting pot, as well as compete for and garner social and economic success. They were pleased to be thrust into a schema of black identity that placed them on top: Caribbean model minorities proving that race is no barrier, unmotivated US-born residents obsessed by race, and Africans from the jungle and primitive tribes. They were, however, put into competition against white ethnics whose mobility was not so constrained by race, and thus subject to many of the same prejudices as the rest of the diaspora. As Caribbean migrants became enveloped in this oppositional discourse, mainstream images of them also became schematized: they were seen as either militant, Garvey-like black nationalists, dangerous inner-city gangsters and Rastafarian drug-runners, or upstanding citizens who are honored to assimilate.

The strategic placement of Caribbean characters in works by writers such as Ralph Ellison and Toni Morrison suggests an ongoing literary engagement with the politics of cultural pluralism. In Ellison's novel *Invisible Man* the nameless narrator finds himself in New York City, the contact zone for him and Ras, the Caribbean exhorter/destroyer, who urges Harlem crowds to rise up against their white oppressors. Ras urges for racial "consciousness" and begs the narrator and his Brotherhood comrade Tod Clifton to open their eyes to the realities of race in America. His unsuccessful attempt to stab Clifton, whom he identifies as one of his "own" (370); his lament over the violence and competition of black against black; and his call for black, yellow, and brown allies all resonate with Marcus Garvey's visions of an international community of sovereign black peoples.[5]

Like Ellison's Ras, Toni Morrison's Soaphead Church from *The Bluest Eye* is a character whose Caribbean migratory history is often neglected in discussions of the major themes of the work. Church is a misanthropic Jamaican immigrant living in the small Ohio community of the novel. Along with the people who hail from all over the South – "Mobile. Aiken. From Newport News. From Marietta. From Meridian" (81) – Church represents the diversity of the black community: one that is grounded in the process of migration and must deal with the legacies of slavery and white supremacy, including their degenerative influence on black male sexuality. In striking contrast to Church, Morrison's Caribbean horsemen in *Tar Baby* are highly ennobled characters. These riders, for whom the Isle de Chevaliers is named, are believed by the black islanders to be the spirits of one hundred former slaves who escaped captivity. Rejecting the powerlessness of slavery and the vulnerability suggested by their blindness, nakedness, and unshod horses, "they gallop; they race those horses like angels all over the hills" (306). As the US-born Son crawls, tentatively walks, and then runs to join them at the end of the novel, he signifies rebirth and the healing of some of the fractures in the African-diasporic community – the fractures that Morrison presages in her epigraph from First Corinthians 1:11: "For it hath been declared unto me of you, my brethren . . . that there are contentions among you." These contentions include the failure of "Philadelphia Negroes" Sydney and Ondine to learn the names of the African-Caribbean workers on the island, or even to recognize their faces; it is therefore a hateful Thérèse, a local island resident, who refuses to speak to the African Americans. Despite the possibilities for pan-African alliances that Morrison suggests by concluding her novel with the imminent union of Son and the Chevaliers, however, the reader must wonder about the potential for these alliances *within* US society: is it significant that the narrative's final action takes place *outside* the political borders of the United States?

In the past few decades, there has been expanding awareness of the literature that focuses on relationships between children of Caribbean immigrants in the United States and their parents' home islands. Although the authors reveal the contradictions of dreams of "Return" to lands to which their characters have never been, in certain ways they still sustain the nostalgic yearning for a Caribbean "home" – a nostalgia that, in many cases, is a borrowed one. US-born children thus exhibit an aura of "ex-isle" as powerfully as their parents do. This can be partially explained by the fact that children from immigrant families often experience a schism of identity: they feel as if they belong partly to both societies, but fully to neither – a fragmentation even more pronounced if they are rejected by, or encouraged by their parents to reject, the US African American community.

In her introduction to *Black Women, Writing, and Identity: Migrations of the Subject* (1994), literary critic Carole Boyce Davies emphasizes the need for crossing borders, whether they be the lines between theory and literature, theory and practice, or actual physical national boundaries. Citing the first move of the conqueror as the drawing up of borders, Boyce Davies argues that diasporic African people, wrenched from their ancestral lands during slavery, are especially harmed by preserving rigid territorial lines because they are kept in a position of "dislocation" (4). Novelists such as Paule Marshall and Edwidge Danticat appear quite positive about the possibilities for crossing borders, spanning cultures, establishing a "Black Atlantic," and finding a Self.

Paule Marshall is arguably the best-known US-born black author of Caribbean descent, and her narratives remain rooted in the spaces of contact between US and Caribbean communities. Her first novel, *Brown Girl, Brownstones*, details the experiences of Selina Boyce, a Barbadian-American girl born and raised in Brooklyn and torn between allegiances to her father and mother. This conflict of affection corresponds to her conflicting alliances to Barbados and the United States. Barbados is the land romantically idealized by Deighton, her father, the classic dreamer who subscribes to a belief in the fast track to success. For him, Barbados is the "home" to which he claims the whole family will one day return. In contrast, the United States is the country in which Silla, Selina's mother, the epitome of responsibility, strives to own property; she clearly perceives the US as a more permanent residence than her husband does.[6]

Silla's and Deighton's contradictory relationships to the States mirror Silla's and Selina's contrasting notions of space, place, and home. The maternal–filial discord is accentuated by the daughter's sense of racial and cultural alienation in the land of her birth – the land that her mother reveres. Selina walks as an intruder in the glittering world of Fifth Avenue because of her race and economic class; she is also estranged from the white women of her college dance troupe because of her race and ethnicity. The young woman's alienation strikes the reader as particularly acute when she peers into a jazz club called the Metropole and feels an affiliation based on the music. The bar can be interpreted as a metaphor for African American culture and community, and the contention between African American and Caribbean people fostered by some members of the Barbadian community in the novel thus seems to dissolve. However, Selina's sense of belonging is problematic in that she is still standing outside the club and thus is physically isolated from the people inside. Notably, all of the Metropole's patrons appear to be white: only the musicians are black. This detail, along with the name of the club, suggests that the position of all African-diasporic peoples in the American (and European) cosmopolitan "metropoles" is marginal, only *seeming* to be "sucked into that roaring center" (214) as Selina believes.

Antiguan author Jamaica Kincaid provides a compelling parallel situation in her novel *Lucy* (1990). The US contact zone allows the protagonist to ruminate on her position as a member of the African diaspora and see the connections between oppressed populations and the colonial and neo-colonial powers that remain in ideological, if not official political, control. Lucy's employer, Mariah, participates in a system that involves bringing poor, African-Caribbean women to the States to care for the children of wealthy white families. She does so without conceding to the racial implications of this transport of bodies, thereby ignoring the history of enslavement and its accompanying involuntary migration in many American societies.[7] At the same time, believing that she is engaged in having Lucy "sucked into that roaring center" (Marshall, *Brown Girl* 224) of social and cultural privilege, she only highlights the resemblance between the US and British metropoles for Lucy: by insisting that the young protagonist focus on the surface beauty of daffodils (emblematic of the present) rather than on her painful experiences as a colonized subject (representing history and the past), she tries to supplant Lucy's Caribbean experiences with her own North American perspective.

By the end of Marshall's *Brown Girl* the reader comes to understand that even though Selina's feelings of estrangement are fostered by her belief that her true home lies elsewhere, her voyage to a Barbadian "homeland' is much more complicated than many critics have claimed. While growing up, Selina, her older sister Ina, and the other Barbadian-American children learn to call Barbados "home," even though the island is an unfamiliar, abstract space. Marshall notably encloses the word in quotation marks to reveal that the concept must be interrogated. And although Deighton has steadily nurtured the illusion of a Barbadian homeland to which the family can and will return, and into which Selina will easily fit despite the fact that she has never visited there, in reality she will be viewed as a stranger and a foreigner. Selina cannot truly "return" to Barbados, a land to which she has never been. She cannot "begin again" (Afterword, *Brown Girl* 322); rather, she must continue along the road she has already begun – a road that began in the United States. The only origins that can be traced without question and complication are Selina's experiences as a cultural creole in her New York City Barbadian community.

Significantly, when Selina first decides to run away with her boyfriend Clive, she makes very nonspecific plans to go "out of the country" (267). "Anyplace" will do; "it doesn't matter" (279). When Selina eventually reveals her travel plans to Silla, she does not explicitly mention Barbados as her destination. She only professes her desire to emulate her mother: "Remember how you used to talk about how you left home and came here alone as a girl of eighteen and was your own woman? I used to love hearing that. And that's what I want" (307). Selina's repetition of Silla's emigration entails leaving one's home as a young woman; it thus becomes clear that Selina is not seeking a lost home in Barbados, but rather leaving a home in the United States in order to become her "own woman." The narrative reveals that the protagonist accepts the land of her experiences as her home, but she must travel outside this often-alienating space in order to find her way. The themes of movement, im/migration, and ex-isle resound like the clang of the bangle that Selina leaves behind her: a not so "frail sound in that utter silence" (310).

Marshall sets up a similarly ambiguous situation in *Daughters* (1991). Like Selina, protagonist Ursa MacKenzie was born in the States, but unlike the principal character of Marshall's first novel, Ursa was raised for fourteen years on the fictional Caribbean island of Triunion before being sent back to inner-city Hartford to attend high school. And although she has lived for the majority of her life in the United States, the adult Ursa conceives of Triunion as her permanent, "true" home for the first portion of the novel. Home is always "there," far away, and even though Ursa visits as often as she can, it comes to represent lack in her life. This is despite the fact that her education, apartment, career, romantic partner, and best friend all appear to locate her permanent homespace in New York. The irony of Ursa's feeling "away from home" while in the bosom of her supposed homeland is striking.

Ursa's mother, Estelle, is an expatriate of the US. Rather than leave the country for political reasons, however, as in the case of many African Americans who fled US soil and racial policies in the 1940s, 50s, and 60s, it is the painful sense of loss that Estelle feels after her parents' fatal accident that prevents her from going back. Significantly, that country is no longer her home. And yet, even though she herself will not return, "she's always made clear that this is where she wants her daughter to be" (256).

About halfway through the narrative, a letter drafted to her parents reveals that Ursa no longer views Triunion as home. She must make a mental note to replace the phrase "come down" with "come home" (250). She later alleges that New York has become "as much home as anywhere else" (254). This comment is loaded with ambivalence, however; it is not an emphatic, definitive identification of the United States as her homespace. The true turn comes at the end of *Daughters*, when Ursa must choose a place to recuperate – both mentally and physically. It becomes clear that the healing she must undergo will take place in New York, and not in Triunion. The night before her flight back to the States, the protagonist imagines the cab ride to her apartment as taking place during "dawn's early light." This phrase from "The Star-Spangled Banner" suggests her allegiance to this nation. At the same time as she anticipates the cab ride, she also looks forward to an herb bath in her New York apartment. The contemplated bath illustrates her incorporation of Caribbean traditional practices in her life; she recognizes the need to preserve the ways of her mothers, literal and figurative.

Amidst her cultural and national reclamations, Ursa realizes that there is no "perfect" space. The island of Triunion has its tensions, as does the United States. Her decision to base her home in the latter – physically, mentally, and emotionally – comes despite all of the troubles she faces there as an African-descended Caribbean-identified woman. Ursa realizes that a "home" of complete security and comfort is a mythological figment. Marshall highlights her message by mirroring Ursa's decisions with Estelle's: the latter has adopted Triunion as her new home despite the problems that she, too, faces as a foreigner.

Besides the border-crossings that occur in *Brown Girl, Brownstones* and *Daughters*, Marshall's characteristic cultural alienation and antagonism, then conflict, bridging, and revelation take place in both *Praisesong for the Widow* (1983) and *The Chosen Place, The Timeless People* (1969). In *Praisesong*, for example, protagonist Avey Johnson has no ties to the Caribbean, but she remembers and reconnects with her African American cultural roots in this space and becomes the emblem of the pan-Africanist subject.

Other more contemporary authors who extend Marshall's paradigm include Elizabeth Nunez, whose novel *Beyond the Limbo Silence* (1998) charts the development of a young Trinidadian immigrant to the United States. Sara leaves her homeland to be educated in a Catholic college in Oshkosh, Wisconsin. There, she experiences the invisibility/hypervisibility paradigm discussed by Dominguez: her white classmates at first refuse to acknowledge her presence; soon after, they reveal their perception of her as a type rather than an individual, and a primitive member of an "uncivilized" society. Local white boys and girls call both the African-Trinidadian Sara and her Indo-Guyanese roommate Angela "niggers," collapsing all racial, ethnic, and national difference under the slur. Intraracial cultural barriers are drawn by Sara's African American lover, Sam, who will not believe that Sara can identify with the Civil Rights struggle – she is a foreigner to him above and beyond anything else. Her St. Lucian friend Courtney warns her: "American slavery lasted longer. Then Jim Crow dug his claws into them. They think no one else is capable of understanding that kind of suffering . . . To them, we're happy, free island natives dancing in the sun to steel band music and calypso" (190). Sara, however, thinks of the five out of 200,000 Caribbean students who receive the opportunity to go to a British university each year, the environmental exploitation of the islands, and the psychological destruction of those who have lost their true identities by accepting the discrimination of colonialism as a natural state of being. In other words, she begins to see the ties between the oppression of African peoples throughout the Americas. Part One of the novel ends with Sara describing her arduous journey to self-realization. "It would begin with resistance . . . my reluctance to accept that I could not separate myself from what was taking place in America in 1963. That I could not be an outsider. It would be a journey that . . . would link me irreversibly to black America" (120). Readers again witness the ways that the migration scenario provides fertile ground for writers to interrogate the viability of a pan-African identity at the same time that they recognize and celebrate ethnic differences.

Interestingly enough, the site of Avey Johnson's re-memory is Carriacou, a small island off the coast of Grenada, which also figures prominently in Audre Lorde's biomythography *Zami: A New Spelling of My Name* (1982).[8] Linda and Byron Lorde, Audre's parents, emigrate to the United States from Grenada in 1924. The emotional draw toward the home island is powerful for both of them; the narrator, like Marshall's Selina Boyce with her father, learns: "This now, here [Harlem], was a space, some temporary abode, never to be considered forever nor totally binding nor defining, no matter how much it commanded in energy and attention . . . Someday we would arrive back in the sweet place, back *home*" (Lorde 13). The words leave Audre in a conundrum because the only place she knows, the land in which she currently resides, is not supposed to be able to define her. In addition, her sense of dislocation is enhanced by her inability to find Carriacou on any map: "so when I hunted for the magic place during geography lessons or in free library time, I never found it, and came to believe my mother's geography was a fantasy or crazy or at least too old-fashioned" (14). Audre is able to discover Carriacou's geographical location and latitude only after her twenty-sixth birthday, once she rejects the myth of Return. "I only discovered its latitudes when Carriacou was no longer my home" (256). In this moment, desire, outsiders' views, and her own self-perception merge together. At the same time, the text ends: "[In Carriacou] it is said that the desire to lie with other women is a drive from the mother's blood" (256). Thus, Audre's lesbianism, her Caribbean heritage, and her relationship with her mother all become inseparably entwined and claimed as essential to her life and her identity as an African American subject.[9]

Similarly, in Marshall's *The Chosen Place, The Timeless People*, the reader's very first impression of protagonist Merle Kimbona embodies cultural amalgamation. A native of the fictional Caribbean Bourne Island, she wears a dress of an "abstract tribal motif . . . which could have been found draped . . . around a West African market woman" and silver earrings engraved with the forms of European saints (4). One learns that she has studied in England, where she married a Ugandan who presently lives with their daughter in his native country. The conclusion of the novel shows her flying to Africa, not by the usual route through the imperial "metropoles" of New York and London, but instead through Trinidad and Brazil, models of cultural creolization, and then Dakar and Kampala.

Marshall's *The Fisher King* (2000) continues the theme of connections between populations of African descent around the world. The epigraph – "You got some of all of us in you, dontcha? What you gonna do with all that Colored from all over creation you got in you?" – applies to Sonny Carmichael Payne, the 8-year-old protagonist who is the quintessence of the African diaspora. Sonny is born in France of a Cameroonian father and French-born mother, Jo-Jo, whose own parents were US-born African American ex-patriates. Furthering the migration theme, Jo-Jo's father's parents migrated to New York City from the Caribbean and her mother's parents migrated from the American South. Jo-Jo's mother's mother, Florence Varina, was named after the Magnolia Grandiflora tree from Varina, Georgia; her father had travelled north with the tree seed, which survived and flourished in a climate antithetical to its natural environment. The seed functions as a symbol for Sonny as well.

Besides Sonny's lineage, his desire for connections between his antagonistic US and Caribbean kin makes him a perfect representative of cultural bridges. Interestingly, his foster mother, Hattie, can see some elements of the diaspora in him, but she willfully ignores others; she notes that his face "reflected them all: Sonny-Rett, Cherisse, Jo-Jo. A triple exposure . . . It contained all three of her loves; moreover, it restored them to her intact" (210). She recognizes those who share her American language and culture, as well as her experience as a US expatriate in France, but she erases the African presence of the baby's father in her description.

Despite Hattie's anxieties about losing Sonny and the connection to the past that she maintains through him, he cultivates relationships with his great-grandmothers, both of whom disapprove of Hattie – African American Florence on the basis of class, and Caribbean Ulene on the basis of ethnicity. Sonny also fosters individual emotional healing for both Florence and Ulene, as well as the possibility of a relationship between the two, where only discord and strife existed before. Florence asserts that the "flood" of West Indians has ruined the street (41), "[b]ringing down the block, the neighborhood" (70). And in the same way that she blames Ulene for birthing the son, Sonny-Rett, whom she perceives as taking her daughter Cherisse away from her, Ulene blames Florence for the same. The political is revealed as deeply rooted in the personal, but with the potential for birthing creativity and change.

The youngest writer examined here who addresses notions of New World identity through the dynamics of the US contact zone is Edwidge Danticat, who emigrated from Haiti to the States in the early 1980s at the age of 12. A similar migration appears in her first novel, *Breath, Eyes, Memory* (1994), which details a young girl's journeys between the Antilles and New York City. Sophie eventually comes to view New York as "a place where you can lose yourself easily" (103) – both in the literal sense of getting physically lost among the buildings, traffic, and crowds of people, and in the metaphorical sense of forgetting one's roots, culture, and identity, despite the fact that places for connection and reconnection exist. A generation later, Danticat revisits the themes first presented by Paule Marshall. Like Marshall's Selina Boyce and Ursa MacKenzie, Danticat's protagonist experiences what might be identified as a pull between the Caribbean, the home of the "soul" and the memory, and the United States, the home of the physical body and everyday life. Also, as in several of Marshall's works, the sense of dislocation and conflicting ideas of "home" seem integrally connected to the protagonist's relationships with her mothers, Martine and Tante Atie.

Contemporary US readers might be tempted to read the initial separation between Sophie and Martine as evidence of Martine's maternal apathy; however, Danticat sets up the novel to reflect the strong communal base of the rural village from which the family comes, the trauma of rape and childbirth that exist as a legacy of slavery in the Caribbean, and the importance of the black family. In other words, the novelist's descriptions of various aspects of Haitian culture resonate with particular African American traditions and point to a common diasporic culture and its connections to Africa. "Othermothers" help rear children. Sugarcane fieldworkers sing songs in the call-and-response tradition (22). Patrons in a New Jersey Haitian restaurant play the dozens (54), and the van driver on Sophie's first trip back to Haiti engages in "toasting," or "speechifying," revealing traditions of word play and emphasis on mental and verbal wit (93). Villagers express joy and the importance of naming and claiming one's own body and one's own children after slavery: "Foi, Hope, Faith, Espérance, Beloved, God-Given, My Joy, First Born, Last Born, Aséfi, Enough-Girls, Enough-Boys, Deliverance, Small Misery, Big Misery, No Misery (6).[10] Storytelling holds an essential place in the culture, whether it be to pass down stories of family members and preserve history, unite the community in the "Krik? Krak!" call-and-response mode, reinforce connections to a cultural heritage and African ancestry, or teach morals and lessons. Sophie's husband Joseph is also key to this theme in the novel; he speaks a Louisiana creole similar to Sophie's Haitian Creole, and, as a musician, he pursues the links between US spirituals and Latin and island music. He describes spirituals as songs about "going to another world": "home, Africa . . . Heaven . . . freedom" (215).

Sexuality is another crucial theme running through the novel, and, similar to its function in Morrison's *The Bluest Eye*, serves the purpose of unifying the black Atlantic. Sophie is severely traumatized by the practice of *testing*; the narrative thus calls into question the double standard by which sexually active, unmarried men are viewed as experienced while women are comparably perceived as "dirty," unattractive, and defective. Danticat also explores the way that rape has become a devastating legacy for the black women of her novel. Martine originally tried to abort Sophie after getting raped and impregnated; strikingly, in the same way that Martine murmurs in her sleep during nightmares of the event, her mother Ifé mumbles at night (109), gesturing towards the legacies of sexual abuse. The inheritance of sexual trauma brings to mind more canonical African American novels like Gayl Jones's *Corregidora* (1975) and Toni Morrison's *Beloved* (1987).

Danticat's protagonist constructs Haiti as a place to which she needs to return in order "to remember" (95). Her phrasing is quite important; she has not claimed it necessary to return permanently, but rather to return temporarily in order to remember her past and her culture. She travels to Haiti on several occasions in order to flee her sexual phobias, marital troubles, and her plagued relationship with her mother. Like the writers discussed before her, Danticat reveals the journey "home" as problematic in that Sophie uses Haiti as a panacea, a hiding place from her relationships. When she returns to Haiti for the first time since her childhood departure, she stays for only a few days. When she travels back to the States, she rejects Joseph's offer to pick her up from her mother's house in New York. "It's better for me if I find my own way back" (186). Not only does the protagonist assert her independence, but she also insists upon her need to complete her journey. She must achieve the full cycle of her life's voyage: from Haiti to the United States as a child, and now again, as an adult, from Haiti to the United States. Sophie's migrations are necessary for her being, both as an Americanized Haitian and a Caribbean American.

On a similar note, Martine refuses to travel to Haiti during her life, wishing only to be buried there. The memory that the island prompts is one she struggles against: her return during life would mean being immersed in the reality of her past and living in the memories of rape. She, too, effectively refutes the romantic notion that all ex-isles need to return to the home island for healing, nurturing, and peace.

As the most visible symbol of the presence of Caribbean migrants to the US, public celebrations like the Brooklyn Labor Day Carnival, a lavish display of Caribbean cultural pride, were at one time perceived by US-born black residents as an antagonistic flaunting of ethnic separateness. However, exhibitions of cultural distinctiveness within the black United States need not isolate individual groups and be used to fragment a potentially powerful community. Instead of being read narrowly as a separatist reaction to US African American society, they can be perceived as opposition to the larger – and predominantly white – mainstream American society: the "annual step out of the melting pot."[11] Celebrations can simultaneously function as emblematic of continual self-creation: "a place where West Indian people create themselves: as foreign nationals, as proud citizens of newly decolonized nations, as striving new immigrants, and as black people. The various incarnations . . . have both responded to and created definitions of race, ethnicity, and nation."[12] Recognizing the multiplicity of cultures embedded within "black" America can only enhance our study and understanding of African American literature.

NOTES

1. Virginia R. Dominguez, *From Neighbor to Stranger: The Dilemma of Caribbean Peoples in the United States* (New Haven: Yale University Antilles Research Program, 1975), p. 32.
2. Many Americans, for example, do not realize that NBA stars Kareem Abdul-Jabbar and Patrick Ewing, Congresswoman Shirley Chisholm, activist Malcolm X, Nation of Islam leader Louis Farrakhan, musicians Monty Alexander, Grandmaster Flash, and Grace Jones, actors Sidney Poitier and Cicely Tyson were either born in the Caribbean, or are of Caribbean descent.
3. For a good number of these highly educated, solidly middle-class migrants, however, scorning African Americans for their lack of social status and schooling was not a matter of ethnocentrism and cultural elitism, but rather of socio-economic class. They would likely have scorned lower-class people from their own island societies as well.
4. In the 1920s, organizations such as the West Indian Reform Association and the West Indian Committee on America encouraged Caribbean immigrants to become citizens, even though for many this move entailed a frightening potential loss – of culture, of a particular history, of homeland, and of possible escape.
5. Like Ras, Garvey was a Jamaican activist who emigrated to the US in the early twentieth century, and, during the 1910s and 1920s, attempted to organize people of African descent and foster an awareness and pride in their African cultural roots. Garvey's Universal Negro Improvement Association (UNIA) was founded to mobilize African Americans to resist racial oppression and fight for political and economic self-sufficiency, and general social equality. During the Harlem riots at the end of Ellison's novel, Ras urges the local residents to stop looting and destroying their own property and take up armed resistance. The carnivalesque atmosphere of the night is epitomized by Ras's appearance on a stallion and reflects the image of Garvey in fieldmarshal's uniforms, plumed hats, and scarlet and blue academic robes during public rallies and demonstrations. Garvey's attempt at signifying an ennobled black race was read as ridiculous and absurd by many, especially those of the black elite. His showiness was praised by Claude McKay, who stated: "Negro art, [certain] critics declare, must be dignified and respectable like the Anglo-Saxon's before it can be good . . . Happily the Negro retains his joy of living in the teeth of such criticism; and in Harlem . . . in Marcus Garvey's Hall with its extravagant paraphernalia, in his churches and cabarets, he expresses himself with a zest that is yet to be depicted by a true artist" (*Home to Harlem*, [Boston: Northeastern University Press, 1987], p. xii).

6. The fact that the couple's perception of Place marks their opposition is crucial. Place is fundamental in the literary tradition of people of the African diaspora, for enslaved ancestors were considered to be property and thus, as critic Sabine Bröck states, "quite literally not allowed to inhabit, let alone own, any physical space." "Transcending the 'Loophole of Retreat': Paule Marshall's Placing of Female Generations," *Callaloo* 10.1 (Winter 1987): 79–90, p. 79. For an extended discussion of the subject of Space and Place in Marshall's novel, see Giselle Liza Anatol, "'I Going Away, I Going Home': Mothers and Motherlands in Paule Marshall's *Brown Girl, Brownstones*," in *Mango Season: Caribbean Women's Writing*, 13.1 (Spring 2000): 43–53.

7. In "Rock-A-Bye Niño: Confessions of a White Mother With a Brown Caregiver," *Mother Jones* 16.3 (May/June 1991): 73, Anne Nelson expresses her doubts regarding the possibility of an ethical relationship between "white mother" and "brown caregiver." She labels any relationship between a white family and an immigrant caregiver of color as "a social relationship that, by its fundamental inequality, presents a dreadful example to the child who is its reason for being" (73).

8. While *Zami* is categorized as a "biomythography" and not a novel, I would argue that its hybrid form, combining biography, myth, the collective stories of a community of women, and geography, allows for its inclusion here.

9. Audre's lover Afrekete's name itself resonates with Africa. In this final relationship, Lorde conveys a strong pan-Africanist message. She is thus able to reject the prejudicial statements against African Americans she heard as a child, when her mother would disdainfully distinguish between Grenadians and "other people."

10. This scene resonates with one in Julie Dash's film *Daughters of the Dust* (Kino International, 1992).

11. Ransford W. Palmer, *Pilgrims from the Sun: West Indian Migration to America* (New York: Twayne Publishers, 1995), p. 21.

12. Rachel Buff, *Immigration and the Political Economy of Home: West Indian Brooklyn and American Indian Minneapolis, 1945–1992* (Berkeley: University of California Press, 2001), p. 117.

PART II

SEARCH FOR A FORM
THE NEW AMERICAN NOVEL

5

ASHRAF H. A. RUSHDY

The neo-slave narrative

The publication of Margaret Walker's *Jubilee* in 1966 defined a subject of representation that would come to predominate in the African American novel for the rest of the twentieth century. Literally dozens of novels about slaves and slavery appeared in the wake of *Jubilee*. Although it would take five more years for the second novel in this tradition to appear (Ernest Gaines's *The Autobiography of Miss Jane Pittman*), and four more for the third (Gayl Jones's *Corregidora*), an African American novel about slavery would become almost annual fare thereafter. Given the paucity of novels about slavery before *Jubilee* and the enduring pervasiveness since, it is natural to inquire about the reasons for this development. What historical or social or cultural events permitted and sustained this new impetus in African American fiction? Since these contemporary narratives of slavery are both formally diverse and yet intellectually indebted to the first form of representation for people of African descent in the New World, the slave narrative itself, it is also worth asking questions about the formal features of this body of work. What is the meaning of the particular aesthetic choices made by authors who were mediating between a nineteenth-century Ur-textual form and a late-twentieth-century period of textual and formal play in American writing? Finally, we must ask, what is the political significance of this body of American fiction? What are we to make of this novel development in American culture at the end of the twentieth century?

The neo-slave narrative may be seen not as an abrupt appearance but rather as a logical continuity in African American writing. Like the first novel published by an African American, William Wells Brown's *Clotel* (1853), Walker's *Jubilee* also draws on the actual life experiences of enslaved Americans and marks its indebtedness to the oral tales of slave life told to its author. *Clotel* marked its lineage from and indebtedness to the earliest form of black American writing by beginning with a slave narrative, Brown's own, and concluded with a statement that many of the episodes recorded in the novel came from interviews with former slaves. Like Brown, who composed his novel by drawing on stories told from the "lips of those who, like [him]self, [had] run away from the land of bondage," Walker bases her novel on what she calls "the most valuable slave narrative of all, the living account of my great-grandmother, which had been transmitted to me by her own daughter."[1] The first neo-slave narrative, then, appears in 1966, but its roots can be traced back a century – to the novel Walker began writing in the 1930s, based on the oral stories she heard in the 1920s, which recounted the experiences of an ancestor and former slave during the 1860s. Seen in this way, *Jubilee* certainly marks a generational continuity with an earlier African American oral and literary tradition.

Walker and her novel, however, are also somewhat anomalous in terms of the contemporary narratives of slavery. For one thing, Walker, born in 1915, belonged to an earlier generation of black writers than the other authors of neo-slave narratives. Their impetus is not so directly connected to the people or the institution they were writing about in their novels. A more reasonable way to understand the emergence of this considerable body of African American writing about slavery is by referring to the social, intellectual, and institutional transformations in American life during and since the mid-1960s.

The most significant social changes, obviously, were connected to and a result of the Civil Rights Movement. Although the full story is much more nuanced and detailed, we can say that the Civil Rights Movement in many ways forced historians undertaking studies of the American slave past to revise their views. Amidst the events of the Civil Rights Movement, the present provided a perspective on the past which historians could use to gauge their assumptions about how oppressed people behaved. When a younger generation of graduate students took to the streets during the Civil Rights and anti-war movements, they learned something new about the dynamics of social agency for change. Seeing that the relatively powerless people in these social movements could actually make history "happen from the bottom up," historians began to re-imagine the possibility of revising their vision of the past and write history "from the bottom up." One very positive result of the Civil Rights Movement on the American academy, then, is that it promoted this revision. As one historian noted, the 1965 march from Selma to Montgomery not only made a statement for voter registration and the pending Voting Rights Act, but it also "linked the academic community to the nation, the past to the present, the professors who were writing our history to the men who were making it."[2] Partly as a result of that cross-fertilization between the streets and the ivory tower, there emerged a new body of historical studies of slavery that took seriously the agency and self-representation of the slaves, their community- and culture-building energies, and the forms of resistance they exhibited.

The Black Power Movement that came about in the mid-1960s augmented that body of writing by producing Black Power intellectuals who contested representations of slavery they found demeaning and uninformed by the new revisionist energies. The work of such notable historians as Eugene Genovese and Martin Duberman was dramatically altered by the interactions and debates they had with Black Power intellectuals like Sterling Stuckey, Michael Thelwell, Vincent Harding, and John Henrik Clarke. As Genovese noted in an essay tellingly entitled "The Influence of the Black Power Movement on Historical Scholarship," the "recent upsurge of political awareness and participation has had an undeniable impact on historians." The Black Power-era debate over William Styron's *Confessions of Nat Turner* (1967) and the Clarke-edited volume *William Styron's Nat Turner: Ten Black Critics Respond* (1968) again focused attention on the representation of slaves. Finally, it is important to point out that the Black Power Movement was a movement that empowered people of African descent, and in this case empowered some to undertake new historical and fictional explorations into the slave past. Sherley Anne Williams recalled that, while the Civil Rights Movement "gave would-be writers of new African-American histories and fictions the opportunity to earn financial security and thus the time to write," the Black Power Movement "provided the pride and perspective necessary to pierce the myths and lies that have grown up around the antebellum period." Black Power, she concluded, gave these black writers "the authority to tell it as we felt it."[3]

The Black Power Movement affected the American academy in more direct ways in 1968 and 1969, when African American students at predominantly white institutions began to agitate and demand Black Studies programs. The inauguration of these programs immediately created a new set of curricula, requiring new books and textbooks, which publishers were then quick to capitalize on. A *Newsweek* story entitled "The Black Novelists: Our Turn" revealed what the article referred to as a "black revolution" in literature and described how publishers were "scrambling to add black writers to their lists."[4] Many black-authored texts immediately began to appear. In 1969, at least six anthologies of slave narratives and interviews were released. In 1970, something like twenty-five black novels were published.

We can sum up the social, intellectual, and institutional changes that directly and indirectly affected the neo-slave narrative in the following way, then. As a result of the Civil Rights Movement, historians began to produce studies of slave life that were newly attentive to the culture and community and resistance of slaves, giving a portrait both closer to the experience of slaves that lent itself more to a rich fictional treatment. The Black Power Movement created a substantial change in American colleges and in African American writers by producing Black Studies programs in the former and giving direction and impetus to the latter. The American publishing industry responded to these changes by commissioning new books, series, anthologies, collections, and seeking out new and promising writers. These are the transformations in American life, I would argue, that enabled those artists who would produce a body of fictional work on slavery that had hitherto not been imagined and has since not been stalled.

The body of work that emerges from so disparate a complex of social and cultural origins, and deals with so varied and complicated an historical experience as American chattel slavery, contains a rich set of formal innovations for conveying that story. One of the remarkable things about contemporary African American narratives of slavery is how experimental the authors have been in developing diverse forms to tell a story that many acknowledge as the most difficult in their careers – what Toni Morrison in *Beloved* (1987) calls "unspeakable things unspoken" and "not a story to pass on."[5] An examination of the first three novels in this tradition will reveal the logic and purpose of the three major forms that these novelists employ: the historical novel, the pseudo-autobiographical slave narrative, and the novel of remembered generations.

In *Jubilee*, Walker set out to produce a narrative that married the "historical novel" (as described by Georg Lukacs) to the "Negro folk literature" she herself was striving to sustain through her own work. Wishing to write a book in which the folk predominate, she was able to produce a world vision in which "characters looking up from the bottom rather than down from the top" are the important ones by which the reader can gauge what is significant. She realizes this political impetus and artistic hope in the novel by primarily focusing on how slaves themselves felt and responded to the world they inhabited. In both the scene of *Jubilee* and in the slaves' discussion of Abraham Lincoln as "emancipator," Walker reveals in her writing what she had described in her theorizing – the importance of having a "world historical figure" like Lincoln become a "minor character seen through the mind of the major characters," who in this novel are the slaves themselves (279–280, 246).[6]

This shift in focus not only allows Walker to describe the brutality of slavery, but it also allows her to show us life from the viewpoint of the slaves who suffered and also fomented insurrections, fled plantations, and created vibrant cultural and religious traditions. In this way, Walker anticipated the wave of historical studies that would emphasize the rebelliousness and sur-vival strategies of American slaves. She also anticipated many of the themes that later novelists would find important. Two are especially worth noting. First, like the authors of so many slave narratives, and subsequently the writers of the early African American novels from Brown's *Clotel* to Charles Chesnutt's *Marrow of Tradition* (1901), Walker attends to the idea of what the black and commodified body of the slave meant to American culture. Walker muses on the ironies of a slave's being "linked by blood" to the master class but "tied to slavery by a black mother" (93). This theme of how mis-cegenation reveals the hidden desires of despotic white men and exposes the hidden familial bonds of black and white Americans, a theme that can also be traced to the origins of the African American novel, would continue to haunt later writers of contemporary narratives of slavery. The second related theme involves the question of how one reconciles an oppressive past. Walker concludes *Jubilee* by meditating on the forgiveness necessary to forge a viable national future out of the ruins of slavery, Civil War, and Reconstruction. At the end of the powerful scene where Vyry rips off her clothing to re-veal the webbed and ridged scars on her back, she forgives the man who had whipped her and testifies that she "ain't got no hate in [her] heart for nobody" (485). Vyry's religious beliefs, which Walker poetically describes as "a spiritual wholeness that had been forged in a crucible of suffering," are held up both as a hope for a nation that would heal as crookedly as the scars on Vyry's body and as "the best true example of the motherhood of her race, an ever present assurance that nothing could destroy a people whose sons had come from her loins" (486).

Walker's remarkable success, then, is that in *Jubilee* she manages magnifi-cently to produce a historical novel, with a third-person narrator, that reveals the dynamics and inner life of a group actively engaged in and responding both to the massive upheaval and turmoil of slavery and Civil War and to the numbing reality of a life that for the slave was "the same as always, drab and hopeless, with always a slender undercurrent of a nameless fear" (150). Later novelists such as Barbara Chase-Riboud in *Sally Hemings* (1979), Louise Meriwether in *Fragments of the Ark* (1994), and J. California Cooper in *The Wake of the Wind* (1998) would also produce historical novels in third-person voices, the first two of which have historical figures as their subjects (Sally Hemings and Robert Smalls). Michelle Cliff's *Free Enterprise* (1993), which has both third- and first-person narration and fluctuates be-tween 1920 and 1858, also takes a historical figure as one of its main char-acters (Mary Ellen Pleasant).

In a 1972 essay, Walker notes that she undertook rigorous archival research amongst the papers and books about slavery in order to "substantiate" her material, to "authenticate" the story she had received from her grandmother's lips, and to use "literary documents to undergird the oral tradition." In a 1973 essay, describing his work on a novel that would appear ten years after *Jubilee* was published, Alex Haley claimed at the end of his research for *Roots*, which led him on a similar archival hunt, that he "trusted oral history now better than [he] trusted the printed page."[7] Appearing five years after *Jubilee* and five years before *Roots*, Ernest Gaines's *The Autobiography of Miss Jane Pittman* (1971) represents in the novel itself this tension between the oral and the literate traditions, between the authority of the archives and the authenticity of the slaves' voices and memories. Like Walker and Haley, Gaines was also ambivalent about the relationship between "what Miss Jane and folks like her have to say" and the "other sources, the newspapers, magazines, the books in the libraries." In an interview conducted a few years after the novel had been published, he noted that he wished the book itself could have transcended the necessarily written form it had to take in the world of American publishing. "I wish I didn't have to write it; I wish no one had to write it, because I think telling a story and talking is so much better. It's too bad that we don't have tapes of those older people talking, so we could listen to this without ever having to read it. That *is* one of my aims – for them, in their folk way, to tell what happened."[8] In *The Autobiography of Miss Jane Pittman*, the history teacher who interviews Miss Jane feels that what was "wrong with them books" he uses to teach African American history is that "Miss Jane is not in them."[9]

Gaines, like Walker, fits the narrative he offers to the form in which he offers it. A story about the century between the end of slavery and the beginning of formal legal equality is told by a woman who had lived that century. A story about the importance of affirming one's own voice, about responding to the voices and books in the library that denied her existence and her humanity, is told in the voice of a former slave, in "Miss Jane's language," in her "selection of words," in the "rhythms of her speech" (vii). And a novel that concludes on the importance of a civil and communal redemption instead of a symbolic one is aptly told by a community of voices that support and reinforce Miss Jane's. "Miss Jane's story," the editor notes, "is all of their stories, and their stories are Miss Jane's" (viii). Gaines's *The Autobiography of Miss Jane Pittman* is the first of the contemporary narratives of slavery to adopt the first-person voice of the former slave herself. Ishmael Reed's *Flight to Canada* (1976), Charles Johnson's *Oxherding Tale* (1982) and *Middle Passage* (1990), and Sherley Anne Williams's *Dessa Rose* (1986) would also later experiment with the use of the slave's voice, casting their novels in the form of what I have elsewhere called "neo-slave narratives," that is, those novels that literally assume the voice of the fugitive slave and employ while deviating from the formal conventions of the antebellum slave narrative.[10]

Like both Walker and Gaines, Gayl Jones is also interested in the interplay between literate sources and oral tales in her novel, *Corregidora* (1975). The narrator Ursa is the granddaughter and great-granddaughter of Brazilian slave women who pass on the story of their incestuous raping at the hands of their master to each generation so that "we'd never forget."[11] They reproduce their stories in oral form not to supplement the written records, as had been the case in *The Autobiography of Miss Jane Pittman*, but to contest the effects of the absence of written records. In Brazil, as Ursa puts it, "when they did away with slavery down there they burned all the slavery papers so it would be like they never had it" (9). Also, like Gaines, Jones is interested in the dilemma of a group whose historical woundedness is both testimony to the evils of the past and yet inhibiting a healthier future. Ursa's grandmother most forcefully expresses this ambivalent situation: "They burned all the documents, Ursa, but they didn't burn what they put in their minds. We got to burn out what they put in our minds, like you burn out a wound. Except we got to keep what we need to bear witness. That scar that's left to bear witness. We got to keep it as visible as our blood" (72). These, then, are the concerns Jones shares with Walker and Gaines. Unlike them, however, Jones also casts her novel almost wholly in twentieth-century America. As we saw, Walker had produced a historical novel set in the nineteenth century, while Gaines had given us the autobiography of a woman whose journey began in the nineteenth and was coming to an end in the twentieth century.

Jones gives us instead a story in which the major action takes place between 1947 and 1969, between the time Ursa undergoes a hysterectomy after her first husband Mutt pushes her down the stairs and the time when they are reconciled twenty-two years later. At the heart of the story, however, is the generational tale of the *Corregidora* women's sufferings, and what Ursa attempts to do in her own narration is to discover to what extent her life is governed by what happened to these enslaved women in the past and to what extent she is able to transcend their suffering while nonetheless finding a means of passing their story on so it would not be forgotten. Ursa's struggle, in other words, is to find a way to bear witness without losing the integrity of her own life, to have a scar testify to the horrors of the past and not the wound itself in her body or in her mind. The answer, in the end, is for Ursa to produce a blues song – a "song that would touch me, touch my life and theirs . . . A new world song. A song branded with the new world" (59) – to do the performative work that the next generation she now can't birth would have done.

The narrative strategy Jones chooses for telling the story of *Corregidora* – in which slavery acts as the historical episode that inhabits and sometimes haunts the present – is innovative and yet also has a long history in African American writing. In some ways, this is the narrative strategy employed by writers in the 1890s, who used slavery to remark on the possible futures facing the nation a generation after the formal end of slavery. In Harper's *Iola Leroy*, slavery is referred to as a "fearful cancer eating into the nation's heart" which, removed by the surgery of war, continues to have "effects" on the nation. It is these effects, the ramifications of the peculiar institution on American racial mores and habits, that form the subject of these novels which trace the lineaments of American racial violence to their origins in slavery. In the words of the eponymous heroine's mother, "Slavery . . . is dead, but the spirit which animated it still lives." In *Contending Forces* (1900), Hopkins uses a narrative of slavery to comment on the blood-ties that link whites and blacks, British and American, as well as revealing the historical source of the contemporary practice of raping black women and lynching black men. The "atrocity of the acts committed one hundred years ago are duplicated today," she writes, "when slavery is supposed no longer to exist." In *The Marrow of Tradition*, Chesnutt exposes the historical roots of the 1898 massacre of black people in Wilmington, North Carolina. At one level, his critique is of humanity itself, of the vaunted patina of society that covers a far more dangerous and lurking element. At the end of the riot, the narrator comments caustically that "our boasted civilization is but a thin veneer, which cracks and scales off at the first impact of primal passion." But, at another level, Chesnutt notes that it is not simply human nature but a particular kind of human nature wrought out of centuries of oppressive practices that is, in fact, the "marrow" of the tradition of violence he traces in his novel. Slavery, he writes, is a "weed [that] had been cut down, but its roots remained, deeply imbedded in the soil, to spring up and trouble a new generation."[12]

Corregidora, too, is in this same tradition. Slavery is the historical force that continues to dictate contemporary racial politics. What makes Jones's novel innovative, though, is that she is concerned more with the ways slavery's effects can be traced through the generational and familial patterns than through the larger social ones. Slavery is the pre-text in *Corregidora* because the slave ancestors who lived through it are the historical actors who give scope and depth to the lives of those familial members who are their progeny. It is not wholly innovative with *Corregidora*, since the main characters of both Zora Neale Hurston's *Their Eyes Were Watching God* (1937) and Ralph Ellison's *Invisible Man* (1952) have slave grandparents who act as either goads or guides to the grandchildren they try to protect with dreams or wily advice. Jones, like the later writers who employ this form, focuses more on ancestors than the earlier novelists, and sees more clearly the ways that a familial secret locked in the slave past continues to haunt and thereby limit the possibilities for the life of the contemporary narrator. Octavia Butler's *Kindred* (1979) and David Bradley's *The Chaneysville Incident* (1981) essentially follow the same pattern of having a lurking family secret in slavery whose solution aids the narrator in moving forward with her or his social and romantic lives.

There are numerous variations on this formal innovation. Borrowing from science fiction, Butler uses time travel to transport her narrator literally from bicentennial Los Angeles back to antebellum Maryland to discover her family secret and origins. In *Crossing over Jordan* (1994), Linda Beatrice Brown sets her novel in the future where the characters resolve the family pain, that began in slavery, from the perspective of 2012. That pain flourished in the mid-twentieth century, and could be healed only by remembering that "there was a life before slavery, a time when we weren't chained by sorrow." Cyrus Colter's *Night Studies* (1979) has a third-person narrator, but is otherwise involved in the same narrative quest in which the main character, the Black Power leader John Calvin Knight, recuperates from an assassination attempt and reconciles himself to the knowledge that he is the last of his "lineal line." Knight unravels the history of his family from its African origins through its experience in America, that "new slave-importing nation of freedom zealots" in order to understand "that vast mystery: the mystery of Blackness."[13]

Although some of the later contemporary narratives of slavery would experiment with and revise these forms, the first three novels in this tradition pretty well defined the three major forms that the latter works would assume or attempt to expand. *Jubilee* set the standard for the third-person historical novel of slavery that took as its subject the personal and political transition from slavery to freedom. *The Autobiography of Miss Jane Pittman* renders the life story of a slave in her own words, replaying the motifs of the antebellum slave narrative and freeing the voice of the former slave to tell her own story. *Corregidora* takes as its subject the continuing traumatic legacy of slavery on later generations by telling the story of how late-twentieth-century African American subjects are tormented by family secrets lodged in the straitened lives of their enslaved ancestors.

Some of the narratives that are less easy to characterize, and fall somewhere amongst these three major forms, are those genealogies or epics of location that also appeared in the 1970s, 1980s, and 1990s. As a genealogy, or, in the terms of its subtitle, "the saga of an American family," Alex Haley's *Roots* (1976) tells the story of the slave experience as part of the overall trajectory of his American family. In another genealogical narrative, Sandra

Jackson-Opoku's *The River Where Blood Is Born* (1998), the narrative is framed by two competing narrators in the afterlife (a gatekeeper who does beadwork and Kwaku Ananse, the spider who does webwork). The narrators trace several generations of black women from Africa to the Caribbean to the United States over the course of two centuries. Two multi-volume epics that explore the meaning of place – Leon Forrest's "Forrest County" trilogy (1973–1983) and Raymond Andrews's Muskhogean County trilogy (1978–1983) – also make slavery something akin to a pre-text in their fictions. For Andrews, this pre-text is almost nonexistent in the first novel, *Appalachee Red* (1978) and barely registers any more in the second, *Rosiebelle Lee Wildcat Tennessee* (1980). The latter mentions one character who was "born a slave," and has a passing reference to how a road came to acquire its name because of the howling sound of whip-scarred slaves that continues to rustle through the pine trees. The final volume, *Baby Sweet's* (1983), gives slightly more attention to the slave past of Muskhogean County because it contains the most explicit narratives about the origins of the settling of the County, which includes the displacement of the original Indians by the Europeans who came with "their Old World furniture and manners . . . and their New World slaves."[14]

Forrest evokes and invokes slavery much more powerfully in his trilogy. The major character in the first and third volumes (*There is a Tree More Ancient than Eden*, 1973; *Two Wings to Veil My Face*, 1983), Nathaniel (Turner) Witherspoon, is revolutionary, as his name suggests, but also repentant because his ancestors had gained their wealth from owning and selling slaves (and creating "special white lightning bleaching creme"). The trilogy as a whole meditates on the dangers of "amnesia" and the necessity of "memory-history." But memory itself is also dangerous, as the second volume attests (*The Bloodworth Orphans*, 1977), since it "destroys as it heals." Part of the danger of memory, as it is in the case of those narratives like *Corregidora*, is that there are "dark secrets of your family, and *that* past, generation unto generation." The dark secret for one character, like that of Witherspoon, is that his fortune is "blood money at the root," because it is a fortune built on the sale and enslavement of humans. As with Andrews's trilogy, the third volume of Forrest's is also the one where slavery appears most persistently, primarily because in that volume the dying Sweetie Reed tells her grandson the full story of their family's legacy. Revisiting the theme of the dialectic of writing and orality, Forrest has Sweetie Reed recognize that her only hope for salvation was in telling "the whole story out loud," while having Nathaniel write out the tale in longhand. Her advice to her grandson is to try to understand the past with a more sympathetic but still incisive perspective. Her mildly confusing advice is: "Don't know too much about what you haven't seen. Get the order of learning your grandfather was always talking about, *troubling, remembering,* and then *revealing.*"[15]

I have dwelt at some length on the formal features of the neo-slave narratives because form itself is so deeply important to all artists, and also because the second half of the twentieth century was a fecund period of formal experimentation in American fiction. More importantly, though, I have attended to the forms employed by these authors of contemporary narratives of slavery because they themselves draw attention to their struggle to find a respectful way to give voice to the historically muted subjects of slavery. Often this struggle manifests itself in the forms they chose to adopt and adapt. Form, as Charles Johnson indicated in one of his neo-slave narratives, is itself a site where deep meaning resides. No form "*loses* its ancestry," he writes; "rather these meanings accumulate in layers of tissue as the form evolves." Changing metaphors, he says that the form will surrender its "diverse secrets" if the modern writer is willing to "dig, dig, dig – call it spadework," he puns.[16] Form, for the others as much as for Johnson, is a matter of grave importance. Walker felt she was revising and emphasizing the popular character of the traditional nineteenth-century historical novel. Gaines wished his readers to have so unmediated an access to the voice of the elders who survived slavery that he wished Miss Jane's voice could be heard directly and not read in his own text. And Jones drew her inspiration from that tradition of African American women's writing from Harper to Hurston in order to carry forward that form of writing which renders the present more meaningful for its visitations to and understanding of the American slave past.

Form, I would also argue, is a site where the politics of representing slaves, slave voices, and slavery is manifestly at stake. We have already examined the social and cultural origins that gave impetus to the authors to produce novels that took up and addressed this episode of the American past. Now we need to explore the significance of what they have done, and continue to do. We need to appreciate how the neo-slave narratives are part of a grander post-Civil Rights-era trajectory involving African American intellectual and social life. We can start that meditation by first turning to the ways one subset of these authors used form itself as a way of raising particular questions about authenticity, control, and appropriation.

In an essay on canon formation, Cornel West comments that "issues of power, political struggle and cultural identity are inscribed within the formal structures of texts." The form where such contestation most clearly evidenced itself was the one I have defined as "neo-slave narrative," that is, those novels written by Gaines, Reed, Johnson, and Williams that assume the voice of the slave and revise the conventions of the slave narrative. These novelists, directly and indirectly, were involved in a heated debate about authenticity and appropriation. Appearing in the wake of the important cultural debate over Styron's *Confessions of Nat Turner* (1967), these authors realized and again raised the question of what was at stake in adopting the voice of the slave in a contemporary novel. Williams stated that she immediately began writing *Dessa Rose* in 1968 as a response to Styron, and the first section of the novel is a direct parody of the jailhouse interview that Styron had borrowed from the original *Confessions of Nat Turner* (1831) by Thomas Gray. Ishmael Reed mocked Styron (and his intellectual forebears) for their inability to comprehend what was at stake in the religious lives of slaves, and he used the analogous case of Harriet Beecher Stowe's "theft" of Josiah Henson's story as an indirect method of raising the question of appropriation. In *Oxherding Tale*, Johnson attempted to situate himself philosophically between those who believed that only an African American author could produce a text that accurately captured the voice of the slave and those who believed in what he insisted on upholding as "universals." In *Middle Passage*, he seemed to have resolved the issue in favor of the former, as he produced a narrative that was transformed from the slave ship's manifest log into a slave narrative – in other words, a book meant to imply mastery over chattel became a text proclaiming the slave's freedom. And Gaines, whose *Autobiography* can likewise be read as a critique of Styron's *Confessions*, has stated that his "criticism of [Styron's] book was with its form."[17]

This contemporary debate over that particular form of writing involving the first-person voice of the American slave hauntingly echoes the nineteenth-century debate over the political truth contained in antebellum slave narratives and the early-twentieth-century debate over the documentary truth value of the autobiographies of slaves for the American historical profession. The voice of the slave, it seems, is doomed to be doubted where it is not absolutely proscribed. It is all the more heartening, then, to see the ways that Gaines, Reed, Williams, and Johnson appreciatively and respectfully attempt to recuperate those voices. The strategy they all share is that of producing a voice that is discontinuous and part of a larger communal voice. We saw how Gaines has others' voices supplement Miss Jane's, as he declares this story to be theirs as theirs, hers. In *Flight to Canada*, Reed gives us a narrator who, in an act of Voudon possession, tells his own life story and the life story of the slave who has commissioned him as a writer. In *Dessa Rose*, Williams produces a chorus of texts – the writing of the white "expert" on slave behavior, the stories of the white plantation mistress, and the recorded memories and voice of the slave Dessa – all of which we discover, only at the end of the novel, to have been the oral rendition of Dessa written down by her son. In *Oxherding Tale*, the story is interrupted by metafictional digressions on the form of the book, and in *Middle Passage* the text is both a record of commercial traffic in slaves and a statement of the slaves' resistance to being commodified. These are all texts that, I think, can be accurately described as ambiguously first-person, suspicious of the coherent subject of narration, and inviting of others' voices. In contrast, it is worth noting that Styron's narrator is both disdainful of any voice other than his own and quite self-consciously absolutist in his individualism. "I shiver feverishly in the glory of self," he proclaims at one point.[18] Against this kind of arrogance, and in respect to the importance of the historical task they are undertaking, Gaines, Reed, Williams, and Johnson produce choral and communal voices in an effort to capture the kind of spirit also evinced in those antebellum slave narratives where the authors realized that they spoke not only for themselves but for a captive community whose voices they represented.

Related to the question of voice, and raising the issue of appropriation in a somewhat different way, is the question of the relationship between orality and textuality, between the spoken word that enlivens and the written one that captivates. We have seen how artists like Walker, Haley, and Gaines found themselves in libraries and archives attempting to supplement the spoken words they heard in their living rooms and on their porches from their grandparents. This tension between the spoken and the written is, of course, an important feature in much African American fiction. While attaining the prohibited literacy is often cast as one of the crucial stages in the progress to freedom in slave narratives and later African American *Bildungsromane*, the written word is also a potent weapon against people of African descent. As Williams puts it in her preface to *Dessa Rose*, "Afro-Americans, having survived by word of mouth – and made of that process a high art – remain at the mercy of literature and writing; often, these have betrayed us." This ambivalent relationship with the written word has produced a kind of double consciousness which Robert Stepto describes as African American culture's simultaneous "distrust of literacy" and "abiding faith in it."[19] In general, in the neo-slave narratives there is much more of the distrust than the faith.

Some of the writers discussed here do genuinely express that ambivalence. Probably Reed's *Flight to Canada* most fully captures the tension. The fugitive slave Raven Quickskill escapes slavery because of his writing – "it was his writing that got him to Canada . . . for him, freedom was his writing" – but he also finds himself endangered because he cannot control the circulation of what he has written. Later, after his poem has revealed to his former master where he is, he wonders whether that made his writing "a squealer? A tattler?" The whole book is framed around the question of how to protect writing so that it is not vulnerable to theft. Employing a Voudon practice, Reed's narrator produces a book in which he "put witchery on the word" so that for any would-be appropriator "to lay hands on the story would be lethal to the thief."[20]

For other authors, writing was a mode that was problematic because it was inefficient. Gaines had wished to be free of the constraints of writing because it was a mode that was inherently limited for capturing the nuances and rhythms of the spoken word. In *The Chaneysville Incident*, Bradley's narrator John Washington finds writing (in the form of the cards on which he has transcribed historical dates and events) to be a constraint on the kind of imagination that will allow him to transport himself fully back into the past. He concludes the novel by setting fire to his written cards. In Octavia Butler's *Kindred*, two professional writers, Dana Franklin and her white husband Kevin, discover that written words can never capture the experience of slavery, even as they realize that it is the only medium they have to reveal what they know. For others, writing was an absence that had to be answered with oral productions. In Gayl Jones's *Corregidora*, the written records of Brazilian slavery are destroyed and therefore the *Corregidora* women have to produce generational tales and blues songs to ensure the survival of their story.

Finally, there are a set of authors of neo-slave narratives who emphatically point out the dangers of writing for the integrity of the slave. Barbara Chase-Riboud's *Sally Hemings* begins with the census taker for Albemarle County misrecording Sally Hemings as "white" in order to save the reputation of Thomas Jefferson. Writing – in this case, official writing sanctioned by the government – is a metaphor for who gets to control definitions of identity and who gets ascribed the authority to report on the American past. Against the official records of the census taker and the writings of the third president of the United States interspersed in the text of the novel, the ex-slave Sally Hemings reports her own memories and inserts her own oral tale. Sherley Anne Williams's *Dessa Rose* likewise begins with an episode in which a white writer attempts to control the voice of a slave, only to find himself thwarted because her voice exceeds the capacity of his mind and text. In the end, we discover that his written words had been subsumed in Dessa's own oral rendition. Writing, in Toni Morrison's *Beloved*, is a danger in every form in which it appears. The newspaper article that Stamp Paid shows to Paul D reveals the infanticide Sethe had committed, but it is unable to report or even to comprehend the motives that made the fugitive slave take the life of her daughter. One of the reasons Sethe escapes slavery is that Schoolteacher, the white man in charge of the plantation, writes a pseudo-anthropological document in which he lists the "human characteristics" of the slaves alongside the "animal ones" (193). No one, "nobody on this earth," Sethe declares, "would list her daughter's characteristics on the animal side of the paper" (251). Later, Sethe would take upon herself a measure of responsibility for Schoolteacher's racism because she feels that she was complicit in helping him produce the materials for his writing. "I made the ink," she tells an uncomprehending Paul D at the end of the novel. "He couldn't have done it if I hadn't made the ink" (271). Writing, for this former slave, is so much associated with misrepresentation that even the physical properties involved in it are tainted.

The answer for many of these authors and characters who are skeptical of writing or believe it positively detrimental is to subvert writing with oral performances. The slaves in all these novels respond by positing their memory as a crucial documentary force in history, their voice as a power equal to the written texts they contest. In the words of the schoolmistress Miss Carey in Cliff's *Free Enterprise*, "Books are fragile things" whose contents "can easily be lost. We must become talking books," she concludes, in order to ensure the safety, the integrity, and the authenticity of the tale told.[21]

Another means by which the writers of contemporary narratives of slavery talk about cultural appropriation is by focusing on the physical appropriation of the slave's body. In *Jubilee*, Walker represents scenes where we see the slave's body abused (at the whipping stand) and commodified (on the auction block). In a scene that would be repeated with variations in later novels, particularly those written by women, Walker shows us the ways that slave women's bodies were subject to and marked by the torture of enslavement. A brutal whipping applied to her body after Vyry attempted to run away "left a loose flap of flesh over her breast like a tuck in a dress." Walker concludes the scene and the section on slavery by noting: "It healed that way" (174). In Butler's *Kindred*, the narrator is physically beaten, whipped, and finally loses her left arm between her 1976 Los Angeles home and her white slave-owning great-grandfather's hold on her in nineteenth-century Maryland. In Williams's *Dessa Rose*, the scar tissue that "plowed through [Dessa's] pubic region" so that her "loins looked like a mutilated cat face," the result of an especially sadistic whipping, is both a marker of how she had been sexually abused by slavery and a sign that the plantation mistress insists on seeing to ensure the validity of the story of the slave's suffering (154). The body of the slave, in *Dessa Rose*, is always on display, always the final determinant of the truth value of her words. The scar that heals on Sethe's back in Morrison's *Beloved* takes the form of a "chokeberry tree," which acts as a sign of others' perceptual distance (16). When Paul D is unable to see the beauty in Sethe, in post-coital *triste*, for instance, he sees nothing but a "revolting clump of scars" (21). When he is able to love this woman, when she becomes truly a "friend of [his] mind" (273), he is better able to appreciate that her body has healed artfully, and he instead sees "the sculpture her back had become," and he cannot rest until "he had touched every ridge and leaf of it with his mouth" (17–18), in the same way that Harker in *Dessa Rose* redeems by kissing Dessa's scars and tells her that they do not "impair" but rather "increase your value" (191).

Turning the language of commodification against itself (from the value of a slave to human value), turning scar tissue into flesh recovered by intimacy, are a few of the ways that these artists show that the body is not only brutalized but reclaimed. Baby Suggs, the grandmother in *Beloved*, who "limps like a three-legged dog when she walked" because of a hip injured in slavery (139), and whose "heart . . . started beating the minute she crossed the Ohio River" into freedom (147), expresses most beautifully the primary lesson of recovery: "Here . . . in this here place, we flesh; flesh that weeps, laughs; flesh that dances on bare feet in the grass. Love it. Love it hard" (88). In various ways and with differing emphases, these artists all show in painful detail the ways that black women's bodies were scarred and dismembered by slavery, and then salvaged and remembered in the acts of free love.

So far, we have seen how the writers of the contemporary narratives of slavery recuperate voice and body, challenge appropriation and commodification, and experiment with the tension between a literacy that captures and an orality that liberates. A final point about the politics of representing slavery in the neo-slave narratives concerns what these artists say about contemporary black subjectivity. Why have so many chosen to represent slavery as the subject from which to make those statements? It would of course be presumptuous to attempt to provide any kind of satisfactory answer that would encompass or even touch on so large and diverse a body of writing. Yet these questions demand some kind of response, some hint of what impelled so many to undertake a task that all acknowledge as daunting and forbidding. I would like to end by briefly making two broad points about the work these novels do.

The first is about contemporary African American subjectivity, about the identity that emerged at the same time as did the neo-slave narratives, in the mid-1960s. In some ways, the Black Power Movement spurred many of these writers to begin their projects. And, although many cultural nationalists and Black Aesthetic intellectuals frowned on such returns to the past, the reclamation of "blackness" as a political category and an ethnic identity necessitated such an archeological project, as it were. To know what the post-Civil Rights "black" subject would be, it was essential to recall the complexity of what the first black American subject had been, not merely to use names inherited from slavery as terms of abuse for those who appeared unresistant to the social order, but to discover the covert and overt acts of resistance that permitted those earlier generations to ensure the survival and birth of this one. In the works of the writers closest in time to the Black Power Movement, Jones, Reed, Butler, Colter, and Williams, their project was one of reclamation of those historical subjects who had suffered first at the hands of owners and then in the intellectual programs of revolutionaries. Reed wished to salvage the "Uncle Tom," as Butler and Williams did the "Mammy," not to celebrate quiescence in the face of suffering but to be just in their assessment of what those who lived through it experienced, and what we, "who never was there," as Morrison puts it (31), did not. It is, yet again, another act of respect, in addition to being an act of historical recovery for the task of providing continuity and parallels for the contemporary African American subject, whose struggles against the inequities of the present would be part of a tradition and mirror the acts of those who struggled in the past.

The second and last point is about the means of recovery, in each sense of that term. Memory is how the past is recalled; memory is also how we heal from that past. Insistently, the artists who produce neo-slave narratives return to what Leon Forrest calls "memory-history," most with an understandable ambivalence toward a force that they, like him, believe "destroys as it heals." What Morrison defines as "re-memory" is, after all, a "place in which things so bad had happened that when you went near them it would happen again" (35–36). This is what makes the story of slavery so utterly difficult a one to tell, what makes it a story one would prefer to pass on rather than to pass on to others. Yet is is also the only way to heal, as so many characters in so many of these novels discover again and again. At the end of *Jubilee*, Vyry strips in the moonlight and asserts her freedom from slavery and hatred, showing that her heart is as healed as the torn flesh above it. At the end of Jones's *Corregidora*, Ursa sings a blues duet with her husband in which each asserts the desire to recover from the "hurt" of the past. It is by sharing memories that recovery is made possible. *Beloved* ends with Paul D wanting to "put his story next to" Sethe's (273), Charles Johnson's *Middle Passage* with Rutherford and Isadora wishing to have their "histories perfectly twined for all time."[22] And it is by sharing those stories and that history with their readers that the neo-slave narrative authors perhaps hope to heal a nation that in many ways still denies its original wound.

What the body of fiction that began with *Jubilee* and continues past this chapter does, at the simplest level, is recover for us a period long-neglected, an institution oft forgotten, and a population of brave souls too frequently denigrated. Ralph Ellison's invisible man begins his meditations on his invisibility by tracing it to the slaves in his family: "I am not ashamed of my grandparents for having been slaves. I am only ashamed of myself for having at one time been ashamed."²³ The contemporary narratives of slavery have helped create a similar sentiment for this generation by so manifestly claiming an important space in American fiction for acts of courage, expressions of love, and endless demonstrations of cultural ingenuity by those people whose enslavement did not cause them to lose sight of their humanity.

NOTES

1. Williams Wells Brown, *Clotel; Or, The President's Daughter: A Narrative of Slave Life in the United States* (London, 1853), pp. 17–55, 245. Margaret Walker, *Jubilee* (1966; Boston: Houghton Mifflin, 1999), p. iii. Hereafter all quotations from all the neo-slave narratives will be taken from the cited edition and noted parenthetically in the body of the chapter.
2. Jonathan Weiner, "Radical Historians and the Crisis in American History, 1959–1980," *Professors, Politics, and Pop* (New York: Verso, 1991), pp. 175, 192, 200; A. S. Eisenstadt, "The Perennial Myth – Writing American History Today," *Massachusetts Review* 7 (1966): 773, 757.
3. Eugene Genovese, *In Red and Black: Marxian Explorations in Southern and Afro-American History* (Knoxville: University of Tennessee Press, 1984), p. 231. Sherley Anne Williams, "The Lion's History: The Ghetto Writes B[l]ack," *Soundings* 76.2–3 (1993): 248.
4. Robert A. Gross, "The Black Novelists: Our Turn," *Newsweek* (June 16, 1969): 94–98.
5. Toni Morrison, *Beloved* (New York: Alfred A. Knopf, 1987), pp. 199, 274.
6. Walker, "How I Wrote *Jubilee*," *How I Wrote* Jubilee *and Other Essays on Life and Literature*, ed. Maryemma Graham (New York: The Feminist Press, 1990), p. 64.
7. Walker, "How I Wrote *Jubilee*," p. 56. Alex Haley, "Black History, Oral History, and Genealogy," *Oral History: An Interdisciplinary Anthology*, eds. David K. Dunaway and Willa K. Baum (Nashville: American Association for State and Local History, 1984), p. 286.
8. Ernest Gaines, "Miss Jane and I," *Callaloo* 1.3 (May, 1978): 37–38. Jerome Tarshis, "The Other 300 Years: A Conversation with Ernest Gaines," *Conversations with Ernest Gaines*, ed. John Lowe (Jackson: University Press of Mississippi, 1995), p. 74.
9. Gaines, *The Autobiography of Miss Jane Pittman* (1971; New York: Bantam, 1989), p. vi.
10. Ashraf H. A. Rushdy, *Neo-slave Narratives: Studies in the Social Logic of a Literary Form* (New York: Oxford University Press, 1999).
11. Gayl Jones, *Corregidora* (1975; Boston: Beacon Press, 1986), p. 9.
12. Frances E. W. Harper, *Iola Leroy Or Shadows Uplifted* (1892; Boston: Beacon, 1992), pp. 216, 217. Pauline Hopkins, *Contending Forces: A Romance Illustrative of Negro Life North and South* (Boston: The Colored Cooperative Publishing Co., 1900), p. 15. Charles W. Chesnutt, *The Marrow of Tradition* (New York: Houghton Mifflin, 1901), pp. 310, 269.

13. Linda Beatrice Brown, *Crossing Over Jordan* (1995; New York: Ballantine, 1996), p. 285. Cyrus Colter, *Night Studies* (Chicago: Swallow Press, 1979), pp. 196, 772–773.
14. Raymond Andrews, *Rosiebelle Lee Wildcat Tennessee* (1980; Athens: University of Georgia Press, 1988), pp. 199, 60. Andrews, *Baby Sweet's* (1983; Athens: University of Georgia Press, 1988), pp. 4, 71.
15. Leon Forrest, *There Is a Tree More Ancient Than Eden* (1973; Chicago: Another Chicago Press, 1988), pp. 3–10, 109, 107. Forrest, *The Bloodworth Orphans* (1977; Chicago: Another Chicago Press, 1987), pp. 41, 340, 218, 174. Forrest, *Two Wings to Veil My Face* (1983; Chicago: Another Chicago Press, 1988), pp. 139, 276.
16. Charles Johnson, *Oxherding Tale* (1982; New York: Grove Press, 1984), p. 119.
17. Cornel West, "Black Critics and the Pitfalls of Canon Formation," in *Keeping Faith: Philosophy and Race in America* (New York and London: Routledge, 1993), p. 41. William Parrill, "An Interview with Ernest Gaines," in *Conversations with Ernest Gaines*, p. 178.
18. William Styron, *Confessions of Nat Turner* (1967; New York: Vantage International Editions, 1992), p. 125.
19. Sherley Anne Williams, *Dessa Rose* (New York: William Morrow, 1986), p. 5. Robert B. Stepto, *From Behind the Veil: A Study of Afro-American Narrative* (1979; 2nd edn.; Urbana and Chicago: University of Illinois Press, 1991), p. 196.
20. Ishmael Reed, *Flight to Canada* (1976; New York: Atheneum, 1989), pp. 88, 85, 13, 11.
21. Michele Cliff, *Free Enterprise* (New York: Dutton, 1993), p. 211.
22. Johnson, *Middle Passage* (New York: Macmillan, 1990), p. 209.
23. Ralph Ellison, *Invisible Man* (1952; New York: Vantage International Edition, 1990), p. 15.

6

CLAUDINE RAYNAUD

Coming of age in the African American novel

Coming of age – reaching the age of "maturity" or "discretion"[1] – is variously a process, a moment, or a scene akin to the structural "scenes of instruction" inherent in African American narratives described by Dexter Fisher (1990).[2] The discovery of American society's racism is the major event in the protagonist's development and in his "education." Emphasis is placed upon being an African American in America, where ownership, belonging, and their negation, and dispossession, are central to the notion of identity. How can one own one's destiny – be self-determined – when one does not own oneself and faces an irrevocable loss? The recognition of belonging takes place within the narrower circles of the family and of the black community, while society as a whole is often viewed as a threat, if not as the enemy. For the black adolescent, "The Man," slang for the white man, translates the contradiction set up by racism between maturation and manhood. Indeed the characters' acquisition of a sense of belonging and its opposite, independence, leads to various questions: What are the major events in the protagonist's growth from individual self into social being? Who and what functions as the "educator" in the African American novel? One's "identity" – as process/trial rather than monolithic category – is at the core of "coming of age." What is the process of becoming of the African American "hero" or central character: self-acceptance as opposed to self-hatred or self-denial? Does the narrative depict the emergence of a stronger individual, better integrated, better self-integrated, both or neither?

Coming of age implies a progress from childhood to manhood or womanhood, a journey towards maturity. Childhood can be either the moment for a happiness never to be retrieved, an age of innocence, or a time already plagued by the torments inherent in the condition of being black in America, as if the protagonist had always already been immersed in experience. Such an opposition helps, for instance, to contrast Langston Hughes's *Not Without Laughter* (1930) with James Baldwin's *Go Tell It on the Mountain* (1953).[3] Overall, the narrators are either adults who recall their youth and years of maturation, or they are adolescents. Narrative resistance often prevents the African American novelist from inventing the device of a child's voice and gaze. When they are children, the realistic conventions of the novel fall apart. Naturalism and realism give way to a modernist text. Like Toni Morrison's Pecola, Alice Walker's Celie, or Sapphire's Precious, the child narrator is caught in a schizophrenic vision, a madness of self-division from which he fails, or attempts, to be free.[4] The ironic and heroic journey of John A. Williams's Robert Youngblood (*Youngblood*, 1954), whose good intentions are constantly thwarted by disillusionment, offers an alternative. In spite of all, he keeps a fighting and optimistic spirit.[5]

The "paradise" of childhood is the scene for the advent of racial consciousness and sexuality, and such knowledge is the occasion for abrupt confrontations, rites of passage, and sensual awakenings. In Zora Neale Hurston's *Their Eyes Were Watching God* (1937), Janie cannot find herself in her class picture since she is the only black child of the group.[6] She literally cannot see her own self. Gordon Parks's *The Learning Tree* (1963) opens with a storm that destroys and kills.[7] The young hero is lost and takes refuge in a barn with an older girl, Big Mabel, with whom he experiences his first sexual encounter. Normally, the protagonists learn from their elders, from the ancestors, with the recurrent figure of the grandmother on the side of strict morality and accommodation. Seldom the beneficiary of formal education, she is both educator and teacher in the cultural sense. Freedom must also be learned along with its corollary, danger. The blues woman is the symbol of such knowledge, an ambivalent or paradoxical one, made of laughter and tears, of resilience and courage in the face of domestic and racial violence, and their various interconnections. The character of the friend, the other young man, Champ, the protagonist's friend in Al Young's *Snakes* (1970) or Guitar, Milkman's alter ego in Morrison's *Song of Solomon* (1978), represents the temptation of a path that should not be taken. This wayward friend is a recurrent type, but the protagonist can also take on his features and be another Bigger Thomas (Wright, *Native Son*, 1940), caught in a trap of hatred, fear and violence.[8]

For the African American writer the narrative of coming of age in America poses the problem of inscribing that fictional moment against the tradition of slavery. The paternalism of the Peculiar Institution placed the slave in the "care" of the master: it infantilized him. "Coming of age" should signal "emancipation" from the "childhood" ascribed by the master to the slave, from servitude and its traces. The names of the protagonists bear the mark of that difficulty since the father's name is handed over to the son. Jimboy is Langston Hughes's father-figure in *Not Without Laughter*; Boy Boy, Eva's husband and one of the male protagonists in Morrison's *Sula* (1973); while

"Milkman" is the anti-hero of *Song of Solomon* as is "Bigger" Thomas, Wright's native son.[9] Mothers and grandmothers also carry in their names the stigma of bondage. Thus, Sissie is the name of the dying mother in the eponymous novel by John A. Williams (1963).[10] In *Trouble the Water* (1989) by Melvin Dixon, the mother has died in childbirth.[11] The grandmother's hatred must be confronted and absolved. A crazed figure, a culprit that should be shot, the father is denied his status. In sum, the protagonists' coming of age is simultaneously contradicted by the fathers' infantile names that they carry into maturity. For the question of lineage, the relationship to the mother and the father, and hence the depiction of the black family, is central to this process of growing up.[12] The relationship to the grandmother is a key link to the construction of a self. Be it Nanny or Big Mama, these exemplary figures are the foundation, the origin of psychic development, their deaths figuring as one of the crucial moments of childhood.

The episode that marks one's coming of age can be grafted onto the broader genre of the *Bildungsroman*.[13] A definition of the term helps envision how it both fails and does not fail to apply to the African American novel that stands at the crossroads of the picaresque novel, the sentimental novel, and the slave narrative per se. The *Bildungsroman* offers the "plot" of an apprenticeship of the concurrent mutual shaping of the protagonist's psyche and his integration into society at large. It is a question of interrogating "one of the most harmonious solutions ever offered to a dilemma coterminous with modern bourgeois civilization: the conflict between the ideal of *self-determination* and the equally imperious demands of *socialization*."[14] Moreover, the hero's life-story – his early years – is related to the historical time of the novel. His or her biography is played up against the background of history in the making. The emergence of a full individual takes shape against the backdrop of historical events and leads to a projection outside the realm of his family, outside the determining forces of history, or even outside temporality. In Ntozake Shange's novel by that name, Betsey Brown's (1985) coming of age takes place within the troubled times of desegregation.[15] Alice Walker's Meridian Hill, whose coming of age has been preempted by an early pregnancy, is born again in the Civil Rights Movement while Anne Moody's narrative, *Coming of Age in Mississippi* (1970), ends with her participation in that same movement (1968).[16] Conversely, Richard Wright's *Native Son* insists on the racial and social determinism of his characters. The utopian thrust of the novel finds in the episode of coming of age or the novel of apprenticeship its most strident expression. Another distinction can be drawn between the *Entwicklungsroman* (development of a subjective individuality) and *Erziehungsroman* (objective process viewed by an educator), thus reopening the fusion effected by the *Bildungsroman*. Within the African

American novel there is this distinction as well. The novel with a didactic purpose shows the positive development of the individual against the combined odds of racism, poverty, and violence, while a more open narrative allows the inner self to be analyzed, as it goes through the expected stages of development: first sexual encounter, racial encounter, choice of school, and finally departure from home.

And yet as the African American novel employs the *Bildungsroman* frame, it effects a critique of coming of age. The traditional European *Bildungsroman* describes the descent or decadence of the hero along with the cynicism inherent in bourgeois values and thus exposes the upstart, the "parvenu." The African American variation leads to a subversion – and even a negation – of the American dream in terms of race relations. In Ellison's *Invisible Man* (1952), coming of age as a literary term corresponds to the gradual deconstruction of the various versions of the narrator's identity. This voice debunks Booker T. Washington's ideal of a school system, the dream of the Great Migration to the urban North, the hope of a political solution through the Brotherhood (the Communist party) and of a religious solution in the satire of the Nation of Islam. Keep that "nigger boy" running . . . and he will never come of age; such is the discourse of the masters/fathers, and false brothers. To know and muster the mechanisms of racism, to understand the workings of his/her oppression rather than fall prey to them is necessary for the black boy or the black girl to reach "adulthood." Yet coming of age is often a precipitation of the stages of life, a distorted or reversed process: work and providing for the family takes the place of formal education (Richard Wright, *Native Son*); motherhood takes place before girlhood. As Maya Angelou notes, her rape makes her a woman before she is a girl. Paule Marshall's Selina feels older than she should be, deprived of her childhood innocence at the end *of Brown Girl, Brownstones* (1953).[17] Celie's repeated rape by her stepfather robs her of her childhood and a "normal" womanhood, rendering her fit only to be a surrogate mother, one without the power or position.

What is repressed in autobiography, that wellspring of African American literature, comes back in these novels for the protagonist's progress is, as critics remark, in novel after novel, a thinly veiled transcription of the author's life. "Biographemes," to use Barthes's term, these insistent recurrent moments of the author's singular story, respond to or echo the progress and trials of the black minority in the US.[18] A case in point is the hatred of John Grimes's father in Baldwin's *Go Tell It on the Mountain*. As a symbol of racist dichotomy, itself supported by the division between good and evil of religious fundamentalism, John Grimes's conversion reads like the chaos of further alienation, false-consciousness. For Baldwin, like many authors of coming-of-age narratives, the genre permits the telling of a story of childhood and maturation within the poetic truth of creative invention. An autobiographical narrative, Moody's *Coming of Age in Mississippi* bears in its title the centrality of the process of growing up, together with the announcement that the South is a strange land for the black adolescent, the territory of a history of suffering and survival. The imprint of the South is also the harbinger of the choice between rebellion and submissiveness for the African American hero or heroine. It becomes a crucial alternative leading to death, self- or other-inflicted, or a critical decision regarding the path of one's life.

The term "coming of age" entails the achievement of the goal: one is finally "of age," mature, ready to face the outside world. The novel contains the proposition of a solution to the formation of the black subject in America. Alternatively, it depicts the impossibility of such a solution, the damage wrought on these black selves by the horrors of history and racism. Such is the lesson of the murders committed by the protagonists (*Native Son*, Ann Petry's *The Street* [1946]),[19] their self-hatred (Selina's boyfriend, Clive), or suicides (Richard, John Grimes's mother's lover). Narrative circularity is a means of recalling childhood events. Hurston's novel starts with Janie coming back from burying the dead. Fulfillment and the round of cyclical time is effected when Janie is left alone at the end of the text. Phoeby has left her. Janie will plant a seed that Tea Cake has given her. John A. Williams's *Sissie* retraces the journey back to the dying mother of the two protagonists, Ralph and Iris. The reader enters their consciousness as they retell their childhood experiences and try to make peace with their mother's troubled legacy. In Ralph's case, it is the crucial question of whose son he actually is, a secret kept by her mother. A question that resounds in numerous novels with the accents of Baldwin's voice: "Whose son are you?" The shattered dreams of the Great Migration explain Sissie's behavior: her love for another man, her despair. Ralph's psychoanalysis is an incursion into these questions: the killing of a man when serving in the army, but also his relation to his mother. Coming of age can only happen at such cost. Toni Morrison's *Song of Solomon* is also circular as Milkman goes back South to recover the history of his people, to learn by heart the children's rhyme that preserves the memory of his genealogy.

The process of coming of age is one of "coming along" (James Baldwin's *Go Tell It on the Mountain*). It is also one of deferral, the postponement of what can never be in this time or in this world. The hero never completes this progress. Most novels end on a note of ambivalence; action is sometimes reaction. Ellison's *Invisible Man* tells the reader that he is about to come out, but the end finds him still underground, maybe speaking for the reader on the lower "frequencies."[20] Morrison's *Song of Solomon* offers an open ending with a flight into the void: death leap or lyrical élan of the African American voice riding the air? Marriage does not conclude this progress. At times it is included in the hero's progress, as in Maud Martha's ordinary and lackluster urban life.[21] More traditionally, the hero leaves his hometown for the city as in Young's *Snakes*. Alternatively, the ending is postponed beyond this world, as Hughes's ending suggests in *Not Without Laughter*, for the "stars beyond" of the spiritual the child hears in the city may be those of afterlife. Such projection is in keeping with an eschatological vision of history: achievement cannot take place in the here and now.

To "build" means to "rememory," to re-member, to tell, to lay one's story next to the other's, as Sethe and Paul D learn to do in Morrison's *Beloved* (1987).[22] Like other women writers, and male writers such as John Edgar Wideman, Toni Morrison, Michele Cliff (*Abeng*), and Jamaica Kincaid (*Annie John*), show that the *Bildungsroman* must be the locus of voices that speak the unspeakable.[23] The construction of a single self must be transmuted into the reconstruction of a collective memory through the poetics of fiction, the prodigy of invention.

Movement in the coming-of-age narrative introduces two of the major metaphors in African American literature: the journey and the veil. The hero or the heroine's development is narrated in terms of a journey from South to North, from North back South, or a flight (to the city). The protagonist of Morrison's *Song of Solomon*, which figures in the black canon as one of the finest variations on the *Bildungsroman*, travels South to find himself. Milkman goes through a rite of initiation in the guise of a hunt and recovers the song that recounts his family's history. He divests himself of the false attributes of materialism to commune with Nature and sings to his aunt Pilate, as she dies after having buried her father's bones, in another ritual of appeasement. Journeys across space coincide with psychological growth. Killing or not killing the father is the central crisis of these novels. Melvin Dixon's *Trouble the Water* tells of the journey back South that helps rebuild the lineage and rekindle the self in the culture of the ancestors by the river. If displacement must be countered, homelessness probed and overcome, the heroes and heroines of the Great Migration travel back South to face the trial of memory. Jordan Henry, Dixon's protagonist, is Milkman's blood brother. Both men have been estranged from their roots by wealth and education. Both must return and resolve what they, or their parents, have fled. Morrison's *Jazz* (1992) also shows Golden Gray, the mulatto son of the master's daughter and the black slave, who goes back to kill the father.[24] The black *Bildungsroman* shows that the father's name must be known to the son: Jake to Jordan, Solomon to Macon, together with a sense of home, a reclaiming of the Southern soil or of a territory, either real or metaphoric, a paternal ground. John Edgar Wideman's *Fatheralong* is the autobiographical counterpart of this lifeline that constructs the African American narrative of adulthood.[25] Where are the fathers? How can one become a father? The parallel interrogation of the link between daughters and mothers is exemplified by Marshall in Selina's brutal opposition to her mother and the final resolution of that conflict in her acknowledgment that she is, indeed, her mother's child.

The veil as a prominent trope recurs in the narrative of adolescent experience. Lifted off or tied on more closely, the veil bespeaks the ambivalence of education; it also separates life from death, slavery from reconstruction, the ghosts from the living, oblivion from the return of the repressed. It can have a ritualized presence not to be denied. In Tina McElroy Ansa's *Baby of the Family* (1989), Lena is born with a veil over her face, a caul, and the old nurse Bloom, who knows the country customs, would have performed the ritual which ensured healing, but the young mother interferes out of ignorance.[26] The novel opposes the rational world of the twentieth century to the ancestral belief in the supernatural. The breach of tradition leads to the child's confusion between the real and the surreal. She sees ghosts and conversely cannot believe in her own reality. She sleepwalks and at the end of the novel is delivered by an incident that resolves her double nature. She is freed from her secret as she catches an owl – a sure sign that there is going to be a death – in her grandmother's house. McElroy Ansa uses the trope of the veil to tell a fable: that of a lack of identity, a "lostness," and a direct communion with the past that is the hallmark of the novels of the period.

Male writers and female writers tackle the coming-of-age journey differently, although to become a man or a woman is equally fraught with difficulty. Diachronically, the variable of sexual difference derives from the opposition between the male and female slave narrative. From Frederick Douglass's *Narrative* comes the prototypical transformation of the "slave [becoming] a man" while the female slave narrative more often critiques conventions of femininity. The confrontation between Hughes's *Not Without Laughter* and Hurston's *Their Eyes Were Watching God* offers an illustration of that major opposition which runs through the novel of formation. Sandy, Hughes's young hero, experiences hardships growing up as a black man in America in a naturalistic tale interspersed with visions of black life in a small Kansas town. His grandmother's strict upbringing contrasts with his young aunt Harriett's blues trajectory and his father's waywardness. His mother, Annjee, works so much that he seldom sees her; she leaves him to his grandmother's care to join her shiftless husband North. Sandy experiences loneliness as, one by one, Aunt Hager's daughters leave her, and as she herself eventually dies of old age. At school and with his playmates, Sandy suffers from the humiliation of Jim Crowism in Kansas: the Free Children's Day Party is for white kids only. Yet the hurt of rejection is compensated by partaking in a collective folklore of hope and survival. Growing up means loneliness as well as communion with the natural world and its round of seasons.

Hager's three daughters symbolize three possible responses to the condition of being black in America: Annjee, the hardworking maid who leaves with her husband and subordinates everything to love; Harriett, the fun-loving daughter who becomes a prostitute; and Tempy, who rejects her race and joins the white community, refusing Negro ways and talk. These three female characters are directions that the young boy can and cannot follow, precisely because of his sex. He finds himself for some time in the guardianship of Tempy, the one who, childless, is a champion of acculturation. Eventually, Sandy is reunited with his mother in Chicago and his aunt Harriett, now a successful cabaret singer, helps him with his education so that he can become what his grandmother wanted him to be: a champion of the black race, like Washington and Douglass.

Al Young's narrative from the 1970s, *Snakes*, echoes Hughes's *Not Without Laughter* in the depiction of a strong grandmother–grandson relationship. Set in Detroit, the novel tells the journey of apprenticeship through music, drugs, and sex. It deploys the choices that must be made between music and education, staying at home and going away, settling down to raise a family and furthering one's horizon. The colorful characters, who represent modulations on a young urban black man's destiny, include an adolescent who quotes Shakespeare, "Shakes," Champ, who succumbs to drugs and violence, and Billy, a musician who deserts the band they had formed to go to New York.

In contrast to these works that weigh the pros and cons of adolescent development, *Their Eyes Were Watching God* is a hymn to experience, love, and freedom. *Their Eyes* is a *mise en abyme* of female ("womanist") education through conversation: Janie's story is told to Phoeby who grows "ten feet higher just from listening to her." Janie's strength derives from the personal choices that have led her to action as she pursues the truth of her dream: "Yo papa and yo' mama and nobody else cant tell yuh and show yuh. Two things everybody's got tuh do fuh theyselves. They got tuh go tuh God, and they got tuh find out about livin' fuh theyselves" (285). The sexual experience at the core of Janie's freedom is that of an orgasm under a pear-tree in bloom. At 40, the older Janie has undergone a transformation that saw her through three different relationships, each emblematic of a link to the black community and to a different economic system. She gradually emerges freer, with a voice of her own. Her grandmother Nanny epitomizes the extreme resilience and the lessons from the days of slavery from which Janie escapes.

Ultimately, the choice is between people and things, relationships and ownership. Janie's first marriage to Logan Killicks is a process of alienation in a rural society, her status no better than that of one of Logan's mules, as she works in his field to improve their livelihood. Her loveless first marriage ends when Janie meets Jody Starks, the black entrepreneur whose determination leads him to become the mayor of the all-black town he has founded. As "de Mayor's wife," Janie's bourgeois status means that she must stop working in Joe's store: "her place is in de home." Gradually reduced to silence, Janie talks back one day and her words "kill" her husband. She then enjoys a freedom that marks a turning point in her story. A young widow, she is courted by Tea Cake, who epitomizes the free-spirited love Janie has been dreaming about all along. She finds that sense of completion in a relationship of mutual respect that she chooses in freedom. Yet her lover Tea Cake is bitten by a rabid dog in the flood that figures an apocalyptic moment in the novel, and Janie must kill him in self-defense. She is then acquitted by an all-white jury. The explicitness of Hurston's treatment of Janie's sexuality and fulfillment contrasts with Hughes's tone; Janie is much older than Sandy, who remains an adolescent. Hughes's is a more sober and traditional tale that nonetheless gives women a central role as life models.

As is to be expected, some of the other works of the African American canon can be described as anti-*Bildungsromane*. Morrison's *The Bluest Eye* (1970) belongs to that category since it retraces from the point of view of the narrator, Claudia McTeer, the gradual descent into schizophrenia of the young black protagonist Pecola Breedlove. Although much older, Ann Petry's Lutie Johnson in *The Street* had paved the way for this dark vision of the self in its relation to the community. Her plight is tragic like that of the mulatto protagonists of the Harlem Renaissance tradition. In her effort to perform the integration she believes in, the suburban domestic cuts herself off from her community and eventually kills a black man at the end of the novel. She loses her self-respect and gives up her struggle, thus signing the defeat of that solution, a consequence of the interrelation of race, gender, and class in American society. In Morrison's novel, Pecola is raped by her father and molested by other children. She is hated by her mother who prefers the young white child of the family she works for. She is also fooled by Soaphead Church, a fake preacher, into believing that he has given her the bluest eye(s)/"I" in the world. Morrison's first novel inscribes the devastation of self-hatred into the black psyche as the deepest destruction of racism. It also denounces the community's scapegoating of the poor black family.

How can the black child construct a self in America? Maya Angelou's autobiography *I Know Why the Caged Bird Sings* can be seen as a mirror and an answer to Pecola's tragic self-alienation.[27] The "I" narrator tells the explosion of the body, the disarray of the senses, the desire for death at the center of the young girl's psychic make-up. As she grows up in the violence of the South of the 1950s, rape, fear of lack of femininity, too many journeys back and forth across the country, must gradually be countered by a determination not to let the internalization of racism, the "razor that threatens the throat," inflict its deadly wound. Maya learns from her grandmother, from her mother, from her brother's experiences, that she must be whole and gather the fragments, overcome self-depreciation. At the close of the book, the mother and the daughter are reunited around the newborn baby, Maya's son. The symbolic circularity of the scene offers the reassurance that maternal and daughterly love, together with the hope of future generations, heals and teaches.

Alice Walker's *The Color Purple* depicts a highly melodramatic childhood. Raped by her father, Celie gives birth to two children from this incestuous relation. Her coming of age, however, is the gradual understanding, through the help of other protagonists, Sofia, Shug Avery, and her sister, Nettie, that she can claim her own beauty, her own self. She ultimately wins back her husband's love and starts her own business. If she is much older than might be expected, this trait is common to a lot of the heroes and heroines of the black novel. The deferral into adulthood of achievement and accomplishment is in direct relation to the weight of the burdens.

Sapphire's *Push*, which explicitly cites *The Color Purple*, tells of the gradual awakening to literacy and to a better self-integration of Precious Jones, a young girl of sixteen raped by her father, a crack addict. She gets pregnant twice by him and her first child suffers from Down's Syndrome. The novel piles up in one single character all the horrors of the ghetto. Precious is illiterate; she is abused by her mother, by her mother's lover; she is obese and learns from her mother that she is HIV-positive. The language of rap and of the urban gangs slowly gives way to more "readable" English under the care of Miss Rain, Precious's instructor in an alternative school system. Precious and her class comrades are Celie and Nettie's sisters and the descendants of Bigger Thomas. The crude vocabulary depicts devastation, yet they teach how love and determination help these downtrodden children. Precious becomes a good mother to Mongol and to Addul; she is independent from her own mother and learns to fight the system, to recover her rights.

Beyond the traumas of the black psyche explored at length in most novels, certain works try to tackle other ways of connecting across the color line by staging black–white relationships. In these cases, the African American novel questions whether racial lines cannot and should not be crossed. *Clover* by Dori Sanders tells the story of a little girl who gradually learns to love her white stepmother after the accidental death of her father.[28] The melodramatic tone is tempered by attempts to write the gradual acceptance of the other woman, the father's wife, the white woman, a reverse lesson in racial tolerance. In Marita Golden's *A Woman's Place*, the three heroines present different ideological positions on various aspects of the African American experience.[29] Religion and marriage are represented by Faith, who converts to Islam and changes her name to Aisha. Creativity and race are embodied by Chrystal, a published poet, who falls in love with a white man. History and place are mined when Serena goes to Africa in search of her self and roots. Marita Golden uses the voices of these young women in a polyphonic structure that recalls Morrison's and Shange's narratives. The voices are both unique and interwoven, each creating a singular path, yet also each entering a fruitful dialogue with the other. Forming this chorus of voices suggests that simultaneity must be thought together with difference just as the dogmatic and dramatic single plot explodes. Morrison's *Paradise* (1998) epitomizes this evolution of a plurality of female voices in the attempt to probe the link between racial purity and individual destiny, between black and white racism, the community and individualism.[30]

Class-lines must also be crossed. Shange's *Betsey Brown* (1985), based on her own life-story, is set in the black middle class. The father is a surgeon, the mother a social worker. With both parents busy and away most of the day, Betsey is a happy child who must be taught that her acts can have terrible consequences, like the firing of their first maid. She also learns, from the easygoing babysitter, the carefree gestures of love. This light narrative breaks the myth of childhood drudgery and tragedy, but it opens the way for a meditation on the difficulty of integration for black children who found themselves a minority in white colleges. It is also the tale of integration and of the black bourgeoisie. The black middle class has integrated the values of white America and the American dream of bettering oneself. Like the other narratives that depict the middle class, it interrogates class and race as it impacts black children.

Another line that contemporary black writers cross is that of homosexual desire. Baldwin's John Grimes struggles with this feeling and Maya Angelou tells her fear of lesbianism in her autobiographical text. *Sula* has been read as a lesbian novel. Morrison declares that hers is a love story. It describes the strong bond that unites two young black girls through the vicissitudes of life. Nel and Sula are a strange pair, brought up in very different households. Helen, Nel's mother, is the quintessence of a desire for integration that leads her to a dull and pathetic conformity. Eva, the grandmother and mistress of Sula's home, is the embodiment of the ancestor: wise, self-sacrificing, cruel, and stubborn. A pariah, Sula grows up to be a creator, an explorer of the margins. She is the community's scapegoat; she transgresses and embodies the dangerous freedom that some of Morrison's heroes and heroines experiment with. She eventually leaves the Bottom to go to college.

Both young girls are bound by a secret: they have accidentally killed a young boy, Chicken Little, while playing with him by the river. The hole in the water that swallowed him only reopens as a return of the repressed memory of that drowning. It is also echoed earlier on by a ritual: the two girls dig a hole in which they bury "useless" bits and pieces. The sexual overtones of this initiatory rite (acknowledgement and covering-up of castration) lead to the broader question of the place of femininity and masculinity in the culture, as well as to the historical destiny. Eva adopts several young boys of different ages, the Deweys. However, through her perception, they gradually appear the same to her and have the same arrested development. Indeed, they never grow up. A morbid echo of that stunted growth, a large number of the men, the Deweys among them, die buried in the collapse of a tunnel that they had built under white authority. *Push*'s Precious Jones fights her homophobia and that of Louis Farrakhan's followers when she is told that her teacher is a lesbian. The novel also features another child whose sexual preference is for women. The reader understands that the sexual abuse that Precious has undergone at the hands of her mother and her lover will leave her helpless in the construction of a positive sexual relation.

The coming-of-age episode is often the result of the writer's use of an omniscient narrator combined with internal focalization when the reader directly enters the adolescent psyche. The use of a first-person narrator is also a powerful medium that serves to expose the torments, the dilemmas. In the case of Baldwin's *Go Tell It on the Mountain*, the device of the "transparent mind" describes the awareness of the protagonist from within. The coming-of-age novel reframes the autobiographical tradition of the conversion narrative and the spiritual autobiography. John's tortured psyche is one where the father's words resound ironically against the reality of the father's violence, itself a reiteration of his own childhood violence. The absurdity and lack of understanding is caused by his feelings of guilt, the trip to the movie house, the hypocrisy and the irony of the Church, and John's consciousness of his sin. Desperately asking for his father's love, John faces rejection: the father loves the son who looks like him, Roy, and negates John, who acts as father substitute to the other children. His hatred of the whites leads the father to find refuge in the clear-cut religious precepts of salvation and damnation. The young man faces sin as the unmentionable act of masturbation; he feels that it has soiled him forever in a world where there is only good or evil. John's conversion at the end echoes in a tragic and ironic mode the communion of the saints and the sinners envisioned by Hughes.

Selina Boyce from Marshall's *Brown Girl, Brownstones* is a complex character, access to whom is given to the reader through the use of internal focalization and omniscient narration. Selina is caught between a romantic father, who dreams of going back to Barbados, where he owns some land (he eventually commits suicide), and a mother whose ambition is to buy a house and to have one of her daughters study medicine or law or make a good marriage. Whereas Selina fights to become independent – she has a lover, she learns ballet dancing and wins an award from the Association of Barbados immigrants – the confrontation of racism at the end of the novel is a trauma that makes her decide to go back to her father's island.

In the context of the autobiographical trace and of actual production of writing, the question of coming of age crystallizes the moment of the writer's vocation, the childhood sources of the transposition of his or her experience into writing. The man- or woman-child bears the burden or the elective status of being the privileged witness and performer of his/her race in the realm of creative writing. A certain reflexiveness in the writing process sends the reader back to his own relationship to race and sexuality, to questioning how much he/she is part of the racial oppression denounced in the pages.

The intensity of this metafictional dimension means that coming of age is no longer limited to narration. The display of the writing and the aesthetics are alluded to in the choice of protagonists who are artists. Selina meets a failed Village artist and is described by her friends as a poetess. She is also an accomplished dancer, the star of the performance that the ballet class gives at the end of the book. Al Young's hero in *Snakes* is a musician, John A. Williams's Ralph, a playwright, and his sister Iris, a singer whose career has taken her to Europe. The narrative of *Lucy* by Kincaid tells more about the writing process and the subject of writing than it does about the "experience" of a young West Indian au pair in the United States.[31]

The Color Purple epitomizes the process of writing as the quintessential life-giving act that enables coming of age: the writing of letters coincides with the heroine's progress. She invents and frees her own self through writing letters to God, to her sister, to the rest of the world, her letter writing coinciding ultimately with the publication of Walker's novel. Her sister Nettie's more conventional letters from Africa establish the distance between a "speakerly" text and its enactment of independence through creativity and a "writerly" text with its dependence on convention and formal education.[32] The rendition of the voice on paper, its foregrounding, meshes with Celie's love for another woman, the blues singer Shug Avery. Similarly, *Push* uses rap language – ebonics – to celebrate Precious's recovery through writing and the incest survivors' sessions. Precious's barely readable first lines written on the page with a translation into English show that her perception is mediated by the trauma of not being able to write and to speak what she experiences. Violence and language are entwined; they echo each other. Vulgarity, insults, physical fights, and hatred are the only recourse for the illiterate, obese, sex-abused child, treated like a domestic by her mother. She finds pleasure in writing and gradually gains self-confidence and independence. From hatred she moves to love, from the spiral of failure to hope for improvement. *Push* is a narrative of redemption. The final section of the book reproduces the texts written by the children in Miss Rain's class; they are all testimonies that coming of age can only happen through literacy and the power of the words.

The reader's edification about the devastation of poverty and alienation, the dark face of the American dream, takes place in the same way. Precious hates the "izms" that her teacher uses and writes "REALITY" in capital letters to fight "realism" and its academic conundrums. The distance between her text and the reality of the writing of young girls' lives can be appreciated by reading Rebecca Carroll's *Sugar in the Raw*, the recorded voices of young black girls in America.[33] Precious Jones contrasts with Ann Petry's Lutie Johnson, a murderer in self-defense. Lutie's last flashback is a memory of her white teacher wondering why they should bother to educate black people. Lutie ponders: "What possible good has it done to teach people like me how to write?"[34]

Coming of age is the necessary transposition of an impossible progress, the creation of a self for an African American subject against the threats of schizophrenia and annihilation. Language serves as the most potent weapon in such an endeavor against the violence of being forever stunted, impeded, erased.

NOTES

1. To deal with this notion would involve going back to Locke and to the genesis of the *Bildungsroman* as the genre that the Enlightenment favored in its acknowledgment that judgment was established as much through sensitivity as through understanding.
2. Dexter Fisher and Robert Stepto, eds., *Afro-American Literature: The Reconstruction of Instruction* (1979; New York: PMLA, 1990).

3. Langston Hughes, *Not Without Laughter* (1930; New York: Scribner, Simon and Schuster, 1969); James Baldwin, *Go Tell It on the Mountain* (New York: Grosset and Dunlap, 1953).

4. Toni Morrison, *The Bluest Eye* (New York: Washington Square Press, 1970); Alice Walker, *The Color Purple* (New York: Washington Square Press, 1982); Sapphire, *Push* (New York: Alfred A. Knopf, 1966). On Morrison's work, see Claudine Raynaud, *Toni Morrison: L'Esthétique de la survie* (Paris: Belin, 1996).

5. John Oliver Killens, *Youngblood* (1954; Athens: University of Georgia Press, 2000).

6. Zora Neale Hurston, *Their Eyes Were Watching God* (1937; Urbana: University of Illinois Press, 1978).

7. Gordon Parks, *The Learning Tree* (New York: Fawcett, 1963).

8. Al Young, *Snakes* (New York: Holt Rinehart and Winston, 1970); Toni Morrison, *Song of Solomon* (1977; New York: Signet Book, 1978); Richard Wright, *Native Son* (1940; London: Picador, 1995). See also his autobiography, *Black Boy* (1940; New York: Harper and Row, 1966).

9. Toni Morrison, *Sula* (New York: Bantam Books, 1973).

10. John A. Williams, *Sissie* (New York: Farrar Strauss and Cudahy, 1963).

11. Melvin Dixon, *Trouble the Water* (New York: Washington Square Press, 1989).

12. These novelistic accounts must be read against the polemics of the Moynihan Report on the black family, *The Negro Family: The Case for National Action* (1965; rpt. Westport: Greenwood Press, 1981).

13. On the *Bildungsroman*, see Mikhail M. Bakhtin, *Speech Genres and Other Late Essays*, ed. Caryl Emerson and Michael Holquist (Austin: University of Texas Press, 1986) pp. 10–59, and *The Dialogic Imagination: Fours Essays by M. M. Bakhtin*, ed. Michael Holquist (Austin: University of Texas Press, 1981); Florence Bancaud-Maënen, *Le Roman de formation au XVIIIème siècle en Europe* (Paris: Nathan, 1998). For a book-length study of the African American and West Indian *Bildungsroman*, see Geta LeSeur, *Ten is the Age of Darkness: The Black Bildungsroman* (Columbia and London: University of Missouri Press, 1995).

14. Franco Maretti, *The Way of the World: The Bildungsroman in European Culture* (London: Verso, 1987), p. 15.

15. Ntozake Shange, *Betsey Brown* (New York: Picador, 1985).

16. Select autobiographies are included as a counterpoint, since they exemplify the process of coming of age within a contractual relationship to the reader which is referential and not fictional. Alice Walker, *Meridian* (1976; London: The Women's Press, 1983); Anne Moody, *Coming of Age in Mississippi: An Autobiography* (New York: Dell Publishing, 1968).

17. Paule Marshall, *Brown Girl, Brownstones* (1959; New York: The Feminist Press, 1981).

18. Roland Barthes, *La Chambre claire: Note sur la photographie* (Paris: Seuil, Gallimard Cahiers du Cinéma, 1980), p. 54.

19. Ann Petry, *The Street* (1946; Boston: Beacon Press, 1985).

20. Ralph Ellison, *Invisible Man* (1952; London and New York: Penguin Books, 1965).

21. Gwendolyn Brooks, *Maud Martha* (New York: Harper, 1953).

22. Toni Morrison, *Beloved* (London: Picador, 1987).

23. Michelle Cliff, *Abeng* (Trumansburg, NY: The Crossing Press, 1984); Jamaica Kincaid, *Annie John* (New York: Farrar, Strauss, Giroux, 1985).
24. Toni Morrison, *Jazz* (London: Picador, 1992).
25. John Edgar Wideman, *Fatheralong: A Meditation on Fathers and Sons, Race and Society* (New York: Pantheon, 1994).
26. Tina McElroy Ansa, *Baby of the Family* (New York: Harcourt Brace, 1989).
27. Maya Angelou, *I Know Why the Caged Bird Sings* (New York: Bantam Books, 1970).
28. Dori Sanders, *Clover* (New York: Fawcett Columbine, 1990).
29. Marita Golden, *A Woman's Place* (1986; New York: Ballantine Books, 1988).
30. Toni Morrison, *Paradise* (London: Chatto and Windus, 1998).
31. Jamaica Kinkaid, *Lucy* (London: Picador, 1990).
32. For a theory of African American literature, see Henry Louis Gates Jr., *Figures in Black: Words, Signs and the "Racial" Self* (New York: Oxford University Press, 1987) and *The Signifying Monkey: A Theory of Afro-American Criticism* (New York: Oxford University Press, 1988).
33. Rebecca Carroll, *Sugar in the Raw: Voices of Young Black Girls in America* (New York: Three Rivers Press, 1997).
34. Petry, *The Street*, p. 436.

7

STEVEN C. TRACY

The blues novel

For many commentators, some of the most distinctively African American elements that readers encounter in African American novels are reflections of the blues tradition. However, the phrase "blues novel" might seem to some to be so incongruous as to approach the level of oxymoron. After all, the two terms comprise widely different genres stylistically. The novel as we know it today, though it has roots in the XIIth Dynasty Middle Kingdom Egyptian prose fiction and appeared in embryonic form in Boccaccio's *Decameron* and *The Arabian Entertainments*, emerged most forcefully in the English literary tradition in the eighteenth century with the work of Samuel Richardson, Henry Fielding, and Laurence Sterne. Novels are traditionally extended written prose narratives with some amount of plot and character development, though the genre has proven very pliable over the years.

The blues as a musical genre, though it has its roots in African modalities that are centuries old, first emerged in America during the period following Reconstruction in the late nineteenth century. The term was applied to the songs of itinerant and frequently illiterate singers whose work was noted and transcribed by folklorists and commentators from outside the tradition in which they were generated until the first blues were recorded in 1920. The blues are traditionally pithy oral lyric works using a variety of loosely fixed structures into which are poured the subject matter of an individual experience that reflects communal interests. The notion that a lengthy, written, narrative work in the European tradition is based upon a brief oral lyric one from the African American tradition thus raises a number of aesthetic, social, and political issues regarding the mixing of these genres that need addressing.

First, we must establish the characteristics of the blues tradition, and then determine in what ways the strategies, styles, and purposes of the blues may be reflected in a written narrative. Since the term "blues" refers to an emotion, a technique, a musical form, and a song lyric, its influence can be manifested in a variety of ways, from the very concrete to the very impressionistic. Though as an emotion "blues" is most frequently associated with sadness, a sadness crucially related to African American experiences in slavery and the Jim Crow era, there are in fact many celebratory, "happy" blues songs that suggest that the blues are not just laments or complaints in their surface content. As such, the blues performance may well not be an expression of sadness but a creative celebration of not only the overcoming of hardship but of the nature of human existence in an imperfect world. African scholar Janheinz Jahn identifies the central theme of the blues as "an individual's right to life and to an intact 'perfect' life," and blues lyrics as reflecting "the attitude caused by the loss of life-force or leading to the gaining of life-force."[1] The blues, then, is an assertion of autonomy and a consolidation of power in the context of a world that wishes to diminish or eliminate that power. When the blues singer sings, "When you see me laughin, I'm laughin to keep from cryin," or "The sun gonna shine in my back door some day," the blues philosophy of endurance in the face of impossible odds, hope in the face of adversity, receives its most direct and forceful expression.

The technique of the blues is the way that the instruments, style, and structure of the music are manipulated to produce and express such ideas. African influences abound: percussion and percussively played instruments; syncopation; call-and-response patterns; growling, buzzing, and straining inflections; blue notes; improvisational predilections; community orientation and function. Of course, these influences are planted squarely into the American environment to help produce art that is not only African, not only American, but African American. The musical form of the blues roughly follows most frequently a 12-bar pattern with a chord progression of I-IV-V. Because the blues is an oral genre practiced in its earliest days for the most part by illiterate or semi-literate, informally trained musicians, performers frequently did not adhere to strict time boundaries but followed their own technique, intellect, or emotions in creating their blues patterns. Therefore, songs frequently tended toward the 12-bar length rather than rigidly following it. The same idea applies to other blues musical stanza patterns such as 8-bar, 16-bar, and 32-bar patterns. Lyric patterns achieve a looseness or freedom in the same way. For example, in a 12-bar blues pattern a singer may follow what has been termed the AAB pattern: one thought sung in roughly four bars, then repeated, not necessarily with identical wording, in four more bars, followed by a thought that somehow wraps up the sentiment in the final four bars, usually with end rhyme. Changes in wording in the repeat lines can serve to add variety, emphasize particular ideas or emotions, or extend the original meaning in some other way. Of course, there are a variety of other lyric patterns, even just for 12-bar blues. Other stanzas of varying musical lengths have similar possibilities for lyric variation. The point here is that the blues provide a basic structure free enough to accommodate individual temperament, abilities, and creativity. Far from being a limited genre, it provides a structured but expansive place for the individual to relate to and express the community, and for artists to touch home base but still express themselves individually.

How such elements as discussed briefly above may find expression in a novel must be considered in as broad a fashion as possible, since creative artists by their very natures employ the resources for their works in a great variety of unique and creative ways. Most immediately, a novel may itself be called a blues, or use some part of a blues lyric in its title, as in Clarence Major's *Dirty Bird Blues* (1996), John A. Williams's *Clifford's Blues* (1999), or James Baldwin's *Tell Me How Long the Train's Been Gone* (1968). In this case, the author provides a clear clue that the reader should be considering the way that characteristics of the blues might be utilized in the novel. The novel may refer to the color blue or use it as an image pattern to evoke some kind of emotion or tradition. In *Their Eyes Were Watching God* (1937), for example, Tea Cake expresses five times the desire to dress Janie in blue. A novelist may make use of language associated with the blues in the language of the narrator or characters, as Zora Neale Hurston did in *Their Eyes Were Watching God*. A novel such as Walter Mosley's *RL's Dream* (1995) might attempt to define or portray the blues and its philosophy through story and technique, or through that definition of the blues ethos attempt to portray its various implications – aesthetic, emotional, psychic, spiritual, communal, and political.

The portrayal of the social and historical context that led up to the birth of the blues as a major expressive African American form that was part of and necessary to its times reflects the spirit of the blues as well. Other novelists might use blues singers as characters or utilize selections from songs or performances, including musical notations, lyrics, or descriptions of performances and audience reactions, as in Alice Walker's *The Color Purple* (1982). Such references to performances might help to highlight the relationship of the performer to the community, or portray social attitudes of one class toward another based on their response to the music. Real blues performers might be named in the text, as either real characters or touchstones or symbols of some idea or spirit, as Langston Hughes uses W. C. Handy in *Not Without Laughter* (1930). Jane Phillips's *Mojo Hand* offers a barely disguised portrait of Lightnin' Hopkins, and Mosley's *RL's Dream* places bluesman Robert Johnson at the spiritual center of the novel.

The traditional subject matter of the blues, which deals most commonly with personal relationships between men and women (though there are blues about or dealing with homosexuality), or the form of the blues lyric, with its call-and-response structure, can also find expression in the novel. Loneliness, frustration, isolation, sexual desire, and such common emotions portrayed in the blues might also find their way into novels as a result of the influence of the blues. In fact, the novelist might employ any number of characteristics associated with the blues in literal or symbolic ways: call-and-response patterns; off-beat phrasing or unexpected accentual patterns that suggest syncopation; techniques of melisma and glissando reflected in the way an author "worries" or handles variously an issue or emotion in the text; the blues singer's "voice masking" techniques that create a persona with a different or alternate voice from the everyday speaking voice; progression by the type of associational thought patterns sometimes found in folk blues.[2]

There are numerous ways in which blues might be utilized in a novel beyond even this brief listing, indicating that a thoroughgoing knowledge of the possibilities of the blues genre and an open-minded consideration of the possibilities for influence is necessary. In all circumstances, the reader must measure the elements the novel portrays against the use of such elements in the blues tradition itself to determine how the novelist accepts, modifies, or alters the occurrence of those elements from the blues tradition in the novel, and why they are employed as they are.

Of course, as always, there are interpretive dangers in making impressionistic connections. Indeed, there are limitations to the discussion provided above. After all, a number of the elements named above may be found in places other than the blues. Such phrases as "easy rider" or "sun gonna shine in my back door some day," though frequently encountered in blues songs, in fact likely originated in communal speech and then found their way into blues songs. Since the philosophy of hope and perseverance in response to overwhelming conditions that usually produce despair is found in places other than the blues, the presence of that philosophy is not necessarily an instance of blues influence. Further, though we encounter call-and-response patterns in blues music, lyrics, and subject matter, antiphony is present in other African American and non-African American music as well. The same could be said of other elements such as percussive techniques, syncopation, and the like. James Weldon Johnson makes prominent use of ragtime in *Autobiography of an Ex-Coloured Man* (1912). Its syncopation and improvisation are brought to bear on his protagonist's attempts to escape his African American hardships, as he plays his practical joke on society while hiding behind the mask of their illusions. When he thinks of embracing his African American-ness, it is through what he believes he can do with ragtime to convince whites of its value, and through it the value of African Americans generally. Thematically, surely loneliness and isolation, while they are encountered in the blues, are subjects dealt with widely.

The question becomes, how can one determine whether novelists are deliberately evoking the blues tradition rather than simply making use of elements that might be found in other sources? And might it be more appropriate to say that novelists are invoking a vernacular music tradition, since African American vernacular musics can share similar subject matter, techniques, and functions? A number of those elements enumerated above, such as syncopation and call-and-response, are found in spirituals, jazz, and gospel music, as well. How many of those elements need to be present, and how crucial must they be to the meaning of the text, before we can call a work a "blues novel"? It is impossible to say definitively. Critics have pointed to the notion of a "blues aesthetic" that informs African American art, as Richard J. Powell explores in a discussion of Aaron Douglas:

> What Douglas sought to tap was a reality that was often raw, unpolished, and marginalized. A reality that was variegated and multifaceted in character. A reality that could be both spiritual and material. A reality that, if we had to come up with a metaphor for all of the above, would be embodied in cultural expression like "the blues." Surely, in an effort to define African American art and/or culture, scholars should acknowledge this thematic and expressive vein within the production of selected twentieth-century works which, by virtue of their respective artists, have a predetermined, *conscious*, basis in a "mystically objective" African-American reality such as in "the blues."[3]

Raw, unpolished, marginalized, variegated, multifaceted, spiritual, and material: indeed the blues can be all of these things (and it can be smooth and polished as well, as evidenced in the work of Lonnie Johnson, Charles Brown, and others). And yet one can also find these elements elsewhere in African American expressive culture. The point here is not to deny the blues as an important force that can embody these ideas. Certainly it can. But we should not automatically think "blues" or "blues music" when these kinds of elements are apparent, when they can occur elsewhere in African American culture, especially in segments of the community that might not embrace the blues as a proper art form (as is sometimes the case in the Christian community that prefers spirituals, jubilees, and gospel music). We must dig out the specific references to the blues as a genre in order to make a firm and reasonable assertion of its presence and influence. Ultimately, to call a work a "blues novel," the blues should likely be present concretely and substantively in its social, historical, political, musical, and/or aesthetic context, its presence necessary to the central meaning of the work. But readers should take care not to rule out other African American music as a source of these elements, and, in fact, be prepared to see how creative artists may be blurring the "boundaries" among the various genres to make a social, political, and aesthetic point.

One other point we must consider is whether there is a differentiation between a blues novel and a jazz novel. There can be an overlap between the two. This is partly because the blues is considered by many commentators to be the soul of jazz, one of its important wellsprings. Early jazz soloists, for example, would play bluesy solos on the chord changes of popular songs as well as in the traditional blues music patterns. Clearly, many of jazz's most important performers have been talented blues players – Louis Armstrong, Count Basie, Lester Young, Charlie Parker, Miles Davis, John Coltrane – and many have rooted their originality and innovations in the blues tradition. Therefore, when writers utilize jazz in their works, they are often by extension referencing the blues tradition as well. However, frequently the jazz tradition is, or jazz performers are, employed to portray or champion the spirit of improvisation, which is by extension a reflection of the quest for or achievement of spontaneity, immediacy, and ultimately, freedom. That intellectual, spiritual, political, and cultural freedom, of course, is firmly planted in the African and African American communal roots that produced African American culture, including spirituals and the blues. But those two genres frequently signify a more "down home" – earthy, direct, lower-class, rural-oriented – connection to African American culture, whereas jazz, in its improvisatory flights, often becomes a symbol for breaking the mental and physical bonds of the slave mentality. This is not to say that the blues cannot be vocally and instrumentally improvisational, but that jazz players tend to emphasize melodic or harmonic improvisation to a broader, more extensive degree. As such, "blues" frequently stands for "down home" tradition, the wisdom of the ancestors made manifest in the contemporary world, still operational and functional. Jazz launches from that dock, still connected by a tether, but with a more intellectually probing journey in mind. This "down home" connection of the blues makes it an obvious and valuable resource for African American novelists seeking to appropriate and personalize the novelistic tradition for themselves and African Americans, without recourse to the traditions of white Christian religious denominations that might be evoked by the spirituals.

Shortly after the first recordings of African American blues artists inaugurated by the release of Mamie Smith's first recordings with jazz accompaniment, authors began to employ blues and jazz to represent, on the one hand, the primitivism and exoticism of African Americans or the lower-class segment of the African American community; and on the other hand, the strength, individuality, and integrity of the folk. Such primitivism and exoticism are represented in part by blues and jazz in Carl Van Vechten's *Nigger Heaven* (1926), with blues lyrics later replaced by some blues penned by Langston Hughes when copyright infringements ensued. Van Vechten also included snatches from spirituals, folk songs, pop songs, and blues, like "My Man Rocks Me" and "World in a Jug," in his panoramic portrait of Harlem. Claude McKay's *Home to Harlem* (1928), with its references to lesbian "bulldiker" blues and "melancholy-comic" blues in a Harlem basement, and his use of such songs as Papa Charlie Jackson's "Shake That Thing" in *Banjo* (1929), as well as Wallace Thurman's evocative description of blues music and dancing in a Harlem night club in *The Blacker the Berry*... (1929), demonstrate this primitivist bent with regard to using blues and jazz to portray African American "low life," as well.

In Nella Larsen's *Quicksand* (1928), the jazz and blues of the Harlem nightclub evoke feelings of the primitive in the protagonist, Helga Crane. Crane is unable to confront the frank sensuality in her life, as is clear from her near-manic inability to acknowledge and deal with the power she could wield over men through her sexuality, especially her fear of facing her feelings for college president Robert Anderson, though her thoughts about him are sexually charged. Helga rushes from the music of the Harlem club fearing that she had not only heard but actually enjoyed the primitive interlude, clearly indicating how society has limited her ability to accept and rejoice in her sexuality. Crane is able to accept that sexuality when it is sublimated, as evidenced in another sexually charged episode. She meets Reverend Green in a storefront church, where religiously ecstatic, writhing women mingle touch, sweat, and passion with God and ceremony before being brought to an exhausted climax. Rebuffed by the cowardly and hypocritical Anderson, Crane runs into the arms of Green, her physicality legitimized in her mind by religion and the institution of marriage, even as it imprisons her in a narrow social role for which she is ill suited. In the end, social conventions render her biologically trapped in a station so different from the place where she began that the ending is nearly unbelievable. However, her status as a middle-class African American woman trained to deny or ignore the joys of sexuality, symbolized in part by the blues and jazz of the novel, make her rapid, seemingly irrational descent plausible. While the novel is not dominated by references to blues and jazz and frequently finds itself in middle- to upper-class surroundings, this central use of the music, as well as Crane's attempts to remain hopeful in the wake of nearly overwhelmingly despairing conditions, especially at the end, suggests the propriety of the label of blues novel in the tradition of the lyrics of women blues singers struggling to achieve social and sexual autonomy.

By the time Langston Hughes's novel *Not Without Laughter* was published in 1930, Hughes had been writing poems under the influence of blues and jazz of "the low down folks"[4] for a decade, and had made them central to the aesthetic he described in his 1926 manifesto "The Negro Artist and the Racial Mountain." Thus, it was no surprise that his first novel was imbued with the spirit of the blues in a variety of ways. For example, Hughes's title may well have specific reference to the blues lyric "laughin to keep from cryin," which Hughes used later as the title of his 1952 short story collection. Hughes's definition of the blues in a review of W. C. Handy's *Blues: An Anthology* as "hopeless weariness mixed with an absurdly incongruous laughter"[5] further associates Hughes's title with the blues tradition. Additionally, a number of characters in Hughes's novel utilize phraseology associated with the blues. So does the narrator, who employs the traditional blues lyric "mailman passed and didn't leave no news" (162), which associates the narrator very closely with the people he is describing in the text and thus closes the gap between artist and community. The speaker comments on and defines the blues explicitly in a variety of places and also characterizes various people in the novel through their responses to blues music. There are, in addition, references to blues songs such as "Jelly Roll," "Careless Love," "Circle Round the Sun," "Easy Rider," and "St. Louis Blues"; blues singers who are main characters in the text: Sandy's father, Jimboy, and Aunt Harriett; the historical blues figure W. C. Handy; and the loneliness of Sandy and Annjee, Sandy's isolation, the frustration of Annjee, Harriett, Sandy, and Hager, and frequent expressions of sexual desire by Annjee, Jimboy, and Sandy that all serve to connect the text to the blues tradition.

Still, since Hughes is attempting to unite various elements of the community in his text, he uses songs and subject matter from both the sacred and secular African American music traditions in tandem to demonstrate how the community is or should not be fractured by its folk heritage. In fact, the sacred and secular are portrayed as being closer to each other than the characters or readers might think. For example, though the blues are associated with sexuality and sin in a number of places in the novel, Hughes portrays Harriett's and Jimboy's bawdy singing and dancing in the yard as being innocent fun, unsullied by the kind of thinking that would make it dirty rather than the celebration of life. Sandy, in fact, finds himself the benefactor of two traditions represented by Hager, on one hand, and Aunt Harriett, on the other. Like the proverbial motherless child of the spirituals, Sandy needs the guidance of a parental figure that is clearly not provided by his own mother and father. He receives it in the form of a call-and-response relation to the two women most important to his life and success. He finds it on the sacred hand from Hager, whose biblical name refers to the long-suffering servant who provides Abraham with a male heir, and is then turned out into the wilderness to bear Ishmael, a wild and embattled outcast who will eventually become the patriarch of a great nation. It is not difficult to see in the protective and committed Hager a history of embattled African American females in slavery, or in the prophecy for Ishmael a prediction of greatness for Sandy as he emerges into adulthood by the end of the text. On the secular hand, he finds nurturance from Aunt Harriett, who has lived as a prostitute, but by the end of the novel, is using her knowledge of the blues traditions and experience in the world of the "bottoms" (a common blues sexual euphemism) to make enough from blues singing to offer Sandy the money to stay in school and raise his social status. Thus, Hughes portrays the coordination of the sacred and secular, oral and written traditions in offering Sandy improved social status in his life. Sandy, for his part, embraces both Hager and Harriett and what they have to offer as valuable, life-affirming figures. Indeed, Hager never loses her love for Harriett, nor Harriett, her love for Hager; nor Sandy his love for both. Hughes brings the two women and traditions together in two important ways. Through his employment of W. C. Handy, with whom Hughes collaborated on the blues song "Golden Brown Blues," as a reference in the text, Hughes conjures the Handy–Tim Brymn composition "Aunt Hagar's Children's Blues," a song which itself mingles sacred and secular traditions in its lyrics. Near the end of the novel, Sandy's memories deliberately juxtapose his grandmother's "whirling" at revival with Harriett's "eagle rocking" in the back yard. By novel's end, Sandy has received sustenance from Hager and Harriett in the form of the important values of support, love, and forgiveness, and has learned to embrace whatever is good in the sacred and secular traditions as a way of making the world more unified and loving.

Zora Neale Hurston's *Their Eyes Were Watching God* (1937) is another quintessential African American blues novel, rooted not only in the blues but in the female blues tradition, one that considers the ways in which women are socialized to accept certain physical and emotional limitations in their lives.[6] A primary emotion portrayed in the text is a "cosmic loneliness" (20) and "infinity of conscious pain" (23) that stems from the types of burdens women such as the sexually abused grandmother and mother of Janie endure. The blues is often described as originating in the lowlands, the bottoms, the muck, down home. Therefore, to embrace the blues is to embrace the muck as the wellspring of honesty, directness, and creativity and to cherish one's origins. This is something that Janie learns to do despite the attempts of her grandmother and her first two husbands to acclimatize her to a somewhat more rarefied life. From her initial embarrassment regarding living in the white folks' yard, she "ascends" through Logan's acres and Joe's wealth to the real pinnacle of her happiness on the muck with Tea Cake, her blues-singing husband, who has played his music at juke joints and fish fries as well as on the front porch. Along the way, she avoids the pitfalls of the middle-class Mrs. Turner, who tries to "class off" by disdaining the darker members of the community as riffraff. Significantly, the establishment she and her husband ran, which is far from a juke joint, is happily trashed by Tea Cake and his friends, who resent her condescension and interference in Tea Cake and Janie's relationship.

The language of the blues is frequently frank, creative, signifying, and poetic, as is the language of the narrator and a number of characters, especially Janie and Tea Cake. Various characters, Janie included, express themselves in language common to the blues tradition: "cool drink of water" recalls the blues ballad "John Henry," while Janie's reference to the difference between her internal and external speech and actions recalls the "when you see me laughin I'm laughin to keep from cryin" motif. References to having the "world in a jug" and being someone's "sidetrack until the mainline comes along" – a common blues double entendre – further recall the language of the blues tradition. In fact, Hurston's novel elevates and celebrates sexuality with an openness and earthiness common to the blues tradition. References to bumble bees and stingers "as long as my right arm" in recordings such as Memphis Minnie's "Bumble Bee" and Margaret Johnson's "Stinging Bee Blues" portray the joys of sex somewhat more directly than Janie's naïve sexual awakening.

A high premium is placed on individuality and originality, with a requisite connection to tradition, in the blues. This is frequently associated with finding a style that presents a distinctive voice that emerges from a community of voices, expressing the concerns and interests of some segment of the community. Hurston's novel is in part about voice, the emergence of a woman's voice, about a woman discovering who she is and expressing herself freely and openly in a language that draws on the idioms and traditions of the community. The effect of Janie's experiences and achievement of such independence on her friend is to brace her, embolden her, make her feel taller and more important, and to increase their intimacy. There is clear double meaning involved when Janie remarks that her tongue is in her friend's mouth. Undoubtedly the tradition of the sassy and independent female blues singer, who exposed frank sexual feelings and issues of domestic abuse (like the much-debated beating that Janie allows Tea Cake to give her) in a public forum, is behind the voice and actions of Janie.

It might even be said that the structure of the novel is similar to the common AAB stanza of the blues: Janie makes the mistake, albeit forced, of marrying Logan, repeats her mistake by running off with Joe, but resolves her dilemma by hooking up with Tea Cake, who accepts the blues and the low-down folks and helps liberate Janie into an appreciation of her own mind and body. In the novel, it is this blues singer who encourages or teaches Janie to be independent (playing checkers, driving, and fishing – the latter two activities common sexual metaphors in the blues) connected to her inner feelings; assertive emotionally and physically; and articulate, to speak the maiden language of renewal, directness, and richness. The narrator's reflection on the experience, something that Ellison describes as fingering the jagged grain of experience, generates a cautionary tale that the audience can identify with and use for relief, advice, and strength. This first-person reflective lament and celebration, presenting communal concerns through personal expression, is blues-inflected throughout.

Finally, the blues philosophy of endurance and hope is reflected in the many references to the horizon in the novel, particularly in looking for transcendence by transforming hardships into personal and artistic triumph. The novel is not only Janie's triumph, but Hurston's as well: her most enduring literary success. This is largely due to her masterful employment of a variety of blues devices in language, structure, imagery, voice, and philosophy to portray the triumph of a woman who learns from the African American vernacular tradition to love and elevate herself to the exalted position she deserves, on the muck where the Lords of Sounds rule. While this is clearly not the exalted place where Nanny envisioned her preaching a great sermon, it is a place where she can demonstrate, as Tea Cake says, that she has the keys to the kingdom. The connection between the sacred and secular traditions, though not quite as intricate and prominent as in Hughes's *Not Without Laughter*, are evident in Hurston's novel as well.

In "Richard Wright's Blues" Ralph Ellison depicted Wright's novel *Black Boy* (1945) as the "flowering of the humble blues lyric" in its portrayal of the young boy's experience, the reflection on the painful realities, and lack of solutions to those problems.[7] Wright was, of course, the dominant African American novelist of the 1940s, a literary naturalist whose influence permeated the African American literary scene. The sense of pessimistic determinism, of being trapped and isolated, that is frequently a characteristic of the naturalistic novel fits well with one of the predominant moods of the blues. William Attaway's *Blood on the Forge* (1951)[8] combines literary naturalism with the blues to present an early African American migration novel that deals with the loss of connection to rural folk roots in the move to an industrial center. His depiction of the decay and corruption of the city looks back to Dunbar's *Sport of the Gods* in its pessimism. Attaway makes a variety of references to the blues, especially in relation to guitar player Melody, in the Kentucky portion of his novel, but once the Moss men reach

Pennsylvania, though their troubles do not disappear, the references to blues all but disappear as they are separated from their roots. As one character, the immigrant Zanski, says, "Plant grow if it get ground like place it came from" (112). Not that they had any choice about leaving. Big Mat's beating of the overseer-like riding boss who has disrespected his dead mother precipitates their departure from an overwhelmingly racist South, clearly no longer viable, for the hope and promise connected with the steel mills of Pennsylvania. However, the predominant images are those of entrapment – in cages, boxcars, and in the dark, in emptiness, by calmness, and on garbage piles. Chapter 2, in fact, can be read as presenting another Middle Passage, the journey to a horrific land and experience where the men have little chance of surviving intact. The North is merely a different setting for the continuing racism. Interestingly, there are a variety of blues songs, such as Sonny Boy Williamson's "Down South Blues," that deal with the promise but ultimate disappointment of the migration North. The restless search for "better times," a euphemism for the escape from racism, is central to the blues. Attaway's novel explores the fearful and hopeful impulse to escape such a life, and shatters the notion that such escape is possible.

As in the Wright and Attaway novels, Ellison's own *Invisible Man* (1952) combines the blues tradition with elements of naturalism, represented by the extreme conditions of control in the "battle royal," as well as existentialism. Like the blues lyric, the novel is a first-person reflective lament-turned-celebration through the creative force of the speaker. Ellison generates an individual voice and style thoroughly rooted in the African American vernacular tradition, offering communal concerns through the voice of an individual member of the community. The heroes of the novel are all connected in some way to the blues. Louis Armstrong, one of the greatest of blues players, is the matrix through which most of Ellison's metaphors in the introduction flow. The concept of invisibility; the creation of poetry; the fluid concept of time related to improvisation, boxing, and violation of chronology in the narrative as it flashes back in Chapter 1; the recognition and management of dichotomies, polarities, and uncertainties – all these are explored in the context of Armstrong's artistry. Armstrong, the preacher, and the boxer are all creators, fighters, and proselytizers as they upset the status quo and push boundaries, syncopators who make observers and listeners aware of the offbeat, the space between the beat, and its importance to overcoming the metronomic regularity and oppressiveness of racist and middle-class existence, as Langston Hughes described it years earlier in "The Negro Artist and the Racial Mountain." Ellison's Armstrong is the musician as unconscious trickster figure whose music employs encoded messages and techniques to communicate social, political, and aesthetic messages to the astute listener.

Significantly, Ellison refers to Armstrong's famous version of the Andy Razaf composition "What Did I Do To Be So Black and Blue?" as he begins to describe Armstrong's prodigious talent. Although the song is not a traditional blues in music or lyric structure, it does convey a sense of the hardships faced by African Americans. The clever wordplay of the title, which refers in one sense to the speaker's skin color (black) and sadness (blue) and in another to the battering and bruising he has endured as an African American (black and blue), is a fitting foreshadowing of the narrator's experiences as portrayed in the novel. Armstrong's creative response to the experiences, to make poetry out of his invisibility, is a fitting strategy for transcending such experiences as well, and a positive example for the narrator/protagonist.

Trueblood, the sharecropper who has had children by his wife and his daughter, is somewhat more problematically heroic. It is difficult to see a man who has committed incest in a positive light, especially when he uses the story of his act for material gain. The fact that, after singing the blues, he accepts his responsibility and faces up to his shortcomings suggests that the blues offers a dose of reality that remind him of his fallibility on the one hand, and his need to persevere and "take care of business" on the other. It is likely best to see Trueblood not as a symbol, as the white townspeople and the black community do – someone to be tittered over, affirming racist stereotype, or shunted aside as an embarrassment to the race – but as an individual who uses the blues either to attempt to atone for his sins or to help create a persona that can help him benefit from his transgressions in a society where the opportunities for benefiting, for an African American, are few.

In Peter Wheatstraw, the blueprint man who sings the blues, Ellison offers a man full of "shit, grit, and mother wit," who is capable of seeing through the illusions and negotiating the deceit present in the urban environment through improvisation – adapting to the changes in the plans. The name itself stems from folk roots related to magic and folk medicine. However, though the name has been connected with a figure in African American folklore, in researcher Leroy Pierson's interview, Ellison acknowledged both performing in the bars of St. Louis with a blues recording artist named William Bunch, whose nom du disque was Peetie Wheatstraw, and adapting his character for use as the blueprint man in the novel. Significantly, this blues singer demonstrates for the protagonist the value of the folk tradition in passing on the wisdom of the elders (which the protagonist had missed from his grandfather), the advantages of wariness and improvisation, and the uses of creativity to combat the narrow or invisible identities allotted to the African American in urban America. Wheatstraw, after all, creates himself, chooses a persona that will help him negotiate his way through the world, one that embraces the African American folk tradition. Bunch was also known as the Devil's Son-In-Law and the High Sheriff From Hell (the character actually uses the former in his speech in the novel), positioning himself as an outlaw and authority figure in opposition to the illusory "good" world ruled by white Americans. His creativity extends to his use of language, which is full of syncopated effects as he names himself, and marked by the techniques akin to the melisma and glissando common to the African American vernacular music tradition in Ellison's employment of typography and spelling in Wheatstraw's sung passages. Even the lyric that Wheatstraw sings, a traditional blues that was recorded by Ellison's friend Jimmy Rushing, presents the folk tradition dealing with one of the protagonist's main faults: the inability to look beneath the surface and escape superficiality. While the lyric focuses on what the woman can do, make love excellently, the protagonist still focuses on the question of how somebody could love someone who looked the way she was described in the song. When the protagonist approaches the yam man slightly later, he is still fixed on how the yams look, and he receives yet another warning about looks being deceiving. Wheatstraw differs from Trueblood in his refusal to "degrade himself for money or goods" or "identify himself in such negative terms as 'nobody but myself.'"9 He is strength, originality, energy, possibility, and, as the veteran at the Golden Day says, people need to understand the possibilities that exist in the world.

Ellison employs Wheatstraw to connect the blues to existentialist philosophy as it was propounded by Jean-Paul Sartre. In the face of radical determinism, Wheatstraw, the "down home" man of flesh and bone, makes his choices and takes responsibility for his actions. He noughts nought by creating an essence for himself that defies racial stereotypes and thus frees him in some ways from the established structures of his world. In this sense, the character Wheatstraw, and Ellison as novelist, are recreating the world by revisioning it. By the end, the protagonist realizes that other people, especially the whites he encounters, are constantly reordering the world, changing the plan, as Wheatstraw puts it. What the protagonist needs to do is participate in the process of choice, recreating himself and noughting the nought of invisibility. And once the mind has been reoriented, not just for the individual but for the masses of people who populate or read the novel, the flesh and blood man can possibly emerge from his hibernation into full and free participation in the world, a point not quite yet reached by novel's end.

There are other elements of the blues present in Ellison's novel, including references to various blues songs. Mary, another positive figure in the text, sings Bessie Smith's "Back Water Blues." Chapter 23 contains a snippet of the blues song "Jelly, Jelly," and in the same chapter a woman is described as playing boogie woogie in church. Ellison may even be subtly referring to a Peetie Wheatstraw song, "First Shall Be Last and the Last Shall Be First," in addition to its biblical source, just before the blueprint man enters the novel. More crucially, we encounter call-and-response effects in the echoes of his grandfather's voice and advice and references to running, vision, and illusion. Armstrong, Wheatstraw, and Rinehart the Bliss Proteus all represent the importance of improvisation. The "down home" connection to roots and earthiness – to community and heritage – which the protagonist unfortunately flees for most of the novel, enters through Armstrong, Jack the Bear, the homeless couple, Mary, Poor Robin (another folk song), Wheatstraw, and the yam man. Finally, the outlook and philosophy of the protagonist is blues-like. The sardonic, laughing trickster who is playing a practical joke on the electric company, and possibly his readers, too (connecting the novel to James Weldon Johnson's *Autobiography of an Ex-Coloured Man*) is in one sense laughing to keep from crying since he has not quite figured out his strategy for literal emergence from his hole. In another sense, he is sending readers his novel because he believes that, although things have been bad, through reconnection to the social, political, and aesthetic wisdom of the elders as reflected in the vernacular tradition, the sun is gonna shine in his back door some day.

Albert Murray, a compatriot of Ellison's who has written extensively about blues and jazz, including assisting Count Basie with his autobiography and relating blues and jazz crucially to African American and American culture, similarly emphasizes the viability of blues and jazz as serious and meaningful art. Underscoring the importance of improvisation as a tool to overcoming adversity, Murray posits in *The Hero and the Blues* (1973) an archetypal blues hero who ventures out to conquer the dragons that endanger human existence with improvisation and experimentation as his weapons. Rooted in age-old community wisdom and traditions, the hero presents not only a victory over adversity, but a path for others to follow in facing that adversity, and, importantly, a self-generated set of standards with which to confront oneself and the world. Murray's novelistic trilogy of *Train Whistle Guitar* (1974), *The Spyglass Tree* (1991), and *The Seven League Boots* (1995) follows Scooter of Gasoline Point, Alabama, whose own success depends on his ability to replicate in his own life the relationship of soloist to group, individual to community, that is found in the successful jazz band, and to confront the tragedy of life with a perseverance, creativity, and dignity akin to that expressed in the blues. The world Murray envisions, then, is imbued with the spirit, passion, and wisdom of the music and the musicians who create it.

There are, of course, other writers post-*Invisible Man* who have continued to write in the tradition of the "Blues School of literature" that Ellison announced his intention to create. In Frank London Brown's *Trumbull Park* (1959), we hear the blues of Muddy Waters and Big Joe Williams against the realistic and naturalistic backdrop of the urban, working-class landscape of Chicago, one of the centers of African American blues and jazz. Brown, a Kansas City native who moved with his family to the South Side of Chicago when he was twelve, was intimately familiar with the jazz and blues of the city, and he published an interview with Thelonius Monk in *Down Beat* in 1958, the year before *Trumbull Park* was published. His novel uses the joys, sorrows, and resolve of the blues to reflect the frequently violent and psychologically harrowing experiences of an African American airplane factory employee and his family as they attempt to relocate to an exclusively white public housing project. Significantly, Brown also joins the blues of "Every Day I Have the Blues" with the spiritual "I Shall Not Be Moved" as a way of demonstrating the relationship between sacred and secular traditions and the need to draw on the entire strength of the community and its traditions to succeed. As Maryemma Graham points out, the nature of the first-person narration "allows for ranges in tone and action necessary to achieve a certain musical effect" (291),[10] working hand in hand with the references to African American vernacular music to achieve a cohesive vision of the events in Buggy Martin's life.

Many other more contemporary novels employ the blues tradition in crucial ways. Alice Walker's *The Color Purple*, for example, returns to the earliest instance of the English novelistic tradition, the epistolary novel, and then reminds us of the prominence of the motif of sending or receiving letters in the blues tradition demonstrated by such blues recordings as "Death Letter Blues" by Ida Cox and "Sad Letter Blues" by Big Bill Broonzy. In another explicit connection to the female blues tradition, Walker explores the oppression and exploitation of Celie, who is finally liberated socially, politically, and sexually at the initiation and under the tutelage of independent, powerful blues singer Shug Avery, who teaches Celie about the sweetness of her own body and the value of embracing her convention-defying sexual orientation. Squeak (Mary Agnes) demonstrates the importance of the voice of the individual through her performance of blues songs, which are initially renditions of Shug's songs but eventually are replaced by songs that address Squeak's own concerns and personality.

With the passing of many first-, second-, and even third-generation blues performers, it is the entry of blues music into the mainstream record-buying market, as evidenced by the flood of blues releases and reissues, that helps to guarantee that novelists will continue to be exposed to the beauty of the blues tradition. Walker herself acknowledged listening to and being influenced by the series of LPs of women blues singers released on Rosetta Reitz's record label, and their inspiration in song translates strongly into Walker's novel. Novelists will, hopefully, continue to find creative and meaningful ways to syncretize the oral blues and written novel traditions, just as the blues themselves adapted African modalities to European and American traditions to create something new and wonderful on American soil. That improvisatory adaptivity, accomplished while retaining the strength and wisdom of the folk past, is another legacy of the blues.

NOTES

1. Janheinz Jahn, *A History of Neo-African Literature* (New York: Grove Press, 1968) p. 172.
2. Glissando, melisma and other musical techniques common to African American vernacular are discussed briefly in Alan Lomax, "Song Structure and Social Structure," *Write Me a Few of Your Lines: A Blues Reader*, ed. Steven C. Tracy (Amherst: University of Massachusetts Press, 1999), pp. 36–37. For a discussion of voice masking, see Robert Palmer, *Deep Blues* (New York: Viking, 1981) p. 35.
3. Richard J. Powell, "Art History and Black Memory: Toward a Blues Aesthetic," *The Jazz Cadence of American Culture*, ed. Robert G. O'Meally (New York: Columbia University Press, 1998), pp. 182–195.
4. Langston Hughes, *Not Without Laughter* (1930; rpt. New York: Scribner's, 1969).
5. Langston Hughes, review of *Blues: An Anthology*, W. C. Handy," *Opportunity* (August 1926): 258. Subsequent references to the text are from this edition.
6. Zora Neale Hurston, *Their Eyes Were Watching God* (1937; rpt. New York: Harper and Row, 1990). Subsequent references to the text are from this edition.
7. Ralph Ellison. *The Collected Essays of Ralph Ellison*, ed. John F. Callahan (New York: Modern Library, 1995).
8. William Attaway, *Blood on the Forge* (1941; rpt. New York: Monthly Review Press, 1987). Subsequent references to the text are from this edition.
9. Steven C. Tracy, "The Devil's Son-In-Law and *Invisible Man*," *MELUS* 15:3 (Fall, 1988): 47–64.
10. Maryemma Graham, "Bearing Witness in Black Chicago: A View of Selected Fiction by Richard Wright, Frank London Brown, and Ronald Fair," *CLA Journal* 33:3 (March, 1990): 291–292.

8

FRITZ GYSIN

From modernism to postmodernism: black literature at the crossroads

A considerable number of African American novels written after 1970 are inspired by postmodernist themes and strategies. The postmodernist novel is essentially antimimetic; it frequently questions the linearity of plot structure, confuses time sequences, blends levels of reality and fictionality, fragments characters, looks at events through several focalizing lenses arranged one behind the other, enjoys unreliable narrators, falls short of expectations, breaks rules, undermines conventions, and sometimes even resists interpretation. All this it does with an excessive blending of wit, irony, and paradox. In short, it favors experimental, avant-garde, progressive literary techniques and approaches.

The engagement with postmodernism as a mode of writing is illustrated in the following declaration of intention by the implied author of Clarence Major's *Reflex and Bone Structure* (1975):

> I want this book to be anything it wants to be. A penal camp. A bad check. A criminal organization. A swindle. A prison. Devil's Island. I want the mystery of this book to be an absolute mystery. Let it forge its own way into the art of deep sea diving. Let it walk. I want it to run and dance. And be sad. And score in the major league all-time records. I want it to smoke and drink and do other things bad for its health. This book can be anything it has a mind to be.[1]

Major precariously situates his novel in a continuously generative linguistic universe; his unconventional use of personification, his application of mixed metaphors, his juxtaposition of images of confinement and liberating impulses, and his propagation of provisionality and uncertainty point to fictional strategies that are no longer satisfied with the foregrounding of irony, ambiguity, and paradox, the hallmarks of the modernist novel.

A detective novel of sorts, *Reflex and Bone Structure* plays with the possibilities of the genre and undercuts any rational attempts to establish a relationship of cause and effect by scrambling the fragments of the two stories of a murder and its investigation and by offering different versions of the first and diverging developments of the second. The victims are Cora Hull, a beautiful, rich, and famous black actress, and Dale, one of her lovers. Dale is a persistent source of frustration for the narrator because of his rare appearance, his vagueness, and because of the narrator's jealousy. Canada Jackson, the third character, is easier to handle, because he is straightforward, socially conscious, and positive. The fourth character is the intrusive author/narrator himself, who seems obsessed with Cora and unable to solve the mystery of her protean existence. Besides juggling with time levels and plot sequences, such as offering alternative versions of Cora's life, e.g. death in a traffic accident, marriage with Fidel Castro, sexual escapades with the narrator, he problematizes his own function as an author by admitting his inability to create round characters, by doing his best to control his figures yet running the risk of being manipulated by them in turn, and thus revealing his own disorientation in the metafictional clinch. This includes emphasis on the written word, as the following example illustrates:

> Cora inspects the word of her mouth. She touches the paper on which her name appears. The word Cora, she thinks, is the extent of her presence. This is a word. She is sitting at the kitchen table, elbows on table. The table has a word that is used by people, like Cora, who wish to refer to it. That word is table. Cora writes her name on the paper. She erases it. It goes away but it is still there. Cora is trapped in herself. (Major, *Reflex*, 74)

Such foregrounding of the signifier ("the word Cora," "the word table") implies a text assuming a life of its own, but it also allows the author/narrator better control over the facts, e.g. the fact that Cora is dead, which he simply ignores. Thus we again encounter the strange juxtaposition of freedom and control: the self-emancipation of language is instrumentalized by a narrator whose deepest urge is to resurrect Cora by re-creating her. Revisiting her empty apartment, he writes: "I climb the steps slowly. Canada probably won't be home. A wasted trip, wasted energy, wasted space. / But the peephole opens and an eye winks. After I've knocked three times. I know I'm crazy but I hope – against all hope – it is Cora. Please person be Cora. Just this once be Cora. You are Cora person. Please" (93). Such metafictional concerns are more than mere games. The author's preoccupation with the self (Cora's, his own) is a concern with himself as an author, with the need to create his own reality, the need to churn out, again and again, his own versions of death – and life.

This novel is thus an example of postmodernist rather than modernist writing. The *modernist* novel is experimental and innovatory in form; it foregrounds the subconscious and unconscious regions of the human mind; it frequently breaks the linearity of plot and often makes use of "new" strategies of point of view, such as the technique of "stream-of-consciousness." Nevertheless, it usually compensates for such breaches of conventional mimetic writing by trying to establish unity, closure, identity, etc. on another (higher or lower) level of discourse. The *postmodern* (or *postmodernist*) novel, on the other hand, is much more radical in these respects, and, above all, it denies or subverts such compensatory measures. For example, it asserts the freedom and autonomy of the literary text while at the same time foregrounding the author's play with language; it presents two-dimensional characters which are then given extremely variable functions, something they could never perform in "real" life (or "real" death, for that matter); it inverts generic plots such as those of crime fiction or the love triangle; and it destabilizes the function of the narrator to the extent that he himself becomes a pawn in the game. *Reflex and Bone Structure* is thus a testimony to the author's engagement with postmodernism, as a *condition* and as a *mode of writing*.

As a *condition*, postmodernism has been characterized, for example, by Lyotard, for whom it refers to the general state of knowledge in times of information technology and the absence of a master narrative,[2] by Jameson, who relates it to the cultural logic of late capitalism[3] and the loss of historical consciousness,[4] or by Baudrillard, for whom it has to do with the cultural production of a "semiurgic society" and the substitution of the simulacrum for the real.[5] These theorists define postmodernism as primarily a concept of philosophy or of cultural theory. As such it has also been claimed by African American scholars, such as Henry Louis Gates,[6] bell hooks,[7] or Philip Brian Harper. The latter postulates the marginalized groups' experience of decenteredness as an age-old postmodern condition:

> if postmodernist fiction foregrounds subjective fragmentation, a similar decenteredness can be identified in US [black] novels written prior to the postmodern era, in which it derives specifically from the socially marginalized and politically disenfranchised status of the populations treated in the works. To the extent that such populations have experienced psychic decenteredness long prior to its generalization throughout the culture during the late twentieth century, one might say that the postmodern era's preoccupation with fragmented subjectivity represents the "recentering" of the culture's focus on issues that have always concerned marginalized constituencies.[8]

De-centering, to be sure, has been around as a critical term in the postmodernist vocabulary for quite some time. Yeats's famous lines: "Things fall apart; / the centre cannot hold; / Mere anarchy is loosed upon the world" in his poem "The Second Coming" (1921) had heralded the fragmentation typical of modernism, but the modernist writers had looked for salvation in formal and mythical countermeasures by making use, however ironically,

FRITZ GYSIN

of older (and "safer") literary and musical forms as well as mythical topics from older literary and religious sources. The postmodern writers, in
contrast, invert or subvert hierarchies, emphasize dislocation, antitotalization, infinite regress, etc., and, together with fabulation, textual play, and
self-referentiality, they mostly valorize the fragments, highlight peripheral
phenomena, focusing on the centrifugal rather than the centripetal forces.
And yet, the above-mentioned African American theorists' re-direction of the
critical focus from the marginal to the central adds a fascinating new angle
to the concept, which also influences our understanding of postmodernism
as a *mode of writing*.

Harper's application of the term to the *condition* of modernist black writing draws attention to the ambiguous quality of postmodernism as a *fictional
mode* inasmuch as it indirectly questions its relationship to modernism, its
antecedent. Although the term "postmodernism" in English was first dis-
seminated by a historian, early usage in literary criticism by Irving Howe
and Harry Levin applies it to late modernist American fiction, whereas critics of the 1960s, such as Leslie Fiedler, Susan Sontag, or the art critic John
Perreault began to see it in opposition to modernism.[9] From then on, and
especially in the writing of Ihab Hassan[10] and David Lodge,[11] the question
as to whether postmodernism is a continuation of modernism or whether
it is its opposite gained prominence in the literary debates. In many practical cases it is both. However, no matter whether continuation or contrast,
David Antin's dictum: "From the modernism you choose you get the postmodernism you deserve"[12] allows us to distinguish between at least two
types of postmodernist theories.

As long as we take as our basis of definition the view of literary modernism
of the kind embraced by T. S. Eliot or Ralph Ellison, who try to counteract
fragmentation by a search for some form of salvation, in myth and ritual,
in folklore, in a return to the roots, etc., we may define the *postmodern*
turn as a radical shift towards dehumanization, subversion of metaphysics,
or "ontological instability." Ihab Hassan and Brian McHale have done this
most succinctly, the latter one, in his second book, even insisting on the necessity to postulate the existence of different postmodernisms.[13] If, on the
other hand, we take as our point of departure the definition of modernism in
architecture, which insists on the totalitarian, i.e. dehumanizing approaches
of modernists such as Mies van der Rohe or Le Corbusier, any *postmodern* attempt would then have to be seen as an attempt to re-humanize the
public space, e.g. by insisting on antitotalization, subjectivity, heterogene-
ity, humor, etc. Linda Hutcheon, in her *Poetics of Postmodernism* is doing
just that, adapting her definitions to those of Charles Jencks, and that is
why she has difficulties accepting in her system some of the more radical

postmodernist writers, such as Barthelme, Brautigan, Elkin, Gaddis, and Oates, and can only make passing mention of Coover, Gass, Sukenick, and Vonnegut.[14]

Most African American postmodernist fiction blends, or oscillates between, approaches implied by those two theoretical positions. This may be due to the strongly ethical and political quality of most black writing, to specific kinds of thematic engagement, or to certain generic preoccupations. As a result, critical and reader response tend to differ remarkably, depending on ideological alignment or aesthetic preference. In some cases, we can even observe a tendency to include some forms of realistic writing, such as Magic Realism (the inclusion of fabulous or fantastic elements in fiction that is otherwise realistic),[15] or certain comparatively new generic developments, such as the jazz novel or even the blues novel, accounts that engage these musical genres in formal and thematic ways, such as making use of call-and-response or attempts at improvisation, on the one hand, or preoccupations with musical history and characters, on the other. This goes to show that the postmodernist mode is in no way limited by strict boundaries, either in production or in reception, that the tendency to experiment, to undermine, or to explode a particular style may be found in a wide range of fictional writing, and that, more often than not, genres, styles, or themes overlap. Moreover, one also encounters texts that show postmodernist traits at some levels and modernist, or even realistic ones, at others. As the postmodern poetics does not advocate a tendency towards harmony, unity, or wholeness, this should not cause any problems. Yet not every leap into fantasy, not every expression of self-reflexivity, not every resistance to closure creates a post-modernist work, any more than every syntactical distortion leads to a modernist example of Joycean stream-of-consciousness. Perhaps it makes sense, then, to restrict the term to those kinds of fiction that predominantly undercut mimesis (the reproduction of external reality), ideology, and "truth," collapse surface and depth, or tend to doubt the foundations of their own existence.

By this definition, arguably the most important player in the field of black postmodernist fiction is Ishmael Reed, whose specialty is satirical parody: of genres, of ideologies, of aesthetic programs, even of religions. His masterpiece, *Mumbo Jumbo* (1972),[16] parodies the detective novel, the Harlem Renaissance, the Jazz Age, Western Culture, and Christianity, propagating the Neo-American Hoo-Doo Church as a contemporary version of the traditional Haitian religion of Voodoo. Through parody, Reed satirizes almost everything under the sun, including racial, cultural, and gender issues, which has made him quite a number of enemies. Apart from his stunning use of the vernacular, his exuberant verbal wit, his successful blending of folklore and caricature, his inventive use of metafictional strategies, and his hilarious deconstruction of history, it is above all the surprising intricacy of Reed's ideological constructions that makes his fiction so challenging (see chapter 12 in this book).

The third significant early postmodernist African American author (besides Major and Reed) is William Melvin Kelley. His innovative potential encompasses forays into the realms of fantasy, myth, and dream as well as the linguistic experiments used to represent them. His third novel, *dem* (1967),[17] is a surrealistic treatment of a white family's disintegration under the spell of black retributive action. Its protagonist risks disappearing into the fantasy world of TV soap opera, and there are early attempts to represent his dreams in language experiments making frequent use of paranomasia (the use of words that sound alike but differ in meaning). Kelley achieved postmodernist fame with *Dunfords Travels Everywheres* (1970),[18] a surrealist satire that blends white-dominated intertextuality with the African heritage to present the African American as a dream-construction. At surface level, the novel tells an unending tale consisting of two separate plots with two different protagonists, partly presented in alternating fragments: a spoof on segregation combined with an account of a clandestine contemporary Middle Passage and a burlesque of a Harlem hustler's maneuverings against the Black Bourgeoisie. Additional depth and actual excitement are provided by a third story, which consists of ironic-prophetic dream-like sequences, in which the two protagonists, the white-obsessed semi-intellectual Chig Dunford and the black-oriented Carlyle Bedlow are offered a possibility to come together and reconstruct the shattered self of the black man, thereby escaping the dismal condition of a spiritually unbalanced world and, as "Blafringro-Arumericans" entering "New Afriquerque," a hypothetical collective myth of a utopian black American nation, which is, however, treated ironically.

Like Ishmael Reed, Kelley thus contrasts and fuses elements of white and black culture; in his case Scandinavian mythology and Nigerian fiction help him oppose the chill of the white man's North to the sun energy of Africa.[19] Unlike Reed, however, he subverts these binary structures by means of audacious linguistic experiments. His "supersaturated black text" (Nielsen 5) signifies on the artificial language practiced in James Joyce's *Finnegans Wake*, making use of spelling experiments to highlight the tension between the visual and auditive effects of puns: "Witches one Way tspike Mr. Chigyle's Languish, n curryng him back tRealty, recoremince wi hUnmisereaducation" (*Dunfords* 49). Yet, in so doing, Kelley does not only provide revisionary comments on modernism, but he also destabilizes essentialist conceptions of Black English (Nielsen 6–7). To paraphrase an illustration by Marieme

Sy, the phrase "grieft of servilization" (*Dunfords* 57), if read aloud, produces "gift of civilization," yet a silent reading suggests connotations such as "grief," "serve," "servile" (Sy 465–466). The words substituted for the originally intended phrase thus, on the one hand, provide an aural/oral version and, on the other, sever this version from its original meaning. Hence, Kelley's rendering of "Chigyle's" dream world foregrounds and at the same time problematizes the vernacular voice, making "writing" essential in ways foreign to his more realistically minded contemporaries among writers and critics.

Major's strategies of radical invention, Reed's satirical parodies, and Kelley's surrealist dislocations testify to these authors' comparatively early appropriation – and transformation – of key issues and central paradigms of American postmodernist writing. But they were not alone in their efforts. Quite a number of their black contemporaries experimented with similar approaches, and additional ones were developed by their successors. One of the central criteria by means of which the postmodernist quality of such approaches might be assessed is the degree to which identity is destabilized and the narrative levels at which such processes take place. Since this issue is inherent in much theory and criticism of African American fiction, I propose to concentrate on this feature and to discuss it by focusing on four selected thematic clusters, namely those of: (1) skin and skin color; (2) ancestry and madness; (3) (hi)story and prophecy; and (4) artist and voice.

1. A central aspect of black identity is, of course, that of skin, and skin has been treated controversially in various ways in postmodern African American novels.[20] This issue can be discussed here in more summary fashion, because the relevant authors are dealt with elsewhere in this book. Whereas recent African American realist and modernist novels concerned with the issue of skin generally provide variations of the themes of passing and of the tragic mulatto,[21] postmodernist writing tends to foreground more exceptional aspects of this topic. Perhaps the most radical postmodernist treatment of skin occurs in Charles Johnson's *Oxherding Tale* (1982) and *Middle Passage* (1990),[22] above all in the mongrel figure of Horace Benbow, aka Soulcatcher, whose chest is tattooed with the victims of his murders, eerie pictures coming alive and melting into each other, providing the ultimate challenge to the protagonist's sense of self and granting him a vision into the liminal region between the worlds of the living and the dead (*Oxherding Tale* 175–176). The topic reappears in *Middle Passage* in the image of the coal-black Allmuseri god, who absorbs people that are sent to feed him and shows them on his epidermis, so that what in the earlier novel appeared as tattoos now functions as a cross-cultural microcosm, exposing the multiplicity and division at the core of black essence and revealing to the

protagonist/narrator that "identity is imagined," that "the (black) self is the greatest of all fictions" (*Middle Passage* 171). Whereas Johnson's epiphanies of skin emphasize the proliferating reflexivity of epidermis, John Edgar Wideman foregrounds color, but again in a subversive manner, namely by making Brother Tate, the no-name protagonist of *Sent for You Yesterday* (1983), an albino.[23] In this way he inverts the issue of black identity, interpreting Brother's mysterious whiteness – or his non-color – as the last stage in the history of racial abuse (484). By exploding the essentialism of skin color, Wideman, like Johnson, makes black and white identity a highly dubious affair and thus contributes to the controversy about race in postmodernist fiction (on Wideman see chapter 15).

2. The second thematic cluster concerns issues of origins and madness. They are tied up in an exemplary way in *The Bloodworth Orphans* (1977) by Leon Forrest.[24] The governing characteristic of Forrest's fiction is excess: of genres, styles, imagery, tales, experiences, relationships, etc.[25] The novel's numerous characters, most of whom perceive themselves as orphans, in their quest for identity desperately try to sound the depths of their family history, only to come up with painful evidence of incest, miscegenation, racism, rape, bloodshed, suicide, and crime of all hues and shades, to a large extent stemming from an almost mythological curse of the Bloodworth family. However, in contrast to classical procedure, this curse finds its own illogical path among the generations of descendants in ever-renewed, repeated, but also dislocated revelations of impropriety, illegitimacy, and guilt. Quite a few characters crack under the burden of such disclosures; others overreact in ways close to insanity. It is as if the plethora of celebrations and outrages, performed (and represented) as an amoral leveling of acclamations and denunciations, functioned to compensate the last (lost) generation of Bloodworth children for their enormous sense of deprivation (on Forrest see chapter 15).

An equally harrowing recreation of communal memory occurs in the first two novels by Gayl Jones. Although the ancestral tale, if untangled, appears, in her case, more linear and focused, the outrage has similar dimensions, and what in the case of Forrest is achieved by excess is here realized by shocking detail. *Corregidora* (1975)[26] problematizes black identity formation by revealing the distortions caused by multiple narrators and focalizers of traumatic tales. Ursa's relentless rendering of the Corregidora family's history of sexual assault allows her to attempt partial psychic recovery from her own mutilation by learning how to question the various constricting functions of ancestral reports and by becoming aware of the slave women's practice of power during and throughout the enforced sexual act. The emphasis on fellatio as a site of female resistance and the protagonist's choice among a series of graded options between loving and emasculating her husband may be read as psycho-political position-taking in a neo-slavery situation, where oppression is predominantly performed by means of rape and enforced prostitution; her final decision to opt for love, expressed in a blues duet with Mutt, has been interpreted as a performance that allows her to reclaim her own desire.[27] (See chapter 5, pp. 93–95.)

The opposite choice – if one can still speak of a choice – is made by the protagonist of Jones's second novel, *Eva's Man* (1976).[28] Eva Medina Canada poisons her lover and then lovingly castrates him by biting off his penis. Leading up to this ironic climax is a series of experiences and accounts of sexual abuse, beginning with a little boy's use of a popsicle stick for his fumbling forays on the passive girl and repeating the same constellation of male aggressiveness and female succumbing to such an extent that critics almost at once have suspected an increasingly unreliable narrator.[29] The shifts among narrative and time levels, together with a less and less comprehensible use of syntax and referentiality, support the growing impression that the protagonist is gradually going insane. Despite detailed communications of the most intimate matters, the experiences rendered remain meaningless, apart from a growing desire of revenge for sexual mistreatment, which is, however, coupled with signs of pathological sexual obsession. The murderess ends up in a prison for the criminally insane, finds understanding and sympathy from a cell mate, and is last seen in a lesbian embrace. Even more than in the case of Forrest, whose use of the Orpheus and Osiris myths suggest additional levels of meaning, Jones's novels offer themselves to multiple allegorical readings, and yet one recognizes an ever-widening gap between the narrative and the attempted psychological, political, or mythological explanations,[30] and it is especially this gap which contributes to the postmodern quality of the novel.

A later version of the dislocation of the self and the concomitant destabilization of identity occurs in Randall Kenan's first novel, *A Visitation of Spirits* (1989).[31] More reticent about sexual details than Jones, Kenan, at the surface level, depicts a case of acute schizophrenia, ingeniously rendered in a flickering interplay between excursions into the occult and the fantastic and glimpses of confused awareness of a frightening present. Structurally reminiscent of Kelley's *Dunfords*, the novel has two separate plotlines, which make contact only at brief moments: the first is an account of the last day (or rather night) of young Horace Cross's losing fight against the inner and outer constrictions to his budding homosexuality; the second consists of his elder cousin, the Reverend James Malachai Greene, recalling a life lived in resignation. The young man's loss of identity leading to his suicide is tied to his refusal to play the part prescribed to him by a history of black suffering and displacement as well as by black refusal to accept his other-ness, his engagement with whites of the same sexual preference. The precise dating of some of the sections provides a rational counterpoint to Horace's necromantic rituals, visions, and nightmares involving demons, wizards, and monsters, as well as visions of earlier versions of himself. By means of a va-riety of styles and modes, present reality and the real and fantastic past are fused. Focalization is never stable, and thus the facts provided by one specific focalizer – or the ways in which these facts are presented – may contest those supplied by another one; for example, information about Horace's death is strangely ignored in James's plotline, then introduced in retrospect, whereas in Horace's plot, the suicide is first rehearsed as a killing of his ghostly dou-ble and only at the end sprung upon the reader in a third-person account of disturbing clinical detail, only to be obfuscated again by a paradoxical assertion of veracity: "Ifs and maybes and weres and perhapses are of no use in this case. The facts are enough, unless they too are subject to doubt" (*A Visitation* 254).

3. A different approach to the destabilization of identity is taken by John Edgar Wideman in *The Cattle Killing* (1996),[32] arguably one of the most significant African American novels of the last fifty years. Wideman's brand of historiographic metafiction relates issues of history and prophecy with the theme of storytelling, but his stories and their tellers, by means of frag-mentation, anachronism, and the permeability of characters, are made to wreak havoc on the identitarian discourses practiced by some of his more modernist-minded contemporaries. Mental disturbance is no issue here; the forces assailing the artist's perception of the self and others are social, moral, and spiritual. Masquerade, disguise, and deception dominate most of the tales told in this novel, whose characters need them to survive in an increas-ingly chaotic world. In typically postmodern fashion, contradictory concepts of time inform the complex arrangement of events and flashbacks; history, story, and the writer's life permeate each other and the characters, so that the process of representation must constantly be renegotiated by the writer: "And who is he anyway, interchangeable with these others, porous, them running through him, him leaking, bleeding into them, in the fiction he's try-ing to write" (*Cattle Killing* 13). That despite his enormously effective use of the vernacular Wideman casts doubts on the power of the griot, of the oral tradition, and thus of the author himself, that he constantly investigates the nature of the truths he encounters, paradoxically gives additional validity to his argument[33].

In a slightly less radical manner, other contemporary novelists play with issues of historical accuracy and thus put the identity of their historical figures at stake. In *Darktown Strutters* (1994),[34] Wesley Brown intervenes in the history of minstrelsy, presenting a fictional biography of Jim Crow, a blend of stereotype and trickster, who questions the issue of masquerade by refusing to blacken up while performing his dances; Charles Johnson constructs a highly ambiguous portrait of Martin Luther King's double in *Dreamer* (1998)[35]; and Colson Whitehead rings the changes on the hero of a famous ballad in *John Henry Days* (2001).[36] Although such novels at first sight seem to be written in a comparatively realistic manner, closer inspection reveals many aspects that make them fit into Linda Hutcheon's postmodern brand of historiographic metafiction, such as the provisionality or indeterminacy of a character's identity, the problematic of reference and representation, or the constructed quality of "facts" (cf. Hutcheon 105–123). These authors "play" with history; they make use of anachronism; or they cast doubt on processes of verification.

4. A fourth way of postmodernist questioning of identity is the author's self-reflective concern with his or her function as an artist, a theme which, more often than not, is developed by choosing a musician as protagonist of the novel. This, again, has become a common topic in recent African American fiction. Postmodernist novels, however, no matter whether they are about musicians or writers, are very rarely "ascent narratives,"[37] and if so, they are parodic and ironical, like the story of the writer Raven Quickskill in Reed's *Flight to Canada* (1976).[38] They rather express reservations about the artist's function, such as in the story of Mason Ellis, the protagonist of Major's *My Amputations* (1986),[39] whose identity and manuscript are stolen by a famous author or an impostor, and who is sent by his sponsoring foundation on a bizarre lecturing tour across Europe, during which he constantly claims to be inventing himself, only to end up in a remote village in Liberia carrying a sealed message that says "Keep this nigger" (*My Amputations* 203). Such weird comments on the establishment of a black voice are frequent in postmodernist African American novels, especially in postmodern jazz fiction, which tends to suspect or even subvert Gayl Jones's postulation of the black musician as the superior artist and model, whom the African American writer ought to emulate.[40] Whereas realist and modernist novels about jazz musicians and their performance tend to focus on specific rhythmical aspects of the black vernacular or even to turn fiction into jazz (cf. Albert Murray, Xam Wilson Cartiér, or some of the authors of short stories collected by Richard N. Albert or Art Lange and Nathaniel Mackey), postmodern authors show a strong tendency to turn jazz into fiction and while so doing to address the anxiety of voice as one of the gaps between the two modes of black performance.

Strategies that are embraced to problematize voice (and, through voice, identity) reach from silencing to indirection and fragmentation.[41] Leon

Forrest, for example, has his protagonist witness a concert in a mental asylum, a one-man-show performed by blind Ironwood "Landlord" Rumble, whose weird musical sermon (related as a story) ends in his physical collapse, leading to his being carried up to his room, to be effectively silenced, whereas his horns, "which he had turned into stunning orchards of beauty and power, now appeared to take on the visage of corroded chains, as they were carted away in huge money-sacks" (*Bloodworth* 315). In Wideman's *Sent for You Yesterday* (1983), Albert Wilkes, the legendary blues pianist, is shot by the police while playing his music, and his successor, the mysterious Brother Tate, after the killing of his son stops talking and communicates by scatting instead, in this way reacting to a nightmare in which he tries to suppress a scream for fear of being sucked out of a dark box car (*The Homewood Books* 341–343).

In these and similar novels, the postmodern problematizing of the musician's voice paradoxically leads to a revaluation of language, but not necessarily of orality. This is interesting, because authors like Forrest or Wideman gained fame by their espousal of the vernacular. It seems that in this fiction the concept of "liberating voices" is challenged, and yet at the same time the artist's concern with writing gains significance. A fascinating example of more recent jazz fiction is the work of Nathaniel Mackey, whose epistolary novels, *Bedouin Hornbook* (1986), *Djbot Baghostus's Run* (1993), and *Atet. A.D.* (2001),[42] written by an acronymic musician and addressed to a mysterious correspondent named "Angel of Dust," convert the performance of music into literary language in a very idiosyncratic manner, in which musicians are sometimes reduced to mouthpieces of the instruments they play or even made to perform silently, merely fingering their instruments. Sound is expressed by silent gesture or related to distorted speech, as in the narrator's "metalecture" on "The Creaking of the Word." At the same time, *visual* imagery and *visual* description abound; bands are given names such as the "Boneyard Brass Octet" or the "Crossroads Choir" (*Bedouin* 165–178); one of the most striking examples is the narrator's explanation of singer Betty Carter's breathless performance of a ballad by focusing on her "facial teasing": "I was struck by her inversion of conventional ventriloquism's motionless lips and expressionless face, by the way the wealth of labial gesture and facial projection she resorted to metathetically altered the ventriloquial formula" (*Djbot* 155). Voice is thus reduced, distorted, or deferred, which to Mackey seems necessary to turn the music into language, and language into writing.[43] Synesthesia is made to foreground and then deconstruct orality; the narrator's stereoscopic vision projects him into the dual personality of Djbot Baghostus / Jarred Bottle – names whose acronyms suggest James

Brown and Damballah[44] – and thus presents identity as a flickering of mystical masks across different layers of reality.

The inversion and subversion of markers of postmodern black literary characterization such as color of skin, mental sanity, historical continuity, and voice are echoed, or twisted and burlesqued in turn in Paul Beatty's satirical novel *The White Boy Shuffle* (1996),[45] which I shall use to wind up this brief survey, because it is not only one of the most succinct successors of Ishmael Reed's iconoclastic fiction but also suggests possible directions in which this fiction may be moving. The surface linearity of Beatty's spoof on the black *Bildungs-* and *Künstlerroman* covers up the fissures and cracks in the life of a pitch-black Californian whiz kid, whose brainpower, sophistication, and creative talent are matched only by his sarcasm, insolence, and occasional cynicism: attitudes that he needs to survive in his new surroundings when his mother moves the family from a white middle-class neighborhood to inner-city Los Angeles. The name, lineage, and educational history of the protagonist are used to satirize the genre of the family novel and especially the current predilection for black autobiographies. Gunnar Kaufmann hails from a clan of self-reliant yet accommodationist folk who exaggerate racial and cultural stereotypes for economic and psychic survival. His intellectual superiority, and particularly his unabashed display of the same, cause him frequent physical damage but also procure lasting friendships with two equally weird characters, Nicholas Scoby, a jazz freak and basketball star, who is constitutionally unable to miss a shot, and Psycho Loco, the insane killer who protects Gunnar against attacks from troublemakers and provides him with a Japanese mail-order bride when he is eighteen.

Despite his dark skin, Gunnar's precociousness makes him appear white to many of his peers. The potential isolation this causes he tries to counteract by joining one of the local black gangs, the Gun-Toting Hooligans, on their occasional masqueraded forays against their enemy gangs. The tone of the narrative, as well as the play with race and gender (they fight in drag), are definitely postmodern, and so is the strange shift of emphasis from the vernacular to the written. For acceptance only comes when Gunnar *writes* a poem and sprays it on the wall surrounding the community he lives in, which turns him into a representative of the weak and downtrodden. And although for a large part of his story Gunnar entertains us by his combination of slapstick and stand-up comedianship, the final chapters turn his hip-hop jargon into relentless, if not to say destructive, "black humor" in the dual sense of the word. The book he finally publishes is sarcastically entitled *Watermelanin,* and the speech he delivers against the acquittal of the white policemen who mistreated Rodney King[46] has unexpected effects: his endorsement of freedom by self-destruction instigates a series of significant suicides, including those of his friend and his father.[47] In a characteristically postmodern way, effect exceeds cause and leads to rather fantastic exaggeration: he discloses the Manhattan Project's secret plan to get rid of the black population by means of a third atomic bomb, Svelte Guy (besides Fat Boy and Little Man, the bombs that were dropped on Hiroshima and Nagasaki), and he goads US state terrorism by having white concentric circles painted on the roofs of the neighborhood, with his own temporary home as the bull's eye. This, by the way, is the place where he defiantly feeds his newborn daughter Naomi. Entropic and apocalyptic echoes of Pynchon and Vonnegut, together with references to suicidal thematics in Morrison and Perry, help create a brand of postmodernist satire full of absurd wit and sarcasm while still enforcing a highly ethical stance. The suicidal poem written by Gunnar's father that ends the novel testifies to this no-nonsense attitude:

> Like the good Reverend King,
> I too "have a dream,"
> but when I wake up
> I forget it and
> remember I'm running late for work.
>
> (Beatty, 249)

Interestingly enough, in this novel, just as in the other ones discussed above, the experimental violations of convention, the insistence on the provisionality of meaning, and the unfixing of identity go parallel with a deep concern for aesthetic aspects of writing, for the novel as a form of art.

NOTES

1. Clarence Major, *Reflex and Bone Structure* (New York: Fiction Collective, 1975), p. 61.
2. Jean-François Lyotard, *La condition postmoderne* (Paris: Minuit, 1979); *The Postmodern Condition*, trans. Geoffrey Bennington and Brian Massumi (Minneapolis: University of Minnesota Press, 1984).
3. Fredric R. Jameson, *Postmodernism, or, the Cultural Logic of Late Capitalism* (Durham: Duke University Press, 1991).
4. Philip E. Simmons, *Deep Surfaces: Mass Culture and History in Postmodern American Fiction* (Athens: University of Georgia Press, 1997), p. 2.
5. Jean Baudrillard, *Simulations*, trans. Paul Foss, Paul Patton, and Philip Beitchman (New York: Semiotext(e), 1983).
6. Henry Louis Gates Jr., *The Signifying Monkey: A Theory of African-American Literary Criticism* (New York: Oxford University Press, 1988).
7. bell hooks, *Yearning: Race, Gender, and Cultural Politics* (Boston: South End Press, 1990).

8. Phillip Brian Harper, *Framing the Margins: The Social Logic of Postmodern Culture* (New York: Oxford University Press, 1994), pp. 3–4.
9. Toynbee in 1947. Cf. Michael Köhler, "'Postmodernismus': Ein begriffsgeschichtlicher Überblick," *Postmodernism in American Literature. A Critical Anthology*, eds. Manfred Pütz and Peter Freese (Darmstadt: Thesen Verlag, 1984), pp. 3–5.
10. Ihab Hassan, *The Dismemberment of Orpheus: Toward a Postmodern Literature* (Madison: University of Wisconsin Press, 1971); *Paracriticisms: Seven Speculations on the Times* (Urbana: University of Illinois Press, 1975); *The Postmodern Turn: Essays in Postmodern Theory and Culture* (Columbus: Ohio State University Press, 1987).
11. David Lodge, *The Modes of Modern Writing: Metaphor, Metonymy, and the Typology of Modern Literature* (London: Edward Arnold, 1977).
12. David Antin, "Modernism and Postmodernism," *Boundary* 2 1 (1972), qtd. in *The New Princeton Encyclopedia of Poetry and Poetics*, ed Alex Preminger and T. V. F. Brogan (Princeton: Princeton University Press, 1993), p. 792.
13. Brian McHale, *Postmodernist Fiction* (London: Methuen, 1987); *Constructing Postmodernism* (London: Routledge, 1992).
14. Linda Hutcheon, *A Poetics of Postmodernism* (New York: Routledge, 1988), pp. 22, 27–29, 52.
15. "Magic realism is a critique of the possibility of representation in that it blurs the boundaries between what is 'magic' and what is 'real' and thus calls into question accepted definitions of either." Brenda K. Marshal, *Teaching the Postmodern. Fiction and Theory* (New York: Routledge, 1992), p. 180.
16. Ishmael Reed, *Mumbo Jumbo* (Garden City: Doubleday, 1972).
17. William Melvin Kelley, *dem* (Garden City: Doubleday, 1967).
18. William Melvin Kelley, *Dunfords Travels Everywheres* (Garden City: Doubleday, 1970).
19. Grace Eckley, "The Awakening of Mr. Afrinnegan: Kelley's *Dunfords Travels Everywheres* and Joyce's *Finnegans Wake*," *Obsidian* 12 (Summer 1975): 27–41; Marieme Sy, "Dream and Language in *Dunfords Travels Everywheres*," *CLA Journal* 25, 4 (June 1982): 458–467; Valerie M. Babb, "William Melvin Kelley," *Afro-American Fiction Writers after 1955*, Thadious M. Davis and Trudier Harris, eds. (Detroit: Gale, 1984), pp. 135–143; Aldon Lynn Nielsen, *Black Chant: Languages of African-American Postmodernism* (New York: Cambridge University Press, 1997), pp. 3–13.
20. Cf. Fritz Gysin, "Predicaments of Skin: Boundaries in Recent African American Fiction," *The Black Columbiad: Defining Moments in African American Literature and Culture*, eds. Maria Diedrich and Werner Sollors (Cambridge: Harvard University Press, 1994), pp. 286–297.
21. Cf., e.g., Raymond Andrews, *Appalachee Red* (New York: Dial, 1978; Athens: University of Georgia Press, 1987); Ralph Ellison, *Juneteenth*, ed. John F. Callahan (New York: Random House, 1999).
22. Charles Johnson, *Oxherding Tale* (Bloomington: Indiana University Press, 1982); *Middle Passage* (New York: Atheneum, 1990).
23. John Edgar Wideman, *The Homewood Books: Damballah; Hiding Place; Sent for You Yesterday* (Pittsburgh: University of Pittsburgh Press, 1992).

24. Leon Forrest, *The Bloodworth Orphans* (New York: Random House, 1977; Chicago: Another Chicago Press, 1987).
25. On excess as a criterion of postmodernist fiction see Lodge, *Modes of Modern Writing*, 235–239.
26. Gayl Jones, *Corregidora* (New York: Random House, 1975).
27. Ashraf H. A. Rushdy, "'Relate Sexual to Historical': Race, Resistance, and Desire in Gayl Jones's *Corregidora*," *African American Review* 34.2 (Summer 2000): 273–297.
28. Gayl Jones, *Eva's Man* (New York: Random House, 1976).
29. Cf. Keith Byerman, *Fingering the Jagged Grain* (Athens: University of Georgia Press, 1985), pp. 181–185.
30. Cf., e.g., Carol Margaret Davison, "'Love 'em and Lynch 'em': The Castration Motif in Gayl Jones's *Eva's Man*," *African American Review* 29.3 (Fall 1995): 393–410.
31. Randall Kenan, *A Visitation of Spirits* (New York: Random House, 1989; New York: Vintage, 2000).
32. John Edgar Wideman, *The Cattle Killing* (Boston: Houghton Mifflin, 1997).
33. Cf. Fritz Gysin, "'Do not Fall Asleep in Your Enemy's Dream,' John Edgar Wideman and the Predicaments of Prophecy," *Callaloo* 22.3 (Summer 1999): 623–628; Kathie Birat, "'All Stories are True.' Prophecy, History, and Story in *The Cattle Killing*," [Ibid: 629–643]: 629–643.
34. Wesley Brown, *Darktown Strutters* (New York: Cane Hill Press, 1994).
35. Charles Johnson, *Dreamer* (New York: Scribner, 1998).
36. Colson Whitehead, *John Henry Days* (New York: Doubleday, 2001).
37. Cf. Madelyn Jablon, *Black Metafiction: Self-Consciousness in African American Literature* (Iowa City: University of Iowa Press, 1997), p. 59. Cf. also Percival Everett, who provides a harrowing parody of Richard Wright's *Native Son* in his novel *Erasure* (Lebanon, NH: University Press of New England, 2001).
38. Ishmael Reed, *Flight to Canada* (New York: Random House, 1976).
39. Clarence Major, *My Amputations* (New York and Boulder: Fiction Collective, 1986).
40. Gayl Jones, *Liberating Voices: Oral Tradition in African American Literature* (Cambridge: Harvard University Press, 1991).
41. Cf. Fritz Gysin, "From 'Liberating Voices' to 'Metathetic Ventriloquism,' Boundaries in Recent African American Jazz Fiction," *Callaloo* 25.1 (Winter 2002): 274–287.
42. Nathaniel Mackey, *Bedouin Hornbook* (Lexington: University of Kentucky Press, Callaloo Fiction Series, 1986); *Djibot Baghostus's Run* (Los Angeles: Sun & Moon Press, 1993); *Atet. A.D.* (San Francisco: City Lights Books, 2001).
43. Cf. several significant contributions in Paul Naylor ed., *Nathaniel Mackey. A Special Issue, Callaloo* 23.2 (Spring 2000).
44. Paul Hoover and Nathaniel Mackey, "Pair of Figures for Eshu: Doubling of Consciousness in the Work of Kerry James Marshall and Nathaniel Mackey," *Nathaniel Mackey. A Special Issue, Callaloo*: 739.
45. Paul Beatty, *The White Boy Shuffle* (New York: Random House, 1996; London: Vintage, 2000).
46. Cf. Ralph Ellison, *Invisible Man* (New York: Random House, 1952), pp. 342–346. In the fashion of Ellison's invisible man's funeral speech on Tod Clifton.

47. Beatty here takes up a topic first developed by Toni Morrison and Richard Perry and exploits it to excess. Cf. "National Suicide Week" at the beginning of Toni Morrison's *Song of Solomon* (New York: Knopf, 1977); cf. Richard Perry. *Montgomery's Children* (New York: Harcourt, Brace, Jovanovitch, 1984). But whereas the earlier two authors connect the suicide theme with the myth of slaves flying back to Africa, Beatty relates his characters' performance of suicide to the Japanese tradition.

9

SUSANNE B. DIETZEL

The African American novel and popular culture

The field of popular fiction is a relatively unexplored terrain in African American as well as American literary history and criticism. Reasons for this exclusion or oversight are manifold and range from academic practices and aesthetic standards that qualify a text for inclusion in the canon, to the politics of publishing, and the stereotypes or myths that persist about African American readers and their reading habits. In the fields of literary criticism and the teaching of African American literature, for example, scholars and critics alike have restricted their efforts to reviewing, promoting, and canonizing only those texts that fit the prevailing aesthetic and literary standards. While this paradigm – the New Criticism and the reading practices it has encouraged – has allowed for the inclusion of a few women writers and writers of color, it has kept in place a rigid division between high and low, or elite and mass culture, an emphasis on invention over convention, and a distinction between literary and commercial forms of literature that have shaped literary scholarship and reading practices to this day. According to the New Criticism and the practices of literary appreciation it has established, the only literature that deserves merit is independently created and does not respond to the demands of the literary marketplace or the audience, as does much of popular fiction. Applying these standards to African American literary texts (and indeed all literary traditions) has pushed much of its literary production out of the classroom, off the bookshelves, and into the dustbin of literary history.

Similar standards and hierarchies exist in the study of popular culture. The field of African American popular culture studies has almost exclusively focused on music, film, and popular (folk) heroes, especially with the emergence and popularity of rap, hip-hop, and black youth culture in the 1980s and 1990s. Popular culture studies in general continues to privilege rap, hip-hop, and black film over romance, mystery, or science fiction writing. Much cultural studies scholarship has focused on the representation or misrepresentation of African Americans in the popular culture at large, and little attention has been paid to the ways in which African Americans have represented themselves in popular genres or in literatures that are written primarily for the entertainment of a black reading public.

The exclusionary practices of the literary marketplace have been equally dismissive of African American popular fiction. Mainstream publishers closed their doors to more than a few black writers and paid little attention to marketing or publicity. Even when a particular work of fiction sells successfully in the black community, it may never appear on the radar screen of *Publishers Weekly* or the *New York Times*. Since the availability of books by African American authors has never been limited to bookstores, those outlets which report to the bestseller lists, black bestsellers have often reached that status outside mainstream economies of book publishing and the book trade. A long history of black publishing exists in America, and African American authors have distributed their work through a network that includes subscription and book clubs, and those venues easily accessible to the black community such as barbershops and beauty parlors, and through author programs or corner stores, church fairs, and community festivals. Finally, popular authors and some "serious" authors have responded to the demands of the black reading public by self-publishing their work.

Given this history, little is known about the popular genres that make up the bulk of African American popular fiction. Stereotypes about this literature continue to persist, influence its study, or perpetuate its neglect. Books that sell by the millions and ensure their authors' celebrity status are easily dismissed as potboilers, their subject matter considered trivial, and their authors accused of "selling out." Recent developments in cultural and literary studies that see popular culture, including popular fiction, as contested terrain, and as a space where meaning is struggled over, however, have provided us with the analytical tools to see these texts as powerful critiques of dominant ideologies and as sites on which cultural and social conflicts are played out. Tracing some of the developments of black popular fiction is one way of assessing the contributions to African American literary production and may suggest the important directions for future study. We expect popular culture to pay attention to trends and formulas but that posture is complicated by changes in technology, the politics of reading, and the ever-changing tastes and demands of a reading public.

How do we define popular fiction? Is it the number of copies a book sells, its genre or formulaic nature, its success as a commodity in the literary marketplace (as a book, for example, that starts a series of spin-off books), or is it its success amongst its intended audience, and the ways in which a book gains momentum, i.e. sales, through word-of-mouth? If a book's or writer's popularity is measured by the number of copies it sells during a particular year, then the honor of being the first black popular novelist goes to Richard Wright, whose *Black Boy* was the first book by an African American author to make the *Publishers Weekly* bestseller list in 1944.[1] *Native Son* sold equally well during the 1940s, as a Book-of-the-Month-Club selection. If, on the other hand, we measure success by the number of novels a particular author has written, Wright's success is easily eclipsed by Frank Yerby, who remains to this day the most prolific African American author. Yerby, who published 33 novels between 1946 and 1985, maintained a steady presence on the bestseller list, and some of his novels sold more than one million copies during their first year. His novels were found on the list six consecutive years, from 1946 to 1952, and then again in 1954. It was not until 1977, however, that an African American author, Alex Haley, the author of *Roots*, made it to the coveted Number One position. Today, the most "successful" African American novelist is Terry McMillan, who reached the bestseller list in 1992 with *Waiting to Exhale* and whose subsequent novels have maintained great commercial appeal. The first "literary" text by a black author to appear on the list is Toni Morrison's *Paradise* in 1998. If "making the list" is the hallmark of popular achievement, then African American classics like Ralph Ellison's *Invisible Man* or Toni Morrison's *Beloved*, which have sold steadily over the years and have made their authors household names, can be considered neither popular nor bestselling fiction.

If, however, we measure the popularity of a literary text by subject matter, by success among its intended audience, and meeting audience demands, then popular fiction has always been integral to African American literature. Not only is African American literature grounded in the oral tradition, the most popular of all cultural practices, but, as some critics have argued, African American literature has had its roots in popular literary forms from its very beginning. Writers such as Martin R. Delany and Pauline E. Hopkins, who are to be found in every anthology of African American literature – and thus could be deemed "literary" rather than popular – liberally drew on conventions of the popular in their writings. Delany's *Blake, or the Huts of America* (1859), for example, has been interpreted as "speculative fiction" for its use of the supernatural and the visionary, and Pauline E. Hopkins created the first black female detective in her serialized novel *Hagar's Daughter* (1901–02). In fact, most of Hopkins's novels would be considered popular fiction today, as they easily combine the genres of romance and mystery into their plots. Moreover, if we assume that black popular fiction is directed at a broad black readership, then its roots are to be found in those black-owned publications such as *The Colored American* and other magazines aimed at African American audiences and which regularly featured literature designed to appeal to a broad readership.

From a contemporary vantage point, African American popular fiction has been and is a growing and constantly shifting field that is governed as much by mainstream market demands, trends, and formulaic conventions inherent to different genres, as by the black literary tradition and the demands of an African American reading public to see itself reflected in literature. The range of African American popular fiction is broad and includes easy-to-read bestsellers, genre or formula fiction, such as the romance, mystery, detective fiction, fantasy and science fiction, as well as pulp fiction, or, as it has also been called, "ghetto realism."[2] African American popular fiction is often grounded in the "real" and the "immediate," making explicit reference to the African American experience and issues of concern to the black community, whether in texts geared to a middle-class female audience or an urban male working-class audience.

For popular fiction to work, to be successful and to attract and maintain a body of devoted readers, it has to embody elements of recognition and identification, "approaching a recreation and identification of recognizable experiences and attitudes to which people are responding," Stuart Hall has pointed out.[3] Or, as one scholar of black pulp fiction has said, "Many readers . . . seek a better understanding of the world in which they live. And these writers provide them with characters and episodes they know and can identify with from their daily living."[4] But rather than just holding up a mirror to African American life and affirming the realities of some aspects of black life, it can also serve as a powerful vehicle of critique, often explicitly indicting the social and political forces that create and maintain racial inequalities.

One of the sources of black popular fiction or genre fiction is to be found in the detective tradition, considered to be the most widely read literary genre. African American writers have been writing in this genre since the early twentieth century when *The Colored American* featured Pauline E. Hopkins's *Hagar's Daughter* and J. E. Bruce's *The Black Sleuth* (1907–09) was serialized in *McGirt's Magazine*.[5] Writing for an audience of middle-class, educated blacks, Hopkins and Bruce used the detective convention to critique racism and to focus on racial uplift. In doing so, Hopkins, Bruce, and those that followed in their footsteps have modified established conventions of both the classical and hardboiled detective genres. Stephen Soitos has pointed out in *The Blues Detective*, black writers "manipulate conventional detective structure and characterization which in turn alters the moral message."[6] In the hands of writers such as Rudolph Fisher, who published *The Conjure Man Dies* (1934) during the late Harlem Renaissance, Chester Himes, probably the most prolific and most misunderstood detective fiction writer, and now Walter Mosley, author of the Easy Rawlins series,

African American detective fiction affirms blackness, attributes the detective's success to his blackness and ability to move in two worlds, and to his use of black vernacular.

Chester Himes, credited with breaking the color barrier in American crime fiction,[7] began writing detective fiction in the 1950s and 1960s while living in Paris as an expatriate. He had already published a number of "social protest" novels in the United States and wrote detective fiction primarily to make money. Himes's expertise and mastery of the genre brought him greater recognition in Europe than in his native country. In his novels, Himes appropriates the hardboiled detective novel through the use of Harlem as a setting and a pair of rather uncharacteristic detectives, Grave Digger Jones and Coffin Ed Johnson, who are as violent and corrupt as the neighborhood they serve. The peculiar and sometimes absurdly comic violence that informs his fiction is often misread as violent, sensationalist, and exploitative. Himes's Harlem series is now considered part of his social protest fiction and as a commentary on the world that produced the criminals his detectives are chasing.

Contemporary African American detective fiction has been flourishing with the 1990 publication of Walter Mosley's *Devil in a Blue Dress* and other novels in the Easy Rawlins series. Focusing on private eye Easy Rawlins, a migrant from Texas living in Los Angeles, Mosley uses the hardboiled genre to comment on and critique race and race relations in postwar California. Like his predecessors Grave Digger Jones and Coffin Ed Johnson, Easy Rawlins benefits from knowing two worlds and solves crimes by moving in both the black and the white community. Coming to writing after a career as a computer programmer, Mosley has published six novels in the Easy Rawlins series as well as a collection of short stories and science fiction. His popular success, especially after the movie *Devil in a Blue Dress* starring Denzel Washington as Easy Rawlins, has made him one of the most recognized African American novelists and a spokesperson for black writers.

Today, much of African American detective and mystery fiction is in the hands of women writers and their female detectives, despite the mainstream success of Walter Mosley. Following the example of Dolores Komo's *Clio Browne* (1988), the first detective novel since *Hagar's Daughter* to feature a black woman protagonist, authors such as Valerie Wilson Wesley, Nikki Baker, and Barbara Neely have not only brought a feminist or womanist perspective to the genre, but they also continue a tradition of subversive representation of the detective figure.

Another source of contemporary black popular fiction is the adventure fiction of Frank Yerby. Yerby's thirty-three novels sold more than 55 million copies during his lifetime. His popularity peaked during the late 1940s and early 1950s. Frank Yerby's novels were predominantly written for and read by a white audience – in fact, many devoted white readers were unaware that he was African American – and many of them fall into the category of the Southern historical romance, or the "costume novel," a term Yerby coined himself.

Yerby's relative obscurity and absence from histories and anthologies of black literature illustrates the dilemma of the (black) popular novelist. Scholarship on his work is virtually non-existent and Yerby has been "criticized for not exploring race issues, and ignored when he did."[8] However, looked at from a contemporary perspective, much of Yerby's fiction can be considered the forerunner of contemporary black popular fiction. Yerby wrote in 1959 in "How and Why I Write the Costume Novel" that "the novelist's job is to entertain." In order to do just that, a novel requires the following ingredients: a picaresque protagonist, a sexy heroine, and a "strong, exteriorized conflict." Together with a "lean, economical plot" and set against a historical background, a novel is to please readers, Yerby argued, to "help them endure the shapelessness of modern existence."[9] This formula also exists in much of contemporary popular fiction. While the antebellum South as a setting has given way to contemporary urban America, and white characters have been replaced with black ones, plotlines remained basically the same. Picaresque protagonists still roam the pages of black popular fiction, although their roguishness has been tempered by thirty years of feminism and the emergence of women writers; heroines are still sexy and beautiful, but for many of them the pursuit of a handsome hero and their eventual submission to his desires may no longer be at the top of their agenda.

The emergence of contemporary African American mass or pulp fiction written exclusively for a black audience can be dated back to the publication of *Pimp: The Story of My Life* and *Trick Baby* in 1967 by Robert Beck, better known as Iceberg Slim. Since the publication of Iceberg Slim's books, the Los Angeles-based Holloway House has become one of the largest producers of fiction aimed at a "mass" African American audience; it has steadily recruited black authors, expanded its list of paperback originals, and has called itself "the World's largest publisher of black experience paperbacks" since the 1970s. Holloway House's list of titles covers a wide range of popular fictions, ranging from what Greg Goode has called "ghetto realism" to detective stories, thrillers, historical novels, romances, family sagas, confession stories, autobiographies, and fictionalized autobiographies, as well as erotica and pornography. Holloway House authors, such as Donald Goines, Joe Nazel, and Odie Hawkins, are extremely prolific and almost rival Frank Yerby as the most widely published African American author. A cursory glance at bibliographies of African American literature shows that Holloway House books command a major part of the African American popular fiction market and thus African American fiction as a whole.

The novels of Holloway House can be considered African American pulp fiction and conform in many ways to standard definitions of the genre. They are printed on cheap wood-pulp paper, their plots are often "lurid and sensational," and much of the action revolves around violence and sex. The books have catchy titles, gaudily illustrated covers, brief and livid summaries of the book's content on the back, and prices as low as $1.95 and no more than $5.95. Written in an easily comprehensible style and language, the novels follow a simple formula and a linear and chronological pattern. The language is descriptive – denotative rather than connotative – and the dialogue often graphic. Characters are simple and one-dimensional, and the plot leaves little room for ambiguity. Plots, however, are varied and manifold, ranging from hustler cautionary tales to threats to the African American community, political intrigues and conspiracies against the African American nation, mistreatments by the justice and legal system, and historical injustices against African American individuals and communities.

Though it constitutes a genre of its own, African American pulp fiction is squarely located within the African American expressive tradition. Most Holloway House novels within the ghetto realism subgenre draw on naturalist novels of the 1940s and 1950s and the "protest" novel and prison autobiography of the late 1960s and early 1970s. They share similarities with commercial African American popular culture such as blaxploitation movies of the 1970s, black action movies of the 1990s, and rap music and videos. Given this heritage, African American pulp fiction barely resembles the escapist and fantastic plotlines that dominate much of the market. On the contrary, in bringing together the African American expressive tradition and popular genres, the pulp fiction of Holloway House represents a site in American popular culture where conceptions about African American life in America are scrutinized and contested. While crime and violence constitute most Holloway House novels, their use is never gratuitous; rather they are used to realistically describe the lives of young, urban males whose only chance at success often lies in crime. In doing so, these novels mirror and validate many of their readers' immediate circumstances and environment, but at the same time create a space where these circumstances can be evaluated, where resistance can be imagined, and where contradictions can be resolved. Scholars have seen these novels as "ghetto cautionary tales," a claim that is easily borne out in the pages of Iceberg Slim's autobiography: "if one intelligent valuable young man or woman can be saved from the destructive slime, then the displeasure I have given will have been outweighed by that individual's use of his potential in a socially constructive manner."[10]

Yet embedded in every cautionary tale is a theme of social protest. While the lifestyle of the hustler is not to be emulated by readers, authors make it very clear that he is a product of his environment where poverty leads to crime, and hopelessness to violence.

Holloway House has consistently appealed to an audience of young, urban, and working-class African American men. The books are easily accessible to a popular audience in the black community: paperback and magazine bookstores in the inner city, newsstands, and supermarkets, barbershops, and pool halls, as well as bookstores on army bases overseas. Not surprisingly, novels by Iceberg Slim and Donald Goines, both Holloway House perennial bestsellers, are used in California prisons as part of the Prison Literacy Act, which ensures prisoners are taught how to read.[11] Given that little has changed in American inner-city black neighborhoods over the last thirty years, authors like Iceberg Slim and Donald Goines enjoy continued success among male members of the hip-hop generation. Iceberg Slim, for example, is referenced in the names of rappers Ice T and Ice Cube, and Donald Goines's and Roland Jefferson's novels have been reissued as part of W. W. Norton's Old School Books line of black pulp fiction reprints.

Today, the tradition of black pulp fiction is carried on by the (S) Affiliated publishing company (financed by actor Wesley Snipes, and edited by Marc Gerald, former editor of the Old School series), which recently started publishing a series of novels about black street life directed at young urban readers and patterned after hip-hop and rap videos. These pulps come with a CD and carry advertising for urban gear; they will be sold not in bookstores, but in record and clothing stores that cater to young black customers.[12]

While African American authors have firmly established themselves in the field of detective fiction, they remain few in science fiction. Until the 1960s, when Samuel R. Delany broke the genre color barrier with the publication of his first novel *The Jewels of Aptor* (1962), virtually no black science fiction writers existed. Gregory E. Rutledge, in one of the few critical assessments of African American science fiction, argues that reasons for the absence of African Americans from the genre include the belief among writers, publishers, and critics alike that (white) readers will not read about black characters, the uneasy relationship between people of color and science, socio-economic conditions that prevented the emergence of writers, and conflicts between the "objectivity" of science and the subjectivity of Afrocentric value and belief systems.[13] Yet, features of science or speculative fiction have been part of African American literature from the beginning. Sandra Govan, for example, argues that elements of the supernatural pervade such texts as diverse as Martin Delany's *Blake* (1859–62), Sutton Griggs's *Imperium in Imperio* (1899), Charles Chesnutt's *The Conjure Woman* (1899), and Edward

Johnson's *Light Ahead for the Negro* (1904).[14] George S. Schuyler's novels *Black No More* (1931) and *Black Empire* (1935), generally considered satires on black life during the Harlem Renaissance, liberally draw on elements of speculative fiction; yet, despite the alternative world they present, the novels have never been considered science fiction.

Authors such as Samuel R. Delany and Octavia Butler, who began their publishing careers in the 1960s and 1970s, have done much to open the field to black authors, readers, characters, and to racial themes in general. Given the popularity and longevity of the genre overall, however, there are few other writers who have been equally successful. The stature of Butler and Delany as science fiction writers is immense; both have received the Hugo and Nebula awards – Butler even was the recipient of a McArthur genius grant – and both have been credited for transcending the genre and becoming "literary" writers. Delany, whose writings include science fiction, autobiography, literary criticism, and theory, has been called "one of the field's pre-eminent stylists," and his novel *Dhalgren* sold half a million copies during its first two years, placing it in the ranks of the top ten bestselling science fiction novels.[15] Moving from space opera to fantasy fiction, and from sword and sorcery tales to science fiction theory, his writings have greatly enriched the genre, partly because issues of race and sexuality are at the center of his writings, and partly because of the highly innovative and literary language he has used. Octavia Butler, who started writing science fiction after she attended a workshop with Delany in the 1960s, was the first African American woman to publish in the field of science fiction. Her many novels, though set in multiple universes, realities, and time periods, squarely fit into the African American (and also the feminist) literary tradition. For example, in her novels *Kindred* (1979), *Wildseed* (1980), and the "patternist" series, Butler reworks the issue of slavery – the power one human, extraterrestrial, or organism holds over another, whether through overt force, physical superiority, or mind control – in creative and innovative ways. Other novels – most notably *Parable of the Sower* (1993) and *Parable of the Talents* (1998) – deal with the establishment of new social orders and communities based on equality, social justice, and religious freedom. Her leaders or protagonists are almost exclusively black women who transcend slavery – mentally and physically – and who move on to create community and generations.

Other black science fiction writers have continued to expand the genre for black readers, black characters, and black subject matter. Charles R. Saunders, for example, writes adventure fantasy about African warriors in the sword and sorcery tradition. His trilogy, *Imaro* (1981), *The Quest of Cush* (1984), and *The Trail of Bohu* (1985), locate the superhero and his mythic quest in Africa and amongst African civilizations. Steve Barnes, who generally writes hard-core science fiction with his co-author Larry Nivens and occasionally writes for the TV and book series *Deep Space Nine*, also writes futuristic action adventures and fantasy novels about alternate worlds where historical realities are reversed and where slaves become masters and masters slaves. His novel *Lion's Blood* (2002) is an inversion of American history, where blacks own plantations in the South and where Irish and French work as slaves. Recently, Barnes's wife Tananarive Due has also contributed to the genre with her novels *The Between* (1996) and *The Living Blood* (2001). Jewelle Gomez is the author of *The Gilda Stories* (1991), a pro-feminist vampire adventure that moves from the period of Southern slavery to the present. More recently, Nalo Hopkinson, a native of the Caribbean who now lives in Canada, won the Warner Aspect First Novel Contest for *Brown Girl in the Ring* (1998), a novel that uses Afro-Caribbean folklore and magic in a futuristic setting. Hopkinson has since published two more books – *Midnight Robber* (2000), a novel, and *Skin Folk* (2001), a collection of short stories – both of which engage Caribbean-inspired themes and magic in the context of other worlds. Walter Mosley has also ventured into the field of science fiction with his novel *Blue Light* (1998), as has Harvard law professor Derrick Bell with his *Faces at the Bottom of the Well* (1992).

In the 1970s and 1980s, literature aimed at black readers was mostly restricted to specialty publishing houses, such as Holloway House and black-owned publishers, and to the occasional African American writer at a major publishing house. Now, almost every major publishing house has added an imprint or series directed at African American readers to its repertoire. Random House, for example, has three imprints: Villard/Strivers Row, named after two blocks in Harlem; One World Books, which focuses on multicultural titles that are mostly African American; and Harlem Moon which acquires hardcover titles for Doubleday, another division of Random House. Warner Books established Walk Worthy Books, focusing on commercial fiction with Christian themes; Dafina, an imprint of Kensington Publishing, has cornered the self-improvement market; and Amistad of HarperCollins publishes both critical works and commercial fiction. This trend was preceded by romance publishers which started imprints directed at black women readers in the late 1980s. Sandra Kitt, the most prolific and well-known black romance writer, published her first black romance for Harlequin in 1985. Today black romances flourish in a market where they have both an independent audience and cross-over appeal. Arabesque books, a romance imprint of Kensington Books, the second largest romance publisher, for example, generates about 10 percent of the publisher's net sales.[16] BET enterprises has launched Sepia, its own imprint of trade paperback and mass market titles.

The market for African American popular fiction experienced an upsurge in the 1990s when the number of hardcover books and paperback originals by black authors rose tremendously, giving rise to a new subgenre in African American popular fiction that some have called "sister-girl" and "brotherman" novels.[17] These sometimes steamy novels cover the ups, downs, and sexual politics of romantic relationship from either a female or male perspective. Changes in the class structure of the black community, the consolidation of the publishing industry that resulted in fewer publishing houses and more attention to bestsellers and money-makers (for example, Yale law professor Stephen L. Carter was paid an advance of $4.2 million for his first novel *The Emperor of Ocean Park*, 2002), and advances in technology that led to new advertising and promotional strategies are responsible for the renaissance in African American mass market publishing we witness today. During the 1980s and 1990s growing class distinctions in the black community increased the number of middle- and middle-upper-class black Americans and subsequently produced a greater market of black readers.[18] For example, a 1994 study showed that "African Americans spend more than $175 million per year on books" and that book purchases in the black community rose by 26 percent between 1988 and 1991.[19] According to industry statistics, these numbers have continued to climb and reader demand for black fiction increased even more in the second half of the 1990s. Some of these changes are visible in the meteoric rise of African American book clubs. The African American Book Club Summit, with more than 350 members, for example, hosts an annual cruise, bringing together readers and authors.[20] Other factors contribute to this shift as well: an increase in black-owned publishing companies, a proliferation of black authors, black writers associations, and writing workshops,[21] and an abundance of websites that deal with many aspects of commercial or mass market literature aimed at black readers. These demographic changes and increased demand for novels by black authors also did not go unnoticed by the mainstream publishing industry. Beginning in the early 1990s, publishers began to look at blacks as customers and consumers whose demands deserve attention and started recruiting black authors who could write in those genres.

The internet and computer technology have greatly contributed to the increased availability of black popular fiction by giving more authors opportunities to publish their works and to promote themselves. Self-publishing, a method of publishing used by black authors in the past, has become easier with technologies such as desktop publishing, on-demand printing, and the dissemination of literature through the internet. Many novels that have become bestsellers among black readers were self-published first. The most famous case in point is E. Lynn Harris's novel about bisexuality, *Invisible Life* (1991), which sold more than 10,000 copies at book parties, in barber and beauty shops, and in black bookstores before it was picked up by Anchor Books. Harris has since published seven more novels and has become one of the most successful and popular black male writers today. Many of the new African American imprints of major publishing houses draw on this reservoir of self-published novels for their catalog.

Much of this revolution in black publishing has been made possible by women readers, writers, editors, and publicity agents. Women, on average, read more books than men do and are also responsible for the book purchases in their household. The African American Literary Book Club (www.aalbc.com) claims that 84 percent of its members/visitors are female, college-educated, and middle-class, a profile that may easily characterize the majority of contemporary African American readers.[22] Author Terry McMillan is generally credited with inaugurating this renaissance in commercial fiction with the publication and success of her novel *Waiting to Exhale* (1992). As mentioned, detective fiction is predominantly written by women, as is romance fiction, and the so-called girlfriend novel to which McMillan has given rise. Talk-show host Oprah Winfrey has also done much to popularize the writings of African American women, such as Toni Morrison and Maya Angelou, but also lesser-known writers, such as Pearl Cleage and Lalita Tademy. Any novel featured on Oprah's Book Club is guaranteed to reach bestseller status and often spawns a cottage industry of related books. Much of the book industry is also headed by women; Toni Morrison was one of the first African American editors at Random House in the 1970s; today most of the imprints mentioned above have black women executive editors, wielding considerable power on what gets published.

While much of the success of black popular fiction today is driven by black readers, it is also true that novels such as McMillan's *Waiting to Exhale* and Mosley's *Devil in a Blue Dress* have had tremendous cross-over appeal. *Waiting to Exhale* not only dispelled the myth that blacks don't read but also showed publishers that white readers will pick up a book by a black author for entertainment. Henry Louis Gates has argued that more and more Americans now have the capacity "to identify with black characters; the black experience is a metaphor for the larger human experience."[23] This ability to identify with the "other," I would argue, is also part of the growing similarity between black and white middle-class readers and their experiences in contemporary suburban America.

Current African American popular or commercial fiction is too large a field to be condensed into a simple formula, but what many of the divergent genres have in common are plotlines that revolve around the emergence and consolidation of a growing black middle class. As such, they can be called black novels of manners that have picked up on Terry McMillan's focus on chronicling the social and love lives of the black petty bourgeoisie. Characters are almost exclusively members of a suburban middle class with college educations, who have overcome, or never even faced, racial discrimination and/or economically disadvantaged backgrounds. They have succeeded in a capitalist society; they may live in predominantly black worlds, but they are not very different from the worlds white characters inhabit in similar novels aimed at white readers. Unlike the African American pulp fiction described earlier that focuses outward, onto the neighborhood and streets and external problems that face the inner-city black community, the contemporary black novel of manners focuses inward, onto creating and maintaining family and relationships. Much like their eighteenth- and nineteenth-century predecessors, contemporary African American novels deal with social customs and mores, the pursuit of happiness and romance, and professional success. Not surprisingly, much emphasis is placed on those material possessions that constitute or mark a new class: education, careers, lineage, houses, taste, and cars to name just a few. Most important, though, is how characters relate to each other in these new social circumstances; women and men, parents and children, gays and straights, all struggle to figure out where one belongs and what blackness means in the twenty-first century.

At this point in time African American popular fiction may have come full circle. Today's authors have become household names and are receiving generous advances for their work; they are making their presence felt in all genres of popular fiction and are reaching readers in unprecedented numbers. They draw on a rich legacy of black popular fiction as they are forging ahead to capture new markets and readers. Since its beginnings at the turn of the twentieth century, African American popular fiction has attempted to balance the demands of its reading public with the conventions and formulas of genre fiction. In this sense, African American popular fiction makes a contribution to the African American literary tradition and to mainstream commercial fiction as well. Readers want to see themselves represented in the texts that they read, and this is perhaps more true for African American readers as a historically excluded population. Whether in science fiction, pulp fiction, or detective fiction, in romance or easy-to-read bestseller, black authors have claimed these genres as their own, modifying and expanding them to write about issues of interest to black readers. As popular fictions with wide distribution networks not limited solely to bookstores, they have the potential of reaching an audience – both black and white – far bigger and more diverse than that of more "literary" novels. Some novels exist within the mainstream, others outside it; some celebrate the achievements of a new class or chronicle love affairs, others critique the virulent racism that keeps large numbers of African Americans disempowered or imagine different worlds altogether where racism is examined. Collectively, they provide a site on which issues affecting African American life can be scrutinized, critiqued, and – depending on the genre – reimagined.

NOTES

1. Michael Korda, *Making the List* (New York: Barnes & Noble, 2001), p. xxiii.
2. Greg Goode,"Donald Goines," *Dictionary of Literary Biography*, Vol. 33: *Afro-American Fiction Writers after 1955* (Detroit: Gale, 1984).
3. Stuart Hall, "Notes on Deconstructing 'the Popular,'" *People's History and Socialist Theory*, ed. Raphael Samuel (London: Routledge, 1981) p. 233.
4. Quoted in Gwendolyn Osborne, "The Legacy of Ghetto Pulp Fiction," *Black Issues Book Review* (September 2001): 50.
5. *Hagar's Daughter* is available as part of Hazel Carby, ed., *The Magazine Novels of Pauline Hopkins* (New York: Oxford University Press, 1988); *Black Sleuth*, ed. John Cullen Gruesser (Boston: Northeastern University Press, 2002).
6. Stephen Soitos, *The Blues Detective: A Study of African American Detective Fiction* (Amherst: University of Massachusetts Press, 1996), p. 4.
7. Charles L. P. Silet, *The Critical Response to Chester Himes* (Westport: Greenwood Press, 1999).
8. Bruce A. Glasrud and Laurie Champion, " 'The Fishes and the Poet's Hands': Frank Yerby, A Black Author in White America," *Journal of American and Comparative Cultures* 23 (Winter 2000): 15–21.
9. *Harper's Magazine* (October 1959): 145–150.
10. Robert Beck, *The Naked Soul of Iceberg Slim* (Los Angeles: Holloway House, 1971), p. 7.
11. *Black Issues Book Review* (Sept. 2001): 56.
12. See: Martin Arnold, "Coming Soon: Paperbacks that Sound Like Hip-Hop," *New York Times* (Sept. 21, 2000).
13. Gregory E. Rutledge, "Futurist Fiction & Fantasy: The *Racial* Establishment," *Callaloo* 24.1 (2001): 236–252.
14. Sandra Y. Govan, "Speculative Fiction," *The Oxford Companion to African American Literature*, eds. William L. Andrews, Trudier Harris, and Frances Smith Foster (New York: Oxford University Press, 1997).
15. James Sallis, *Ash of Stars: On the Writings of Samuel R. Delany* (Jackson: University Press of Mississippi, 1996), pp. x, xv.
16. Theola Labbe, "Black Books in the House" *Publishers Weekly* (Dec. 11, 2000): 36.
17. For the increased purchasing power of African Americans in the 1980s and 1990s and the response of American capitalism to it, see Robert Weems, *Desegregating the Dollar: African American Consumerism in the Twentieth Century* (New York: New York University Press, 1998).
18. "The Trouble with Success," *Publishers Weekly* (Dec. 12, 1994): 33.
19. African American Book Club Summit, http://www.pageturner.net/Cruise/index.htm

20. For a useful introduction to the black writer's market, see Jewell Parker Rhodes, *Free Within Ourselves; Fiction Lessons for Black Authors* (New York: Main Street Books, 1999).
21. "In the Market for Romance," *Black Enterprise* (Dec. 1996): 62.
22. http://aalbc.com/aalbcdemographics.htm
23. Quoted in *The New York Times*, July 26, 2001.

SELECTED MAJOR WRITERS OF THE POPULAR NOVEL

Nikki Baker
Steven Barnes
Robert Beck
Connie Briscoe
Octavia Butler
Bebe Campbell Moore
Samuel R. Delany
Eric Jerome Dickey
Tananarive Due
Donald Goines
E. Lynn Harris

Odie Hawkins
Chester Himes
Nalo Hopkinson
Sandra Kitt
Terry McMillan
Walter Mosley
Joe Nazel
Barbara Neely
Charles R. Saunders
Valery Wilson Wesley
Frank Yerby

PART III

AFRICAN AMERICAN VOICES
FROM MARGIN TO CENTER

10

JERRY W. WARD JR.

Everybody's protest novel: the era of Richard Wright

In the early years of the twenty-first century, a discussion of the American protest novel or of Richard Wright as a protest novelist is an exercise in retrospection. It seems from certain angles of critical thought that literary history demands a deliberate, not always happy, effort to remember things past. The glance back privileges the claims of history over the speculations of aesthetics. It is especially necessary to let history speak in the case of Wright and the African American novel. Our postmodern sense of aesthetics can betray us and muddle our understanding of the necessity for protesting social policies and cultural beliefs through the mechanism of the novel. Looking backward helps us to remember at least two points. The African American novel originated in the nineteenth century as the use of literacy and writing more for purposes of enlightenment than for the pleasures of entertainment. Richard Wright stands in a special relationship to the form he sought to develop, because he did not abandon the original purposes of the black novel for the sake of being modern. He stuck to the purpose of using fiction to illuminate conditions and possibilities as they affected blacks and whites in America, particularly in matters of social psychology. The novel, for Wright, was a weapon against culturally sponsored ignorance as well as a medium for expressing his intellectual and artistic vision.

Contemporary criticism of fiction can still find some salience in examining the problem novel, the sociological novel, or the novel grounded in social realism. To understand Richard Wright historically, we must deal with artistic uses of language that have special targets. It would be rare to find any fictions, especially those from former imperial domains, described simply as works of protest or complaint. They are more commonly considered as instances of writing back, a gesture involving more parity than does the asymmetrical power relation implicit in the very notion of protest. Wright was indeed writing back. In twentieth-century literary usage, "protest," a word inextricably associated with "race," might be taken as a pure product of America. Protest was a pejorative code word for work of inferior artistic accomplishment. Unless we want to play games that ignore or blatantly revise the language of history, we initially accept that Richard Wright's novels from *Native Son* (1940) to *The Long Dream* (1958) are instances of protest fiction. We thereby admit a "fact" about the reception of Wright's novels within his lifetime, and that "fact" compels us to remember that African American fiction was as excluded from the canon of American literature as were African American citizens from the right to vote in Mississippi. Thus, we acknowledge the books were read at the time of their publication more closely as documents that had a kind of outlaw status in the republic of letters than as genuine examples of literature. The admission begins to expose something about ideological commitments and reading habits in the past. And it may inspire us to take a fresh look at what the word "protest" obscures.

At the same time, we must assert that Wright's novels do not fit well in a box marked "protest," the confining space accorded them in the 1940s and 1950s. Protest is a position, not a genre. Wright's novels can be read more fruitfully outside that racist box, and we do not need to beg the question of whether Wright created propaganda or literature. His novels instruct; they challenge beliefs about the human condition. They remain in dialogue with the past and the present, responding to and transcending the situational imperatives of their time. They enable us to trace dynamics and thematic strategies in the tradition of African American fiction. Wright's unique development of the *thesis novel* or the *novel as essay* was a landmark moment in American and African American literature. In a sense that readers are only recently beginning to understand, Wright did succeed in the task of writing *everybody's* protest novel.

To cast light on why Wright's novels were almost simultaneously praised and condemned as instances of protest fiction, we might contrast James Baldwin's seminal essay "Everybody's Protest Novel" (1949) with Ann Petry's "The Novel as Social Criticism"(1950). Baldwin and Petry describe the minefield and the boundaries that Wright chose to risk crossing. First published in the June 1949 issue of *Partisan Review*, Baldwin's essay was a brief against the American protest novel, the epitome of which he took to be Harriet Beecher Stowe's *Uncle Tom's Cabin* (1852). Baldwin demanded that there be a distinction among genres. The protest novel, he contended, too often resembled the pamphlet, and the demands of pamphleteering hindered the novelist in his true pursuit, the discovery and revelation of truth. Truth, for Baldwin, was not reducible to a proposition or an assertion. On the contrary, it was a constituent of lived action, a willed commitment to "the human being, his freedom and fulfillment; freedom which cannot be legislated, fulfillment which cannot be charted."[1] Baldwin's protest against protest fiction, then, is balanced upon understandings of what freedom and fulfillment might be. However the words *freedom* and *fulfillment* are defined, it is clear that Baldwin objects to the impossibility of protest loosening them from the constraints of its own discourse. Protest also fails to be an adequate pathway toward "truth." It champions the importance of rules, of that which can be legislated and charted (or perhaps chartered). The protest novel, with its avowed aim of bringing greater freedom to the oppressed, displaced "truth" with matters that ultimately would cause the death of freedom. The protest novel did violence to language and credibility. To argue for the value of the protest novel on the grounds of its intentions and on the premise that the good of society took priority over style or characterization led to the confusion of literature with sociology. Like others who have argued from such aesthetic principles, Baldwin was convinced literature must not be tainted by social use.

In arguing against the validity of the protest novel because it blurred generic boundaries, Baldwin was not promoting an African American view of what literature should be. The very utility many black readers assumed was a given in literature made protest novels self-defeating. Like sociology, the protest novel supported a passion for categorizing. Thus, human beings are transformed into ciphers and real problems are made comfortably remote. Baldwin accused *Native Son* of falling into the trap of the protest novel, of reinforcing the social framework it was designed to challenge, of failing to destroy the myth of black inhumanity. Wright failed because Bigger Thomas was less a character than a categorization unable to transcend the status of stereotype.

By linking the problems of art and sociology with problems of philosophy and theology, Baldwin indeed raised complex questions about the limits of the protest novel as a genre, about the status of Wright's fiction, and, by extension, the interrelations of black and white American literature. Baldwin's specialized use of language precluded his seeing alternative meanings of protest in the realm of literature, meanings that Ann Petry read accurately.

Writing in defense of her own novel, *The Street* (1946), as a work involving social criticism, Ann Petry was keenly aware that critical dismissal of protest literature was a matter of fashion, a way of promoting the idea of art for art's sake. She argued that all great novels were a species of propaganda, reflecting the writer's awareness of the political, economic, and social events of her or his time. Dickens, Tolstoy, Hemingway, Steinbeck, Dostoevsky, George Eliot, and Wright all projected such an awareness in the medium of fiction.[2]

Petry confronted what Baldwin ignored. Uncle Tom and all his children were icons of accusation in the context of American literature. Proposing that the story-line for many novels of social criticism emerged from *Uncle Tom's Cabin*, Petry pointed to a crucial matter in reader-response. Attitudes toward African Americans in the 1940s were still influenced by arguments to justify slavery, and these attitudes could not be divorced from how a largely white readership in the 1940s and 1950s read literature. Consigning protest novels to the status of the extra-literary was clearly a defensive posture, a way of denying the importance of the emotional pain and guilt readers actually experience. Literature does not evade truth; it may provide readers with an overdose of "truth," real and imaginary.

Committed to the full range of truth, Petry championed *Native Son* as a fine example of the novel as social criticism. Wright's characterization of Bigger Thomas was remarkable. People might talk about Bigger as if he actually existed. She recommended that any novelist planning to write about race relations in America should "reread *Native Son* and compare the small talk which touches on race relations with that found in almost any novel on the subject published since then [1940]" (1117). It was Wright's fidelity to the language of human interaction that made his novel powerful; his mastery of technique was, from the perspective of a fellow novelist, more important than his "sociology." If readers failed to discriminate between documents that were the results of disciplined investigation and works that came from a novelist's social awareness, blame should be located in the community of writers. The confusion was in the mental "eye" of the beholder, not in the creative imagination of novelists. Petry made clear why a description of Richard Wright as a protest writer secures his place in literature as a tradition. And her retort to the position Baldwin held should make us aware that the critical response to African American novels was often a deformation of how they were actually read. This is particularly true of the critical response to Richard Wright.

After the publication of *Uncle Tom's Children* (1938), short stories that were powerful depictions of the racial climate in the American South, Richard Wright was acclaimed as an extraordinarily gifted and promising young writer. When his second book, *Native Son*, was published in 1940, it was received as a rare first novel, a magic mirror which revealed as yet unexamined psychological monstrosities to the American public. Everyone who read it was forced to acknowledge the uncanny accuracy of Wright's vision or to become exceptionally defensive in retorting that such horrors as Wright described could not happen in America. Given the dynamics of racial understanding and misunderstanding in 1940, Wright's novel was indeed a phenomenon, being just enough of a work of art and just enough of a polemical treatise to keep readers off balance. Wright made the nemesis of race in the United States the subject of his novel. It was impossible for American readers to be untouched by its stinging indictment and by the specter of the novel's main character Bigger Thomas.

Native Son appeared one year after John Steinbeck's *The Grapes of Wrath*, and the social criticism in both novels invited comparison. Both were indebted to the kind of fiction proletarian writers produced in the 1930s. Yet, Steinbeck's critique of the American economy, of labor exploitation, and the plight of those forced to migrate from the Midwest to California because of drought and a flagging economy did not stem from the same political tradition as Wright's novel. Steinbeck protested the harshness of nature, class discrimination, and capitalism. He was not protesting about the emotionally charged subject of race and environment. Like Wright, he provided an uncompromisingly realistic story about unfortunate people; on the other hand, Steinbeck did not explore areas of feeling and social concern as incendiary as those Wright surveyed. *Native Son* was a novel designed to induce fear and trembling.

Out of his experiences in the South and the North, out of a vision of social realities fine-tuned by his association with the Communist Party, Wright boldly outlined a frightening aspect of race in America: the possibility that incipient pathology among young adolescents who were consistently denied the chance to develop healthy psycho-social identities might manifest itself in extreme violence. *Native Son* asserted that deferred dreams might explode in the Bigger Thomases of America.

The question raised by the novel's thesis was ultimately this: given the racial mores of America or the racial contract[3] that governed life in the United States, would it ever be possible for black men and white men who were linked by a common history to achieve a common humanity? As Wright would propose five years later in *Black Boy* (1945), the answer depended on whether the language and concepts used by whites and blacks came to have identical referents. The question was not new, but Wright's posing the question from the perspective of a "bad nigger," a nihilistic teenager, was. Wright had created a new kind of African American novel, one that invited not sympathy but pangs of complicit, national guilt. Wright added a new twist to the penchant in certain nineteenth-century black novels for integrating recognizably literary discourse with arguments often kept at a safe distance from "literature." The first two parts of the novel, "Fear" and "Flight" were a ripping story of despair and crime. "Fate," the third part, was a full-blown essay on economic determinism and racial outcomes disguised as a lawyer's defense of a guilty client. Wright had stripped the black novel of the literary decorum obtained in earlier works by such novelists as Charles Chesnutt, Paul Laurence Dunbar, James Weldon Johnson, Nella Larsen, Zora Neale Hurston, and Langston Hughes. In its palpable violations of the expected, *Native Son* was a formal objective correlative for its subject matter. Wright was demanding that his readers refashion their reading habits and feel the onus of his question.

Wright had slipped the yoke and changed the joke with regard to the criteria for literary judgments. *Native Son* provided a fine dilemma. Critics and general readers were obligated to select new criteria in accord with their political ideas, beliefs about literature, and racial identification. Interpretation of Wright's shocking presentation of race was the crucial problem. Race was an old theme in American fiction, a major theme since the appearance of James Fenimore Cooper's Leatherstocking novels in the early nineteenth century. But race in America was more than a mere concept of classification.

It was an ingrained feature of the American mindset, at once overwhelming and personal. Did the unrelenting "objectivity" of *Native Son* overshoot the bounds of literary realism and naturalism?

Judging from the initial critical responses to *Native Son*, we might surmise that critics knowingly mixed their concerns for the novel as art with their deeper concerns regarding emotional reaction and racial actualities. Moreover, both Marxist and non-Marxist critics set up Wright as a golden calf for the sake of literary politics. Wright's own intentions to express spiritual hunger, oppression, and some of the horrors in American life in writing the novel, which he spelled out in the essay "How 'Bigger' Was Born," were overvalued or undervalued or ignored. Many of the newspaper reviews emphasized the "power" of the novel to thrill or frighten. Used loosely, the word "power" might describe any number of states of feeling.

Such description allowed critics to avoid dealing seriously with Wright's novel as art. Some reviewers took a clue from Dorothy Canfield Fisher's introduction to the novel. Fisher located the novel's primary value in its treatment of black adolescent psychology. Wright had sought to obviate a simple reading of relations between the oppressor (Dalton, the slum-lord philanthropist) and the victim (Bigger Thomas) through a careful use of symbolism. Fisher vacillated between admitting that Wright's novel was comparable to the work of Dostoevsky in its wrestling with a human soul in hell and describing the novel as "the first report in fiction we have had . . . from those whose behavior-patterns give evidence of the same bewildered, senseless tangle of abnormal nerve-reaction studied in animals by psychologists in laboratory experiments."[4] Fisher set the pattern for interpreting Wright's novel as an imaginative social document, as a book worthy of comparison with a major Russian novelist, and as an innovative contribution to American literature. Wright's accomplishment was compared with that of Dostoevsky, Dreiser, and Steinbeck. It was noticed that Wright, unlike Dreiser, did not permit readers to think out his main character in realistic terms, because he insisted on making authorial interpretation of character. Authorial intrusion made Bigger Thomas too articulate and not recognizable as a stereotype of the lower-class Negro. This spoiled the story and the possibility of sympathizing with the tragedy of the Negro race. It was precisely Wright's intention to preclude such sympathy. As he had recognized in his "Blueprint for Negro Writing" (1937), one of the major faults of the African American novel up to the early twentieth century was its begging white America to acknowledge the humanity of black people. If *Native Son* had the potential of alienating white readers and aggravating existing prejudices, it was a risk Wright could not avoid.

It was not the possibility of alienating black or white readers that figured strongly in the response by most black critics. Alienation was one of the costs of telling the truth. The dominant idea that recurred in African American reviews of *Native Son* was that literature had moral effects, that these effects could be translated, if the readers were "responsible," into social action. The Platonic notion that literature could change society was shared in varying degrees by liberal white and Marxist critics. However, for many of the Marxists, *Native Son* was not sufficiently proletarian. Some black critics took the notion to its logical extreme: *Native Son* was neither "literature" nor social document but a literal weapon in racial struggle. This radical view is instructive, for it reminds us that Wright's work was then and continues to be caught in the cultural wars between those who hold fast to some form of black nationalism in their literary politics and those who insist that all literature should function within the shadows of the universal.

One of the great moments in American literary politics that has much to reveal about responses to the African American novel and to Richard Wright himself was initiated by David L. Cohn's review in the *Atlantic Monthly* and Burton Rascoe's "Negro Novel and White Reviewers" in *The American Mercury*. These provoked Wright into making public replies.

Cohn took the position that Wright had written a study in hate that did not discriminate between good and bad whites and that used Bigger Thomas as a racial symbol. Wright's placing the responsibility for Bigger's plight on white society did not conform to fact. Fact, for Cohn, was that black rights were gradually being extended throughout the United States and that blacks had no monopoly on injustice. He could not understand why Wright seemed to call for a second Civil War to free the black masses. Cohn conveniently forgot that there was a quite legitimate struggle for civil rights in the United States. He was offended that Bigger's lawyer was a Jew, because it seemed that Wright was not paying sufficient attention to Jewish history and several centuries of oppression. No Jews behaved like Bigger Thomas. Cohn accused

Wright of lacking an adequate vision of history and the laws of expedience; the end result of the novel would only make what Cohn called "a tolerable relationship intolerable."[5]

Wright replied to Cohn in the June 1940 issue of *Atlantic Monthly*. He was keenly aware that the social climate of America made it more difficult for a black to reply to a Jew than to a white American. He refused Cohn's recommendation that black action be modeled on Jewish experience, because expedience did not guarantee liberation. Moreover, Wright understood that Cohn implied he should judge the plight of blacks in a relative rather than a specific sense. Wright was forthright in saying he did not wish to be a traitor to his race or to humanity, that he was an artist, not a scientist. If Cohn's recommendations were a model of how racial history ought to be conceived, they went against the grain of Wright's social experiences and beliefs.

Reacting negatively to the praise Wright's novel had received, Rascoe saw intellectual anarchy among critics who went haywire about anything that seemed to be a social document exposing so-called "conditions." Rascoe lashed Wright for his violations of aesthetic decorum. In addition to aesthetic violations, Wright had written a novel in which the message was loathsome. Just as Cohn invoked the collective Jewish experience to undermine the validity of Wright's historical expectations, Rascoe used his personal experience to prove that Wright's thesis about the impact of environment was unfounded. He had observed Wright's very civilized behavior at the Dutch Treat Club and Wright's success in making money.[6]

In a letter to the editor of *The American Mercury*, Wright suggested that Rascoe had introduced unheard-of criteria into literary criticism. His personal life had nothing to do with the merits of his novel. Wright asserted that he did not create literature to satisfy aesthetic expectations or pander to public tastes. He wrote out of the background of his experiences, and he had the right to depict the actions of people he did "not agree with, Aristotle to the contrary!"[7]

Wright's treatment of the nemesis of race in *Native Son* did secure him a place in American literary history, but it also made him subject to the oppressive forces operative in the literary establishment of the 1940s. The pressure of being the most visible black novelist in America might have hastened his decision to choose exile.

The novels Wright produced during his exile in France (1947–1960) bear the marks of his quite different experiences as a black man in the United States and as an acclaimed writer in Europe; they are also testaments to Wright's maturation as an artist. *The Outsider* (1953) and *The Long Dream* (1958) received mixed responses. When read in relation to Wright's earlier fiction, the first seemed a radical departure and the second, an attempt to recover the thematic rhythms of his early short fiction about the American South. *Savage Holiday* (1954), which gave evidence of Wright's strong interest in psychoanalysis and the need to free himself from matricidal impulses, was deemed a potboiler that did not merit critical attention.[8]

It is not difficult to understand why critics avoided *Savage Holiday*. Initially published as an Avon paperback, the novel explored the psychological illnesses of Erskine Fowler, a white insurance executive in New York. Behind a mask of harmony and order, Fowler is a most insecure person. He is simultaneously attracted to and repulsed by his neighbor Mabel Blake, a woman of easy virtue, who provokes his long repressed Oedipal impulses. Fowler is responsible for the accidental death of her son Tony, and he feels tremendous fear and guilt. He transfers his guilt feelings to Mabel, blaming her for being a bad mother and a loose woman. At the height of his outrage, he murders her with a butcher knife and then surrenders himself to the police. Wright's surgical exploration of Fowler's psychopathology was well written, but the critics remained silent about the novel. They seemed to know that a black writer's exposure of potential criminality among the model citizens of America would have little success with postwar readers in the early 1950s.

From the vantage of critical evaluation, *The Outsider* was a worthier target. How did Richard Wright's distance from his native land and from the Communist Party affect his fiction? Was his second novel technically superior to *Native Son*? Had Wright become a world-class artist? The critics who interpreted *The Outsider* most successfully were those who saw it as an experiment in representing a larger sense of human possibilities than was present in *Native Son*. Influenced by his reading of Kierkegaard's philosophy, Dostoevsky's *Crime and Punishment*, and Camus's *The Stranger*, Wright departed from the expected limits of protest to present a complex meditation on the spiritual malaise of the twentieth century.

In the story of Cross Damon, a working-class intellectual, Wright embodied a critique of Communism through the prisms of race and existential longing. Damon is a man quite dissatisfied with the "normal" responsibilities of a social being; he longs for the absolute freedom that is possible only outside the process of history. When a subway accident frees him to fashion a new identity, Damon finds himself caught in a web of protective lies, political bad faith, and cold-blooded violence. By shifting the grounds for violence from the sociological domain of *Native Son* to the realms of philosophy and the human condition, Wright advanced the black novel in a new literary dimension. Those who expected Wright to be the voice of his people or to rehash stereotypes were disappointed.

The young, radical Lorraine Hansberry considered Cross Damon to be "the symbol of Wright's new philosophy – the glorification of – nothingness." Indeed, in a moment of ideological correctness, Hansberry accused *The Outsider* of being "a propaganda piece for the enemies of the Negro people, of working people and of peace" and Wright of having become a writer who negated the reality of the black struggle for freedom.[9] Wright's new interest in philosophy was not welcomed by critics who felt he should focus on matters of race. Writing for the influential *Saturday Review*, Arna Bontemps dismissed the novel's philosophical importance with a provocative metaphor: "He [Wright] has had a roll in the hay with the existentialism of Sartre, and apparently he liked it." In a strained attempt to redeem *The Outsider* for Negro literature, Bontemps identified Cross Damon's problem as woman, not the problematics of alienation.[10] Critical assessment of Wright was again swinging between the poles of art and propaganda, for his achievement was being measured against the backdrop of spectacular anti-Communist witch-hunts in the American Congress and the growing momentum of black demands for civil rights.

One of the more balanced assessments came from Henry F. Winslow's review in *The Crisis*. Winslow recognized that Cross Damon had "the peculiar perspective of standing at once *inside* and *outside* of our culture." Winslow judged *The Outsider* to be worthy of comparison with the work of Homer and Strindberg, an achievement "hardly equaled by any other American novelist who ever lived." He concluded that Wright's novel was "an eloquently articulate reading of the handwriting on the iron walls of contemporary civilization."[11] A few of the positive reviews gave special notice to the fact that although Cross Damon was a Negro character, the subject matter of the novel was not the plight of the Negro. Orville Prescott applauded this fact, because it allowed readers to take a greater interest in Wright's ideas, in Wright's finding cogency in the nihilistic depths. "That men as brilliant as Richard Wright," Prescott asserted, "feel this way is one of the symptoms of the intellectual and moral crisis of our times."[12] In his sophisticated review of the novel, Granville Hicks noticed that it was "one of the first consciously existentialist novels to be written by an American." Despite what Hicks called Wright's "persisting clumsiness of style," he was pleased that *The Outsider*, like *Invisible Man*, was only "incidentally a book about Negroes." It was a book about twentieth-century man, one that "challenges the modern mind as it has rarely been challenged in fiction."[13] It is indeed remarkable that what is arguably Wright's most powerful and haunting work of fiction was positioned between the rock of racial and political specificity and the hard place of the universal.

In *The Long Dream* (1958), the last novel published before his death, Wright returned to the American South as a primal scene for the drama of race, and he drew upon his memory of the South to create for his protagonist, Rex "Fishbelly" Tucker, a childhood and a youth that actual circumstances made it impossible for him to enjoy. To be sure, *The Long Dream* was a return to the subject of relations between blacks and whites that Wright had explored in *Uncle Tom's Children*. A far more accomplished writer than he had been twenty years earlier, Wright focused his story on the problems of growing up as a black male in a Southern middle-class environment, on the bonding between father and son, and on racial hypocrisy. To the extent that we might argue for an autobiographical dimension in the novel, it would concern Wright's unattainable dream of a positive relationship with his own father.

In his exploration of the family narrative, Wright created a novel that seems to complement Chester Himes's *The Third Generation* (1954), a powerful exploration of an ill-fated relationship between a mother, visually "white," who abhors the fact of her blackness, and a son, who is ultimately unable to deal with the contradictions of color-consciousness. Nevertheless, it was not Wright's aim to probe that kind of social pathology. The pathology he did explore was that constituted by *de jure* segregation and by the fact that some whites were willing to sponsor black criminal activities when they could share the profits. The stakes for such transgressions of racial mores are high. Fishbelly's father is murdered by his silent partner, the local Chief of Police, when it is discovered he has been smart enough to save incriminating evidence regarding their complicity in illegal practices. The novel is an elaborate tale of living the ethics of Jim Crow, a fleshing out of the autobiographical sketch that had been appended to the second edition of *Uncle Tom's Children*. Unlike *Native Son*, *The Long Dream* had no comprehensive ideology or philosophy embedded in its structure. It was a multilayered exposure of dilemmas that always deferred the American Dream for a Southern black family that yearned to be upwardly mobile. It was to some degree Wright's coming to terms with his feelings about race in America after more than a decade of exile from his native land. Well informed about the struggle to secure civil rights after the United States Supreme Court decision of May 1954, in *Brown v. Board of Education*, regarding equality in educational opportunity, Wright was not blind to the fact that the American South was changing rapidly. At the same time, Wright knew that change could be cosmetic rather than systemic. What he exposes in *The Long Dream* are the deep structures of racial behaviors and the habits of the heart that remain constant despite change, that transform dreams into nightmares.

Given that the protagonist, like Wright himself, chose exile in France, the novel sent a message that not enough had changed in America since 1946. It was not a message to be welcomed by those most optimistic about racial progress.

One of the major criticisms of *The Long Dream* was that Wright himself had refused to change. Saunders Redding, one of the most respected black American critics of the time, found numerous flaws in the narrative. There was too much repetition, apathy displaced knowledge, and the characterizations were not convincing. The book was sensational, and the plot moved with "spasmodic haste." Redding associated the technical flaws in the novel with what he took to be the deadly effects of Wright's exile.[14]

Redding associated Wright's technical flaws or shortcomings in verisimilitude with a lack of adequate information about progressive change in America's racial contract. Or, as James Baldwin might have repeated, Wright was once again rejecting the artistic obligation to accept life. From hindsight it does not surprise us that Wright's severest critics in the late 1950s received *The Long Dream* as a brash violation of the "rules" for acceptable African American fiction. We must recall that Ralph Ellison's *Invisible Man* (1952) and James Baldwin's *Go Tell It on the Mountain* (1953) had set new standards for representing the Negro's life experiences in the United States. Mining classical western motifs and narrative structures, the potentials of symbolism, and the potential of American humor to provoke laughter, Ellison had succeeded in convincing readers that black Americans were thoroughly integrated in the fabric of American civilization.

Baldwin's novel had exploited the ancient themes of guilt and conversion. Even if these themes were elaborated in a world apart, the murky world behind the racial veil, they were sufficiently related to matters that preoccupied Hawthorne and Faulkner and narrated in a manner Henry James might have found appropriate for the art of fiction. Neither novel protested overmuch about the dominant, complacent sentiments of mid-twentieth-century Americans. *The Long Dream* was an assault, a throwback to the jeremiads of the 1930s, a wake-up call for which the liberal readers of the late 1950s did not feel prepared.

The reviewers for such pacesetting intellectual journals as *Commonweal* and *Partisan Review* were forthright in claiming that Wright was a crusader, not a writer, that *The Long Dream* was a mere "scaffolding of an idea," not a work of art. Wright spent his talent for ideas, not art, and he could not deliver a balanced judgment because his vision of race reflected a black point of view. Indeed, William Dunlea, the reviewer for *Commonweal*, felt that Wright's racial interests outweighed his concern for art to the extent that *The Long Dream* was "the most racist of all the author's anti-racist fiction."[15] Writing for *Partisan Review*, Irving Howe was discerning enough in his judgment to note that the novel was deeply psychological, "a nightmare of remembrance." And Maxwell Geismar likewise noted that Wright was returning to the trauma of his early youth and adolescent experiences. The novel was uneven as fiction, but it was "true" in the sense that literature about depression and tragedy is true.[16]

Granville Hicks saw a new direction in Wright's work. He was convinced Wright was moving closer to Ralph Ellison, subordinating racial preoccupations to more existential concerns. Nevertheless, *The Long Dream* was closer to *Native Son* than to *The Outsider*. Wright had not moved close enough, had not put sufficient distance between himself and the urge to illustrate what it meant to be a Negro in America. Wright's interest in violence could be understood but not admired on literary grounds. In a surprising twist of the critical knife, Hicks contended that the source of Wright's power, his use of symbols, was problematic; Wright was not a realist but a person who used and was used by symbols. Despite the fact that Wright was fully capable of touching his readers' emotions, Hicks believed there were few signs of growth in Wright's artistry.[17] Wright, to be sure, was deeply wounded by criticism that suggested he had not moved as a novelist far beyond the limits of *Native Son*.

Just as in a qualified sense Wright might be acclaimed as the novelist who wrote everybody's protest novel, equally strong qualifications must be used in speaking of the era of Richard Wright. It is a bold act of critical license to propose that Richard Wright dominated the African American sector of the American literary scene between 1940 and 1958. Wright's steady production of fiction and nonfiction from the publication of *Native Son* to his death in 1960 did ensure that he was discussed by serious readers and considered the leading black writer of the time. His early association with the Communist Party, as Addison Gayle has described in detail, did make him one of the favorite targets for such government agencies as the Federal Bureau of Investigation (FBI), Central Intelligence Agency (CIA), and the US Department of State during the Cold War period.[18] Fame alone, however, is not a sufficient warrant for hasty fabrication of literary periods. It does not honor Wright to give his name to a moment of literary history that can all too easily be deconstructed.

Our understanding of the African American novel deepened by considering the period 1940 to 1960 as one of complicated transitions. Black fiction was evolving in concert with the efforts of black Americans to secure their constitutional rights as full citizens of the United States and to destroy the legal and extralegal barriers that precluded full participation in American social and political life. Novelists were as varied in their aesthetics and ideas about the function of literature as were the social activists who operated under the umbrella of the Civil Rights Movement. The ideas of solidarity and unity of purpose that emerged after 1960 with the advent of the Black Arts/Black Aesthetic Movement did not obtain for most African American novelists of the 1940s and 1950s. They pursued their craft much along the attitudinal lines Langston Hughes had drawn in his 1926 manifesto "The Negro Artist and the Racial Mountain." What did obtain for the novelists was Richard Wright's leadership in providing models of yoking literary experimentation with social criticism of America's racial problems.

Wright's novels were examples of how one might incorporate ideas about history and race, philosophy, modernism and change, human psychology, politics and capitalism in a racist culture, gender, sexuality, language, and action in fiction. Wright was indeed singular in his sustained commitment to creating fiction that assaulted consciousness, an American literature that sought to provoke and strengthen human awareness of the struggle for meaning in a world that seemed progressively alienating.

It is most judicious to read the novelists who followed Wright in time as artists who are linked to him within the pattern of call-and-response, which is a central feature of African American literary tradition and of situated uses of literacy in African American cultures. To be sure, Wright's influence can be traced in works that overtly deal with his dominant themes as well as those novels that offer strongly contrasting perspectives on being and race. For example, William Attaway's second novel, *Blood on the Forge* (1941), shares Wright's concerns with the negative rewards for Southerners who migrate to the North in quest of "better opportunities," but Lloyd L. Brown's *Iron City* (1951) is a counterweight to Wright's preoccupation with the black character as victim. The early novels of Chester Himes – *If He Hollers Let Him Go* (1945), *Lonely Crusade* (1947), *Cast the First Stone* (1952), and *The Third Generation* (1954) – do have affinities with Wright's use of naturalism in addressing the racial situation in America; Himes, however, was far more committed to the portrayal of individual characters and less to the task of integrating a thesis with an imaginative narrative. Despite Ellison's denials, it is apparent that he embeds the special perspective of Wright's novella "The Man Who Lived Underground" in the structure of *Invisible Man*. Ann Petry's *The Street* (1946) may be considered a womanist or feminist complement to Wright's exploration of the city and race, but it is more important that Petry's novel is itself within the tradition of black women novelists' engaging issues of race, gender, and class as is Dorothy West's *The Living Is Easy* (1948). And it is sobering to remember that Gwendolyn Brooks's novel *Maud Martha* was published in the same year as Wright's

The Outsider. With its fine poetic techniques and focus on the inner life of a woman, *Maud Martha* is quite remote from Wright's masculine, polemical interests in existentialism and the impossibility of absolute freedom. Brooks did not use fiction as a megaphone for announcing rage. In short, the works by Wright's most immediate contemporaries are not exactly in a school of naturalism and social realism for which Richard Wright served as headmaster. Our ongoing study of the African American novel must respect the integrity of their individual talents. It is far better to honor Wright for the place he quite obviously occupies in the tradition of African American novels: that of the twentieth-century Prometheus who appropriated the fire writers still use in exploring the universe of fiction and protesting its absurdities.

NOTES

1. James Baldwin, "Everybody's Protest Novel," in *Notes of a Native Son* (Boston: Beacon Press, 1968), p. 15.
2. Ann Petry, "The Novel as Social Criticism," *Call and Response: The Riverside Anthology of the African American Literary Tradition*, eds. Patricia Liggins Hill, *et al.* (Boston: Houghton Mifflin, 1998), pp. 1114–1119.
3. See Charles W. Mills, *The Racial Contract* (Ithaca: Cornell University Press, 1997).
4. "Introduction," *Native Son* (New York: Harper & Brothers, 1940), p. x.
5. David L. Cohn, Review of *Native Son*, *Atlantic Monthly* (May 1940): 659–661.
6. Burton Rascoe, "Negro Novel and White Reviewers," *The American Mercury* (May 1940): 113.
7. Richard Wright, "Rascoe-Baiting," *The American Mercury* (July 1940): 376–377.
8. See Claudia Tate, *Psychoanalysis and Black Novels: Desire and the Protocols of Race* (New York: Oxford University Press, 1998). Tate's brilliant discussion of *Savage Holiday* is invaluable for reassessments of Wright's life and works.
9. Lorraine Hansberry, Review of *The Outsider*, *Freedom* (April 1953): 7.
10. Arna Bontemps, Review of *The Outsider*, *Saturday Review* (March 28, 1953): 15–16.
11. Henry F. Winslow, "Forces of Fear," *The Crisis* (June–July 1953): 381–383.
12. Orville Prescott, Review of *The Outsider*, *New York Times* (March 18, 1953): 29.
13. Granville Hicks, "The Portrait of a Man Searching," *New York Times Book Review* (March 22, 1953): 1, 35.
14. Saunders Redding, "The Way It Was," *New York Times Book Review* (October 26, 1958): 38.
15. William Dunlea, "Wright's Continuing Protest," *Commonweal* (October 31, 1958): 131.

16. Irving Howe, "Realities and Fictions," *Partisan Review* (Winter 1959): 133; Maxwell Geismar, "Growing Up in Fear's Grip," *New York Herald Tribune Book Review* (November 16, 1958): 10.

17. Granville Hicks, "The Power of Richard Wright," *Saturday Review* (October 18, 1958): 13.

18. See Addison Gayle, *Richard Wright: Ordeal of a Native Son* (Garden City: Anchor Press/Doubleday, 1980).

11

HERMAN BEAVERS

Finding common ground: Ralph Ellison and James Baldwin

Placing James Baldwin and Ralph Ellison side by side, as contemporaries who chose to write novels for the purpose of limning the depths of the American scene, is a critical enterprise that insists as much on a critical leap forward as it does a harkening back. The reasons for this, of course, have a great deal to do with the state of American literary and racial politics in the years following World War II. At that time, with the Civil Rights Movement bringing about calls for racial integration and equal protection under the law for African American citizens, there grew to be a great need for black writers to fulfill the role of articulating what would come to be understood as "the black experience," by an audience often bewildered by the malevolence of Malcolm X and the Nation of Islam and the unwavering insistence by Martin Luther King Jr. that justice could only be achieved by peaceful means. How could a people deemed at one time so incapable of eloquence and critical thought suddenly be so persistent in their claims for equality, in their demands that their humanity be fully recognized? Who among them could bring clarity to their motivations?

To be sure, African American writers had, as early as Phillis Wheatley and David Walker, taken seriously the need to "speak truth to power," aiming their messages toward a readership that was consciously thought of as white. With the publication of Richard Wright's *Native Son* in 1940, there emerged on the literary scene a novel meant to sound the alarm for whites that their negligence and hostility were soon to be repaid a thousandfold by blacks angry at their mistreatment. Tracing the origins of the protest novel back to Harriet Beecher Stowe's *Uncle Tom's Cabin*, Baldwin observed in "Everybody's Protest Novel," published in 1949, that the purpose of the protest novel was to bring "greater freedom to the oppressed."[1] He rejected Wright's *Native Son* on similar grounds, insisting that what was needed was fiction that limned the contours of African American experiences more carefully in order to articulate the complexities of those experiences. Similarly, Ellison would insist that, because he saw no distinction between "art and protest,"

Invisible Man was the product of a more complete vision, one that included anger, but also irony and comedy alongside the tragedies that often marked black life.

Thus, any attempt to engage in a comparative discussion on James Baldwin and Ralph Ellison must focus on the relationship between woundedness and narrative. Invariably, their fictions treat men who are injured by their circumstances and thus are forced to find ways to give narrative shape and breadth to the damage done them. Even a cursory analysis of their respective novels leads to the conclusion that each understood suffering to be an inimical part of black life. Ellison's and Baldwin's characters are engaged in attempts to fashion for themselves adequate narrative space, to become agents, actors, and subjects.[2] At the level of plot, their characters must contend with the fact that their injuries often leave them isolated and alone, incapable of articulating the extent and nature of their injuries or, conversely, so aware of their wounds that they ponder them to the exclusion of everything else. In some instances, they are prone to acts of forgetting, of trying to distance themselves from injury; to view it as an aberration rather than as a consequence of their embattled presence. What this means is that these protagonists have to confront the obstacles that grow up between injury and telling.

But there are profound variances in terms of how Baldwin and Ellison approach the wound. For Ellison, the wound becomes something the hero must embrace wholeheartedly, prompting the story of how he received it, as well as how he has come to understand it as the symbolic capital intrinsic to a life lived free of illusion, whereas in Baldwin the wound is the only readily available sign that pain is meaningful. Narration in his fiction, then, seeks to achieve a moral legibility that will allow his characters to understand their problems as outgrowths of toxicity and contamination. Perhaps a better way to work out the difference between Ellison's and Baldwin's symbolic use of injury is that the older writer, relying on African American folk materials like the blues, understood the wound as the cure, while Baldwin's close proximity to the Civil Rights Movement led him to distrust such a conclusion; for the former, then, the wound is part of the ritual of becoming, while the latter values the wound for its diagnostic potential. Thus, the wounds both writers depict call for testimony, if only because the act of testifying is the only way their characters can make their way to sanity and wholeness.

In Ellison's writing, suffering is rendered in tragicomic terms. Believing in the liberating potential of mythopoetic chaos, Ellison's novels embrace the idea of death and rebirth, often beginning with the Gothic construct of being buried alive and investing that construct with an irony that turns it on its head. Thus, in *Invisible Man*, we find that his narrator is living underground in a basement of an apartment on the edge of Harlem. But rather than making this death-in-life into a symbol of his protagonist's demise, Ellison instead refashions it into hibernation. "I have been hurt to the point of abysmal pain, to the point of invisibility," Ellison's hero relates in the Epilogue of the novel.[3] In *Juneteenth* (1999), Reverend Hickman preaches a sermon over the prone body of his young protégé, Bliss, who lies in a coffin. At the sermon's climax, Bliss sits up in the coffin, as if he has risen from the dead, to signify the rebirth embodied by the end of black enslavement. Again, death functions to shift the reader's attention away from the sense that it involves finality and toward the notion that death involves the transgression of boundaries. These boundaries must be transgressed, Ellison's novels insist, if we are to emerge on the other side and thus enter into a new level of consciousness. Pain, therefore, is necessary to the process because it marks the ritual process the hero must endure in order to achieve insight.

Baldwin's novels provide us with characters whose suffering can take both spiritual and physical forms. Indeed, two of his characters, Leo Proudhammer in *Tell Me How Long the Train's Been Gone* (1968) and Arthur Montana in *Just Above My Head* (1979), suffer heart attacks (in the former, life-threatening; in the latter, life-ending) that signify, on the one hand, that these are men who have suffered psychic wounds that take on physical manifestations and, on the other, that they are mortal, that no matter how heroic they may be, they cannot transcend their physical limitations. Like John Henry in African American folklore, their hearts give way while they are engaged in the Herculean task of trying to remake the world.

John Grimes of *Go Tell It on the Mountain* (1952) and Rufus Scott of *Another Country* (1962) endure suffering of a different sort. For them, the very air they breathe serves as a constant reminder of how their lives are beset by hatred and bitterness. Each of them falls, albeit with distinctly varied results. In John's case, he undergoes a spiritual journey that leads him to accept a judgmental and punishing Christianity as the price of belonging. Rufus drives his lover insane, abandons his life as a jazz musician, and in a state of total emotional disrepair, opts to commit suicide.

Neither Fonny in *If Beale Street Could Talk* (1974) nor David of *Giovanni's Room* (1956) is fated to die a physical death. But their suffering denotes the "life in death" each endures within the realm of social death. Each man is caught up in a web of criminality and guilt that threatens to destroy him: Fonny is falsely accused of rape and thus must find ways to ward off the despair and hopelessness he knows the wider society wants him to embrace; David's life is marked by his inability to give or receive love. As he ponders marriage to a woman he does not love, his gay French lover is being executed for murder.

Though none of his novels achieve the level of accomplishment demonstrated in *Invisible Man*, Baldwin can nonetheless be regarded as an important commentator on American race relations. Unlike Ellison, who sought to understand the ways black and white embody their common origins, Baldwin's novels assume a greater interest in matters of racial injustice. It would be misguided, though, to suggest that race is their primary concern, since they are ultimately distinguished by their unflinching attention to sexuality. While one might conclude that this applies only to his depiction of homoerotic encounters, a more accurate portrayal of Baldwin's fiction would highlight the manner in which he works out the relationship between sexuality and power; thus relationships of all types get represented in his work. Indeed, Baldwin was among the first African American novelists to explore sexuality as an integral part of African American identity. His contribution to the novelistic tradition comes in the form of his ability to imagine the problem of American identity in terms of both sexuality and race. In looking at the six novels Baldwin produced, we can understand how sexuality is used to map the contours of power, as an index of his characters' ability to love, and as a way to alter the terms upon which we base notions of racial progress. It is in this way, however, that we can begin to understand the "common ground" Ellison and Baldwin stake out as novelists. Both men wanted to expand our sense of what constituted the human potential for self-recovery. Ellison insisted that black life, even at its most downtrodden, is marked by a resilience and style that can best be understood through the blues. Baldwin, while seeking to understand American racial injustice, wrote fiction that argues for the ways morality is rendered legible through the ability to love.

Ralph Ellison's first novel was the product of over eight years of labor, begun as World War II was drawing to a close and completed while America was in the midst of the Korean War. Though he had some brief flirtations with the radical left, Ellison had come to consider himself an outsider in the realm of secular politics, preferring instead to understand America as a ritual site where the mythic and symbolic revealed the deep structure of the national project. This is reflected in the structure of *Invisible Man*, which begins with a Prologue and ends with an Epilogue. These sections constitute the novel's "narrative present." The twenty-five chapters occurring between them are related as an extended flashback that chronicles twenty years in the protagonist's life. This structural delineation is important because it allows us to account for the novel's radical tonal shifts. In the Prologue and Epilogue, Ellison employs a rhetorical playfulness similar in tone to that found in Dostoevsky's *Notes From the Underground*. Chapters 1 through

25 adopt a more varied tone, one moment reflecting a surrealism that renders all rhetorical surfaces suspect, enacting the maneuvers necessary to convey a tone more rollicking, able to contain circumstances both absurd and tragic, the next moment, a tone beset by pathos and anger.

The novel begins with the protagonist relating the moment of his grandfather's death, where he provides the narrator with cryptic advice that, due to its ironic nature, will take the entire novel to decipher. After he tells the narrator's father that he has been "a spy in the enemy's country," and that his obsequiousness has been a mask he has assumed in order to plot his oppressors' demise, the grandfather states, "Live with your head in the lion's mouth. I want you to overcome 'em with yeses, undermine 'em with grins, agree 'em to death and destruction, let 'em swoller you till they vomit or bust wide open" (*Invisible Man* 16). What follows from this is the narrator's maddening struggle to first understand, and then apply, his grandfather's injunction. Thus, after being expelled from college, nearly being lobotomized, recruited as an organizer for the Brotherhood, and pursued by a black nationalist named Ras the Destroyer, the narrator comes to realize that, to the people he seeks to influence, he is "transparent as air" (575).

In the novel's penultimate scene, the hero discovers that the Brotherhood plans to incite a riot in Harlem, not as a way to bring about change, but to use the moment for rhetorical capital. As he moves through Harlem, amidst scenes of looting and violence, the hero realizes that he has been a pawn of the Brotherhood all along. But just as he reaches this conclusion, he is pursued by Ras the Destroyer and his men who see him as the scapegoat and seek violent retribution. Eluding them, the hero ends up in a dark basement where, in order to have light, he has to burn all the important documents in his briefcase. Symbolically, he undergoes a ritual death that leaves him reborn in the role of writer. As the novel draws to a close, the hero ruminates on his grandfather's advice and observes:

> Could he have meant – hell, he must have meant, the principle, that we were to affirm the principle on which the country was built and not the men, or at least not the men who did the violence. Did he mean say "yes" because he knew that the principle was greater than the men, greater than the numbers and the vicious power and all the methods used to corrupt its name?
>
> (*Invisible Man* 574)

Writing his memoirs, the "invisible" narrator achieves a new level of self-consciousness – and conscientiousness – when he proposes, "The fact is that you carry part of your sickness within you, at least I do as an invisible man. I carried my sickness and though for a long time I tried to place it in the outside world, the attempt to write it down shows me that at least half of it lay within me" (*Invisible Man* 575). Having reached such a conclusion, Ellison's hero engages in a commentary on African American citizenship, as well as the state of black writing. The passage above stands as an implicit critique of Wright's social realism, which tries, "to place it in the outside world," insisting that the blues offered a way to understand that self-recovery lies in the act of metaphorizing trouble; to do so is, in Ellison's mind, an act of self-realization that has the power to transform a nation.

As David Yaffe observes, in the time between the publication of *Invisible Man* in 1952 and *Juneteenth* in 1999, "Ellison's inability to produce a follow-up to *Invisible Man*, was the bane of his existence."[4] After Ellison's death in 1994, his literary executor, John Callahan, undertook to assemble a coherent piece of fiction from the numerous drafts and sections he left behind. Following Fanny Ellison's injunction that the novel have "a beginning, middle, and end," Callahan culled enough material to publish "a single, self-contained volume." As a result, *Juneteenth* revisits the territory covered in *Invisible Man*, making use of "African American folktales, the blues, the dozens, the swing and velocity of jazz." It is a novel that has a great deal to say about the responsibilities that come with freedom as well as the posturing that accompanies a life in politics. However, it could just as easily be argued that *Juneteenth* is a novel that ruminates on the vagaries of race in American culture, including a serious treatment of what it means to "pass" from black to white in light of the fact that blacks and whites share a past neither wishes to claim. Finally, it is a novel that explores the struggle on the part of the son to break free of the influence of the father. As the novel begins, Senator Sunraider is making a speech before Congress, extolling the virtues of American citizenship. Significantly, Sunraider's speech partakes of the rhetorical flourishes to be found in the black sermonic tradition even as he renders a speech characterized by race-baiting and mean-spiritedness. In a strange turn, he calls for Americans to spurn memory in favor of more forward-looking policies. "Thus again," he asserts, "we must forget the past by way of freeing ourselves so that we can reassemble its untidy elements in the interest of a more human order."[5]

However, the moment is cut short when an assassin shoots Sunraider and leaves him near death. In the hospital, in a state of delirium, Sunraider calls for the Reverend A. Z. Hickman. The remainder of the novel demonstrates Ellison's strategic depiction of the wound as the force prompting the voicing of memory. We find out that once upon a time, Senator Sunraider was a young boy named, significantly, Bliss. The name comes from Hickman, who is present at the time of his birth and who chooses the name because "that's what ignorance is." Raised by Hickman among blacks, young Bliss acquires a reputation for being a great preacher, much like Hickman, who refers to himself as "God's Trombone." Ellison contrasts the improvised, collaborative format of the sermon against the seductive, illusory world of cinema. While watching a silent film, Bliss sees a woman he takes to be the mother who abandoned him at birth. Undertaking to find her, Bliss passes out of the black world, opting to "become" white and eventually being elected to the US Senate. The novel's ending, which leaves Sunraider/Bliss's condition in doubt, signals Ellison's belief that for all its racialist contradictions, its reliance on the cult of personality, and its subsequent elisions of human complexity, America is an unfinished project, one we will have to imagine and improvise into being.

If Ellison's novels move away from social realism to embrace surrealism and the expansive, open-ended possibilities of myth, James Baldwin's *Go Tell It on the Mountain* (1953) fuses the *Bildungsroman* and the spiritual conversion narrative in order to traverse the concatenations of Baldwin's life. It seems fitting, then, that *Go Tell It on the Mountain* should involve life in the Pentecostal church, in which Baldwin served for three years as a child preacher. Thinking about the men and women who people the Temple of the Fire Baptized and the fact that many of them were probably Southern migrants whose lives were characterized by the move from segregated, sometimes dehumanizing, conditions to Northern cities in which their living conditions were no less segregated and their prospects no less bright, a child preacher would be reason to celebrate. Setting maturation and aspiration against salvation, the novel's protagonist, John Grimes, is a young boy entering puberty at the same time that he feels pressured to become Saved, a predicament which crystallizes in the novel's first words: "Everyone had always said that John would be a preacher when he grew up, just like his father."[6] The problem, the reader quickly discovers, is that John's biological father is dead and thus the "father" to which people refer is his stepfather, Gabriel Grimes, a deacon in the Temple of the Fire Baptized, who looks at John and sees "the face of Satan" (27).

Go Tell It on the Mountain is distinguished in its use of the "limited" narrator, whose omniscience we must depend upon to understand the characters' motivations apart from their declarations of religious devotion. For example, though John assures his mother that he will "try to love the Lord," one of the novel's most poignant scenes has John watching a film whose main character is a woman dying of tuberculosis amidst a life of debauchery. John views the film and concludes that he wants "to be like her, only more powerful, more thorough, and more cruel; to make those around him, all who hurt him, suffer . . . and laugh in their faces when they asked pity for their pain" (39). Baldwin describes this woman in hyperbolic terms:

> She walked the cold, foggy streets, a little woman and not pretty, with a lewd, brutal swagger, saying to the whole world: "You can kiss my ass." Nothing tamed or broke her, nothing touched her, neither kindness, nor scorn, nor hatred, nor love. She had never thought of prayer. It was unimaginable that she would ever bend her knees and come crawling along a dusty floor to anybody's altar, weeping for forgiveness. (39)

There are two aspects of this description that make it worthy of comment. First, Baldwin makes a radical break from both racial and sexual convention when he has his main character, a black male, be inspired by a white female, and indeed, a white female who manifests what might be described as a masculine posture. The significance of this needs to be understood as Baldwin's effort to subvert, once more, the impulse so deeply entrenched in African American fiction by male writers, that black men should look within the race for models of behavior. By having John identify spectatorially with a white female who embodies transgressive behavior, Baldwin insinuates John's sexual difference and articulates the manner in which Baldwin advocates an alternative strategy for the formation of a black male subjectivity that eschews the notion that masculinity and femininity are mutually exclusive sites in favor of a consciousness that seeks to manifest the best characteristics of both. In many ways, the conflict is a metaphor for what may have been Baldwin's own ambivalence: the novel as the announcement of his dissatisfaction with Christianity with its final scene of "salvation" suggesting nonetheless that the novel came into being through spiritual struggle.

Go Tell It on the Mountain marks the passage of his protagonist from sin to salvation or from guilt to redemption, but Baldwin's second novel, *Giovanni's Room*, offers a protagonist, David, whose "innocence" is nonetheless destructive to those who try to care for him. As the novel ends, set to return to his home in the United States, David tears up a letter announcing the day his former lover, Giovanni, is to be executed. Symbolically, the wind blows pieces of the letter back onto him, as if to convey the persistence of memory and the tangibility of his guilt. The novel has depicted David's homosexual relationship with Giovanni in order to suggest the ways that socially constructed categories like "gay," "straight," "man," or "woman," ultimately undermine human beings' ability to reach outside themselves. If the first novel was about the desire to escape, Baldwin's second novel informs us that without the capacity to love there is little chance of escape, which means fragments of the past stay with us in spite of our best effort to eschew them.

Set in and around Paris, *Giovanni's Room* (1956) is distinctive in the history of the African American novel because all of its characters are white. Though Baldwin would not have viewed this as an avoidance of racial themes, it does provide the reader with a reason to understand the novel as a rumination on what Baldwin sees as the kind of self-delusion that leads whites to scapegoat blacks. As Kemp Williams has observed, "Baldwin utilizes [in *Giovanni's Room*] a metaphor pervasive in western cultures: the body as container for the emotions."[7] Thus, the reader sees the things that happen *in* David as opposed *to* him. Because of this, he is a catalyst for disaster; his self-absorption leads him to hurt people because he is lacking in anything resembling empathy for the suffering of others. When he decides to abandon Giovanni, he can only think of his own discomfort and shame. Baldwin's plot provides him with a way to dramatize the ways that the instantiation of guilt can completely undermine our personality. In this sense, the novel can be read as both sexual and racial allegory.

Published to mixed reviews, Baldwin's third novel, *Another Country* (1962), revisits the intersection between race and sex portrayed in *Giovanni's Room*.[8] What makes this novel a departure from the earlier novels, perhaps, is its deeper and more resonant investment in social protest. Unlike his first two novels, which featured characters who exist removed from the wider world, *Another Country* revels in its portrayal of characters who come together across lines of race, class, and sexual preference. In this, the novel demonstrates that it is possible for individuals to love and care for one another, irrespective of their background. But, of course, Baldwin's intention is to suggest that love happens in the world, and thus it is jeopardized by the fragility of the human spirit and the human propensity for disloyalty.

Baldwin begins the novel with Rufus Scott, a jazz drummer, who, as the novel begins, can be found wandering the streets of New York, "so tired . . . that he scarcely [has] the energy to be angry; nothing of his belonged to him anymore."[9] The novel's first section deals with Rufus's demise. In a moment meant to suggest the depth to which he has fallen, Baldwin shows us Rufus's life on the night he meets Leona, a good-hearted white woman from the South who falls in love with him, only to be driven insane by his distrust and self-loathing. We see Rufus up on the bandstand, playing drums in "the last set of his last gig," only seven months before. Baldwin includes a metaphorical gesture that states directly the novel's thematic tension. As Rufus accompanies him on drums, a young saxophone player launches into a solo that begs insistently, "Do you love me? Do you love me? Do you love me?" (*Another Country* 9). This is an important question, not only because it forms the question that will render Rufus's impending suicide so tragic, but also because it hangs over every relationship in the novel. There is Rufus's best friend, Vivaldo Moore, a struggling writer who becomes romantically involved with Rufus's sister, Ida. There are Richard and Cass Silenski, whose marriage suffers after Cass has an affair with Eric, an Alabama-born actor who is bisexual and involved with Yves, his French lover.

At the novel's core lies the issue of integrity and the struggle to maintain it in the face of the constant assaults directed at those who dare to love. The novel suggests that who we are as individuals, our ability to construct a unified sense of self, is reliant on the ability to love unconditionally, which makes it possible to place what we have on the line. What each character, save Eric, fails to understand is that there is no safe haven; love cannot provide a refuge from a hostile world. Indeed, it is Eric alone who is capable of giving and receiving love without any hint of self-recrimination or loss of integrity. It is not that Eric is lacking in self-consciousness, but his bisexuality symbolizes his ability to accept love from whomever comes his way, be they male or female. Unlike David, who believes that homosexuality is an evil to be shunned and a reason to feel shame, Eric understands that love is inalienable, irrespective of where it comes from or in what quantity. Thus, he can bring himself to romantic encounters with Cass, Vivaldo, Yves, and Rufus and be present in the moment, a trait that Baldwin admires and believes that humans should emulate fully. It is perhaps for this reason that we can regard *Another Country* as a novel that best reflects Baldwin's admiration for the nineteenth-century novelist Henry James. For in a manner that is reminiscent of James, *Another Country* provides us with characters whose talents lie in their presentations of legible surfaces that the novel's limited omniscient narrator reveals to be manifested on false premises and self-delusion. In a novel that is much longer than either *Go Tell It on the Mountain* or *Giovanni's Room*, Baldwin's ambitious undertaking often goes awry in *Another Country*. The reason, as Albert Murray would later lament, is that Baldwin's Rufus Scott seemed to reflect such one-dimensionality that one could not believe that a jazz musician would be so bereft of personal resources. Moreover, Murray insisted, the Harlem Baldwin creates is one which reflects more in the way of sociological analysis than it does in terms of its complexity. In that sense, then, *Another Country* failed to achieve its artistic ends.

While Murray's remarks, which appear in his book *The Omni-Americans*, do possess merit, one has to consider, nonetheless, that his analysis considers Baldwin's fiction solely in terms of its role as racial discourse. We must contend with the novel's tenacious approach to the question of what it means to search for love. Ultimately, the novel reflects Baldwin's sense that love is doomed when it adheres to the categorical boundaries imposed by American society. Thus, when we look at Rufus's relationship with Leona, we can see that Baldwin's decision to imprison her in an insane asylum is indicative of his belief that the invalid categories that grow out of race and sexuality are the sign of the nation's inability to come to grips with its history. *Another Country* is meant to dramatize the destructive potential denial and dishonesty can unleash.

Baldwin published his fourth novel, *Tell Me How Long the Train's Been Gone* (1968), six years after the publication of *Another Country*. What distinguishes this work is Baldwin's use of a bisexual black man as the protagonist/narrator. In this instance, Leo Proudhammer, a black actor who has gained some measure of success, must attempt to conceptualize a role for himself in the black resistance movement. In a novel written at the end of the 1960s, published in the year of Martin Luther King Jr.'s death, the novel is perhaps an effort on Baldwin's part to ruminate upon his own celebrity. Though critical reception of the novel was less than enthusiastic, it is worthwhile to consider John Roberts's assessment of the novel as an ambitious effort that fails because its reach exceeds its grasp.[10]

An appropriate connection can be made between *Tell Me How Long the Train's Been Gone*, written in Baldwin's "middle period," and his last novel, *Just Above My Head* (1979), because Baldwin portrays two men: Leo Proudhammer and Arthur Montana, artists who have achieved great public stature but whose status does not spare them the inner turmoil shared by all black men. Further, both novels use the parable of the Prodigal Son as a structuring principle for their plots. Leo and Arthur are similar in that both men have intense relationships with their older brothers. In Leo's case, he begins his life admiring his brother Caleb, whose life takes a variety of turns, ranging from time in prison to a life as a minister. For Arthur, it falls to his brother, Hall, to narrate his story. Both texts reflect the irreconcilability to be found in the parable; the older brother comes to be the arbiter of the younger brother's tale. For Leo and Caleb, they fall into a state of conflict when the latter embraces Christianity and thus comes to be in judgment of Leo's lifestyle. For Hall, his act of narrating Arthur's life, speaking for him when he cannot speak for himself, is a way for him to seek healing and understanding of his own life.

But what also distinguishes these books is that they allow the reader to consider the role of the black artist in contemporary society. Though the 1960s marked a time when black artists achieved a level of visibility among whites previously unheard of, Baldwin's experiences in the public sphere led him to question his effectiveness as a writer. *Tell Me How Long the Train's Been Gone*, as John Roberts suggests, reflects "Baldwin's internal struggle with his role as an artist/celebrity and civil rights spokesman during the 1960s. The black celebrity has two choices: he can become a 'fatcat,' as Leo is labeled at one point, and withdraw into the protective shell of his success, or he can use his status as a symbol for the black community."[11]

In response to such anxieties, Baldwin attempted to explore the pressures a racist society places on black men and women trying to love one another. In *If Beale Street Could Talk* (1974), Fonny Hunt, a sculptor, is in love with Clementine (Tish) Rivers, who is pregnant with his child. After a confrontation with a racist policeman, Fonny is accused of raping a Puerto Rican woman, who promptly disappears from New York, making it next to impossible for Fonny to prove his innocence. Though she is young and undereducated, Baldwin's decision to narrate the story from Tish's point of view strains credibility to near the breaking point. For example, Baldwin requires Tish to comment on the American legal system, but it seems clear that he cannot raise the novel above the level of melodrama. Indeed, to characterize Baldwin's later fiction in this way is appropriate, given his propensity to incorporate social commentary into his work. But Baldwin's use of melodrama also reflects the time period in which he is writing. At a time when Baldwin may have felt ambivalent about how he was being received in the black community, a novel in which a black man is imprisoned despite his innocence allowed him to manifest moral legibility through the juxtaposition of characters in situations where there is a clear delineation between good and evil.

As Keneth Kinnamon has suggested, the antagonist in *If Beale Street Could Talk* is the American legal system.[12] Hence, Tish must bear the narrative responsibility for commenting on matters that she is either too young to know about or lacking in the educational experiences necessary to form an opinion about. The novel ends with Tish entering labor and Fonny being released from jail after posting bond. Inexplicably, however, his father, despondent over his plight, has committed suicide. It represents a pyrrhic victory because the woman who accused Fonny of raping her has gone insane. Baldwin has given us a glimpse through flashback of what Fonny and Tish's lives will be like: Fonny will be an artist, and Tish will have the baby and care for the household. Thus, the novel's progressive gesture of giving a woman voice is undone by Baldwin's inability to push the plot beyond the confines of melodrama. Moreover, the novel lacks the weightiness of *Another Country* or *Giovanni's Room* because nothing happens *inside* the characters. Rather, things happen *to* them and they react. Baldwin's abandonment of the modality found in the Jamesian novel of manners leads him away from the nuanced characterizations to be found in his earliest fiction, particularly *Go Tell It on the Mountain* and short stories such as "The Manchild," "Sonny's Blues" and "This Morning, This Evening, So Soon." More than *Another Country* perhaps, *If Beale Street Could Talk* incorporates elements of protest that, as Murray insisted, are evocative of the sociological problems to be found in the black community and Baldwin's constant assertion that love is the only weapon that can withstand the assault. The problem is that his ability to produce believable characters is compromised by his capitulation to popular trends.

Baldwin's last novel, *Just Above My Head*, published in 1979, revisits many of the themes which readers of his fiction would, then, have found familiar. He takes the opportunity once again to portray Christianity as morally bankrupt and perverse. Indeed, his characters are only able to assume moral coherence when they abandon it. We have two brothers: Hall and Arthur Montana. Hall is narrating the story in the wake of Arthur's death of a heart attack. As Darryl Pinckney wrote concerning the novel's limitations, Hall's narration "becomes more urgent and elliptical, as if he were uneasily aware that the story he wished to tell were too large."[13] Pinckney points to several moments in the novel where Baldwin glosses over crucial information, as if the story's epic sweep were more important than nuance or detail. One aspect of the book that Pinckney and others recognize is that the homosexual, in this case Arthur, is no longer the figure outside.

The effect of this, when Baldwin allows it, is that Hall is an articulate spokesman for what Warren Carson describes as "a definitive statement of black masculinity."[14] And indeed, we see that sexual practices do not, in any way, compromise Baldwin's sense that masculinity issues form a different space in the cultural imagination. Rather than suggesting that racial identity is the foundation of masculinity, Baldwin instead reveals sexuality as the means for black men to discover the true substance of their humanity. In such a scheme, the men and women in *Just Above My Head* can collaborate rather than contend with one another. Though there are certainly figures in the novel who are victims – Crunch, for example, ends up institutionalized; Peanut is abducted and murdered by white supremacists; Red becomes a heroin addict – ultimately, Baldwin suggests that male bonding is the way to liberation. What makes Baldwin's emphasis on masculine power different, as Carson insists, is his constant (since 1954) call for men to acknowledge their mutual need, to escape what he referred to as the "Male Prison."

In looking at the respective careers of James Baldwin and Ralph Ellison, it is clear that each has made lasting contributions to American letters and in the process forced us to reimagine what it means to be human. However, this common ground is by no means easily traversed when we consider the fact that Baldwin's stature as a novelist is overshadowed by his public life and

Ellison's public life was thrust upon him by the success of his idiosyncratic approach to the American character in *Invisible Man*. Certainly, Baldwin's novels work to diagnose America's ills by dramatizing what happens when love is compromised. It could be that the most effective way to link Baldwin and Ellison is to propose that their respective fictions are peopled by prodigals and pilgrims. What they share is the sense that black life, though often a "lowdown, dirty shame," is nonetheless worthwhile.

NOTES

1. James Baldwin, *Nobody Knows My Name* (1955; rpt. New York: Dial Press, 1961), p. 18.
2. Michel-Rolph Trouillot asserts that "history involves peoples in three distinct capacities: 1) as agents, or occupants of social positions, 2) as actors, in constant interface with a context, and 3) as subjects . . . as voices aware of their vocality." See *Silencing the Past: Power and the Production of History* (Boston: Beacon Press, 1995), p. 23.
3. Ralph Ellison, *Invisible Man* (1952; rpt. New York: Vintage Books, 1982). All subsequent references are to this edition and will appear parenthetically in the text.
4. David Yaffe, "Ellison Unbound," *The Nation*, March 4, 2002: 34–36.
5. Ralph Ellison, *Juneteenth* (New York: Vintage Books, 1999). All further references to the text will appear parenthetically in the remainder of the essay.
6. James Baldwin, *Go Tell It on the Mountain* (1952; rpt. New York: Dell Publishing, 1981), p. 11. All further references to this novel will be acknowledged parenthetically in the text.
7. Kemp Williams, "The Metaphorical Construction of Sexuality in *Giovanni's Room*," *Literature and Homosexuality*, ed. Michael J. Meyer (Amsterdam: Rodolpi: 2000), p. 27.
8. In his treatment of Baldwin's novels, John W. Roberts notes that reviews in *The New York Times* alone reflect the mixed response. As Roberts observes, the *Times Book Review* refers to the novel as "strained," while the daily book column "hailed [the novel] as 'brilliantly and fiercely told,'" *Dictionary of Literary Biography*, vol. xxxiii (Farmington, MI: Gale Group Publishing, 1989), p. 11.
9. James Baldwin. *Another Country* (1962; rpt. New York: Vintage Books, 1990), p. 3. All further references to this novel will appear parenthetically in the text.
10. Roberts, *Dictionary*, p. 13.
11. *Ibid.*, p. 14.
12. Keneth Kinnamon, "James Baldwin," *American Writers*, ed. Leonard Unger (New York: Scribner, 1974), pp. 47–71.
13. Darryl Pinckney, "Blues for Mr. Baldwin," *Critical Essays on James Baldwin*, ed. Fred L. Standley and Nancy V. Burt (Boston: G. K. Hall, 1988), pp. 161–166.
14. Warren J. Carson, "Manhood, Masculinity, and Male Bonding in *Just Above My Head*," *Re-viewing James Baldwin: Things Not Seen*, ed. Quentin Miller (Philadelphia: Temple University Press, 2000), pp. 215–232.

12

PIERRE-DAMIEN MVUYEKURE

American Neo-HooDooism: the novels of Ishmael Reed

Because reading Reed's fiction is like savoring and devouring *Gombo Févi* or *Gumbo à la Creole*, two metaphors that Reed develops in the poem "The Neo-HooDoo Aesthetic" and the novel *The Last Days of Louisiana Red* (1974), a thorough analysis of Reed's novels must start by recognizing their underlying postcolonial discourse, African Diaspora reconnection, and multicultural poetics. Because so far very little attention has been directed toward the intertextuality that pervades his work (novels, poems, plays, essays), Reed has been rightly complaining about both readers and critics' failure to investigate the allusions used in his work. By failing to both investigate the multiplicity of allusions in Reed's novels and to regard Neo-HooDooism as a poetics of multiculturalism, critics have either misread or misinterpreted Reed's novels. In his *Writin' Is Fightin': Thirty-Seven Years of Boxing on Paper* (1990), Reed complains that when he "set out to add fresh interpretations to an ancient Afro-American oral literature by modernizing its styles so as to reach contemporary readers," he knew that his work would be greeted with controversy. He further states that he knew that some critics "would dismiss the material [included in his work] as arcane, when millions of people in North, South, and Central America, the Caribbean, and Africa are acquainted with the structures [he] used" (137).[1] By "ancient Afro-American oral literature" Reed refers to the folklores and stories from Vodoun/Voodoo and HooDoo religious systems (from Africa and the African Diaspora), the dozens, the toasts of the Signifying Monkey (in which the monkey subverts the power of the lion and the elephant) as well as Native American myths (of the raven in *Flight to Canada* [1976] and coyote in *The Terrible Threes* [1989]), Asian, and other world oral traditions. It is out of this "ancient Afro-American oral literature" and Voodoo/HooDoo traditions that Reed has developed his multicultural and global writing style called Neo-HooDooism.

On the other hand, readers and critics have been complaining that Reed's books are difficult to read because of their numerous subtexts, their non-Aristotelian plots (or artistic arrangement of events), and their stock, flat

characters – in almost all of the nine novels. Reed returns the favor by
having characters either mock the conventional ways of writing novels or
proclaim their being in favor of Aristotelian aesthetics and round characters. The point to be made here is that Reed always has many non-related
things (Syncretism) going on at the same time (Synchronicity), while his
readers and critics tend to follow a straight line or one thing at a time in
their reading. Robert Gover has cogently pointed out that as "a houngan
[a Voodoo priest] of his novels," Ishmael Reed is not only "hard on his readers," but he seems to take them for granted by assuming that "they already
know the basics of Voodoo or are quick-witted enough to pick them up by
osmosis." What is more, Reed "is a tireless researcher and he writes to send
his readers scurrying to their dictionaries and libraries."[2]

While Reed's work seems to be concerned with de-centering Judeo-
Christianity in order to affirm African-based identities, it seems to do so
within a global perspective made possible by his Neo-HooDooism. Thus,
Reed's aim is not simply to assert "the blackness of blackness"[3] or an
Afrocentric aesthetic in the manner of Amiri Baraka, Molefi Asante, and others, but that his writing goes beyond the reconnection to African spirituality
in order to create a multicultural space for all cultures and modes of being
and thinking. Reed has argued that his idea of Neo-HooDooism differs from
"the Black Nationalist approach," because he sees "West African imagination as capable of being inspired by many different cultures," while "the
Black Nationalists are mono-cultural. The absorptive capacity of 'Neo-
HooDooism' incorporates European ideas as well as Native American
ideas."[4] In Reed's fiction, the decolonization process hinges not only on
appropriating the language of the master but also on liberating his writing
by both forging his writing style out of ancient African-based traditions and
enmeshing them with those found in the "New World." Interestingly, black
characters (South American or North American) who are endowed with the
knowledge of these ancient African-based traditions and the cultural interdependence that exists between the latter and American traditions are those
who survive and are positively portrayed in Reed's fiction – missing this
point has misled many critics to label *The Last Days of Louisiana Red*
(1989) and *Reckless Eyeballing* (1986) misogynistic novels. On the other
hand, those characters who lack the historical knowledge of slavery, colonialism, and neo-colonialism, tend to become colonial collaborators.

Just as language is central to any colonial, postcolonial, or neo-colonial
experience – every colonial or imperial oppression begins by controlling language as a medium of communication – so is it pivotal to Reed's fiction (as
it has always been in African American literature). It is not a coincidence
then that his first novel, *The Free-Lance Pallbearers* (1967), addresses such

issues as "the bastardization of the tongue," and *Japanese by Spring* (1993), his most recent novel, abrogates and appropriates the English language by using Yoruba and Japanese languages and cultures, all made possible by Neo-HooDooism. To borrow from Ashcroft, Griffiths, and Tiffin, Reed and his characters understand that it is through language that "a hierarchical structure of power is perpetuated, and the medium through which conceptions of 'truth,' 'order,' and 'reality' become established."[5] Reed's writing cogently demonstrates that the liberation of any oppressed people begins by recovering the language of communication just as the liberation of the so-called minority or colonized writer starts with tampering with the Word. Not only does Reed's writing re-place the language and text of the master, but it also elaborates its own theory of writing whereby it achieves its liberation: Neo-HooDooism. Further, Reed's novels demonstrate how African American literature is part of African oral tradition, not a subcategory of Western literature, by abrogating Western novelistic forms and appropriating them to both express his African American experiences and establish true multicultural American and global realities.

As Reed has argued in his *Shrovetide in Old New Orleans* (1978), Voodoo is "the perfect metaphor for the multiculture," because it "comes out of the fact that all these different tribes and cultures were brought from Africa to Haiti" with "all their mythologies, knowledges, and herbal medicines, their folklores, jelled" (232–233). In an essay in *Writin' Is Fightin'*, Reed explains that it is this multicultural aspect underlying Voodoo that attracted him to study and write on Voodoo, for "there seems to be no room" for "intellectual meanness" in African-based religious systems. Indeed, Voodoo "could mix with other cultures with no thought of 'contamination,' or 'corruption,' but usefulness." In this light, Catholic saints could perform the functions of African gods, just as in Guadeloupe "the gods of the immigrant Indians were added to the neo-African pantheon, and a curry dish, with Indian origins, has become the national dish of this Caribbean country" (141). Reed further theorizes Neo-HooDooism in three poems: "The Neo-HooDoo Aesthetic," where Gumbo is used as a metaphor for syncretic writing insofar as the amount of ingredients to make *Gombo Févi* or *Gumbo Filé* rests entirely on the cook/artist; "Catechism of a Neoamerican Hoodoo Church," in which the poet declares that, unlike computers, writers are not programmable and their pens are free; and "Neo-HooDoo Manifesto," in which the origins of Neo-HooDoo are traced back to Africa via Haitian Voodoo. Equally important, Neo-HooDoo is linked to dance and serves as the matrix for African American expressive cultures: several blues, R&B, and rock and roll musicians are named Neo-HooDoos. As the poem suggests, central to Neo-HooDooism is the belief that "every man is an artist and every artist / a priest," and people can bring their "own creative ideals to / Neo-HooDoo." The poem cites Charlie "Yardbird (Thoth)" Parker as an example of "the Neo-HooDoo / artist as an innovator and improviser" (*New and Collected Poems* 21). Not only does Charlie Parker get mentioned in every one of Reed's novels after *The Free-Lance Pallbearers*, but also on the back cover of *Conversations with Ishmael Reed*, Reed is quoted as saying that if anyone was going to compare him to anybody, then compare him to "someone like Mingus and Charlie Parker, musicians who have a fluidity with the chord structure just as we have with the syntax or the sentence which is our basic unit." Not only do all Reed's novels depend on improvisation of scenes and characters, an improvisation the essence of which Reed finds in jazz musical forms such as Be-Bop, but for almost four decades Reed has also been arguing that in order to survive slavery, Reconstruction, lynching, Jim Crow, imperialism, and other colonizing systems, Africans in the "New World" have had to improvise on little that had been left of African traditions. As Reed points out in his introduction to *19 Necromancers From Now* (1970), a multicultural anthology of American fiction, Neo-HooDooism allows him to write more effectively by returning "to what some writers would call 'dark heathenism' to find original tall tales, and yarns with the same originality that some modern writers use as found poetry – the enigmatic street rhymes of some of Ellison's minor characters, or the dozens. I call this *Neo-hoodooism* [my emphasis]; a spur to originality."[6] That is, Reed is a "necromancer," a visionary and prophet who possesses his "vision of reality" and is "from the culture of the underground – the conjurer," a descendant of "the conjure people" who can be found in other cultures.[7] In this light, Reed views the African American artist as a "necromancer," "a conjuror who works JuJu upon his oppressors; a witch doctor who frees his fellow victims from the psychic attack launched by demons of the outer and inner world" (*19 Necromancers* xviii). Reed points to the fact that the Mayans and the Egyptians regarded the writer as "a necromancer, soothsayer, priest, prophet; a man who opened doors to the divine" (xx).

The Free-Lance Pallbearers sets Reed's literary Neo-HooDooism in fiction in motion for his subsequent novels. In it Reed collages parodies of the toasts of the urban ghetto traditions, Vincent McHugh's *Caleb Catlum's America*, Franz Kafka's *The Metamorphosis*, Voltaire's *Candide*, Ralph Ellison's *Invisible Man*, Charles Wright's *The Wig*, Booker T. Washington's *Up From Slavery*, the German voodoo film *The Cabinet of Dr. Caligari*, Nathaniel West's *The Dream Life of Balso Snell*, Dostoevsky's *Crime and Punishment*, Daffy Duck cartoons, and voodoo aesthetics (to name a few), from which stem the fantastical landscape, the style, the protagonist, and the narrative. Parodying (signifying[8] upon) these literary and popular texts – which Reed has recently called "a mixing and sampling technique" or the gumbo style (*The Reed Reader* xiv) – is part of Reed's Neo-HooDooism and multicultural poetics, for Reed feels that these texts have been neglected, though they are part of American culture. *The Free-Lance Pallbearers* signifies upon the idea of the American Dream that Bukka Doopeyduk, the protagonist, is so obsessed with that he leaves college, where he was expected to become "the first bacteriological warfare expert on the colored race" (4), "to start at the bottom and work [his] way up the ladder" through "temperance, frugality, thrift" and studying the book of the Nazarenes. More specifically, Bukka Doopeyduk studies the Nazarene manual hoping to overthrow HARRY SAM, the name of both a dictator and a country, and become one of the Nazarene bishops. But like the protagonist in *Invisible Man*, Doopeyduk eventually not only discovers that HARRY SAM is a dictator and a murderer of children, but he also realizes that alienating himself from the black community and blindly embracing American myths about hard work and its rewards can only lead to disappointment and disillusionment. Indeed, any attempt to escape from tyranny throws Doopeyduk into a state of utter confusion in a country filled with excrement and waste – HARRY SAM is a head of state who governs while sitting on a toilet and whose sexual practices are anal. Reed seems to suggest that Doopeyduk mainly fails in his quest because he is alienated from black cultures, including his dislike of the black dialect for the fear that the assistant dean of arts and sciences and the students from the University at Buffalo would circulate a petition about the "ADULTERATION OF HER TONGUE" (100).

That language is an issue in *The Free-Lance Pallbearers* is indicated in the opening paragraph where Doopeyduk, the "I" narrator, reveals that he lives in HARRY SAM, a "big not-to-be-believed out-of-sight, sometimes referred to as O-BOP-SHE-BANG OR KLANG-A-LANG-A-DING-DONG" (1). This phrase, repeated as a leitmotif throughout the novel, certainly introduces and foreshadows the slang and Be-Bop language of the 1950s – jazz drummer Max Roch has called Ishmael Reed "the Charlie Parker of American fiction."[9] Not only has Reed expressed his admiration for Parker, but he has also compared his way of writing plots to Parker's Be-Bop style and jazz. Writing laudatorily about the "technical innovations" of Be-Bop and emphasizing the latter's influence on "American style in fashion, manners, and language," Reed notes that Be-Boppers "invented words long ago consigned to the slangheap by out-of-touch grammarians."[10] More directly, Reed has argued that just as Parker improvised on Cole Porter's "Night and Day" and produced "something more than what it was," so does he improvise on "the western form" to create new and more viable forms – understand multicultural forms – of writing.[11] Clearly, the term "Bop" in the phrase above is part of the black vernacular insofar as it designates "an innovative form of jazz started in the 1940s by Charlie Parker (the Prince of Bop)" and several other jazz musicians such as Dizzy Gillespie and Thelonius Monk, in which "innovation was the key: melody and harmony were open-ended; anything could happen in bop."[12] Clarence Major reminds us that Be-Bop designated a style of scat singing or unconventional playing of an instrument. Ultimately, such a phrase and several others in *The Free-Lance Pallbearers* demonstrate how in this novel Reed de-centers the English language and form of the novel in order to make room for other languages such as black dialect, Be-Bop language, Chinese – the last message of the novel has been supposedly glossed from the Chinese – and Yoruba. It is worth noting that in this first novel Reed introduces HooDoo through the back door of Hollywood insofar as Voodoo is perceived as a bad thing; indeed, Doopeyduk gets hoodoooed by his wife's grandmother who thinks that he is a failure. In *Yellow Back Radio Broke-Down* (1969), Reed studies Voodoo further and begins to chart its origins from West and Central Africa via Haiti to New Orleans.

Yellow Back Radio Broke-Down represents a major shift from *The Free-Lance Pallbearers* not simply as a HooDoo Western, the first of its kind, but also by the way it moves from a Hollywood-type idea of Voodoo to a well-documented concept of HooDoo as a North American version of Dahomean and Haitian Voodoo. At the same time, it transforms an oral form of Voodoo folklore into a written form of a HooDoo Be-Bop Western novel. That is, *Yellow Back Radio Broke-Down* illustrates Neo-HooDooism (Neo-HooDoo Aesthetic) and its application to the cultural character of the American West and the Western genre. Reed's abrogation and appropriation of the Western hinge on his premise that the Western is traceable to both African Voodoo and African American HooDoo insofar as when in Voodoo and HooDoo *loas* (spirits) ride/possess human beings (who become their hosts), the latter become horsemen and horsewomen. Therefore, Reed "would naturally write a Western, here again using traditional styles of Afro-American folklore but enmeshing such styles with popular forms with which readers could identify"[13] The very syncretic and synchronistic nature of Neo-HooDooism allows Reed not only to question the colonial world of the American West and the Western, but also to reappropriate and to reinvent the American West and the Western through Loop Garoo Kid, a black HooDoo cowboy and houngan (Voodoo priest), as a hero of the Western. The result is a multicultural and multiethnic Western. Using his HooDoo powers against Drag Gibson and his acolytes, and helped by the Native American Chief Showcase and his science fiction technique mixed with Native American trickster characters, Loop Garoo Kid transforms the

Western into a HooDoo Be-Bop Western (scatting like Charlie Parker) that accommodates African Americans, Native Americans, women, children, Chinese, Germans, and Christians, with their differing linguistic and cultural views. In the novel, Loop Garoo Kid is presented on the one hand as a demonic figure and the apocryphal twin of Christ, and as a HooDoo houngan/priest who is both the lord of the lash and the master of conjuration, on the other. For Drag Gibson, however, Loop Garoo represents the forces of disorder and evil just like the Bacca Loup-gerow *loas* of Haitian Voodoo.[14] Additionally, the character Loop Garoo originates from Africa via Haiti, for the "slaves were brought from Haiti to New Orleans, so you get a Loup Garou in Haiti who's a female and you get a Loup Garou in New Orleans who's male [and who has] got leather and a lasso."[15] Kid, of course, is a reference to William Bonney, better known as Billy the Kid, who has been considered the epitome of the bad man in the Western. Through Loop Garoo, Reed reverses the belief system in the Western according to which good prevails over evil: it is the supposedly demonic Loop Garoo who epitomizes good, order, compromise, and a sort of harmony among races, genders, cultures, and religions. On the other hand, the law and order that Drag Gibson represents are nothing but oppression, repression, and corruption. When Drag Gibson fails to fight the Loop Garoo's HooDoo forces, he invites the Pope from Rome to come and save Christianity from the evil Loop Garoo. But it turns out that Loop Garoo and the Pope know each other from Heaven from where Loop Garoo was chased by the Father for allegedly plotting a coup against Jesus Christ. Nevertheless, the Pope strips Loop Garoo of his protective mojo/charms and leaves him at the hands of Drag Gibson, but only after entreating him to go back with him to prevent the Virgin Mary from singing the blues. With the Pope in the novel, Reed theorizes how, despite the Catholics' efforts to wipe out Voodoo and other African traditional religions, the latter have survived in the African diaspora by mixing with Catholic saints and Native American mythologies. Not only does the Pope characterize Loop Garoo's HooDoo as "scatting arbitrarily, using forms of this and adding his own. He's blowing like that celebrated musician Charles Yardbird Parker – improvising as he goes along" and "throwing clusters of demon chords at you," but he defines HooDoo as "an American version of Ju-Ju religion that originates in Africa [Dahomey and Angola]." What is more, the Pope acknowledges that Europeans have attempted to falsify the history of Sub-Saharan Africa by hiding the facts and claiming the history of North Africa as their own (153).

A study of *Yellow Back Radio Broke-Down* would be incomplete if it did not include Reed's criticism against critics' prescriptive rules about writing novels – this is central to Neo-HooDooism. Responding to Bo Shmo's neo-social realist criticism, Loop Garoo utters what both underlies Neo-HooDooism and describes Reed's fiction career: "what if I write circuses? No one says a novel has to be one thing. It can be anything it wants to be, a vaudeville show, the six o'clock news, the mumblings of wild men saddled by demons" (36). Loop Garoo is initially part of a circus from New Orleans (ambushed and killed by Gibson's men), and the novel is itself a circus, a vaudeville show Western in which Gibson and his Yellow Back Radio town are saddled by "demons" sent by Loop Garoo. Reed further reclaims the artistic freedom for African American creative writing when he lets the children of the Yellow Back Radio town proclaim that they have decided to create their own fiction (16). This means that one "can speak accurately of the psychological history of a people if one knows the legends, the folklore, the old stories which have been handed down for generations, the oral tales, all of which tells" where one's people come from, "which shows the national mind, the way a group of people look at the world," which one can establish by "reconstructing a past" that Reed calls Neo-HooDooism whereby people can have their "own psychology rather than somebody else's."[16]

Mumbo Jumbo (1972) will always have an important place in African American literary and critical traditions: it inspired Henry Louis Gates to elaborate his theory of the Signifyin(g) Monkey in his seminal work *The Signifying Monkey: A Theory of African-American Literary Criticism* (1988). It is also clear that Reed's novel inspired E. L. Doctorow's *Ragtime*. *Mumbo Jumbo* is Reed's dissertation about the manifold aspects of Voodoo and HooDoo and the role of Africa and Haiti in the origins of African American literature and culture. The novel involves a considerable amount of research on Haitian history, Voodoo, and HooDoo, psychology, Western history, Christianity and its link to colonization, world history, the history of dance, and American history, just to name a few – Reed wrote *Mumbo Jumbo* after a trip to Haiti in 1969. Throughout *Mumbo Jumbo*, Reed "profanes" Western words by "beating them on the anvil of Boogie Woogie [Blues, Cakewalking, the Congo, Jazz, ragtime, Jes Grew, Neo-HooDoo(ism)], putting [his] black hands on them so that they shine like burnished amulets" and demonstrates how European civilization benefited from other civilizations, including African and Asian[17] If in *Yellow Back Radio Broke-Down* Loop Garoo Kid indicts Christianity for trying to eliminate African-based religions and cultures, the HooDoo detective and HooDoo therapist PaPa LaBas – based on the figure of Legba (Fon) or Esu-Elegbara (Yoruba), the Western Voodoo *loa* of the crossroads and interpretation – of *Mumbo Jumbo* cogently proves how Greek civilization, the foundation for European civilization, is Egyptian-derived. Not only does *Mumbo Jumbo* theorize how Africans in the Diaspora have succeeded in retaining and re-creating African religious beliefs, but it also shows how Reed has created an African-based multicultural poetics to negotiate the historical, social, political, and cultural conditions of Africans in the "New World." Through syncretism and synchronicity, Reed parodies the classical idea of the novel by turning *Mumbo Jumbo* into "a polyphonic novel," a collage of detective fiction, prose, poetry, drawings, ads, footnotes, photographs, a partial bibliography of 104 titles, the Harlem Renaissance, Egyptian and Greek mythologies, European myths, *The Conjure-Man Dies*, and *De Mayor of Harlem*. These are a few of the intertexts that make *Mumbo Jumbo* a multicultural novel *par excellence*. Indeed, the paratextual insertions in *Mumbo Jumbo* move away from the center of the main narratives by pointing to themselves while at the same time moving to the center of the main narratives whose multicultural underpinnings they compound. In other words, the footnotes and excerpts challenge those who do not acknowledge their sources and borrowings while at the same time enriching the multiculturalism of *Mumbo Jumbo*. In conjunction with the partial bibliography, they function as a response to PaPa LaBas's criticism against Hinckle Von Vampton, a stand-in for Carl Van Vetchen, that the "white man will never admit his real references. He will steal everything you have and still call you those names. He will drag out standards and talk about propriety" (194).

Through visual illustrations, footnotes, quotations from other books, newspaper clippings, and poems, *Mumbo Jumbo* rewrites the technique of realism and authentication used in many slave narratives. Besides these subtexts, the novel contains an international and multiethnic group of "art-nappers" called the *M'utafikah*, whose role is to steal and repatriate art and religious objects that European colonizers embezzled and stored in museums the world over. More important, Jes Grew, the latest manifestation of Neo-HooDoo and the point of conflict in the novel, is a metaphor for multiculturalism. Although its detractors such as the Atonists call it a plague, it becomes clear that it is a form of possession related to Voodoo and HooDoo through dances and songs. In Reed's poem "Neo-HooDoo Manifesto," we learn that "Neo-HooDoo is a litany seeking its text / Neo-HooDoo is a dance and Music closing in on its own words / Neo-HooDoo is a Church finding its lyrics."[18] That is, being an African diaspora phenomenon that originates from Haitian and African Voodoo, Neo-HooDoo must keep improvising and blending with other South and North American oral traditions, something similar to jazz riffing. Asked how to catch Jes Grew, the Haitian houngan detective Benoit Battraville advises Nathan Brown to ask Bessie Smith, Louis Armstrong, musicians, painters, and poets (*Mumbo Jumbo* 152). At the end of his lecture in the Epilogue section, PaPa LaBas emphatically declares that the "Blues is a Jes Grew, as James Weldon Johnson surmised. Jazz was a

Jes Grew, which followed the Jes Grew of Ragtime. Slang is Jes Grew too" (214). Throughout *Mumbo Jumbo*, Jes Grew appears as multiracial, multiconscious, and multilingual, as people it possesses begin by dancing and speaking in tongues.

In *The Last Days of Louisiana Red* (1974), PaPa LaBas reappears as a Neo-HooDoo detective who is sent to Oakland, California, to investigate the murder of Ed Yellings, an Osiris-type HooDoo therapist who is murdered because he was trying to get rid of Louisiana Red, a neo-slave mentality that leads African Americans to kill and hold one another down like crabs in a barrel. The signifyin(g) revisions (parodic intertexts) include Cab Calloway's song "Minnie the Moocher" (thus we have the character of Minnie Yellings), Egyptian Antigone, Sophocles's *Antigone* and *Oedipus at Colonus*, Richard Wright's *Native Son*, the *Amos 'n' Andy Show*, *The Picayune Creole Cook Book*, the Congolese history in the 1960s, the detective story, and Marie Laveau and Doc John of nineteenth-century New Orleans. The preface from *The Picayune Creole Cook Book* about gumbo-making foreshadows all these intertexts and bears on the meaning of the novel as a whole insofar as Ed Yellings is in the gumbo business – "Business" and "Work" are code names for Voodoo and HooDoo to avoid detection. As an example of Reed's syncretism and synchronicity at work – several disparate elements from different cultural and time periods are brought together and given twists so that they happen at the same time – Ed Yellings's children are shaped after characters in Sophocles's *Antigone*: Minnie the Moocher is Antigone (Reed makes it clear that the original Antigone was Egyptian), Wolf Yellings is Eteocles, Street Yellings is Polynices (but also Bigger Thomas), Sister Yellings is Ismene, and PaPa LaBas is Creon, while Ed Yellings parallels Oedipus and is compared to Osiris because of his being a HooDoo therapist with polytheistic approaches. Through Ed Yellings, Reed explores the psychological effects of slavery/colonization on the slave/colonized and tackles black male–black female relationships. In a sense, Ed Yellings functions as a HooDoo therapist, not unlike Frantz Fanon in Algeria, who strives to redress the psychological effects of slavery and colonialism as represented by Louisiana Red. Despite some dialogues that some feminist critics have labeled misogynist, the novel cogently suggests that black male characters are not better portrayed than their female counterparts; the latter actually come out of the novel in a better shape than the former. As is the pattern in Reed's poetics of multiculturalism, characters such as Chorus in *The Last Days of Louisiana Red* blame Christianity for the decline of Greek drama and charges that Christianity has excluded "the dance and life from Greek Drama/-Religion (in early plans for the Greek Amphitheater there was included a seat for the Priest of Dionysus)."[19] Later in the novel, Chorus accuses Antigone of being "a monoculturalist with a twist" who worships "one God [Hades]" and wants "to make it with Death" (87). In Reed's Neo-HooDooism, monotheism is to polytheism what monoculturalism is to multiculturalism. Contrary to what some critics argue, Reed in this novel does not have any problem with matriarchy and the black woman: Sister Yellings and Ms. Better Weather evince the fact that Reed has a variety of female characters and that matriarchy is not a problem in the novel. Throughout *The Last Days of Louisiana Red*, both women are constantly praised (and contrasted to Minnie) not only for helping Ed Yellings and later PaPa LaBas, but for also understanding the necessity to preserve the Solid Gumbo Works as a representation of African cultural retention in North America. They also know that it is disastrous for any black woman, and for any black man for that matter, to let a white man such as Max Kasavubu manipulate her against her own people.

Like previous novels, *Flight to Canada* (1976) suggests that characters who survive the displacement caused by slavery are those who possess the knowledge of "ancient Afro-American oral literature," which can allow them to trick the master as well as to use the acquired writing skills as someone would use HooDoo. *Flight to Canada* rewrites the slave narrative and the historical novel, revisits the American Civil War, and discusses slavery (old and contemporary), Abraham Lincoln, Harriet Beecher Stowe and her *Uncle Tom's Cabin*, Alfred Lord Tennyson and his *Idylls of the King*, Tom Taylor's *Our American Cousin* (during the performance of which Lincoln was shot), the Native American myths of the raven, Edgar Allan Poe's "The Raven," "The Fall of the House of Usher," and "The Cask of Amontillado," Phillis Wheatley's "To His Excellency, General Washington," *Gone With the Wind*, Frederick Douglass, William Wells Brown, Henry Bibb, Ezra Pound, T. S. Eliot, and the politics of race, ethnicity, and multiculturalism. As can be noticed, the implicit Neo-HooDooism in this novel allows Reed to incorporate variegated references from different cultures and traditions and in so doing closes the gap between slavery, the Civil War, and the present Bicentennial Year, as well as the future. Although on the surface it is the story of Raven Quickskill, an escaped slave who flies on a jumbo jet (in nineteenth-century America!) to Canada but eventually comes back to the plantation to be freed by Uncle Robin and to write the latter's biography, *Flight to Canada* is a comment upon the present plight of African Americans, Native Americans, Jewish Americans, and other minority groups in America. Through Raven Quickskill, a trickster character, Reed shows how African American writers, as well as other American writers, can benefit from borrowing from other traditions; a further suggestion is that slavery affects everybody, not just blacks. Just as literacy as a pathway to freedom underlies most slave narratives, so is it a main theme in *Flight to Canada*. The quest for literacy and freedom is so poignant that the novel moves from an oral tradition of Voodoo and HooDoo to a hybridized HooDoo literary text. Quickskill, indeed, sees his writing as "his HooDoo. Others had their way of HooDoo, but his was his writing; his typewriter was his drum he danced to."[20] Another example is Uncle Robin – he is a subversive version of Uncle Tom – who, aware of the power of language, masters the master's language and uses it to subvert the subjugating power of slavery by rewriting Swille's will and inheriting his property.

The Terrible Twos (1982) and *The Terrible Threes* (1989) – two novels in a trilogy series; Reed has been writing *The Terrible Fours*, a novel which, according to Ishmael Reed (the character) in *Japanese by Spring*, begins in Rome where the detective Nance Saturday (from the two previous novels) has finished helping the Pope deal with his creditors – are probably the most misunderstood and unappreciated novels of Reed's. Not only have they received scathing reviews, they have also been neglected.[21] Yet a closer analysis reveals that *The Terrible Twos* and *The Terrible Threes* are as successful and as undergirded by Neo-HooDooism as Reed's previous novels. What confuses critics is the fact that Reed has appropriated Rastafarianism and Calypso, aesthetics borrowed from the Caribbean traditions and used by several Caribbean writers (Orlando Patterson, V. S. Naipaul, Sam Selvon, Earl Lovelace, and Derek Walcott) into his Neo-HooDooism to make a social commentary on the plight of minorities in the US and American foreign policies towards the so-called "Third World" countries. In *The Terrible Twos* and *The Terrible Threes*, Reggae and Calypso are both the latest manifestations of Neo-HooDooism and bridges between Africa, South America, and North America. Just as Rastafarianism in Jamaica and Calypso in Trinidad are postcolonial discourses used to make social commentaries, so, in turn, they are used by Reed (through Black Peter) to charge America, its politicians, and its religious leaders with behaving like Scrooge and the two-year olds, as they say "ho" to poor and minority people. Given the sheer amount of images and symbols of Rastafarianism and references to Calypso, any reading of *The Terrible Twos* and *The Terrible Threes* must take into account Rastafarian theology and Calypso aesthetics. The confluence of these aesthetics shows that in the two Christmas novels characters such as Dean Clift and Nola Payne, though initially endowed with "dissonance," are constantly searching for cultural "consonance"[22] found in the variations of the myths of Black Peter and St. Nicholas, myths that are latent in Christmas mythology, under positive vibrations[23] and sounds of Reggae and Calypso. In these two novels, whose structure is loosely based on Charles Dickens's *A Christmas Carol*, Reed uses Christmas as metaphor to explore cultural oppression, social and economic inequalities, and how the US government (stand-in for the Reagan–Bush administrations) and big corporations coalesce to monopolize Christmas to benefit the rich who can afford it. In *The Terrible Twos*, Bob Krantz, an advisor to President Dean Clift, implores the Heavenly Father to send him a signal that "Operation Two Birds, a plan to save all of Thy Christian work from being overrun by the forces of the anti-Christ . . . is the right ting to do" (104). In *The Terrible Threes*, Rev. Clement Jones, a faith healer and televangelist, concocts a plan to "drive the infidels out of the country. They will have to convert to Christianity or leave" (10). Parallel to this colonialist setting is the story of Black Peter and St. Nicholas, culled from myths from all over the world, in which Black Peter and St. Nicholas try to rectify things in the US by appearing to President Dean Clift (and taking him to visit the American hell to see what happened to Harry Truman, Rockefeller, and Eisenhower because of their actions) and Nola Payne, a Supreme Court Justice, and several members of Congress.

Because critics have failed to investigate the parodic intertexts (signifyin(g) revisions embedded in *Reckless Eyeballing* (1986) and because of the way the latter handles multiculturalism in regard to (neo-)colonialism, anti-Semitism, feminism, race, and gender issues, critics have erroneously charged this novel with misogyny and wrongly labeled Reed a misogynist, a label that has been following him and his work since Michele Wallace's (in)famous "Female Troubles: Ishmael Reed's Tunnel Vision." Purporting to review *Reckless Eyeballing*, the essay ends up being a personal attack on Reed for "feminist baiting" and anti-black women's progress. A close textual analysis reveals the opposite: in *Reckless Eyeballing* Reed rather signifies upon and pays homage to African American women's fiction by abrogating and appropriating the novels of Toni Morrison (*Sula*), Alice Walker (*The Color Purple*), Gayl Jones (*Corregidora*), Zora Neale Hurston (*Their Eyes Were Watching God*), Michele Wallace's unpublished work, Toni Cade Bambara (*The Salt Eaters*), and Paule Marshall, particularly by critiquing the way they portray black male characters and how the latter mistreat black female characters. Tremonisha Smarts's play *Wrong-Headed Man*, for example, draws its scenes and characters from Gayl Jones's *Corregidora* and Alice Walker's *The Color Purple*, just as Randy Shank's argument about why white boys love Tremonisha is a signifyin(g) revision of Sula's dialogue about why white women and men love the black man in *Sula*; the narrator also directly comments on how difficult it is for Sula to be independent, since people at the Bottom want her to be submissive. Thus, understanding *Reckless Eyeballing* requires one to explore and analyze the signifyin(g) revisions and parodic intertexts from African American women's fiction as the underpinnings of Reed's Neo-HooDoo discourse or poetics of multiculturalism with focus on decolonization, ethnicity, race, gender, and sexuality. It is worth noting that discussing Velma in Reed's novel is natural because in *The Salt Eaters* Toni Cade Bambara revises Reed's *The Last Days of Louisiana Red* by teaching Minnie the art of Voodoo healing about which she is accused of not caring in Reed's novel. Gayl Jones has also returned the favor by signifyin(g) on Reed's Neo-HooDooism in her recent novels such as *The Healing* (1998) and *Mosquito* (1999).

To these black women's texts within *Reckless Eyeballing* one has to add Scott Joplin's ragtime play *Treemonisha* from which Reed draws the character of Tremonisha, Emmett Till about whom Ian Ball, the protagonist, writes *Reckless Eyeballing*, a play whereby he hopes not only to get off the sexist list he got on after writing *Suzanna*, but also "to distance himself from the misogynistic attitudes that have ruined the work of some of his [black male] contemporaries."²⁴ In addition to being a "Southern term for a black man who looks at a white woman the wrong way, sometimes with dire consequences,"²⁵ the term "Reckless Eyeballing" is an important metaphor from a multicultural perspective insofar as Ian Ball contends that on one level his play is about people who intrude "into spaces that don't concern them" (*Reckless Eyeballing* 81). Earlier in the novel, Jake Brashford accuses Jewish writers (Updike, Malamud, Wolfe) of stealing black material and writing about blacks. The ironic twist here is that in this novel Reed is already writing about Jewish people and their experiences, including the Holocaust, a case of cultural reckless eyeballing. Throughout Reed's *Reckless Eyeballing*, it is clear that whatever Ian Ball says about black women and their collaboration with the enemy (white feminists and white men) is not to be taken seriously because he is a "double-headed" character (an Obeah woman hoodooed him when he was born), a Legba figure, who "has a way of talking out of both sides of his mouth, as though he were of two heads or two minds" (127). Like Benjamin "Chappie" Puttbutt in *Japanese by Spring*, Reed's ninth novel, Ian Ball changes his mind and switches sides whenever it benefits him. Thus, overlooking the fact Ian Ball is a Neo-HooDoo trickster can only lead to a misreading of *Reckless Eyeballing*. Despite the bitter satire against radical black feminism, the novel does offer some empathy for black women in America. At the end of the novel, not only does Tremonisha Smarts reject Becky French's white radical feminism, but she also develops from a black-male-bashing black feminist into a caring mother and a womanist.²⁶

As is always the case with Reed's novels, *Japanese by Spring* (1993) contains more than one plot and subplots. On the surface, it is the story of Benjamin "Chappie" Puttbutt (named after two black American generals: Benjamin O. Davis, Chappie James, and some echoes of Colin Powell), an African American professor at Jack London College in Oakland, California, who is more interested in getting tenured than in the cause of his people.

For three years since he was hired, he has been spending time commuting between Eurocentrists and Afrocentrists. To the black students, Puttbutt is an "Uncle Tom," because he argues that affirmative action is a form of quotas and that blacks should negotiate instead of being confrontational – here Reed was prophetic and ahead of Proposition 109 in California. Throughout the novel, Puttbutt's hallmark is the fact that he changes his mind like revolving doors. While in the 1960s, he belonged to the Black Power Movement and believed that black was both beautiful and the future, in the 1980s he became a feminist and memorized works by Zora Neale Hurston and Sylvia Plath, because he wanted the feminists in the Department of Humanities to vote for his tenure. In the 1990s, convinced that the twenty-first century was going to be a "yellow" century, Puttbutt learned Japanese "to take advantage of the new global realities."[27] One of the new global realities is that the Japanese would take over the US, just as Dr. Yamato (one of the ancient names for Japan) takes over Jack London College and renames it Hideki Tojo No Gaigaku (Hideki Tojo University) after the Japanese prime minister hanged for war crimes following World War II. Further, Dr. Yamato renames the student union Isoroku Yamamoto Hall, after the general who masterminded the attack on Pearl Harbor. As a result of the "Orientalization" of Jack London, Puttbutt becomes the second man in command, an opportunity for him to get even with those who voted against his tenure. Of course, Puttbutt and Dr. Yamato are just two voices among hundreds of voices and references from Africa, Europe, Asia, South America, and the Middle East, not to mention literary and nonliterary names such as Rodney King, Anita Hill and Clarence Thomas, Colin Powell, Saddam Hussein, Shakespeare (whose *Othello* Puttbutt reads as racist), Arthur Schlesinger and his *The Disuniting of America*, Milton (after whom the racist and monoculturalists at Jack London College are named Miltonians), and Plato (whose philosophy Dr. Yamato calls rubbish), just to name a few. Truly, *Japanese by Spring* is a jazz composition, not unlike Charlie Parker's, filled with improvised calls and responses among various instruments. It is an improvisation, "like a jazz musician stating a song and dancing around it elliptically" (*Japanese by Spring* 128).

It must be noted that until *Japanese by Spring* Reed had learned about Voodoo and HooDoo cultures second-hand via Haiti and then Africa. With this novel, however, he learns an African language and goes directly to African oral traditions of the Yoruba people. Equally important, in *Japanese by Spring* Reed achieves the highest degree of Neo-HooDooism – thus the highest degree of postcolonial writing and discourse (the highest degree of abrogating and appropriating the English language), African diaspora reconnection, multicultural poetics, and globalism, by writing in three languages:

English, Yoruba, and Japanese. While Benjamin "Chappie" Puttbutt is learning Japanese because he thinks that English will be obsolete in the 1990s US, his nemesis Ishmael Reed is learning Yoruba from a Nigerian houngan and bookstore owner in Oakland, California. Concerning Yoruba, Reed has argued that not only do black people "still speak Yoruba," they "speak English with a Yoruba syntax" and "drop their verbs." Further, Reed wanted to explore "some of the literature of the Yoruba civilization, and when one does, one can see some of the retention that has happened [in the African diaspora]."[28] As for Japanese, Ishmael Reed (the character), convinced that languages die unless they expand and borrow from other languages, argues that English is already "hungry for new adjectives, verbs and nouns" and can use "some more rhythm from a language like Japanese, which sounded like as though it were invented for bebop. Atatakakatta, past tense for the word warm. Doesn't it sound like a Max Roach attack? . . . It could use some Yoruba drumtalk" (*Japanese by Spring* 50). Ishmael Reed also studies Yoruba to "end the jazz poetry hype" – everybody claiming to be a jazz poet. Having realized that speaking and reading Yoruba is like reading a song sheet, he sees Yoruba as a jazz language, the "foundation of jazz. The language that was the only real jazz poetry" (123). Clearly, Ishmael Reed appears in his own novel to challenge Puttbutt's views against affirmative action, racism, multiculturalism, and ethnic studies on college and university campuses across America. But there is another important reason Ishmael Reed is in the novel: to challenge and poke fun at "the death of the author" proclaimed by Derrida, Barthes, and Foucault whom he discusses in the novel.

As can be noticed, one of the challenges for readers of *Japanese by Spring* (and other Reed novels) is not only to have a Gargantuan knowledge of world history and cultures, but also to be able to navigate between three linguistic centers: English, Yoruba, and Japanese. In the Epilogue section of *Japanese by Spring*, for example, Reed has purposely left the song to the Yoruba god Olódùmarè, "Àwá Dé O, Olórun" [Here We are Olorun (God)],[29] untranslated, and there is no way of surmising its meaning from the context. One has then to either be a speaker of Yoruba or find someone who speaks it to do the translation. Knowing that the song praises Olódùmarè for being the Creator (first verse), for his glory and unblemished love on earth (third verse), and for owning today, yesterday, and everyday (second, fourth, and sixth verses) helps one realize that in the song Reed expresses a Neo-HooDoo concept: time past is time present and future, which allows Reed's novels to draw from as many cultures and texts from different times as possible and to compress them in one time frame of the parodying novel. *Japanese by Spring* further suggests that Reed's ultimate message in all his nine novels is that Americans can overcome (neo-)colonialism, mono-culturalism, and bigotry by not only learning about other cultures, but also by learning an extra language in addition to English. The best example is Professor Crabtree, a former Miltonian who used to argue that Africa did not have the Tolstoys and the Homers, who learns Yoruba and even leads the song of praise to Olódùmarè. In other words, Reed's Neo-HooDooism encourages characters to "reckless eyeball" other cultures as a means of surviving in an increasingly multicultural and multiethnic American society and global world.

NOTES

1. Ishmael Reed, *Writin' Is Fightin': Thirty-Seven Years of Boxing on Paper* (New York: Atheneum, 1990), p. 137.
2. Robert Gover, "Interview with Ishmael Reed," *Black Literature Forum* 12.1 (Spring 1978): 14.
3. For more on the "blackness of blackness," see Henry Louis Gates's chapter on *Mumbo Jumbo* in *The Signifying Monkey: A Theory of African American Literary Criticism* (New York: Oxford University Press, 1988), p. 217.
4. Joseph Henry, "A MELUS Interview: Ishmael Reed," *Conversations with Ishmael Reed*, ed. Bruce Dick and Amritjit Singh (Jackson: University Press of Mississippi, 1995), p. 211.
5. Bill Ashcroft, Gareth Griffiths, and Helen Tiffin, *The Empire Writes Back: Theory and Practice in Post-Colonial Literatures* (New York: Routledge, 1989), p. 7.
6. Ishmael Reed, ed., *19 Necromancers from Now* (Garden City, NY: Doubleday, 1970), pp. xvii–xviii.
7. Joseph Henry, "A MELUS Interview," p. 210.
8. For more on signifyin(g) and signifyin(g) revisions, see Gates's *The Signifying Monkey*.
9. Praise found on the back cover of Ishmael Reed's novel *The Terrible Threes* (New York: Atheneum, 1989).
10. Ishmael Reed, *Shrovetide in Old New Orleans* (Garden City: Doubleday, 1978), p. 108.
11. Al Young, "Interview with Ishmael Reed," *Conversations with Ishmael Reed*, ed. Bruck Dick and Amritjit Singh, p. 44.
12. Clarence Major, *Juba to Jive: A Dictionary of African-American Slang* (New York: Penguin Books, 1994), p. 57.
13. Ishmael Reed, *Writin' Is Fightin'*, p. 137.
14. In *Tell My Horse*, Zora Neale Hurston remarks that in Haiti the Bacca Loupgerow belong to the order of the Petros and the Congos, especially the "Congos of the open field or woods," who are "recognized as evil, but one must feed them to have better luck than others" (167).
15. Gover, "Interview with Reed," 14.
16. Peter Nazareth, "An Interview with Ishmael Reed," *Conversations with Ishmael Reed*, ed. Bruce Dick and Amritjit Singh, p. 186.

17. Ishmael Reed, *Mumbo Jumbo* (Garden City: Doubleday, 1972), p. 114. All further references to the text will appear parenthetically in the remainder of the essay.

18. Ishmael Reed, *Conjure* (Amherst: University of Massachusetts Press, 1972), p. 25.

19. Ishmael Reed, *The Last Days of Louisiana Red* (New York: Random House, 1974), p. 25. All further references to the text will appear parenthetically in the remainder of the essay.

20. Ishmael Reed, *Flight to Canada* (New York: Random House, 1976), p. 88.

21. As a sample of negative reviews, see Stanley Crouch in *The Nation* 234.20 (1982), Ivan Gold in *The New York Times Book Review* July 18, 1982, Robert Towers in *The New York Review of Books* 39.13 (1982), or Michael Kransy in *San Francisco Review of Books*, January–February, 1983.

22. I borrow these terms from Leonard E. Barrett Sr.'s *The Rastafarians: Sounds of Cultural Dissonance* (Boston: Beacon Press, 1988).

23. Here I am referring to the late Bob Marley's famous song "Positive Vibration" from the *Rastaman Vibration* CD (Islands, 1976).

24. Ishmael Reed, *Reckless Eyeballing* (New York: St. Martin's Press, 1986), p. 127.

25. Ishmael Reed, *The Reed Reader* (New York: Basic Books, 2000), p. xxiv.

26. For more on the concept of womanism, see Alice Walker's definition in *In Search of Our Mother's Gardens: Womanist Prose* (New York: Harcourt Brace & Company, 1983). See also Chapter 14.

27. Ishmael Reed, *Japanese by Spring* (New York: Atheneum, 1993), p. 5.

28. Steve Cannon, *et al.*, "A Gathering of the Tribe: A Conversation with Ishmael Reed," *Conversations with Ishmael Reed*, ed. Bruce Dick and Amritjit Singh, p. 37.

29. For the translation of this I received help from T. Temi Ajani from the University of Florida in Gainesville.

13

MARILYN MOBLEY McKENZIE

Spaces for readers: the novels of Toni Morrison

These visions are traditional. I knew them by heart as did the rest of the congregation, but it was exciting to see how the converts would handle them. Some of them made up details. Some of them would forget a part and improvise clumsily or fill up the gap with shouting. The audience knew, but everybody acted as if every word of it was new.

> – Zora Neale Hurston, *Dust Tracks on a Road*

Every literary work *faces outward away from itself*, toward the listener-reader, and to a certain extent thus anticipates possible reactions to itself.

> – Mikhail Bakhtin, "Discourse in the Novel"

I have to provide the places and spaces so that the reader can participate.

> – Toni Morrison, "Rootedness: The Ancestor as Foundation"

In the introduction to one of Toni Morrison's often-cited interviews, critic Claudia Tate observed that "while her stories seem to unfold with natural ease, the reader can discern the great care Morrison has taken in constructing them."[1] Over the span of nearly thirty years, from *The Bluest Eye* in 1970 to *Paradise* in 1998, the Nobel Laureate has not only continued to take great care in the construction of each novel, but she has also commented on the role of the reader in the construction of meaning. In fact, in one interview, Morrison says, "[t]o make the story appear oral, meandering, effortless, spoken – to have the reader *feel* the narrator without *identifying* that narrator, or hearing him or her knock about, and to have the reader work with the author in the construction of the book – is what's important. What is left out is as important as what is there."[2] Indeed, as readers have attempted to explicate, analyze, critique, and evaluate Toni Morrison's writing, some have lamented about the challenges her novels pose for the reader, while others take pride in filling in the hermeneutic gaps with the historical, cultural, and political meanings they believe her stories invoke. To assess the significance of Morrison's novels, it is critical to interrogate how her narrative aesthetic and cultural politics have shaped spaces for readers to enter her texts and how an even larger, diverse body of interpretations have emerged from the community of readers than she might have ever anticipated. An examination of the seven novels published between 1970 and 1998 reveals that the narrative and literal spaces of her texts are a window into her narrative poetics, her cultural politics, and many of her ideas on the meaning of life itself.

Morrison's first novel, *The Bluest Eye* (1970), actually focuses the reader on domestic space as represented in an elementary school primer. The meanings of house and home circulate throughout all of her novels, but in the first novel of her literary career, the house has some particular meanings that foreshadow the story inside the body of the novel. First, it frames the story of how racial difference affects the social dynamics of the community where the MacTeers and Breedloves live. Most readers recall Dick and Jane primers with pictures of blond-haired white people and no people of color whatsoever. The novel can be read as an exploration of the psychic consequences, particularly for black girls, of being marginalized, not only in the earliest textbooks used in elementary schools, but also in their everyday lives both in and outside school. The domestic space of their home, therefore, was a possible refuge, unless, of course, the inhabitants of the household had internalized the racial and racist views of the larger society, as the Breedloves did. Second, the references to house and home in the opening passage inscribe, through the literal spacing of words on the page, the ways in which language shapes, mirrors, and defies reality. Third, references to house and home in Morrison's first novel focus on the space in which a black girl's identity first comes into manifestation. Ironically, *The Bluest Eye* directs the reader's attention to the act of reading itself; and the elementary primer suggests the schoolhouse as the space second to home where language takes on meaning, where a child must connect the signs and symbols with what they mean for her life. Thus, the movement from a perfectly grammatical passage, with appropriately placed spaces and punctuation, gives way to less space and appropriate punctuation, to no spaces between words. The order and apparent logic of the primer gives way to chaos, total disorder, and a loss of meaning that foreshadow Pecola Breedlove's descent into madness after she endures incest, rape, pregnancy, and the illusion that blue eyes will make her beautiful.

Yet we enter the novel through the narrative voice of Claudia MacTeer, and it is through this narrator and her retrospective reading of Pecola's demise, and the community's complicity in that demise, that the reader learns the layers of meaning inscribed in this novel. The narrator's ability to assess the fate of Pecola and the community, to tell the story in all its complex beauty and tragic ugliness, creates a new space for her to go on with her own life based on her illumined perspective, in sharp contradistinction to Pecola, whose descent into madness represents a freedom in her own mind, but a tragic enclosure inside the narrow spaces of disconnection from community and the larger society forever. By the time readers finish the novel, they have ventured into domestic spaces where economic depravity dictates when and how people love, where taboos of rape and incest traumatize and sabotage black girlhood, where racism in the larger world shapes and constrains the options men and women have to imagine themselves as whole, acceptable human beings, and where people both in and outside the community exploit the most vulnerable. But Morrison's readers are not permitted the luxury of venturing into Claudia and Pecola's respective worlds unscathed, as disinterested spectators or as mere eavesdroppers on someone else's tragic story. Morrison deftly creates an intimacy between the narrator and the reader that she then disrupts with the plural pronouns, "we" and "our." Of course, Claudia understands, at the end of the narrative, how she and her community are implicated in what happened to Pecola, but the repetitious, insistent use of the plural pronoun in the final paragraphs of the novel suggest that the reader may too be implicated:

> All our waste which we dumped on her and which she absorbed. And all of our beauty, which was hers first and which she gave to us. All of us – all who knew her – felt so wholesome after we cleaned ourselves on her. We were so beautiful when we stood astride her ugliness. Her simplicity decorated us, her guilt sanctified us, her pain made us glow with health, her awkwardness made us think we had a sense of humor. Her inarticulateness made us believe we were eloquent. Her poverty kept us generous. Even her waking dreams we used – to silence our own nightmares. And she let us, and thereby deserved our contempt. We honed our egos on her, padded our characters with her frailty, and yawned in the fantasy of our strength.[3]

By the time the reader comes to the end of this passage, she discovers how she may also be complicit in the condemnation and demise of an innocent child who has internalized the racial gaze into what Morrison calls "racial self-loathing."[4] In many regards, the novel lulls the reader into Pecola's story only to shift, in the final pages, into exposing how the familiar phenomenon of scapegoating operates in the society at large. In other words, the reader is not allowed to get off the hook as a mere voyeur. Instead, Morrison writes the conclusion of the novel in such a way as to invite the reader to come to terms with his or her own "complicity in the demonization process Pecola was subjected to."[5] Nevertheless, the beauty of the prose and the clarity of the narrator's understanding in retrospect what she did not understand as a child, all point to Morrison's ability, even in her first novel, to help readers discern how art could be both "unquestionably political and irrevocably beautiful at the same time."[6]

In Morrison's second novel, *Sula* (1973), she creates a different kind of time and space. She leaves the world of children, literacy, and the complications that racism and poverty create for young people and moves on to the adult world of female friendship. But even this novel begins with an aesthetically riveting description of a place called the Bottom and illustrates how space gets racialized and shapes our understanding of our identity and the options available to us. Even before the reader meets Nel and Sula, the two protagonists, she learns about the social space that has transformed a black neighborhood into an exclusive country club. In a passage that describes a familiar form of regentrification, in which less economically able citizens are displaced by those who can afford to buy the land and force those who once claimed it as their own to relocate, Morrison seems almost prophetic in anticipating how urban phenomena are changing public and private spaces. Indeed, the text mirrors how many communities have had to grapple with the implications of such relocations of people and the attendant redistribution of resources throughout much of the last three decades of the twentieth century and the early months of the twenty-first century as well. The novel introduces the "nigger joke," and the black people who were the brunt of it, to provide a historical and geographical context for the narrative that will follow. Having established this racialized context, however, she writes that the people had little time to be preoccupied with the racism that contributed to their fate or their location. Instead:

> [t]hey were mightily preoccupied with earthly things – and each other, wondering even as early as 1920 what Shadrack was all about, what that little girl Sula who grew into a woman in their town was all about, and what they themselves were all about, tucked up there in the Bottom.[7]

With these words, Morrison creates two different spaces at once for her readers. On one hand, the readers get a window into how black people in Medallion were reading the text of their own lives; on the other hand, readers learn that the text of their lives is much more complex than any racialized reading of it could contain. Thus, as early as her second novel, Morrison was already creating a space for her readers to consider simultaneously how race does and does not matter for the stories she needs to tell.

Once she introduces her readers to Medallion and to Shadrack, its most eccentric citizen, a shell-shocked World War II veteran who, when he returns from war, institutes a National Suicide Day, she then introduces Nel Wright, the friend of the woman for whom the novel is named. Morrison organizes this novel, therefore, by gradually moving the reader in from the neighborhood and its history into the particular story of two households and the daughters that emerge from them respectively. The reader learns about Nel's oppressive household through her mother, through the layers of meaning available in how Helene treats her daughter, teaches her to conform, and contains her emergent sense of her identity. Morrison introduces the Peace household as one that is the antithesis of the order and containment of the Wright home. Sula's wild and chaotic household with its seemingly endless stream of boarders and male lovers taught her virtually nothing about intimacy and love, but a great deal about sex and using men for entertainment purposes. While Nel is described as a girl whose strict mother "drove her imagination underground," Sula's personality is best summed up in the following description:

> In a way, her strangeness, her naivete, her craving for the other half of her equation was the consequence of an idle imagination. Had she paints, or clay, or knew the discipline of the dance, or strings; had she anything to engage her tremendous curiosity and her gift for metaphor, she might have exchanged the restlessness and preoccupation with whim for an activity that provided her with all she yearned for. And like any artist with no art form, she became dangerous.[8]

Each an only child, when Nel and Sula meet, they feel the "ease and comfort of old friends. Because each had discovered years before that they were neither white nor male, and that all freedom and triumph were forbidden to them, they had set about creating something else to be. Their meeting was fortunate, for it let them use each other 'to grow on.'"[9]

At the center of the novel, of course, is the story of a friendship gone awry, of gender politics both in and out of marriage, and of the consequences of life decisions. In prose that is at times poetic and riveting, Morrison enables her readers to bear witness to how these two women have read the choices their culture and community made available to them. Inside the text of the novel, she reveals how familiar intimate spaces such as home, marriage, and even friendship can estrange one from oneself and from others. By rendering such familiar spaces unfamiliar through a pariah figure such as Sula, Morrison challenges the readers' notions of right and wrong, good and evil, even love and hate. For example, on her deathbed, despite the fact that she has slept with Jude, her friend's husband, and broken the connection that made them friends, Sula asks Nel to consider that maybe she, not Nel, is the good one. Like Nel after Sula's death, Morrison's readers are left to question their own values, their own choices, and how their reading of others reveals more about who they are than they might suspect.

Song of Solomon (1977), Morrison's third novel, moves literally and metaphorically in and out of space and time. With the folktale of flying Africans and the history of one family's connection to that folktale at the center of the novel, Morrison constructs several spaces for the reader to come into a narrative of African and African American history and culture. In a style that will characterize Morrison's later novels, *Song of Solomon* begins *in medias res*, literally bringing the reader into a space with no points of reference for understanding what is happening. As a consequence, the reader, like the onlookers down below, bears witness to Mr. Robert Smith's leap into space from the top of Mercy Hospital without having much of a context for understanding the how and the why of his actions. Unlike the onlookers, however, the reader does not have the benefit of "word of mouth news"[10] to prepare them for the North Carolina Mutual Life Insurance agent's decision to commit suicide. Yet, as with the first two novels, before Morrison introduces the reader to the male protagonist, Milkman Dead (Macon Dead, Jr.), she first establishes the hostile spaces to which black people had become accustomed. She also illustrates how they subverted the power of racist practices through the linguistic practices of renaming hostile spaces such as Doctor Street to Not Doctor Street and Mercy Hospital to No Mercy Hospital to document how they had been excluded. The reader also learns that it is the illiterate status of Milkman's grandfather that accounts for the family surname. In other words, at the same time that the reader learns about the immature 32-year-old Milkman whose cultural illiteracy makes him unable to adapt to his own community or historical moment, the reader also learns that his grandfather was illiterate and did not know that a drunken agent at the freedman's bureau had inscribed errors into the very papers that were supposed to declare his freedom from enslavement. Confusing the status of his father – dead – with the place of his birth – Macon – the history of Milkman Dead's family is almost presented as yet another "nigger joke." Morrison deftly weaves multiple stories into one grand narrative, moving in and out of the past and present, illustrating that a mature sense of identity requires an understanding of the interdependence of both.

As the novel unravels the story of Milkman Dead's birth, the story of his family and the history of his ancestors, the reader is lulled into a story of how intimate spaces can contain names with history, lives full of secrets and misunderstandings, and communities replete with what Morrison refers to as "unspeakable things unspoken."[11] With references to the familiar forms of black vernacular, and even elements of classical mythology that resonate with many readers, Morrison brings the reader into intimate contact with strange people and unfamiliar events to reveal the various and sundry ways black people have survived oppressive spaces and unjust treatment through language, music, and cultural practices. Pilate, Milkman's aunt, is represented as a griot figure without a navel, who Macon Dead, Sr. (Milkman's father), considers strange, unkempt, and unworthy of his son's love. Yet she is the very person who has the key to the mysteries of his family history and his identity in the present. Though she lives outside the town in a space that intensifies her pariah status, she teaches her nephew to defy time and space and that "if you surrendered to the air, you could *ride* it."[12] In essence, it is Pilate who enables Milkman to undertake an initiation journey into his family history, into the history of black people, and into a mature knowledge of how the people and places of his past and present are interconnected.

When we turn to Morrison's fourth novel, *Tar Baby* (1981), we discover the author's desire to take her readers to yet another understanding of space and time. Using a contemporary setting in the Caribbean with a young black woman with an almost postmodern sense of her racial identity, Morrison again disrupts familiar ideas about race, class, identity, and culture to provide some new ways of reading them. She begins *in medias res* once again and provides a view of a lush Caribbean setting into which a black male stowaway intrudes. But before Morrison elaborates on his intrusion, she delineates how colonial powers disrupted the serenity of this place by importing slaves, using them to clear the land and to reconstruct a man-made paradise. In language that is as lush as the landscape whose destruction she is describing, Morrison carefully reveals how this time it is the river, not a community of people, that is "evicted from the place where it had lived, and forced into unknown turf,"[13] but it is not a stretch to suspect she is connecting this eviction to the kidnapping of African people throughout the diaspora and to the ways in which black bodies have been rendered into service for colonial powers. Having established the setting, the novel then moves into the intimate space of the island winter home on the Isle des Chevaliers, where Valerian and Margaret Street have established a luxurious, yet unfulfilling life for themselves. The novel focuses, however, not so much on this couple as on the relationship between the niece of their servants, Jadine, and the intruder, Son. In a novel that takes on the gender politics of the late 1970s, Morrison invites her reader to construct meaning from some disparate pieces of information about the Streets, who have a wayward son, whom Valerian describes as a "cultural orphan;"[14] about Margaret, Valerian's vacuous wife, whose secret crime of child abuse interrupts the larger narrative of Jadine and Son's love affair; about the ongoing conflict between the indigenous peoples of the island and Sydney and Ondine; about the failed interracial love affair between Jadine and her white lover in Paris that precipitates Jadine's return home to her benefactors; and about Jadine's ultimate decision to return to Europe after she cannot resolve the conflict between herself and Son. Morrison once again uses familiar elements of house and home, but she demands that her reader read these spaces in ways they may not have anticipated. The novel requires a rethinking about black identity in nationalist terms when Son questions Jadine's education at the Sorbonne, which was financed by the generosity and patronage of the Streets. It also requires a rethinking about Jadine's claims for her European education and her enlightened sensibilities, which offer her no way of appreciating Son's Southern roots or the Philadelphia roots of her aunt and uncle and other black people. The novel also invites readers to consider the claims of capitalism as it manifests itself in colonialist practices that keep the colonized in poverty even after the colonizers have departed. Readers cannot overlook the unpaid and poorly paid labor that has made the island paradise possible. Nor can they overlook how Morrison has lifted cultural dynamics from the familiar public and private spaces of her first three novels on the mainland of the United States and located them in the Caribbean to reveal how those dynamics might, in a different place, remain the same. Though the novel seems to anticipate easy readings of race, identity, and even class, Morrison complicates easy readings of all these terms as the assessment of Jadine and Son indicates near the end of the novel:

> This rescue was not going well. She thought she was rescuing him . . . He thought he was rescuing her . . . Each was pulling the other away from the maw of hell – its very ridge top. Each knew the world as it was meant to be or ought to be. One had a past, the other a future and each one bore the culture to save the race in his hands.[15]

Thus, *Tar Baby* ends with unresolved contentions and suggests that neither of these lovers has a monopoly on how to read culture, the text of Son's own life, or the text of how Jadine's life is connected to those of the community from which both have emerged. At a cultural moment in the late 1970s and early 1980s when questions of identity, multiculturalism, and diversity were beginning to be hotly contested, Morrison entered into the fray with a novel that took readers into familiar spaces of myth and folklore to ask more questions than it answered.

Toni Morrison's last three novels have often been referred to as a trilogy about excesses of love. *Beloved* (1987), the Pulitzer Prize-winning novel about a formerly enslaved woman's attempt to kill all her children rather than see them enslaved in accordance with the Fugitive Slave Law, was clearly about excesses of mother love. Some readers have chosen to read Sethe's act as an act of revenge to deprive her slavemaster of his property. The second in the trilogy, *Jazz* (1992) – the story of Violet and Joe Trace, whose marriage crisis results in his affair, the murder of his teenage lover, and Violet's attempt to deface the corpse of her husband's lover at the funeral – is clearly about excesses of romantic love. *Paradise* (1998) represents the third novel in the trilogy, the story of an all-black town that attempts to murder the women who have turned to a convent outside town for solace and female community. Here is Morrison's narrative about the excesses of religion or the love of God. The novels all move from the public sphere in which black people live, negotiate their lives with one another and with the larger white society, but each novel then moves inside to more intimate spaces. Each explores the ways in which black people's lives are simultaneously about race and not about race. Beyond the constraints of enslavement in the public spaces of plantations that have devastated Baby Suggs, Sethe, and the Sweet Home men, is the reality that black people had interior spaces of thoughts and feelings that few novels had explored. Shifting the view from the slavemaster and his deeds to the interior life of enslaved people, Morrison offers readers a new way to read the slave narrative. Moving back and forth in time, narrating the novel through the aesthetics of memory rather than the chronology of linear time, the reader enters into the emotional past of slavery without denying the reality of its more familiar brutal dimensions. As a result, the novel enables readers to consider enslavement from a new perspective of how black people were able to endure, to survive, when they did not own their bodies, their children, or anything but their own minds. Ironically, though Baby Suggs suffered from the "sadness [that] was at her center, the desolated center where the self that was no self made its home . . . never having had the map to discover what she was like"[16] and though the same could be said for Beloved, the ghost who returns to haunt her mother and her house, Baby Suggs is also able to inspire the enslaved community with a psychic strategy for enduring a peculiar system that was designed to destroy them but did not: "You got to love it. This is flesh I'm talking about here. Flesh that needs to be loved."[17] Even after Baby Suggs dies, Sethe remembers her sermons in the clearing and tries to "listen to the spaces that the long-ago singing had left behind,"[18] for some clue as to how she is to carry on without her mother-in-law's sage wisdom and command that they sing healing into their circumstances.

By using an aesthetic narrative style that mirrors the improvisation of jazz, in the novel by that name, Morrison takes the reader away from the public spaces associated with the Harlem Renaissance with its literary salons, artistic productions, and white patronage to the private spaces of black folk trying to eke out a living after traveling from the South to the North. While

they are lured into reading the City as a new, open space for their freedom
to flourish, they are, nevertheless, torn between "when to love something
and when to quit . . . Word was that underneath the good times and the
easy money something evil ran the streets and nothing was safe – not even
the dead."[19] So the novel explores through a very improvisational rendering
of the multiple readings of what happened, not only from the characters
themselves, but even from the narrator. In fact, the narrator's distrust of her
own reading of the events renders her unreliable and thus leaves the reader
once again to fend for herself:

> I was so sure, and they danced and walked all over me: Busy, they were busy
> being original, complicated, changeable – human, I guess you'd say, while I
> was the predictable one, confused in my solitude into arrogance, thinking my
> space, my view was the only one that was or that mattered.[20]

By the time the reader finishes the novel, all she really knows is that a couple
had a crisis, a young woman was married, the couple reconciled, and it all
took place against the backdrop of one of America's most exciting artistic
and cultural moments.

The excesses of religious love produce another kind of arrogance in
Paradise. Black people who had once been excluded from white towns move
west and form all-black towns, only to give in to a form of exclusionary
practice of their own on the basis of an intraracial color line. The novel
exposes the various ways in which this all-black paradise unravels because
of the ways in which their religious and gendered orthodoxies break down
into violent arguments about everything from the history of the town, to the
meaning of the oven, its central edifice, to the character of the women who
seek refuge in the convent on the outskirts of town. Again exposing the ways
in which communities create pariah figures and then denigrate them and the
spaces in which they reside as inferior, Morrison brings to bear the history
of the state and the church in a novel that exposes racial and intergenera-
tional hostilities. Even the familiar space of the church with all its sacred
meanings gets deconstructed in this novel for the ways in which it exposes
the hypocrisies and secrets of domestic space. At the wedding of two of the
main characters, one of the two ministers present realizes the problem with
the town of Ruby is that there were

> two editions of the official story: One that nine men had gone to talk to and
> persuade the Convent women to leave or mend their ways; there had been a
> fight; the women took other shapes and disappeared into thin air . . . Richard
> didn't believe either of the stories rapidly becoming gospel . . . But because
> neither had decided on the meaning of the ending and, therefore, had not been
> able to formulate a credible, sermonizable account of it, they could not assuage

> Richard's dissatisfaction . . . As for Lone, she became unhinged by the way the
> story was being retold; how people were changing it to make themselves look
> good.[21]

By the time the reader finishes this complex novel of racial history, a town's history, and a community of women's stories, there are more questions than the usual one of who is the woman referred to in the first line "They shoot the white girl first."[22] The reader realizes there are other larger questions such as what gave the men the right to believe they had read the lives of the women correctly, that the women were doing anything out at the convent besides listening to one another's stories, singing, and offering a healing touch to those whose lives had been brutal, torn, tragic. The reader realizes that while each of the three religious denominations named thought it had a monopoly on truth, none did. All are therefore implicated in the demise of the paradise they had once enjoyed. And, as is the case at the end of *Sula*, the reader is left to ponder just where the source of good and evil really does lie.

More importantly, however, all of Morrison's novels so far challenge the reader to move from familiar to unfamiliar interpretations of life and living. Rendering the novel through a lens of complex narrative aesthetics, she invites readers into the cultural politics of race, gender, class, age, and even religion to entertain new readings of the text of their own lives, the nation, and the global community. While the challenge of such complex renderings of relationships and history may be more than readers like or are accustomed to, the beauty with which Morrison pulls her readers into these spaces makes it all worthwhile and tempts them not to give up, but to "rest before shouldering the endless work they were created to do down here in Paradise."[23] Inside the space of her novels is a form of uneasy rest, therefore, encouraging readers to return to their lives with new ways of making meaning of them.

NOTES

1. Claudia Tate, *Black Women Writers at Work* (New York: Continuum, 1984), p. 119. The first epigraphs at the beginning of this essay are from Zora Neale Hurston, *Dust Tracks on a Road* (Urbana: University of Illinois Press, 1984), p. 220; Mikhail Bakhtin, "Discourse on the Novel," *The Dialogic Imagination*, ed. Michael Holquist (Austin: University of Texas Press, 1981), p. 257; and Toni Morrison, "Rootedness: The Ancestor as Foundation," *Black Women Writers 1950–1980: A Critical Evaluation*, ed. Mari Evans (New York: Anchor Books, 1984), p. 341. The views I am expressing in this critical essay are adapted from my forthcoming book, tentatively titled, "Spaces for the Reader: Toni Morrison's Narrative Poetics and Cultural Politics."
2. Morrison, "Rootedness," p. 341.
3. Morrison, *The Bluest Eye* (New York: Plume, 1970 rpt. 1994), p. 205.

4. Morrison, "Afterword," *The Bluest Eye*, p. 210.

5. *Ibid.*, p. 211.

6. Morrison, "Rootedness," p. 345.

7. Morrison, *Sula* (New York: Bantam Books, 1973), p. 5.

8. *Ibid.*, p. 16.

9. *Ibid.*, p. 44.

10. Morrison, *Song of Solomon* (New York: Knopf, 1977), p. 3.

11. Morrison, "Unspeakable Things Unspoken: The Afro-American Presence in American Literature," *Michigan Quarterly Review* (Winter 1989): 1–34.

12. Morrison, *Song of Solomon*, p. 337.

13. Morrison, *Tar Baby* (New York: Plume, 1981), p. 9.

14. *Ibid.*, p. 145.

15. *Ibid.*, p. 269.

16. Morrison, *Beloved* (New York: Plume, 1981), p. 140.

17. *Ibid.*, p. 88.

18. *Ibid.*

19. Morrison, *Jazz* (New York: Knopf, 1992), p. 9.

20. *Ibid.*, p. 220.

21. Morrison, *Paradise* (New York: Knopf, 1998), pp. 296–297.

22. *Ibid.*, p. 3.

23. *Ibid.*, p. 318.

14

LOVALERIE KING

African American womanism: from Zora Neale Hurston to Alice Walker

Zora Neale Hurston's work in the woman-centered narrative, particularly *Their Eyes Were Watching God* (1937), connects African American women's literary production in the second half of the twentieth century to African American women's literary production in the nineteenth century. Alice Walker epitomizes this connection in her acknowledgment of Hurston's significance in *In Search of Our Mothers' Gardens: Womanist Prose* (1983), the volume prefaced by Walker's four-part womanist aesthetic.[1] Critics and other readers recognize Walker's resurrection of Hurston's exuberant spirit in Shug Avery of *The Color Purple* (1982).[2] Walker pays tribute to Hurston and other black foremothers who paved the way, even under the most difficult circumstances.[3] She acknowledges, as well, the efforts of her sisters in struggle in the mid-twentieth-century social movements: "Women have, over the last twenty years, really forged a community of readers, writers, and activists. That is what we're seeing. We're seeing that feminists and womanists have actually come of age, so that we are able to talk to each other."[4]

One happy offshoot of the social transformation that took place during this period was an unprecedented flowering of African American women's literature. What the growing body of literature lacked, however, was a means for assessing its value as art.[5] In "Toward a Black Feminist Criticism" (1977), Barbara Smith broke new ground, calling for the serious work of articulating a black feminist approach to black women's literature. Though Walker had published the title essay for her 1983 collection of womanist prose in 1974, it was in "One Child of One's Own" (1979) that she invoked Virginia Woolf's famous essay to point to the failure of white feminists to give serious consideration to African American women's art. Responses to Smith and Walker's combined call to fill this void in literary criticism would ultimately spawn a small cottage industry and launch numerous academic careers.[6]

Walker's womanist aesthetic takes shape in the context of addressing this issue, and its implications have been far-reaching.[7] It is less a means for judging the value of black women's art than it is a framework for imagining the black female subject in the process of achieving *wholeness*. Madhu Dubey finds that, "Walker's womanist ideology affirms a psychological wholeness that is communally oriented and is explicitly opposed to the self-sufficient individuality of bourgeois humanist ideology."[8] In *Katie's Canon*, womanist theologian Katie Cannon uses Walker's definition of womanist as "a critical, methodological framework for challenging inherited traditions for their collusion with androcentric patriarchy as well as a catalyst in overcoming oppressive situations through revolutionary acts of rebellion."[9] In "Womanizing Theory" (1998), Clara Juncker describes Walker's articulation of a womanist aesthetic as an attempt to womanize theory: "Walker deconstructs Harold Bloom's *Anxiety of Influence* and his theory of aggressive misprision with the harmonious chorus of women writing/inviting/rewriting women in 'In Search of Our Mothers' Gardens.'" Her autobiographical, poetic, elliptic and multivocal discourse . . . signifies, moreover, her difference from dominant cultural theoreticians and theories."[10] Though Walker's aesthetic has been labeled by some as both polemic and essentialist, ultimately, and for our purposes here, it serves as the basis for the womanist cosmology that becomes increasingly evident in Walker's novels.

One of Walker's earliest written articulations of her womanist aesthetic appears in her 1981 review of Jean Humez's *Gifts of Power: The Writings of Rebecca Cox Jackson, Black Visionary, Shaker Eldress* (1981). She writes that she could "imagine African American women who love women (sexually or not) . . . referring to themselves as 'whole' women . . . as 'round' women . . . who also have concern, in a culture that oppresses all black people . . . My own term for such women would be 'womanist'."[11] Walker further explains that the term would need to express the "spiritual and the concrete and it would have to be organic, characteristic, not simply applied. A word that said more than that they choose women over men . . . than that they choose to live separate from men." The word would also affirm "connectedness to the entire community and the world."[12] She defended her choice of terms to Audre Lorde, pointing out that her use of "womanist," rather than "black feminist," was "a necessary act of liberation to name oneself with words that fit." She pointed to Lorde's own celebration of that position in works such as *Zami: A New Spelling of My Name* (1982). In addition, "womanist" offered more room for changes, "sexual and otherwise," and was more "reflective of African American women's culture, especially Southern culture."[13] The idea of an inherent, or built-in, flexibility becomes increasingly evident as one considers Walker's work in the novel *vis-à-vis* her articulation of a womanist aesthetic through her art.

Using the format for a typical dictionary entry, Walker sets out her womanist aesthetic as the preface for *In Search of Our Mothers' Gardens*. The first component of the definition invokes the black vernacular and provides details about the womanist attitude:

> Womanist 1. From womanish. (Opp. of "girlish," i.e., frivolous, irresponsible, not serious.) A black feminist or feminist of color. From the black folk expression of mothers to female children, "You acting womanish," i.e., like a woman. Usually referring to outrageous, audacious, courageous or *willful* behavior. Wanting to know more and in greater depth than is considered "good" for one. Interested in grown-up doings. Acting grown up. Being grown up. Interchangeable with another black folk expression: "You trying to be grown." Responsible. In charge. *Serious.* (xi)

Walker's first three novels, set primarily, though not exclusively, in the South, evidence her commitment to reclaiming and valorizing the rural Southern black vernacular, specifically that of Georgia, Mississippi, and Alabama. This is most pronounced in *The Color Purple* (1982) where Celie composes her letters to God and Nettie in her own familiar idiom, in a way that does not "feel peculiar" to her mind. Though Walker includes the straightforward statement that a womanist is a "black feminist, or feminist of color," the qualities associated with the womanist are not confined to racial, gender, or other categories. The womanist subject is at once precocious and determined, someone whose thoughts and actions place her "ahead of the game," perhaps even in the position of visionary. She is direct and assertive, a person who willingly and aggressively takes responsibility for her own life, and who claims the right to full existence.

Walker's definition of the attitude exhibited by the womanist subject is broad enough, and flexible enough, to invoke Maria Stewart's boldness in making political speeches to men *and* women long before society deemed it proper for a woman (let alone a black woman) to do so.[14] Thus, while we must continue to credit Walker for having set down the terms for a womanist aesthetic, her acknowledged debt to certain foremothers, who served as trailblazers, is as apparent as is her own influence on a growing body of women's literature and criticism worldwide. The most obvious of these is Zora Neale Hurston, whose exuberant spirit is easily recognizable in Walker's definition of the womanist attitude. Along with Hurston, Walker directly invokes Harriet Tubman, escaped slave and Underground Railroad conductor, in setting out her definition; and she also draws from a documented legacy of African American women who exhibited the kind of courageous, willful, audacious, *womanish* behavior that Walker includes as part of her definition. Implicit in Walker's description of the womanist approach to life is the spirit of women such as Rebecca Cox Jackson, Jarena Lee, Zilpha Elaw, and Sojourner Truth, who went against the grain and challenged prevailing notions about what women (who were also of African descent) could and could not do.[15] One is reminded also of Harriet Jacobs's agency in her direct challenge to legal and social structures that made it permissible for a white man to demand her total submission to his will.[16]

That Walker was *theorizing* womanism long before she officially entered the neologism into literary history is also clear.[17] More than a decade before Walker spelled out her womanist aesthetic, the character of Ruth Copeland exhibited aspects of the womanist attitude in *The Third Life of Grange Copeland* (1970). Precocious and womanish as a young girl, Ruth clearly exhibits the attributes of the potential womanist subject, the kind that will survive *whole* in subsequent works. Likewise, the title character of *Meridian* (1976) epitomizes the courageous, willful behavior of the womanist subject, though critics disagree as to whether she becomes a fully realized subject. Meridian Hill, whom we might consider a projection of Ruth's potential into the immediate future, exemplifies the spiritual resolve of real women like Ruby Doris Robinson-Smith and Fannie Lou Hamer. We first encounter Meridian in the immediate aftermath of the Civil Rights Movement, which serves as the present moment of the story. She is *staring down* a tank (and the white men who operate it) in a small Mississippi town in order to integrate the local freak show. In another willful act, she brought the bloated body of a drowned black child to a city council meeting to convince them that integrating the public swimming pool was the right thing to do. Years before, she had the audacity to refuse the responsibility of motherhood in giving her own child up so that she could attend college. Compared to the type of virginal young ladies the college sought to mold, however, Meridian seemed outrageous (94). Her womanist resolve led her easily into the Civil Rights Movement, though when the Movement began to move away from nonviolence, she found it difficult to embrace the idea of killing for the revolution without first contemplating the implications to her soul. Walker recasts Meridian's contemplative nature in exemplary characters throughout her subsequent novels.

In her Pulitzer Prize-winning third novel, *The Color Purple*, Walker achieves a previously unrealized depiction of the womanist approach to life in the character of Shug Avery. Like Meridian Hill, Shug Avery is comfortable choosing an alternative to mothering. She leaves her children to pursue a career as a blues singer, an act considered scandalous by many. She expresses a free, open, fluid sexuality that is not bound by prefixes, which serves as further evidence of her willful, audacious, and even courageous approach to life. Sofia also displays the womanist attitude in refusing to allow Albert (her future father-in-law) to define her out-of-wedlock pregnancy in negative terms. Her life experiences mandate that she fight back when Harpo tries to dominate her, and she even survives the horrible series of circumstances set in motion when she rebuffs the white mayor's wife's offer of a job as her maid.

As the primary subject/narrator of *The Color Purple*, Celie must develop the womanist attitude, which Shug and Sofia already possess when she first encounters them, in order to undergo successfully the womanist process of transformation. Centered on the reciprocal relationship between Celie and Shug, *The Color Purple* begins with Celie as adolescent mother and victim of her stepfather's lust and ill-treatment. Celie is subsequently turned over to a husband who continues the abuse. The stunted relationship between Alfonso and Celie's mother, as well as that between Celie and her husband, mirrors the dysfunctional and tragic Copeland marriages from Walker's first novel. However, the womanist process, which Shug's appearance incites, propels the reciprocal relationship that rescues Celie from a fate similar to those Mem and Margaret suffered. In communion with Shug, Sofia, and/or Celie, other characters – Mary Alice, Eleanor Jane, Albert, Harpo – begin to exhibit signs of the womanist mindset.

Lissie, of *The Temple of My Familiar* (1989), is Walker's neologism made flesh. She is living history, exemplifying the womanist spirit of knowledge. She is Shug Avery magnified, responsible, outrageous, audacious, contrary, and whole. She embodies the womanist attitude as a result of having acquired the wisdom that comes with experiencing life from a variety of perspectives through multiple incarnations through time. Interestingly, Walker chooses the name Lisette for the French woman who exhibits the womanist attitude in *Possessing the Secret of Joy* (1992). Everything about Lisette's association with Adam – the fact that he is married, black, and American, the fact of her intentional out-of-wedlock pregnancy, the way she raises their son, and even her attempts to reach out to Adam's wife, Tashi – suggest that she is audacious, willful, and courageous. Prior to volunteering for what Walker refers to as female genital mutilation, Tashi had exhibited similar proclivities in her relationship to Adam and, generally, by daring to operate outside the narrow constraints of societal conventions. Tashi experiences a rebirth of her womanist spirit after she kills M'Lissa, her village *tsunga*.

Finally, Magdalena is the budding womanist in *By the Light of My Father's Smile* (1998). In this novel, Walker sends a family of fake missionaries to Mexico to live among a group of natural Indians.[18] Mr. and Mrs. Robinson are upwardly mobile, black middle-class, agnostic anthropologists, who pose as missionaries in order to qualify for the funds they need for field research. Unable to see the natural lifestyle of the Mundo in terms other than static and impoverished, Mr. Robinson tries to free them from their ignorance.[19] Eventually, he takes on the role of fake priest, and becomes "sucked into the black cloth" as Manuelito, the Mundo Indian who is Magdalena Robinson's soulmate, tells him. With this arrangement, Walker sets up a startling contrast between the natural (what is revealed to the Mundo through thousands of years of observing nature) and the artificial (what has been codified and handed down in written form). Manuelito asks Mr. Robinson point blank: "Did you really think we did not know we should love one another; that the person across from us is ourself? That stealing is bad; that wanting what other people have is hurtful to us? That we are a part of the Great Spirit and loved as such?" (148). Such questions reduce the drama surrounding the biblical story of the Ten Commandments to melodrama. Mr. Robinson's teaching of an ideology that he does not himself embrace, however, is the ultimate sign of disrespect for the Mundo and their natural way of life. The point is brought home in the act that provides the central conflict for the Robinson family.

Angered and frustrated by his daughter's womanish behavior, Mr. Robinson attempts to control Magdalena by beating her severely with the belt that was a gift from soulmate Manuelito. In effect, he drives Magdalena's budding womanism underground. In the afterlife, Manuelito explains to Mr. Robinson that the Mundo had bestowed the name Mad Dog on Magdalena because they recognized her as embodying the wisdom the mad dog realizes as a result of being separated from its mind. The Mundo practice such temporary separations, through herbal means, so as to avoid the kind of artificial life into which Mr. Robinson had fallen. They see in the mad dog the potential for gaining the wisdom not found in logic. After her father beats her in order to suppress her womanist proclivities, Magdalena buries her natural, audacious, willful spirit beneath layers of self-destructive fat. She will not forgive her father, and thus, like him, she exists in a state of static spiritual development for the rest of her corporeal existence. In the afterlife, Magdalena and her father receive another chance to achieve *wholeness*.[20] More than her five previous novels, *By the Light of My Father's Smile* reveals the womanist process in an almost pragmatic manner.

The second component of Walker's womanist aesthetic describes the womanist *vis-à-vis* her relationships with others and with herself, stresses connectedness over separatism, encourages an acceptance of a collective past as it is exhibited in the many hues of the African diaspora, and celebrates a legacy of resistance to oppression:

> 2. *Also*: A woman who loves other women, sexually and/or nonsexually. Appreciates and prefers women's culture, women's emotional flexibility (values tears as natural counterbalance of laughter), and women's strength. Sometimes loves individual men, sexually and/or nonsexually. Committed to survival and

wholeness of entire people, male *and* female. Not a separatist, except periodi-cally, for health. Traditionally universalist, as in: "Mama, why are we brown, pink, and yellow, and our cousins are white, beige, and black?" Ans.: "Well, you know the colored race is just like a flower garden, with every color flower represented." Traditionally capable, as in: "Mama, I'm walking to Canada and I'm taking you and a bunch of other slaves with me." Reply: "It wouldn't be the first time."[21]

Walker's womanist is in touch with her own fluid sexuality, which she shares at her discretion and pleasure with women and/or men. The womanist em-braces and openly expresses her sexuality in relationships with others. In *The Color Purple*, Walker gives us the Celie/Shug/Albert triad. Though Walker posits sexuality as a *good thing*, relationships can be sexual or not sexual. Celie and Albert learn to coexist as friends without interacting sexually. Lissie provides a veritable history of human sexuality in *The Temple of My Familiar*. Nevertheless, she and husband Rafe continue to enjoy a close in-timate relationship even after he no longer desires her sexually. They form a triad with Lissie's lover, Hal. Tashi's story represents the importance of unencumbered sexuality via negativa in *Possessing the Secret of Joy*. Though she is unable to experience sexual joy after her voluntary circumcision, Tashi does not condone her husband's affair with Lisette until after she has killed M'Lissa. It is Lisette who willingly accepts her role in the triad, who ex-presses her sexuality freely, and thus better exemplifies this aspect of the womanist. Walker begins her Acknowledgments at the end of *By the Light of My Father's Smile* by thanking the spirit of Eros, for the novel celebrates the erotic. The novel's central conflict arises as a result of Mr. Robinson's attempt to suppress his adolescent daughter's burgeoning sexuality.[22]

Though Walker's process is supposedly de-centered, the quest for personal and communal *wholeness* is the one aspect of the process that is most ap-parent in all six of her novels.[23] In this project, she employs recurring motifs of the spiritual journey or questing self, rebirth and transformation, the uni-versality of pain and suffering, and a holistic view of life that brings her idea of connectedness into full relief. At issue is the condition of the soul, and it is not simply a matter of the individual soul. She or he who achieves wholeness, or who aspires to achieve *wholeness*, bears the responsibility for showing others the way, *for lifting as they climb*. One imagines a chain, or a continuum, of humanity with each leading the next.

In *The Third Life of Grange Copeland*, Walker represents this idea in Grange's relationship to Ruth, and in Ruth's resolve to someday lead the way. Set in rural Georgia, the novel spans some sixty years from the early 1900s to the 1960s. Grange Copeland's journey comes packaged in three phases: He lives his first "life" as a tragic sharecropper turned brute, his second "life" as a southern migrant in the hostile North, and his third "life" as the somewhat enlightened and regenerated worldly guide for his grand-daughter, Ruth. Grange envisions for Ruth the possibility for "joy, laughter, contentment in being a woman . . . Survival was not everything. He had survived. But to survive *whole* was what he wanted for Ruth" (298).[24] The degeneration of Grange's soul, charted in the first part of the novel, gives way to a regenerative process in the second part, which leads Grange to the point of giving up his life for Ruth's sake.

The difference between Meridian Hill's spiritual development in *Meridian* and that of Grange Copeland is obvious, for Meridian's soul is never in the degenerated condition of Grange's. Indeed, Meridian Hill seems to move – spiritually and temporally speaking – from the point where Ruth is situated at the end of *The Third Life of Grange Copeland*. In her developing consciousness, Ruth points out certain weak aspects of her grandfather's spiritual development. She also recognizes the task ahead of her. Near the end of the novel she tells Grange, "I'd be bored stiff waiting for black folks to rise up so I could join them. Since I'm already ready to rise up and they ain't, it seems to me I should rise up first and let them follow me" (275–276). Ruth's words are manifested in Meridian's exemplary life as a willful and courageous civil rights worker, who ultimately serves as a spiritual guide for others.

Importantly, the questing subject of *Meridian* is a black woman, and the primary setting is still the American South. For most of her journey, Meridian, an avid civil rights worker, ponders the question of whether she would kill for the revolution. The question invokes the moment when the nonviolent Civil Rights Movement gave way to the more aggressive Black Power Movement. It is in her incessant pondering of this question about taking a life that we understand her soul to be highly evolved. Indeed, some critics see Meridian as destined for sainthood in her devotion to her calling, and certainly in her suffering; however, as Walker knows from experience, dedicated civil rights work was often physically and emotionally debilitating. People who live with the constant anxiety of being attacked develop nervous conditions and suffer a variety of physical ailments, including the loss of hair and weight.[25] If Meridian's physical suffering qualifies her for sainthood, then there were many others who would also qualify. Meridian actively rejects the role of Christian martyr when she says that Jesus Christ and Martin Luther King Jr. should have refused death as an option and simply left town. She follows her own advice and leaves town, but not before preparing the way for Truman Held, who takes Meridian's place in the community.

Truman will, in turn, light the way for former wife Lynne, who will light the way for the next seeker, and so the chain goes.

In *The Color Purple*, the chain becomes a circle of reciprocity that begins with the central relationship between Celie and Shug, when Shug arrives to serve as Celie's guide in her quest. That their relationship is reciprocal is clearly illustrated when Shug explains how and why she came to compose a song to Celie. The reciprocal relationship between Celie and Shug radiates outward to form an ever-widening cooperative community that includes Sofia, Albert, Harpo, their children, Mary Alice, and, ultimately, Eleanor Jane. The primary setting is rural Georgia, with Walker once again raising the taboo subject of physical and sexual violence within the black community. Epistles (Celie's letters to God, Nettie's letters to Celie, and Celie's letters to Nettie) comprise the narrative. Walker's growing optimism is reflected in her decision to cast the story as a romance, allowing for Celie's happy ending and, in a sense, giving the dead sharecropper wives of her first novel a chance for subject status.[26] (Celie's story also resembles the subgenre of African American literature known as the freedom narrative, in its movement from slavery to freedom, and in some of its built-in plot devices.) It is Shug Avery who gives voice to a universal relatedness: "one day . . . it come to me: that feeling of being part of everything, not separate at all." She likens the feeling to satisfying sex. Celie echoes Shug in directing her final letter: "Dear God. Dear stars, dear trees, dear sky, dear peoples. Dear Everything. Dear God. Thank you for bringing my sister Nettie and our children home" (286).

In her next novel, Walker expands the universal consciousness that Shug and Celie express. The cooperative community that Walker imagines in *The Temple of My Familiar* appears boundless, extending to all of creation, the condition of the soul more significant than ever, her womanist ideas given full rein. *The Temple of My Familiar* continues Walker's discourse on the communal quest for wholeness, culminating in a realization of oneness, an ideal unity among the living. There is no self and other, only the self and the familiar. In *Anything We Love Can Be Saved* (1997), Walker writes of a "central dream" in which she

> saw that our essential "familiar" is our own natural, untamed, "wild" spirit and that its temple is the cosmos, that is, freedom. This dream came complete with temple, familiar, Lissie and Suwelo, and the understanding that I was writing a "romance" (that is to say, a wisdom tale, memory, adventure) that was less about the relationships of human beings to each other than about the relationship of humans (women, in particular) to animals, who, in the outer world, symbolize woman's inner spirit. (118)

Walker extends and expands her idea of connectedness to depict relationships that transcend time, geographical space, and even the human form. She explains that she understood upon reaching *Temple*'s final chapter that "Hal had been instructing Suwelo about how to live – with women, with children, with other men, with animals, with white people. Con Todos!" (119). The "central dream" of *Temple*, Walker tells us, is about "our collusion with the forces that suppress and colonize our spirituality" (118). In *Temple*, Suwelo epitomizes the colonized mindset, most notably in his attitude toward his wife, Fanny Nzingha, and in his approach to the American history that he teaches for a living. Arguing that *Temple* signifies on Western metaphysical dualism, Ikenna Dieke asserts that in Walker's *The Temple of My Familar* that:

> For Alice Walker, artistic creativity is nothing but a deliberate act of giving form to a vision of the underlying or hidden links in the great universal chain of being . . . From the predominately Gothic vision in *The Third Life of Grange Copeland*, to the somewhat Camusian pastiche in *Meridian*, to the vision of the great gender divide-and-conquer in *The Color Purple*, Walker moves into *The Temple of My Familiar* and creates a salutary vision of reality, which points toward a monistic idealism in which humans, animals, and the whole ecological order coexist in a unique dynamic of pancosmic symbiosis. (129)

Meridian's sense that killing would irreparably harm her soul, and Shug Avery's acknowledgment that all of creation is connected are both implicit in *Temple*'s vision of universal symbiosis. Even in Walker's first novel, the cyclical nature of oppression depicted in the multigenerational family saga connects it to Walker's more recent novels. For example, Grange Copeland's final acts in Walker's first novel serve a disruptive function that parallels Tashi's killing of the village *tsunga* in *Possessing the Secret of Joy*.

By killing the *tsunga*, Tashi (as representative African woman) symbolically breaks the tradition that stood between her and *wholeness*. Walker uses the subject to illustrate the continuum (through time and space) of physical and spiritual damage that a single harmful act sets in motion. An addendum to *The Color Purple* provides the information that the Johnson family (Samuel, Corinne, Adam, Olivia) and Nettie arrived at Olinka the same day that Tashi's sister Dura, apparently a hemophiliac, bled to death after being circumcised by M'Lissa. Tashi had greeted them in tears. Hence, Samuel's fundamental question, which Adam remembers, "Why is the child crying?" (161). The question evokes the memory of Tashi's tears and questions the psychic well-being of the community that produces the crying child. Samuel's question conjures up the image of the toddler, Brownfield Copeland, spending his days alone and un-nurtured while his sharecropper parents enrich the landowner through their unrequited labor. We are reminded of the adolescent Celie, bleeding from her stepfather's rape, forced to groom her rapist even as the blood oozes down her legs. With Samuel's question, Walker lets no one "off the hook"; anyone who turns an apathetic eye or ear is complicit.

Possessing the Secret of Joy gives us the character M'Zee, or Carl. M'Zee is Lisette's uncle, a psychologist who feels that in witnessing Adam's and Tashi's suffering, he is being brought home to himself. He sees in them a self he has often felt "was only halfway at home on the European continent." In other words, he shares Tashi's (Walker's character from *The Color Purple* who reappears in this novel) suffering: "Harm to one is harm to the many" (84). Adam realizes too late in his marriage that he had always considered Tashi's suffering as "something singular, absolute" rather than part of a "continuum of pain" (165). Tashi's spiritual freedom is connected to the symbolic act of killing her *tsunga*, an act for which she resolutely accepts her death sentence. The letter Tashi composes to long-dead Lisette the night before her scheduled execution is a preview of the tone and style of narration for Walker's sixth novel, *By the Light of My Father's Smile*. In that novel, spirits (or angels) tell the story and work out in the spiritual realm those issues that remained unresolved at the time of their physical death.

Pierre, the son of Adam and Lisette, raises the question of connectedness another way in *Possessing the Secret of Joy*. He ponders whether the Marquis de Sade's "cruelty to women is somehow lodged in the collective consciousness of the French . . . like the zest of Rabelais, the wit of Molière" (138). Similarly, as the title character of *Meridian* considers the central question of whether she is willing to kill for the revolution, she wonders how killing for the revolution will affect the music of succeeding generations of African Americans. The question invokes the history of African American music. If the spirituals expressed the suffering of enslavement, and the blues grew out of the Southern rural experiences of Jim Crow apartheid, what kind of music would come from the collective and eager embrace of violence? How could Meridian/Walker have foreseen the birth of "gangsta" rap?

Walker's womanist process advocates separatism as a temporary solution for the sake of healing. In *Possessing the Secret of Joy*, Tashi speaks of "The secret place *I* come to heal myself" (84). Womanist wisdom suggests healing the self before attempting to heal others. Though her first novel came long before Walker set out the terms for the womanist process, one notes the limited progress Grange Copeland made toward healing himself during a period of separation from his Southern community before he was able to assist his granddaughter. Meridian Hill's frequent retreats give her the space for rejuvenation so that she is able to carry on her activist work. Shug

Avery understands fully the idea that occasional separations are a must for her continued resilience. Even Celie realizes that it is in everyone's best interest that she exit rural Georgia soon after she finds the cache of Nettie's letters that Albert has kept from her for years. Walker demonstrates via negativa that Tashi's attempt to retain a connection to the Olinka, regardless of circumstances, proved detrimental to her well-being.

The idea of temporary, occasional separation for the sake of health comes packaged in completely different terms in *By the Light of My Father's Smile*, however, for here the separation takes place internally. The Mundo take an *herbal separation from their minds* once a year to avoid falling into the complacent belief that logic explains everything.[27] Manuelito explains that the separation allows them to take in the knowledge they need to maintain their natural lifestyles. Magdalena, at puberty, existed in such a state before the beating. Mr. Robinson's soul cannot rest until he understands and acknowledges fully the harm he inflicted directly to Magdalena and, indirectly, to Susannah. Walker connects Mr. Robinson's negative turn to his fake practice of Christianity.

Walker's valorization of connectedness (the opposite of separatism) allows her to trace a continuum of pain and suffering and continue the development of her idea of the universal. She also illustrates through plot, theme, and narration how harmful acts become part of the individual or collective psyche and come to bear on ensuing generations. Yet, the focus is on healing, rather than blame. Healing begins with accepting responsibility.[28] The Brownfields, Alberts, and Alfonsos of the world must accept responsibility for their own deeds regardless of what has come before, just as Mr. Robinson's ignorance of *the natural way* is no excuse for the psychic harm he inflicts on Magdalena in *By the Light of My Father's Smile*. Magdalena must, in spite of the beating, take responsibility for her own soul's well-being and give her father the unconditional love that her mother had shown toward him.

This aspect of the womanist is expressed in Walker's third component, from *In Search of Our Mothers' Gardens* which also emphasizes sensual pleasure:

> Loves music. Loves dance. Loves the moon. *Loves* the Spirit. Loves love and food and roundness. Loves struggle. *Loves* the Folk. Loves herself. *Regardless.* (xii)

Like female subjectivity, sensual pleasure and unconditional love find little healthy expression in Walker's first novel. Nevertheless, their profound absence speaks volumes and makes it ripe for exploration on that basis. The sharecropper existence, as Walker portrays it, is fraught with pleasure denying hardship. The pleasures young couples take in each other, in being with each other, and in their experience of the natural world, are soon casualties of the sharecropper life. Though the space of Josie's club offers some possibility for the experience of sensual delights, time and again it becomes, like its owner, a misused space. In Josie we see an early manifestation of Magdalena Robinson (*By the Light of My Father's Smile*) in the sense that the way each woman expresses (or does not express) her sexuality is directly related to unfinished business with her father. Both Grange Copeland and his son misuse Josie, Grange as an escape from the brutal reality of his sharecropper life, and Brownfield as revenge for his father's abandonment. Grange's wife, Margaret, commits suicide after her husband abandons her (first emotionally, and then physically). Grange's degenerate offspring, Brownfield, subsequently kills his wife, Mem, whose name is from the French for "same," which underscores the cyclical nature of Copeland family violence. Brownfield even tries years later to destroy Ruth's chances for a meaningful life. Margaret, Mem, and even Josie, clearly end up as victims, which leaves Ruth as the novel's only potential expression of a womanist subject.

In *Meridian*, sensual pleasure and erotic love take a back seat to the important work of the Civil Rights Movement and Meridian's own spiritual journey. Meridian's pleasure manifests itself spiritually as ecstasy (57), though Walker notes that critics have tended to overlook the "whole sublayer of Indian consciousness" in Meridian, in which one recognizes an appreciation of natural things, including trees, birds, and the desert.[29] In *The Color Purple*, this aspect of Walker's womanist process is most evident in Shug Avery. Shug, the artist, is earthy; she celebrates the sensual and treats the world to music that comes directly from her soul. Her music invites dancing, and it is important to remember that Shug's concept of God/Goddess (the *philosophy* of connectedness or relatedness at the core of *The Color Purple* and which Walker expands in subsequent works) is consistent with her healthy embrace of all the sensual pleasures. Shug Avery expects and allows herself the orgasms that Hurston's Janie Crawford was able to achieve only after she extricated herself from an outdated narrative about African American women's sexuality. She is a fitting personal (hands-on) guide in Celie's experience of sensual pleasure.

Lissie is Shug's highly developed counterpart in *Temple*, and, like Shug, she shares the stage with other women and men, including Zedé, Carlotta, Fanny, Arveyda, and Hal. Significantly, most of these characters are artists. Tashi, of *Possessing the Secret of Joy*, is also an artist, but Tashi is alienated from the sensual pleasures as a result of her circumcision. Her husband, Adam, finds in Lisette a friend and lover who deliberately and lovingly fulfills the missing aspect of his relationship with Tashi. Lisette gives birth to the deeply sensitive Pierre, who dedicates his life to the fight against the practice of female circumcision. It is Pierre who tells Tashi that "the greatest curse in some African countries is not 'son of a bitch' but 'son of an uncircumcised mother,'" (274).

Walker best develops the third component of her definition in *By the Light of My Father's Smile*. Manuelito and his Mundo clan are a natural people, the folk, who celebrate the sensual pleasures. They live their lives in accordance with nature's cycles. For the Mundo, music is so important that they believe one who makes the transition from the physical world to the spiritual world while singing will experience "self-assurance on the path of death" (148). Subtitled, "A Story of Requited Love, Crossing Over, and the Sexual Healing of the Soul," *By the Light of My Father's Smile* is first and foremost a thorough enactment of that part of Walker's womanist aesthetic concerned with embracing sensual pleasure and expressing love for self, others, and all things, unconditionally. This last aspect is reflected in Magdalena's need to love her father despite the harm he inflicted on her. Mr. Robinson (and the traditions upon which he relies for support) does as much harm toward driving Magdalena's healthy sense of herself underground as Alfonso and Albert did toward driving Celie's sexuality and self-esteem underground in *The Color Purple*. Manuelito serves as Mr. Robinson's spiritual guide, leading him gently toward the enlightenment he needs in order to reconcile with Magdalena.

According to Manuelito, the Mundo had allowed the Robinsons to stay and interact with them because Mr. Robinson was always making love to his wife, a sign of the quality they treasured as a natural acceptance of sensual pleasure and a natural appreciation for women. Essentially, the Mundo came to realize after thousands of years how closely their routines were tied to the cycles of the moon, and how closely women are connected to the moon and its rhythms. They are in synchronization with nature, and thus, part of everything. Manuelito explains that a "woman's tides, her blood tides connect with moon," and during a certain period, women just do not want to be bothered. Manuelito recalls that his mother, "during such times, would actually throw things" at his father (208–209). Since the Mundo "love to make love," this is a gloomy time for them. They also recognize by the condition of the moon when a woman is most likely to become pregnant, and since they cannot afford many children, they are careful during that time. This simple remedy to unwanted pregnancy and the economic hardship that comes with it places the responsibility on both men and women, and it makes absurd the kinds of violent responses we see in Mr. Robinson, as well as in Josie's father (*The Third Life of Grange Copeland*).[30] The Mundo believe that woman is neither the purveyor of some original calamity nor of a gender subordinate to man. Her ability to create life should cause celebration, not incite fear and violence. This, among other reasons, is why they barely tolerated the missionaries who came to them with the story of Original Sin, which they see as anti-woman. They use the cycles of the moon not only for birth control, but also to help them (men and women) to coexist harmoniously. In the afterlife, Manuelito explains to Mr. Robinson the Mundo belief that the "cathedral of the future will be nature . . . In the end, people will be driven back to trees. To streams. To rocks that do not have anything built on them" (193). Thus, in her sixth novel, Walker brings to the surface the Native American consciousness that lay beneath the surface in *Meridian*.

The fourth component of Walker's womanist process is comprised of a single straightforward statement that has, nevertheless, invited much critical analysis:

Womanist is to feminist as purple to lavender.   (xi–xii)

To enhance our understanding of the last component of Walker's womanist aesthetic, it is important to consider the other three components, as well as how Walker enacts her womanist project in her own fiction. The first component set out the proper womanist attitude or approach to self-actualization. Though it specified that a womanist is a black feminist or a feminist of color, the qualities Walker delineates for the womanist are qualities that anyone might exhibit. Walker has demonstrated this time and again in her fiction. The second component focuses on relationships, and here Walker tries to avoid the self-and-other split that drives Western dualism. This becomes increasingly explicit in her novels and is probably best developed in *The Temple of My Familiar* and *By the Light of My Father's Smile*. The third component invites the unbridled expression of love of all living things, an appreciation for the natural world and its cycles, and the experience of sensual pleasure. The focus on connectedness, both in her articulation of womanism and in her representation of it in her novels, would indicate a tendency toward inclusiveness rather than exclusiveness.[31] Her attention to illuminating the limitations of Western dualism and the binary oppositions that undergird it would be grossly undermined by her own failure to avoid setting up her own false dichotomies. The differing views of critics suggest, however, that the matter is up for debate.

Dorothy Grimes writes that the analogy is "apparently intended to capture the texture and intensity of *womanist* as opposed to *feminist*."[32] Consistent with her charge that Walker's model is idealist and essentialist, Tuzyline Jita Allan offers that "even with the filter of metaphor, the last statement fails to conceal the deep lines of division drawn here between black and white feminists. Walker sets up (black) womanism and (white) feminism in a binary opposition from which the former emerges a privileged, original term and the latter, a devalued, pale replica."[33] Maria Lauret believes that the final component of Walker's definition *absorbs* the white feminist (lavender) "into her project and *radicalises* it to the point of no return."[34] This last idea would be in keeping with Walker's focus on connectedness. Purple, a more intense color than lavender, is not merely the result of adding black to lavender. It also symbolizes the place of those black women in American society who, like Celie, must find a way to resist multiple oppressions related to race, class, gender, and sexuality, and to survive whole. Obviously important is the relationship between this particular component of womanism and the title of Walker's best-known novel, *The Color Purple*. Linda Abbandanato points out that purple is "encoded within the novel as a sign of indomitable female spirit."[35] The audacious, self-loving, overtly and fluidly sexual Shug Avery utters the important insight that explains the connection between the concept of God/Goddess and the presence of the color purple in nature.[36]

In an early assessment of Walker's work, Barbara Christian noted her attention to the recurring motif of the "Black woman as creator" and how the black woman's "attempt to be whole relates to the health of her community."[37] A womanist is pro-woman, not anti-man. Against a binary world view, Walker uses her novels to resist the implication of Western dualism that man should dominate all of nature, including woman. Ultimately, she constructs a womanist cosmology, which is most apparent in her fourth and sixth novels. The communal relationships Walker depicts, particularly in her last three novels, transcend time, space, the physical realm, and even the species we call human – which includes its own subcategories. Whether Walker's womanist aesthetic is flexible enough to include her hopeful vision of wholeness for an ever-expanding community is clearly a subject for the kind of critical debate that makes Walker cringe.[38]

NOTES

1. The title essay for this volume had been published almost a decade earlier, in 1974.
2. Walker tells us that she not only knew people in her own life with the nickname Shug, but she also found a character named Shug in Hurston's work (Walker, "Anything We Love Can Be Saved: The Resurrection of Zora Neale Hurston and Her Work," *Anything We Love Can Be Saved* (New York: Random House, 1997), p. 46. In her Dedication to *I Love Myself When I Am Laughing . . .* (1979), Walker describes Hurston in terms that she will later use to articulate her womanist aesthetic (1–5). In "Alice Walker's Life and Work: The Essays" (*Alice Walker*, New York: St. Martin's Press, 2000), Maria Lauret offers a comparative examination of Walker and Hurston and their works. She suggests that Walker's definition

of womanism "presents less a political analysis of black women's oppression, let alone a programme to end it, than a depiction of a positive role model" (18–19).

3. See Walker, *In Search of Our Mothers' Gardens* (New York: Harcourt Brace Company, 1983).

4. Sharon Wilson, "A Conversation with Alice Walker," *Alice Walker: Critical Perspectives Past and Present*, ed. Henry Louis Gates and Kwame Anthony Appiah, (New York: Amistad, 1993), pp. 319–325.

5. Smith demonstrated the need for this new approach by first reviewing the glaring omissions of black women's work in studies of American literature, American women's literature, and African American literature. She pointed out that even black women critics failed to take into consideration the connections among "the politics of black women's lives, what we write about, and our situation as artists" (133). Next she offered a black feminist assessment of Toni Morrison's *Sula* (1973) to further demonstrate that a black feminist approach might lead to additional insights about a given text. Walker's infamous challenge to Patricia Meyer Spacks and white feminists in general in "One Child of One's Own" is included in *In Search of Our Mothers' Gardens*, pp. 361–383.

6. Walker's articulation was only a small part of an ongoing and evolving project that included the work of critics such as Hazel Carby, Barbara Christian, Deborah McDowell, and Mary Helen Washington, to name only a few. Tuzyline Jita Allan locates Walker's "'womanist' ethos" in "the middle ground between McDowell's not-so sanguine expectations and Carby's hearty historicization." It "embodies both the frustration and the promise of black feminist criticism" (Tuzyline Jita Allan, "Introduction: Decoding Womanist Grammar of Difference," *Womanist and Feminist Aesthetics: A Comparative Review* [Athens: Ohio University Press, 1995], p. 5).

7. See, for example, Joseph Ajibola Adeleke, "Feminism, Black Feminism and the Dialectics of Womanism," *Critical Essay on the Novel in Francophone Africa*, ed. Aduke Adebayo (Ibadan: AMD Publishers, 1996); Ikenna Dieke, ed., *Critical Essays on Alice Walker* (Westport, CT: Greenwood Press, 1999); Ana Maria Fraile-Marcos, "'As Purple to Lavender': Alice Walker's Womanist Representation of Lesbianism," *Literature and Homosexuality*, ed. Michael J. Meyer (Amsterdam: Rodolpi, 2000), pp. 111–134; Clara Juncker, "Womanizing Theory," *American Studies in Scandinavia* 30.2 (1998): 43–49; Maria Lauret, *Alice Walker* (New York: St. Martin's Press, 2000); and Meera Viswanathan and Evangelina Mancikam, "Is Black Woman to White as Female Is to Male? Restoring Alice Walker's Womanist Prose to the Heart of Feminist Literary Criticism," *Indian Journal of American Studies* 28. 1–2 (1998): 15–20.

8. Madhu Dubey, *Black Women Novelists and the Nationalist Aesthetic* (Bloomington: Indiana University Press, 1994), p. 4. The emphasis on the collective community in her work connects Walker to writer and activist Frances Ellen Watkins Harper and her insistence in the late nineteenth century that black people could ill afford to indulge in America's notion of the rugged individualist. Other connections lie in the attention both give to representing the qualities of the true man (or natural man in Walker's case) alongside the qualities of the true (or natural) woman, and in the relationship between art and activism.

9. Katie Cannon, *Katie's Canon: Womanism and the Soul of the Black Community* (New York: Continuum, 1995), p. 23.

10. Clara Juncker, "Womanizing Theory," p. 46.
11. Alice Walker, "Gifts of Power: The Writings of Rebecca Jackson," *In Search of Our Mothers' Gardens*, pp. 71–82.
12. Alice Walker, *In Search of Our Mothers' Gardens*, p. 81.
13. Alice Walker, *Anything We Love Can Be Saved*, p. 81.
14. See Richardson "Preface," *Maria W. Stewart* (Bloomington: Indiana University Press, 1987), p. xiii.
15. All these women breached societal expectations of their behavior so as to live the fullest possible lives. This is not to suggest that these women identified as feminists; however, Walker's adjectives for the womanist attitude would apply to their assertive behavior in challenging conventions related to gender. Born free in 1795 in Horntown, Pennsylvania, Rebecca Cox Jackson was a charismatic itinerant preacher who later founded a community of Shakers in Philadelphia that was predominantly black and female. Among other things, the dual-gender concept of deity initially attracted Jackson to the Shaker faith. Her literary legacy includes the spiritual autobiography, *Gifts of Power*. See Jean Humez, "Rebecca Cox Jackson," *African American Women in America*, Vol. 1, ed. Darlene Clark Hine (Brooklyn: Carlson Publishing, Inc., 1993), pp. 626–627. Born free but very poor in Cape May, New Jersey on February 11, 1783, Jarena Lee's family was forced to hire her into service when she was only 7. It was around 1811, as a member of Philadelphia's Bethel African Methodist Episcopal Church that Lee felt called to preach. She faced instant resistance from the founder and minister in charge, Richard Allen, who believed the Methodist discipline precluded women from becoming preachers. Some eight years later, however, she would gain Allen's endorsement as a preacher, but only after her own bold and spontaneous demonstration of her ability to exhort (see Jualynne E. Dodson, "Jarena Lee," *African American Women*, vol. 1, ed. Clark Hine). Born free near Philadelphia around 1790, Zilpha Elaw was drawn to Methodist evangelism at an early age. After marrying, bearing a child, and moving to Burlington, New Jersey, she continued her religious devotion; it was during a Methodist camp meeting in 1817 that she fell into a "trance of ecstasy." Following that event, she began to offer prayers for others at public meetings as an itinerant preacher, and eventually – after the death of her husband – she moved to Philadelphia to begin her ministry. Elaw would later brave the dangers inherent in carrying her messages into the slave states. Her memoirs contain revealing information about how women were received as public speakers in early nineteenth century America (see Gayle T. Tate, "Zilpha Elaw," *African American Women*, vol. 1, ed. Clark Hine). Sojourner Truth is the well-known nineteenth-century formerly enslaved woman who became an abolitionist and women's rights activist. Born in slavery as Isabella Bomefree around 1799 in Ulster County, New York, Truth is best remembered for her challenging speeches. See Nell Irvin Painter, "Martin R. Delany," *Black Leaders of the Nineteenth Century*, ed. Leon Litwack and August Meier (Urbana: University of Illinois Press, 1988), pp. 149–171.
16. See Harriet A. Jacobs, *Incidents in the Life of a Slave Girl*, ed. Jean Fagan Yellin (Cambridge: Harvard University Press, 1861, rpt. 1987).
17. Consider, for example, the resistance Barbara Christian expresses in "The Race for Theory" (1987; *Within the Circle*, ed. Angelyn Mitchell [Durham: Duke University Press, 1994], pp. 348–359). In response to the mandate that black

feminist critics articulate a theoretical framework in which to situate African American women's literature. Likewise, Katie Geneva Cannon (referencing an essay by Hortense Spillers) asserts that we need to be aware of entangled power relations within society whereby "certain people whether by accident, design, providence, or the most complicated means of academic currency exchange high-handedly dictate the specific disciplinary aims, setting the parameters as well as the agenda, for each field of study" (24). In Walker's womanist aesthetic the privileging of so-called high theory becomes another offshoot of Western dualism.

18. We learn in this novel that "Indian," rather than a politically incorrect term for Native Americans, is derived from the Greek words meaning "in God."

19. The fact that the Robinsons are anthropologists evokes the history of Hurston's own experiences as an anthropologist, who lived among the folk and collected a wealth of folk materials.

20. Here, Walker again holds out hope for those women and men who, in her previous novels, were not allowed this achievement in their corporeal lives.

21. Alice Walker, *In Search of Our Mothers' Gardens*, Preface, p. xi.

22. Walker seems to be strongly indebted to Audre Lorde's "Uses of the Erotic," *Sister Outsider: Essays and Speeches* (Freedom, CA: Crossing Press, 1984), pp. 53–59.

23. See John O'Brien, "Alice Walker," *Alice Walker: Critical Perspectives Past and Present*, ed. Henry Louis Gates and Kwame Anthony Appiah (New York: Amistad, 1993), p. 33, or Walker *In Search of Our Mothers' Gardens*, p. xi.

24. Madhu Dubey concludes that the novel's "heavy reliance on psychological realism collapses its alternative notion of a whole identity into the humanist model of full individuality . . . Its strict adherence to the formal elements of realism obstructs the novel's ideological aim of liberating a radically new vision of community and political change, as well as of black identity" (*African American Women Novelists* 112).

25. Real-life examples of Meridians exist in women such as Ruby Doris Robinson, Anne Moody, Fannie Lou Hamer, Gloria Richardson, and many others.

26. See Molly Hite, "Romance, Marginality, Matrilineage: *The Color Purple*," *The Color Purple*, Model Critical Interpretations Series, ed. Harold Bloom (Philadelphia: Chelsea House Publishers, 2000), pp. 89–105, who argues that the romance serves as the most likely structural paradigm for assessing the merits of *The Color Purple* and *Their Eyes Were Watching God* (92).

27. Walker discusses the usefulness of temporary mental excursions in an early interview in Claudia Tate's *African American Women Writers at Work*, 179. If one considers Captain Falcon's articulation of Western dualism – featuring the bifurcated Mind that cannot but enact the Self and Other split – in Charles Johnson's prizewinning novel, *Middle Passage* (1990), this idea makes perfect sense.

28. Walker points out in the Afterword to *The Third Life of Grange Copeland* that the violence she depicts in the novel, such as the killing of Mem by her sharecropper husband, is based on real examples of oppressed persons taking out their rage on one another in her childhood community of Eatonton, Georgia. Walker wanted to illustrate the futility of their actions. The very real fact of Brownfield's oppression by the dominant society in no way excuses his oppression of Mem (343, 345).

29. Claudia Tate, *Black Women Writers at Work* (New York: Continuum, 1983).

30. Certainly Magdalena's awakening sexuality recalls Janie Crawford's expreience of pleasure under the pear tree, and the pleasing smell of basil and other spices

Mattie Michael experiences during her *seduction* in Naylor's *The Women of Brewster Place* (1982).

31. Tuzyline Jita Allan asserts that Walker's womanism is essentialist because she defines a womanist as a black feminist or feminist of color, which "excludes white feminists whose creative vision approximates the womanist ideal . . . or who might choose to incorporate aspects of womanism in their writing . . . . It also assumes that by virtue of being black or nonwhite, a feminist is necessarily womanist" (*Womanist and Feminist Aesthetics* 93). Madhu Dubey, in addressing Walker's full definition, concludes that "womanism . . . may be interpreted as an attempt to integrate black nationalism into feminism, to articulate a distinctively black feminism that shares some of the objectives of black nationalist ideology. Taking the term 'womanist' from a black folk expression, Walker distinguishes her ideology from white feminism" (Madhu Dubey, "'To Survive Whole': The Integrative Aims of Womanism in *The Third Life of Grange Copeland*," *African American Women Novelists*, p. 107).

32. Dorothy Grimes, "Mariama Ba's *So Long a Letter* and Alice Walker's *In Search of Our Mothers' Gardens*: A Senegalese and an African American Perspective on 'Womanism'," *Global Perspectives on Teaching Literature: Shared Visions and Distinctive Visions*, ed. Sandra Ward Lott *et al.* (Urbana: National Council of Teachers of English, 1993), p. 66.

33. Tuzyline Jita Allan, *Womanist and Feminist Aesthetics*, p. 6.

34. Maria Lauret, "Alice Walker's Life and Work: The Essays," in *Alice Walker*, p. 21.

35. Linda Abbandonato, "Rewriting the Heroine's Story in *The Color Purple*," *Alice Walker: Critical Perspectives Past and Present*, ed. Henry Louis Gates and K. Anthony Appiah (New York: Amistad, 1993), p. 306.

36. One might also consider Walker's description of African American women's vaginas in "One Child of One's Own" as the color of raspberries and blackberries (which Abbandanato recalls) as well as her suggestion that white feminists have problems envisioning them.

37. Barbara Christian, "Alice Walker: The Black Woman Artist as Wayward," *Black Women Writers: 1950–1980*, ed. Mari Evans (New York: Anchor, 1984), p. 457.

38. In an interview, Walker explains her dislike of critics: "Criticism is something that I don't fully approve of, because I think for the critic it must be very painful to always look at things in a critical way. I think you miss so much. And you have to sort of shape everything you see to the way you're prepared to say it, instead of the way it reveals itself to you. Amen," (Sharon Wilson, "A Conversation and Alice Walker," *Alice Walker: Critical Perspectives Past and Present*, ed. Henry Louis Gates and Kwame Anthony Appiah, p. 320).

15

KEITH BYERMAN

Vernacular modernism in the novels of John Edgar Wideman and Leon Forrest

Recent work in African American literary studies has attempted to define an "Afro-modernism," an aesthetic position that participates in the project of modernity while not being subsumed by or subordinated to the "high" modernism of the early twentieth century. While Houston A. Baker has identified this practice as "mastery of form/deformation of mastery,"[1] Richard Powell and others have defined it as a "blues aesthetic,"[2] clearly linking it to the African American vernacular tradition. While these are highly useful constructions, they are not quite adequate to much of modern and contemporary black writing. These theorizations have created a "difference from" high modernism when at least some artists – Robert Hayden, Gwendolyn Brooks, and Ralph Ellison are clear examples – have chosen to position themselves within the tradition of T. S. Eliot, James Joyce, and William Faulkner. At the same time, they have also made use of the vernacular tradition, but this should not be surprising, since many of the "high" modernists themselves, whether in poetry, fiction, or the visual arts, found the vernacular to be an important resource. The two authors under consideration here, John Edgar Wideman and Leon Forrest, are part of this grouping. While Fritz Gysin, in an earlier chapter in this volume, locates them within the context of postmodernism, they have both explicitly positioned themselves as modernists, at least in some aspects of their work. It is therefore useful to explore that identity as one means of grasping their connection to black postmodernism.

"Modernism" has been one of the most fluid terms of critical discourse. It is often associated with a specific period, a set of ideas and values, a collection of artistic practices and products, or a list of names. Michael Levenson, in his introduction to the *Cambridge Companion to Modernism*, has wisely chosen to suggest some characteristics rather than a strict definition of the movement: "the recurrent act of fragmenting unities (unities of character or plot or pictorial space or lyric form), the use of mythic paradigms, the refusal of norms of beauty, the willingness to make radical linguistic experiment, all often inspired by the resolve (in Eliot's phrase) to startle and disturb the public."[3] In addition to these formal traits, modernists saw themselves interrogating the foundations of culture. As Sara Blair notes, "In the moment of Modernism, 'culture' itself – what constitutes it, whose property it is, how it identifies or informs national or racial bodies – is a deeply political issue. And this fact, it can be argued, is modernism's most important contribution to the politics of its moment, and to those of ours."[4] In this second sense, African American writing can be said to have always been modern, at least since Phillis Wheatley exercised, in David Trotter's term, a "will-to-literature."[5] The very existence of black literary expression raised questions about the validity of a whites-only American culture.

"Vernacular" is also a term with variant meanings, especially in the context of the modern era. Its origins are in discussions of language use, as in Dante's choice to write in Italian rather than Latin, "the language or dialect native to a region or country." But in folklore studies, it has more general connotations, fitting better Webster's other definition, "a style of artistic or technical and esp. architectural expression employing the commonest forms, materials, and decorations of a place, period, or group." Within African American culture, the vernacular includes the conventional genres of folklore (tales, songs, beliefs, material culture) as well as performative aspects of storytelling, call-and-response, verbal contests, and religious practices. These mostly oral forms and practices are generally understood as constituting the basis of African American culture; not surprising considering that, for most of American history, blacks have been legally or socially forced into a situation of illiteracy and thus had to rely on oral tradition to sustain and nurture their culture. In addition, the very otherness of the vernacular generates much of its power. It is, after all, as Paul Arnett says, "language *in use* that differs from the official languages of power and reflects complex intercultural relationships charged with issues of race, class, region, and education."[6] It serves as counter-memory to the narratives of the dominant order. Moreover, Arnett adds, "vernaculars acquire additional moment because in recent history they have been among the few genuinely uncontrollable cultural energies" (xxii).

If vernaculars have this critical and subversive authority, then it is not unexpected that modernists, committed to "startling and disturbing the public," would find them of great use. What better source for undermining the claims of cultural power than the suppressed elements of the culture itself? What better perspective than the point of view of those forced to exist behind and below the authority figures of the society? Thus, the voices of the Dublin streets or of Mississippi blacks and poor whites or of jazz clubs can speak effectively of the sham that is modern society. Moreover, their very "rawness" expresses a vitality that civilization has lost.

In twentieth-century African American writing, the vernacular has had a consistent relationship to that writing which considered itself "new." Whether it was the blues-influenced poetry of Langston Hughes, the folk voices of Zora Neale Hurston, the jazz-inflected fiction of Ralph Ellison, or the street talk of the cultural nationalists, what has constituted the generational shifts in black writing has been the incorporation of African American cultural elements. Recent work on the Harlem Renaissance has suggested that it is this feature that marks it as one of the "modernisms" of the twentieth century, one that has been ignored because of the critical bias in favor of high modernism.[7] Ellison's break with the protest tradition associated with Richard Wright can be understood precisely as his willingness to use modernist methods in conjunction with vernacular elements.

Vernacular expression, especially in African American culture, focuses on process more than product, especially since the product, in Alice Walker's phrase, is for "everyday use."[8] It is the style of storytelling, sermonizing, or blues singing that is crucial, in part because the content is already known to the audience. As in modernism, technique is central to establishing the authority of the artist. "Mastery of form" defines the reputation of the creator and the quality of the creation. But Baker's other term, "deformation of mastery," is also relevant. Because the materials of folk art are always old, the vernacular artist must "make it new" by signifying on the work of other artists.[9] Such acknowledgment can take the form of parody, of renaming, of homage, or of direct borrowing. In this process, both similarity to and difference from the source are recognized, just as they are in T. S. Eliot's "Tradition and the Individual Talent." Thus, while modernism and vernacular art are very different in their purposes, registers, and engagement with social reality, they share aspects that make them available for African American writers.

While Leon Forrest and John Edgar Wideman bring these elements together in their writing, they do so in very different ways. What Sara Blair says about the distinction between high modernists and Harlem modernists is relevant here: "If the landscape of modernity reads to Eliot and company as a symbolic wasteland, it appears for other writers to be a Mecca, a metropolis of multivalent possibilities."[10] Forrest, for example, assumes no inherent conflict between modernist technique and vernacular expression. Quite explicitly taking Joyce and Faulkner as two of his models,[11] he sees in their methods a means of rendering cultural experience that is rich and complex, often bordering on chaos. Given his understanding of African American life and history, realistic representation would simply not work; like Ellison, he embraces experimentation as the best way to tell his stories. In contrast, Wideman has a much darker vision and has seen the relationship between modernism and the vernacular as much more vexed. According to his own statements and the arguments of James Coleman, the relationship is almost exclusionary: connection to modernism means disconnection from black tradition and its expressive forms.[12] In this career narrative, Wideman spent his first three novels creating himself as a modernist, with a special emphasis on alienation as a theme; after a break of several years that involved educating himself in black culture, he began writing a very different fiction, one devoted to depicting families and communities and to challenging the dominant social order. What this model overlooks is his continued practice of modernist technique and, moreover, in good modernist fashion, his ongoing critique of the *cultural* failings of American society.

The work of Leon Forrest is characterized by its richness of voices and storytelling. In all of his fictions, stories are embedded within stories and narrative voices recreate the voices of other speakers in endless play. In addition, there are constant allusions to other literary and cultural texts, including Shakespeare, Melville, Dostoevsky, Joyce, Faulkner, and Ellison, as well as the Bible. Stylistically, he makes use of stream of consciousness, dream sequences, visions, monologues, song lyrics, repetition, elements of epic, and the fragmentation of time. Like Faulkner, he generates his own world through interconnected narratives across novels. While Forrest is very much aware of the social deprivation that blacks have suffered in American history, he is primarily concerned with demonstrating the resources that they bring to that situation. Most of his major characters are orphans, but out of that condition they manage to engender communities built on the possibilities of the vernacular.

There Is a Tree More Ancient Than Eden (1973) describes the coming of age of Nathaniel Witherspoon. While the present time of the story is only a day, it moves through three generations of his family, dating back to slavery. Nathaniel is potentially Joyce's Stephen Dedalus or Faulkner's Quentin Compson, a son lost in the world without immediately apparent familial or cultural resources. His mother has died and his father is absent from the present time of the narrative. But while Forrest's protagonist must experience loss and come close to despair, he never reaches a point of complete isolation. From the beginning of the novel, he is presented with options, from the family, the community, and the culture. The novel is structured in five parts (with a sixth added in a 1988 edition) that are linked by theme and imagery much more than plot. In the first part, "Lives," we are given biographies of some of the characters who will appear in the book, but these are less factual accounts than they are complex narratives that blend documents, legends, personal statements, and passages of prose-poetry. The point is not to provide information, but rather to suggest the range of responses available to a young black man. These include open resistance to oppression, religion, drug addiction, or some form of endurance that occasionally required acts of deception, or "Tomming." But Forrest is careful to depict the latter option as a device of survival and not an act of betrayal. He says of Louis Armstrong: "Press-music-money magnates always kept out of the news the very substantial contributions Armstrong made to the freedom movement, as they enjoy dividing Dipper from the young and his own people on the shaky grounds that he was a 'Tom' when in the end it was from the people themselves that Armstrong's towering and revolutionary power issued."[13] The statement serves not only as a defense of the musician, but also of Forrest himself and all other black artists who appropriate elements of Western culture into their work. By espousing the legitimacy of a spectrum of life choices and of all the cultural possibilities for one who is both black and American, the author sets up a dialectic for his protagonist in which there is simultaneously too much and too little to choose from in shaping his identity. The biographies show both the potential and the danger of each choice for one seeking black manhood. The next two sections are structured as call-and-response, in which Nathaniel first envisions himself as a fallen angel, with linked narratives of African American men who have had to struggle alone in a racist society. This "Nightmare" section is followed by "The Dream," in which the religious faith of Hattie Breedlove shows how the lost individual can be sustained by the community. But here, too, the path is one of struggle: belief does not eliminate suffering nor justify it; rather it makes it possible to endure. The following section, "The Vision," links that personal suffering to a national narrative of racism. In a surreal, apocalyptic allegory, Nathaniel sees a black man crucified and dismembered as a sacrifice for the society. The result is not healing but the end of time. The original final part, "Wakefulness," brings Nathaniel face to face with his responsibility for himself. He is able to grieve for what he has lost, but also to go forward. But going forward, in a gesture that combines modernist and vernacular perceptions, does not mean taking on a unitary identity, but rather becoming one capable of endless change: "Upon this earth young man you will learn the advantages of changing your name and your ways when attempting to ford dangerous, marshy country" (*Tree*, 155).

What *There Is a Tree* does on the individual level, *The Bloodworth Orphans* (1997) does on the communal level. It is a complex of narratives about a family and a community that draws on myth and epic to construct and problematize identity and origins. Nathaniel Witherspoon is again part of the story, but now primarily as a collector of the stories of others. What he discovers, consistent with modernist themes, is that the quest for identity, especially for African Americans, is doomed as long as it is a search for origins. Virtually every character is an orphan seeking an actual or substitute father. Since the "Bloodworth" of the title refers to a Southern slaveholding family that produced a number of unacknowledged mixed-race children, the novel is a metaphor of the racial history of the United States. Thus, for the characters, to discover one's origins in fact would be to discover one's illegitimacy; this situation leads to the repeated use of the spiritual "Scandalize My Name" in reference to these figures. Through religion, through artistic expression, or through sheer personal power, they attempt to come to terms with what might best be called their blues conditions. But no matter how good or beautiful they might be, their obsession with origins leads to disaster. Incest, murder, rape, mob violence, and apocalyptic riot run through the text as the outcome of their quests. The only solution offered is one similar to that of *There Is a Tree*; as Nathaniel and one of the older black Bloodworth orphans escape the riot, they pick up an abandoned baby. By doing so, they constitute themselves as a family of the "lost-found," those seeking not origins but a new beginning. Identity again is not recovered but invented within history and by making use of the cultural elements of African American life. In Forrest's fictional world, the modern self is the blues self.

Two Wings to Veil My Face (1983) would seem to return to the personal story of Nathaniel, but in fact engages much larger issues. The frame situation is that he has been called to the bedside of his grandmother, Sweetie Reed, presumably to learn why she refused to attend her husband's funeral several years earlier. However, the narrative quickly takes another direction. First, she insists that her grandson write down everything that she says; she rejects his offer to simply tape-record it. The moment marks a movement from the oral to the written tradition. It shifts narrative from the vagaries and imperfections of vocal retelling to the permanence of the written word. Ironically, this demand is necessitated by the very orality of the complex story she tells. It is a tale of many voices, in different time periods. It is also a tale of unreliability, in which she recreates the voices of her untrustworthy father and husband. To validate her own version of reality, she must capture their "lying tongues" with precision and must make her telling the final one. But of course her obsession with them raises questions about her own reliability; in her demonizing narration, she recalls Faulkner's Rosa Coldfield. And, further, as the text eventually shows, Nathaniel himself has a strong investment in what her history reveals.

In recording this history of the Reed and Witherspoon families, Forrest makes use of a range of vernacular devices, including sermons, spirituals, call-and-response, folktales, and beliefs about curses, conjuration, and healing. In this sense, he roots the story in everyday Southern culture as much as Faulkner did. In doing so, he creates a sense of a shared humanity against which to measure both the inhumanity of racial and gender oppression and the deep fallibility of human beings. The dominant culture, which insists on absolute control, generates its own disasters when it exercises that power through miscegenation and greed. I.V. Reed loses his wife Angelina and his daughter Sweetie (temporarily) when a group of whites kidnap and enslave them despite the fact that the Civil War is over. But he gets little sympathy from other blacks, even when Angelina is killed, because of his reputation as a lying Uncle Tom, a reputation even his daughter accepts.

But in an irony typical of modern fiction, it is from I.V. that Sweetie learns the devastating truth about herself: that it was Angelina and not herself who was promised to Jericho Witherspoon as a reward for ransoming them. With Angelina's death, Sweetie became the substitute bride. Furthermore, she reveals to Nathaniel that, because she could not bear children, Jericho's son (Nathaniel's father) was the product of a liaison with Lucasta Jones. Thus, the family history, which the young man had taken as the one stable element in his life, turns out to be a narrative of deceit, illegitimacy, and orphanhood. But this very deprivation becomes possibility, for now Nathaniel has a more complex view of the grandfather he idolized, a greater respect for the woman he believed to be his grandmother, an awareness of the variety of ways African Americans (and whites) engaged the nation's history, and a more sophisticated sense of human fate and responsibility.

In *Divine Days* (1992), Forrest shifts to a different narrator and focuses his attention on everyday black life in Chicago (though, in a clearly self-referential gesture, he calls it Forest County). The first-person voice of the novel is Joubert Jones, a novice playwright who returns to the city after two years in the Army. Forrest has stated that, in creating a young artist as protagonist in a massive work (over 1,100 pages), he intended his book to be compared to Joyce's *Ulysses*.[14] The author claims all of American and world culture as the context for his fictional creation. His narrator's speech and thought, like that of other characters, is filled with acknowledged and unacknowledged literary and cultural references. Homer, Greek dramatists and philosophers, Shakespeare, Milton, Melville, Emerson, Russian novelists, Joyce, Faulkner, Ellison, Baldwin, and Alice Walker, among others, are alluded to through quotation or parody. But *Divine Days* is not intended as imitation; rather, its author sought to create something that could stand alongside and be measured against Joyce's masterpiece. While also an urban work and structured within a narrow time frame, it does not depend on the complex referential structure that Joyce employed. Rather, it offers its own mythic figures, which emerge from, and are connected to, the black community. It employs a wide range of artistic and intellectual characters, from trickster preachers to black nationalist painters to Shakespearean scholar-barbers to journalists to barstool raconteurs, and they are shown to have a wide knowledge of Western, Eastern, and black vernacular cultures. In addition, each of the characters has a story to tell, even if it must be articulated by someone else. In this sense, the novel is a narrative cornucopia, out of which Jones must choose his material and give it dramatic shape.

He assumes that he already knows where to look and what to do, but he is constantly being challenged in his assumptions. He has two dichotomous figures – W. A. D. Ford, a trickster who becomes the head of a religious cult, and Sugar Groove, legendary for his sexual prowess and good works – about whom he is writing plays. But as he seeks more information about them, he gets caught up in more mysteries and more stories. He supports himself by working in his Aunt Eloise's bar and by writing occasionally for the neighborhood newspaper. Each job lends itself to narrative possibilities, and he attempts to collect and assess them for their dramatic potential. But such distance from his material is not acceptable within the community, and he is repeatedly forced to engage the lives around him. Thus, Forrest resolves for himself one of the key issues of modern art by insisting on a dialectical relationship between the artist and the world: aesthetic determinations must be connected to human experience and not detached from it. This point might be considered the essence of his vernacular modernism: artistic creation is a form of call-and-response in which the artist is neither identical with the audience (or world) nor separate from it. All of the cultural materials are available to be used, but they must be used in a way that sustains and nurtures the relationship. When Jones violates this principle, he causes disasters, whether comic or tragic.

In *Meteor in the Madhouse* (2001), a posthumous collection of novellas, Forrest comes back to Joubert Jones and attempts to bring together many of the issues he has raised. In one sense, the pieces are material that could not be worked into *Divine Days* but are clearly related. By this point, Jones has become a very successful playwright and is returning to the city. His current responsibility is his cousin, Leonard Foster, who has been admitted to a psychiatric hospital. Leonard's wife seeks some understanding of his condition from Joubert, who was raised with him. In recounting this history, he hears again in his head the voices and stories of the community. In this way, Forrest makes the connections that bring together his fictional world. We learn, for example, that Leonard's mother was Lucasta Jones, Nathaniel Witherspoon's grandmother. As in the Witherspoon case, she is deprived of the opportunity to raise this child. So to the orphans we now add the child-deprived mother; appropriately for her "blues" experience, she always listened to the music of Billie Holiday. We also learn that Joubert's father was the illegitimate son of a Bloodworth and that Joubert himself was orphaned when he was 12. As in the earlier works, most of this information is communicated through stories told in various voices, though filtered through Jones's consciousness. Even within individual novellas, the fragmentation of narrative found in the novels is apparent. To tell a story sequentially for Forrest violates a principle of the play of memory and storymaking. *Meteor* ends with the death of Joubert Jones and thus the center for the narratives. But as this final work suggests, the telling of tales is endless; there are always new versions and additional layers. What brings order out of this apparent chaos is not a preconceived structure that contains the material, but rather the skill of a master storyteller who, like the folk artist, has and communicates a sense of the organic form through which he works.

If the fiction of Leon Forrest followed some organic pattern merging modernism and the vernacular from the beginning, a similar pattern in John Edgar Wideman's Homewood trilogy was achieved after years of very self-conscious effort. As noted earlier, James Coleman has argued that a fundamental shift in Wideman's work moved him from a high-modernist perspective in his first three novels to a fully vernacular one in the writing since. It can be shown, however, that his fiction retains many of the earlier qualities, including wasteland and apocalypse imagery, narrative experimentation, the unreliability of memory and historical representation, and a thematics of the relationship between artist-intellectual and community. At the same time, the vernacular is present in his work from the beginning and is sometimes, but not always, central to the later work. Moreover, his texts frequently transgress genre boundaries, especially between fiction, history, and autobiography, meaning that folk expression operates within an experimental context.

The first three novels – *A Glance Away* (1967), *Hurry Home* (1969), and *The Lynchers* (1973) – are clearly within a modernist mode in their use of stream of consciousness, of frequent literary allusion, and of an atmosphere of despair, impotence, and violence. In each, central characters are highly self-conscious and even intellectual figures alienated from the world around them. And while the novels are set in African American communities, there is relatively little engagement with the ordinary life of that world. Wideman's technique in these works includes unclear shifts between exterior and interior worlds, making it often impossible to distinguish between fantasy and reality. He also changes narrative perspectives without clear markers, thereby momentarily disorienting readers.

Despite these modernist qualities, all of which serve to reinforce a sense of hopelessness, the little hope apparent in the texts comes through vernacular expression. *A Glance Away*, for example, opens with the larger-than-life figure of DaddyGene, a legend in the community both for his skill as a paper hanger and his capacity for wine. He breaks through the pretense and anxiety of his wife and his daughter, who has just given birth. He is a life force against which the despair and ineffectiveness among others can be measured. He is an early version of John French, who plays an important role in the Homewood trilogy. Here he disappears after the first few pages, in part because the themes of alienation and despair cannot operate in his presence. Similarly, late in the book, Eddie, DaddyGene's grandson and the central black character, remembers a church service the two of them had witnessed in his childhood. What he recalls is the sheer joy of the participants, including the dancing of a huge man named Tiny. But, though the novel is set on Easter Day, he refuses to draw any message from the memory and returns to the hopeless present.

Similarly, *Hurry Home* focuses primarily on the irresponsible and alienated experience of Cecil Braithwaite, who abandons his new wife to pursue law school and then refuses to take up his profession. One of the few moments of pleasure occurs as he works in a vernacular space, the neighborhood beauty shop. As he does a "process" on the hair of his male client, he meditates on the process of art as the truly creative aspect, far more important than the completed product. It is virtually the only moment in the novel that transcends the drabness and futility of lived experience.

The Lynchers is the most pessimistic of these early works, in part because, though it is the one most centered in the African American community, its central characters can find no life-affirming qualities there. There are references to spirituals, blues, jazz, religious services, and even the teaching of black history, but none of it offers them any alternative to the frustration that has led them to plot the lynching of a white policeman and the attendant murder of a black woman. Despite a three-page prose poem on the beauty of street basketball, the key plotter remains dismissive of the character of the black people for whose benefit he plans the action. Nothing in the culture can save him from his mad scheme nor deter two of the others. The one who finally grasps its fundamental insanity and inhumanity is the one most removed from identification with the culture. Thus, in this text, which incorporates all the modernist techniques of the others, cultural expression only reinforces the despair. What we see, then, in these early texts, is an artistic choice to subordinate the vernacular, not because it is either irrelevant to black life or inappropriate for a modernist text, but rather because it challenges the despair Wideman assumes is central to modernism. Unlike Forrest, he does not see at this point in his career the possibilities of a more dialectical perspective.

After *The Lynchers*, Wideman took an eight-year break from writing fiction; during this time, he reestablished connections with his family and the Pittsburgh neighborhood of several generations of his family. The result was the Homewood trilogy: *Hiding Place* (1981), *Damballah* (1981) – a collection of stories – and *Sent for You Yesterday* (1983). In it, he creates a family history very similar to that of the Widemans and the Frenches from whom he descended. The narrative foregrounds storytelling as the principal method by which the history is kept alive. Pieces of stories are repeated in different contexts, or the same story is told from different perspectives. Folk expressions, religious beliefs, secular and sacred music, legends, and street language are present throughout the narratives. Moreover, in these works, as in later ones, they make a difference.

But it is important to understand the nature of that difference. The world of Homewood is a dangerous, deteriorating space. Work is hard to find, buildings are decaying, alcoholism and drug addiction are common, racism and violence are rampant, and there is little hope for escape. One key figure is Tommy, who is accused of one killing (*Hiding Place*) and imprisoned for another (*Damballah*); another is Albert Wilkes, a blues pianist who killed a policeman and is later killed by the police. In one story, Tommy's description of Homewood as a wasteland goes beyond anything found in T. S. Eliot. What the vernacular culture does is create a "blues" environment; that is, it enables the characters to see the world for what it is, but to believe that the resources – of family, history, cultural expression – can enable survival. It does not guarantee survival, and, in fact, these fictions are not significantly more optimistic than the earlier ones. What becomes clear is the shared humanity of the characters. One hope in these works is the black artist-intellectual, who has a prominent role in "gathering up" the stories. He is the one who listens to the narratives and uses them to reassure others that survival is possible. Unlike the earlier novels, here he is invested in preserving not only the stories but also the voices through which they are told. Consistent with this view of the writer's role, Wideman entitled a later collection *All Stories Are True* (1993).

After the Homewood trilogy, Wideman mostly turned away from family stories to engage larger social and historical issues. In doing so, he has continued to display a modernist sensibility rather than resorting to critical realism. He often conducts narrative experiments in his short fiction. The title story of *Fever* (1989), for example, uses medical dictionaries, diaries, court records, natural histories, and letters, as well as several voices to tell the story of the yellow fever epidemic in eighteenth-century Philadelphia and by metaphoric extension, the story of racism in America. "Newborn Thrown in Trash and Dies," from *All Stories Are True*, transforms a news item from the *New York Times* into a highly allegorical story told by the newborn. "Surfiction" interweaves parts of a short story by Charles Chesnutt with a commentary on it in the context of a recounting of a disturbing creative writing class in which the professor becomes a voyeur through the pieces submitted by his husband and wife students. In such works, he might easily be understood as part of black postmodernism.

The novels that Wideman has published since the Homewood trilogy have focused on the urban black communities of Philadelphia and Pittsburgh, but they have been engaged less with cultural experience and more with social and political issues. *Reuben* (1987) continues the emphasis on storytelling, but the stories are those of troubled individuals with little interest in communal resources. The title character, a mysterious figure in the neighborhood, is in some ways a classical trickster figure, but the author uses him primarily to raise the modernist theme of appearance and reality. Resolutions are achieved, not through his efforts or through faith or music, but rather through real or imagined acts of violence. This gives the text a surreal quality, as it becomes difficult to distinguish fantasy from reality.

Philadelphia Fire (1990) continues the wasteland imagery as it depicts the literal holocaust that was the city's 1985 response to MOVE, a radical black organization. The conceit of this fictionalized account is that an expatriate writer returns to try to find the small boy who was the only survivor of the police bombing of the house and subsequent fiery destruction of several city blocks. The creation of Cudjoe reasserts the role of the outsider artist-intellectual in Wideman's fictional world. Again, as in the trilogy and *Reuben*, his primary function is to collect and make sense of the community's stories. But the narratives he gathers, with difficulty precisely because he is seen as an outsider, serve not to nurture shared values and histories, but to indict the political order for its inhumanity. The history that is recorded in the text is a national, not a local one, recorded in books, not voices. Even the memorial service at the end of the novel, designed as a ritual of remembrance, uses no forms of indigenous expression. The drumming that runs through the scene links it to Africa, not Philadelphia's black community. And, finally, the service itself, though affecting for Cudjoe, is a failure in that the city, including its black citizens, largely ignores it. Its importance is private, not public, and thus reinforces the pessimism that pervades Wideman's fiction.

In *The Cattle Killing* (1996), Wideman creates another outsider narrator, but one who refuses to be alienated despite the attitudes of others. As in "Fever," he sets the story in the time of the yellow fever epidemic. The principal narrator describes himself as an itinerant African preacher who attends to mostly white congregations in rural Pennsylvania despite their often hostile reaction to him. When the disease comes, he takes care of the sick, even those who would rather die than be attended to by a black man. On his journey toward Philadelphia, he encounters a black woman who he seeks to keep alive by telling her the stories of his encounters. Thus, he is another example of Wideman's definition of the writer as a collector and reteller of tales rather than a creator out of only the imagination. The author also uses another art form to fully develop his ideas. The narrator meets Liam and his wife, a black man and white woman who have emigrated from England, where they both suffered from a white male society. To their neighbors they present themselves as widow and servant. In the presence of the narrator, Liam begins speaking after years of silence caused by the witnessing of various cruelties. He also resumes his painting, taking his wife as his subject. What Wideman emphasizes in his art is experimentation, work that seems more like abstract expressionism than the representation we would expect. But what the narrator sees through his method is an effort to capture the deep truth of the wife's being. This is contrasted to the work of an English artist he served who participated in grave-robbing and illegal autopsies in order to learn how to draw women. Liam's art, in contrast, is life-affirming and life-enhancing. Like the narrator's (and by extension, Wideman's) storytelling, his painting shows the human reality of ordinary experience without sacrificing it. But this does not mean that art has much power in the world. While the narrator is gone, Liam and his wife are killed by their white neighbors who have discovered their secret. This becomes simply another of the terrifying, traumatic stories the narrator must tell.

Two Cities (1998) is a narrative of mourning: death and its effects on the living is one of the central themes. One of the central characters has lost both of her sons to ghetto violence; another recalls the ghosts of his old neighborhood; the third knew John Africa (perhaps) before he was killed in the MOVE bombing. In this sense the book is a lamentation for the cities of Philadelphia and Pittsburgh. But it is also a claim for the restorative possibilities of art, when all the vernacular options fail. The church, the music clubs, the basketball games, and the family stories can offer little more than temporary respite from the pain of everyday life. The shift in point of view from Mallory to Robert Jones to Kassima serves to demonstrate the ways these forms only intensify the suffering.

Art, in the formal and not vernacular sense, offers the only nurture available. Mallory discovers his creative potential in taking photographs and experimenting with their development. At the same time, he begins writing letters to the sculptor Alberto Giacometti, not because he expects a response, but because he feels him to have a similar understanding. The mourning theme is brought into conjunction with this when Kassima and Robert discover the full extent of Mallory's art after his death; he has asked Kassima to destroy all the photographs. What the two of them come to see is the ways in which he captured the vernacular world through his camera. That which has died or otherwise disappeared can be given renewed life through his art. He finds the humanity in the environment, even photographing gang members who are otherwise responsible for so much of the destruction. He also resolves the problem of the outsider artist; his distance from his subjects is seen merely as a necessary eccentricity, since the photographer must disappear behind the camera. Also, he usually asks permission to take the pictures and thus collaborates with his subjects in the creation of his art. Because he then seeks some deep truth in the processing of the negatives, he experiments with them and produces work that he believes speaks only to him. This is why he wants Kassima to burn them. But through his death, the examination of his work, and the final gesture of speaking for him, she is restored to hope and belief in the future, though without any illusions. Thus, art and the artist give back to the community what it has lost. Mallory calls his photography a "blues" art, because he finds both life's troubles and the power to endure them through it. Through him and his work, Wideman finds a modernist image of the value of his own art. In a sense, this is a return to high modernism, in that it is only the artist who can make use of cultural materials to give whatever meaning might be found in the wasteland that is contemporary society.

What we see, then, in the fiction of Leon Forrest and John Edgar Wideman are two different versions of the interaction of a Western aesthetic and African American material. And in both, it is important to understand this interaction not as the joining of antithetical elements but rather as a means by which the optimal possibilities for storytelling can be achieved. Leon Forrest, in the tradition of Ralph Ellison, sees African American culture as a hybrid that has always contained widely diverse components. While the world may be chaotic, racist, and filled with suffering, this wealth of resources makes not only survival but also hope always likely. Wideman is much more pessimistic, given his sense of the unending racism of American society. While he has a sense of the beauty of the vernacular realm, his essentially modernist reading of the world as a wasteland leads him to emphasize the fragility of that beauty and of even the most sophisticated art.

NOTES

1. Houston A. Baker Jr., *Modernism and the Harlem Renaissance* (Chicago: University of Chicago Press, 1987), p. 15.
2. See Richard J. Powell, ed., *The Blues Aesthetic and Modernism* (Washington, DC: Washington Project for the Arts, 1989).

3. Michael Levenson, ed., *The Cambridge Companion to Modernism* (Cambridge: Cambridge University Press, 1999), p. 3.
4. "Modernism and the Politics of Culture," *Companion to Modernism*, ed. Levenson, p. 158.
5. "The Modernist Novel," *Companion to Modernism*, ed. Levenson, p. 78.
6. Paul Arnett and William Arnett, eds., *Souls Grown Deep: African American Vernacular Art of the South, Volume 1: The Tree Gave the Dove a Leaf* (Atlanta: Tinwood Books, 2000), p. xv.
7. Much of the discussion on modernism and the Harlem Renaissance has focused on Langston Hughes. In addition to Baker, see Larry Scanlon, "'Death is a Drum': Rhythm, Modernity, and the Negro Poet Laureate," *Music and the Racial Imagination*, eds. Ronald Radano and Philip V. Bohlman (Chicago: University of Chicago Press, 2000), pp. 510–553; Anita Patterson, "Jazz, Realism, and the Modernist Lyric: The Poetry of Langston Hughes," *Modern Language Quarterly* 61.4 (2000): 651–682; Peter Brooker, "Modernism Deferred: Langston Hughes, Harlem and Jazz Montage," *Locations of Literary Modernism: Region and Nation in British and American Modernist Poetry*, eds. Alex Davis and Lee M. Jenkins (Cambridge: Cambridge University Press, 2000), pp. 231–247; Robert O'Brien Hokanson, "Jazzing It Up: The Be-Bop Modernism of Langston Hughes," *Mosaic* 31.4 (1998): 61–82; and Arnold Rampersad, "Langston Hughes and Approaches to Modernism in the Harlem Renaissance," *The Harlem Renaissance: Revaluations*, eds. Amritjit Singh, William S. Shiver, and Stanley Brodwin (New York: Garland, 1989), pp. 49–71.
8. See the short story "Everyday Use," in *In Love and Trouble* (New York: Harcourt Brace Jovanovich, 1973).
9. This use of the term "signifyin(g)" is from Henry Louis Gates, *The Signifying Monkey: A Theory of Afro-American Literary Criticism* (Oxford: Oxford University Press, 1988).
10. "Modernism and the Politics of Culture," *Companion to Modernism*, ed. Levenson, p. 166.
11. See Keith Byerman, "Angularity: An Interview with Leon Forrest," *African American Review* 33.3 (1999): 442.
12. See James W. Coleman, *Blackness and Modernism: The Literary Career of John Edgar Wideman* (Jackson: University Press of Mississippi, 1989), including the interview with Wideman that constitutes the Appendix.
13. *There Is a Tree More Ancient Than Eden* (New York: Random House, 1973), pp. 34–35.
14. Byerman, "Angularity," 440.

BIBLIOGRAPHY

This list includes works cited and further reading provided by the contributors. Many of them contain extensive bibliographies of their own.

Primary works

The Anglo-African Magazine, Volume 1 – 1859. Facsimile. Introd. William Loren Katz. New York: Arno Press and the New York Times, 1968.

Albert, Richard N., ed. *From Blues to Bop: A Collection of Jazz Fiction*. Baton Rouge: Louisiana State University Press, 1990.

Andrews, Raymond. *Appalachee Red*. New York: Dial, 1978; Athens: University of Georgia Press, 1987.

   Baby Sweet's. 1983; Athens: University of Georgia Press, 1998.

   Rosiebelle Lee Wildcat Tennessee. 1980; Athens: University of Georgia Press, 1988.

Angelou, Maya. *I Know Why the Caged Bird Sings*. New York: Bantam Books, 1970.

Anon. *Narrative of the Uncommon Sufferings, and Surprizing Deliverance of Briton Hammon*. Boston: Printed and sold by Green & Russell, 1760.

Anon. "Patrick Brown's First Love." New York's *Anglo-African Magazine*, September, 1859.

Attaway, William. *Blood on the Forge, A Novel*. Garden City: Doubleday, Doran, 1941.

Baldwin, James. *Another Country*. 1962; New York: Vintage Books, 1990.

   Giovanni's Room. New York: Dell Publishing, 1956.

   Go Tell It on the Mountain. New York: Dell Publishing, 1952; New York: Laurel Publishing, 1981.

   If Beale Street Could Talk. New York: New American Library, 1974.

   Just Above My Head. 1979; New York: Dell Publishing, 2000.

   Nobody Knows My Name. 1955; rpt. New York: Dial Press, 1961.

   Notes of a Native Son. Boston: Beacon Press, 1955.

   Tell Me How Long the Train's Been Gone. New York: Dell Publishing, 1968.

   "Everybody's Protest Novel." *Notes of a Native Son*. Boston: Beacon Press, 1968.

Bambara, Toni Cade. *The Salt Eaters*. 1980; New York: Vintage Books, 1992.

Barnes, Steve. *Lion's Blood*. New York: Aspect/Warner Books, 2002.

Baudrillard, Jean. *Simulations*. Trans. Paul Foss, Paul Patton, and Philip Beitchman. New York: Semiotext(e), 1983.

Beatty, Paul. *The White Boy Shuffle*. New York: Random House, 1996; London: Vintage, 2000.

Beck, Robert. *The Naked Soul of Iceberg Slim*. Los Angeles: Holloway House, 1967.
  Trick Baby. Los Angeles: Holloway House Pub. Co. (distributed by All American Distributors Corp.), 1967.

Behn, Aphra. *Oroonoko, or, the History of the Royal Slave. A True History*. London: William Canning, 1688. Rpt. in Aphra Behn; *Oroonoko, Rover, and Other Works*. Ed. Janet Todd. London: Penguin, 1992.

Bell, Derrick. *Faces at the Bottom of the Well*. New York: Basic Books, 1992.

Bellamy, E. *Equality*. 1897; New York: AMS Press, 1970.
  Looking Backward, 2000–1887. 1888; New York: Penguin, 1982.

Blackson, L. D. *The Rise and Progress of the Kingdoms of Light and Darkness; or, The Reigns of Kings Alpha and Abandon*. 1867; Upper Saddle River, NJ: The Gregg Press, 1968.

Bontemps, Arna. *Black Thunder*. New York: Macmillan, 1936.
  God Sends Sunday. New York: Harcourt Brace, 1931.

Bradley, David. *The Chaneysville Incident*. 1981; New York: Harper & Row, 1990.

Brooks, Gwendolyn. *Annie Allen*. 1949; Westport: Greenwood Press, 1971.
  Maud Martha. New York: Harper, 1953.

Brown, Linda Beatrice. *Crossing over Jordan*. 1995; New York: Ballantine, 1996.

Brown, Frank London. *Trumbull Park, A Novel*. Chicago: Regnery, 1959.

Brown, Lloyd. *Iron City*. New York: Masses & Mainstream, 1951.

Brown, Wesley. *Darktown Strutters*. New York: Cane Hill Press, 1994.

Brown, William Wells. *Clotel: Or, the President's Daughter, a Narrative of Slave Life in the United States*. London: Partridge & Oakey, 1853.
  Clotelle: A Tale of the Southern States. Boston: J. Redpath, 1864.
  Clotelle; or the Colored Heroine: A Tale of the Southern States. Boston: Lee & Shepard, 1867.
  Miralda, or, The Beautiful Quadroon in the New York *Weekly Anglo African*. Dec. 8, 1860 to Mar. 15, 1861. The first two installments have been lost.
  Narrative of William W. Brown A Fugitive Slave Written by Himself. Boston: Published by the Anti-Slavery Office, 1847.

Bruce, J. E. *The Black Sleuth*. Boston: Northeastern University Press, 2002.

Butler, Octavia. *Kindred*. Garden City: Doubleday, 1979.
  Parable of the Sower. 1993; New York: Warner Books, 2000.
  Parable of the Talents. New York: Seven Stories Press, 1998.
  Wildseed. New York: Warner Books, 2001.

Carroll, Rebecca. *Sugar in the Raw*. New York: Crown Trade Paperbacks, 1997.

Cartiér, Xam Wilson. *Be-Bop, Re-Bop*. New York: Available Press, 1987.
  Muse-Echo Blues. New York: Harmony Books, 1991.

Chase-Riboud, Barbara. *Sally Hemings*. New York: Viking Press, 1979.

Chesnutt, C. W. *"To Be an Author": Letters of Charles W. Chesnutt, 1889–1905*. Ed. J. R. McElrath Jr. and R. C. Leitz III. Princeton: Princeton University Press, 1997.
  The Colonel's Dream. 1905; Upper Saddle River, NJ: The Gregg Press, 1968.
  The Conjure Woman. 1899; Ridgewood, NJ: Gregg, 1968.
  The House Behind the Cedars. 1900; Athens: University of Georgia Press, 1988.

The Journals of Charles W. Chesnutt. Ed. R. Brodhead. Durham: Duke University Press, 1993.

Mandy Oxendine. Urbana: University of Illinois Press, 1997.

The Marrow of Tradition. 1901; Ann Arbor: University of Michigan Press, 1969.

Child, Lydia Maria. *Letters of Lydia Maria Child*. With a Biographical Introduction by John G. Whittier and an Appendix by Wendell Phillips. Boston: Houghton, Mifflin and Company, 1883.

"The Quadroons." *Fact and Fiction: A Collection of Short Stories*. London: William Smith, 1847. 13–17.

Clarke, John Henrik. *William Styron's Nat Turner: Ten Black Critics Respond*. Boston: Beacon Press, 1968.

Cliff, Michele. *Abeng*. Trumansburg, NY: The Crossing Press, 1984.

Free Enterprise. New York: Dutton, 1993.

Colter, Cyrus. *Night Studies*. Chicago: Swallow Press, 1979.

Cooper, J. California. *Family*. Garden City: Doubleday, 1991.

The Wake of the Wind. New York: Doubleday, 1998.

Crafts, Hannah. *The Bondwoman's Narrative*. 1850s. Unpublished manuscript. Ed. Henry Louis Gates Jr. New York: Warner Books, 2002.

Cullen, Countee. *Color*. 1925; New York: Arno Press, 1969.

Danticat, Edwidge. *Breath, Eyes, Memory*. New York: Soho Press, 1994.

Dash, Julie. *Daughters of the Dust* [feature film]. 1992.

Delany, Martin R. *Blake, or, the Huts of America. A Tale of the Mississippi Valley, The Southern United States, and Cuba. 1859–62*. Introd. Floyd J. Miller. Boston: Beacon Press, 1970.

Delany, Samuel R. *Dhalgren*. 1974; Boston: Gregg Press, 1977.

The Jewels of Aptor. London: Gollancz, 1968.

Detter, T. *Nellie Brown; or, The Jealous Wife*. 1871; Lincoln: University of Nebraska Press, 1996.

Dick, Bruce and Amritjit Singh, ed. *Conversations with Ishmael Reed*. Jackson: University Press of Mississippi, 1995.

Dixon, Melvin. *Trouble the Water*. New York: Washington Square Press, 1989.

Doctorow, E. L. *Ragtime*. New York: Bantam Books, 1975.

Douglass, Frederick. *The Claims of the Negro, Ethnologically Considered*. Rochester: Press of Lee, Mann & Co., 1854.

Narrative of the Life of Frederick Douglass. An American Slave, Written by Himself. Boston: Published by the Anti-Slavery Office, 1845.

"The Heroic Slave." *Frederick Douglass' Paper* (March 4, 1853: 1; March 11, 1853: 1; March 18, 1853: 1; March 25, 1853: 1–2).

"The Heroic Slave." *Autographs For Freedom*. Ed. Julia Griffiths. Boston: John P. Jewett and Company; London: Low and Company, 1853. pp. 174–239.

Dove, Rita. *Thomas and Beulah*. Pittsburgh: Carnegie-Mellon University Press, 1986.

Dreiser, Theodore. *American Tragedy*. New York: Heritage Press, 1954.

Du Bois, W. E. B. *Dark Princess: A Romance*. New York: Harcourt Brace, 1928.

The Quest of the Silver Fleece. 1911; Boston: Northeastern University Press, 1989.

Souls of Black Folk. 1903; New York: Fine Communications, 2003.

Due, Tananarive. *The Between*. New York: HarperCollins, 1995.
    The Living Blood. New York: Pocket Books, 2001.
Dunbar, P. L. *The Fanatics*. 1901; Miami: Mnemosyne Pub. Inc., 1969.
    The Love of Landry. 1900; New York: Negro Universities Press, 1969.
    The Sport of the Gods. 1902; New York: Dodd, Mead, 1981.
    The Uncalled. 1898; New York: AMS Press, 1972.
Eliot, T. S. *The Waste Land*. London: Faber & Faber, 1961.
Ellison, Ralph. *The Collected Essays of Ralph Ellison*. Ed. John F. Callahan. New York: Modern Library, 1995.
    Going to the Territory. New York: Vintage-Random, 1987.
    Invisible Man. 1952; New York: Vintage Books, 1982.
    Juneteenth. Ed. John F. Callahan. New York: Random House, 1999.
    Shadow and Act. 1964; New York: Vintage Books, 1972.
Equiano, Olaudah. *The Life of Olaudah Equiano, or Gustavus Vassa, the African*. Ed. Joslyn T. Pine. New York: Dover, 1999.
Faulkner, William. *The Sound and the Fury*. New York: Random House, 1956.
Fauset, Jessie Redmon. *The Chinaberry Tree: A Novel of American Life*. 1931; College Park: McGrath Publishing Co., 1969.
    Plum Bun: A Novel Without a Moral. New York: Frederick A. Stokes, 1929.
    There is Confusion. New York: Boni & Liveright, 1924.
Fisher, Rudolph. *The Conjure-Man Dies: A Mystery Tale of Dark Harlem*. 1932; Ann Arbor: University of Michigan Press, 1992.
    The Walls of Jericho. New York: Alfred A. Knopf, 1928.
Fitzgerald, F. Scott. *The Great Gatsby*. 1953; New York: Scribner, 1961.
Fleming, S. L. B. *Hope's Highway*. 1918; New York: G. K. Hall, 1995.
Forrest, Leon. *The Bloodworth Orphans*. New York: Random House, 1977; Chicago: Another Chicago Press, 1987.
    Divine Days. New York: Norton, 1992.
    Meteor in the Madhouse. Evanston: Northwestern University Press, 2001.
    There Is a Tree More Ancient Than Eden. 1973; Chicago: Another Chicago Press, 1988.
    Two Wings to Veil My Face. 1983; Chicago: Another Chicago Press, 1988.
Fowler, C. H. *Historical Romance of the American Negro*. 1902; New York: Johnson Reprint Corp., 1970.
Freeman, Gosden and Charles Corell, *The Amos 'n' Andy Show*. 1928; or CBS Situation Comedy. The Amos 'n' Andy Show. June 28, 1951–June 11, 1953.
Fulton, D. B. *Hanover, or the Persecution of the Lowly*. 1900; New York: Arno Press, 1969.
Gaines, Ernest. *The Autobiography of Miss Jane Pittman*. 1971; New York: Bantam, 1989.
Gates, Henry Louis Jr., ed. *The Classic Slave Narratives*. New York: New American Library, 1987.
Golden, Marita. *A Woman's Place*. 1986; New York: Ballantine Books, 1988.
Gomez, Jewelle. *The Gilda Stories*. Ithaca: Firebrand Books, 1991.
Grant, J. W. *Out of the Darkness: or, Diabolism and Destiny*. 1909; Freeport, NY: Books for Libraries Press, 1972.
Gray, Thomas R. *The Confessions of Nat Turner, The Leader of the Late Insurrection in Southhampton, VA*. Baltimore, 1831.

Greenlee, Sam. *The Spook Who Sat by the Door*. New York: R. W. Baron, 1969.

Griffiths, Julia, ed. *Autographs For Freedom*. Boston: John P. Jewett and Company; London: Low and Company, 1853.

Griggs, S. E. *The Hindered Hand; or, The Reign of the Repressionist*. 1905; New York: AMS Press, 1969.

    Imperium in Imperio. 1899; New York: Arno Press, 1969.

    Overshadowed. 1901; New York: AMS Press, 1973.

    Pointing the Way. 1908; New York: AMS Press, 1974.

    Unfettered. 1902; New York: AMS Press, 1971.

Grimes, William. *The Life of William Grimes: The Runaway Slave, Written by Himself*. New York: n.p., 1825.

Haley, Alex. *Roots*. Garden City: Doubleday, 1976.

Harper, Frances Ellen Watkins. *A Brighter Coming Day: A Frances Ellen Watkins Harper Reader*. Ed. w/Introd. Frances Smith Foster. New York: The Feminist Press, 1990.

    Iola Leroy; or, Shadows Uplifted. 1892; Boston: Beacon Press, 1897.

    Minnie's Sacrifice. 1869. In *Minnie's Sacrifice, Sowing and Reaping, Trial and Triumph: Three Rediscovered Novels by Frances E. W. Harper*. Ed. Frances Smith Foster. Boston: Beacon Press, 1994.

    Sowing and Reaping. 1876–1877. In *Minnie's Sacrifice, Sowing and Reaping, Trial and Triumph: Three Rediscovered Novels by Frances E. W. Harper*. Ed. Frances Smith Foster. Boston: Beacon Press, 1994.

    Trial and Triumph. 1888–1889. In *Minnie's Sacrifice, Sowing and Reaping, Trial and Triumph: Three Rediscovered Novels by Frances E. W. Harper*. Ed. Frances Smith Foster. Boston: Beacon Press, 1994.

    "The Two Offers." New York *Anglo-African Magazine* September, 1859: 288–291; October, 1859: 311–313.

Harris, E. Lynn. *Invisible Life*. Atlanta: Consortium Press, 1991.

Henderson, David. *De Mayor of Harlem: The Poetry of David Henderson*. New York: E. P. Dutton, 1970.

Henderson, George Wylie. *Ollie Miss*. New York: Frederick A. Stokes, 1935.

Hildreth, Richard. *The Slave; or, Memoirs of Archy Moore*. 2 vols. Boston: John H. Eastburn, 1836.

Himes, Chester. *Cast the First Stone*. New York: Coward McCann, 1952.

    If He Hollers Let Him Go. 1945; New York: Thunder's Mouth Press, 1986.

    Lonely Crusade. 1947; New York: Thunder's Mouth Press, 1986.

    The Third Generation. 1954; New York: Thunder's Mouth Press, 1989.

Holmes, C. H. *Ethiopia: The Land of Promise (A Book with a Purpose)*. 1917; New York: AMS Press, 1973.

Hopkins, P. E. *Contending Forces: A Romance Illustrative of Negro Life North and South*. 1900; New York: Oxford University Press, 1988.

    Hagar's Daughter: A Story of Southern Caste Prejudice. 1901–1902; *The Magazine Novels of Pauline Hopkins*. Ed. Hazel Carby. New York: Oxford University Press, 1988.

    Of One Blood; or, The Hidden Self. 1902–1903; in *The Magazine Novels of Pauline Hopkins*. New York: Oxford University Press, 1988.

    Winona: A Tale of Negro Life in the South and Southwest. 1902; in *The Magazine Novels of Pauline Hopkins*. New York: Oxford University Press, 1988.

"Reply to Cordelia A. Condict." March 1903; in *The Norton Anthology of African American Literature*. Ed. H. L. Gates Jr. and N. Y. McKay. New York: W. W. Norton, 1997. 594–595.

Hopkinson, Nalo. *Brown Girl in the Ring*. New York: Warner Books, 1998.

Midnight Robber. New York: Warner Books, 2000.

Skin Folk. New York: Warner Books, 2001.

Howard, J. H. W. *Bond and Free: A True Tale of Slave Times*. 1886; College Park: McGrath Pub. Co., 1969.

Hughes, Langston. *Not Without Laughter*. 1930; New York: Scribner's, Simon and Schuster, 1969.

The Weary Blues. New York: A. A. Knopf, 1926.

"The Negro Artist and the Racial Mountain." In *The Norton Anthology of African American Literature*. Ed. Henry Louis Gates Jr. and Nellie Y. McKay. New York: W. W. Norton, 1997. Vol. 1, 267–1,271.

Hurston, Zora Neale. *Jonah's Gourd Vine*. Philadelphia: J. B. Lippincott, 1934.

Seraph on the Suwanee. New York: Scribner's, 1948.

Their Eyes Were Watching God. 1937; Urbana: University of Illinois Press, 1978.

Jackson-Opoku, Sandra. *The River Where Blood is Born*. New York: One World, 1997.

Jacobs, Harriet. *Incidents in the Life of a Slave Girl: Written by Herself*. Ed. Jean Fagan Yellin. 1861; Cambridge: Harvard University Press, 1987.

Johnson, A. E. *Clarence and Corinne; or, God's Way*. 1890; New York: Oxford University Press, 1988.

The Hazeley Family. 1894; New York: Oxford University Press, 1988.

Light Ahead for the Negro. 1904; New York: Grafton, 1975.

Martina Meriden; or, What Is My Motive? Philadelphia: American Baptist Publication Society, 1901.

"Afro-American Literature." *The New York Age*, 30 January 1892.

Johnson, Charles. *Dreamer*. New York: Scribner, 1998.

Middle Passage. New York: Atheneum, 1990.

Oxherding Tale. Bloomington: Indiana University Press, 1982.

Johnson, J. W. *Along This Way: The Autobiography of James Weldon Johnson*. 1933; New York: Viking, 1968.

The Autobiography of an Ex-Coloured Man. 1912; New York: Hill & Wang, 1960.

Jones, Gayle. *Corregidora*. New York: Random House, 1975.

Eva's Man. New York: Random House, 1976.

The Healing. Boston: Beacon Press, 1998.

Mosquito. Boston: Beacon Press, 1999.

Jones, J. M. *Hearts of Gold*. 1896; College Park: McGrath Pub. Co., 1969.

Kelley, William Melvin. *dem*. Garden City: Doubleday, 1967.

Dunfords Travels Everywheres. Garden City: Doubleday, 1970.

Kelley-Hawkins, E. D. *Four Girls at Cottage City*. 1895; New York: Oxford University Press, 1988.

Megda. 1891; New York: Oxford University Press, 1988.

Kenan, Randall. *A Visitation of Spirits*. New York: Random House, 1989; New York: Vintage, 2000.

Killens, John O. *And Then We Heard the Thunder*. 1962; New York: Knopf, 1963.
    Youngblood. 1954: Athens: University of Georgia Press, 2000.
Kincaid, Jamaica. *Annie John*. New York: Farrar, Straus, Giroux, 1985.
    Lucy. New York: Plume, 1990.
Komo, Dolores. *Clio Brown*. Freedom, CA: Crossing Press, 1988.
Komunyakaa, Yusef. *Neon Vernacular*. Hanover: University Press of New England, 1993.
Larsen, Nella. *Passing*. New York: Alfred A. Knopf, 1929.
    Quicksand. New York: Alfred A. Knopf, 1928.
Locke, Alain. ed. *The New Negro: An Interpretation*. New York: A. & C. Boni, 1925.
Lorde, Audre. *Zami: A New Spelling of My Name*. Trumansburg, NY: Crossing Press, 1982.
McElroy Ansa, Tina. *Baby of the Family*. New York: Harcourt Brace, 1989.
McHugh, Vincent. *Caleb Catlum's America*. New York: Stacpole Sons, 1936.
McKay, Claude. *Banjo: A Story Without a Plot*. 1929; New York: Harvest/HBJ, 1957.
    Harlem Shadows. New York: Harcourt, Brace and Company, 1922.
    Home to Harlem. 1928; Boston: Northeastern University Press, 1987.
McMillan, Terry. *How Stella Got Her Groove Back*. New York: Viking, 1996.
    Waiting to Exhale. Boston: G.K. Hall, 1993.
McPherson, James Alan. *Elbow Room*. 1977; New York: Scribner, 1987.
Mackey, Nathaniel. *Atet. A.D.* San Francisco: City Lights Books, 2001.
    Bedouin Hornbook. Lexington: University of Kentucky Press: Callaloo Fiction Series, 1986.
    Djbot Baghostus's Run. Los Angeles: Sun & Moon Press, 1993.
Major, Clarence. *Dirty Bird Blues*. San Francisco: Mercury House, 1996.
    My Amputations. New York and Boulder: Fiction Collective, 1986.
    Reflex and Bone Structure. New York: Fiction Collective, 1975.
Marshall, Paule. *Brown Girl, Brownstones*. 1959; New York: The Feminist Press, 1981.
    The Chosen Place, The Timeless People. 1969; New York: Vintage, 1992.
    Daughters. New York: Plume, 1992.
    The Fisher King. New York: Scribner Paperback Fiction, 2001.
    Praisesong for the Widow. New York: Plume, 1983.
Meriwether, Louise. *Fragments of the Ark*. New York: Pocket Books, 1994.
Moody, Anne. *Coming of Age in Mississippi: An Autobiography*. New York: Dell Publishing, 1968.
Morrison, Toni. *Beloved*. New York: Plume, 1987.
    The Bluest Eye. 1970; New York: Plume, 1994.
    Jazz. New York: Knopf, 1992.
    Paradise. New York: Alfred A. Knopf, 1998.
    Song of Solomon. New York: Knopf, 1977.
    Sula. New York: Bantam Books, 1973.
    Tar Baby. New York: Plume, 1981.
Mosley, Walter. *Blue Light*. Rockland, MA: Compass Press, 1998.
    Devil in a Blue Dress. New York: Norton, 1990.
    RL's Dream. New York: W.W. Norton, 1995.

Murray, Albert. *The Hero and the Blues*. Columbia: University of Missouri Press, 1973.

The Omni-Americans. 1970; New York: Vintage Books, 1983.

The Seven League Boots. New York: Random House, 1995.

The Spyglass Tree. New York: Random House, Pantheon, 1991.

Train Whistle Guitar. New York: McGraw-Hill, 1974; Boston: Northeastern University Press, 1989.

Naylor, Gloria. *The Women of Brewster Place*. New York: Penguin, 1982.

Nunez, Elizabeth. *Beyond the Limbo Silence*. Seattle: Seal Press, 1998.

Palmer, Robert. *Deep Blues*. New York: Viking, 1981.

Parks, Gordon. *The Learning Tree*. New York: Fawcett, 1963.

Perry, Richard. *Montgomery's Children*. New York: Harcourt Brace Jovanovich, 1984.

Petry, Ann. *The Street*. 1946; Boston: Beacon Press, 1985.

Phillips, J. J. *Mojo Hand*. 1966; Berkeley: City Miner Books, 1985.

Picayune Times, ed. *The Picayune Creole Cook Book*. 1901; New Orleans Applewood Publishers, 2003.

Pryor, G. L. *Neither Bond Nor Free: A Plea*. 1902; New York: AMS Press, 1975.

Reed, Ishmael. *Flight to Canada*. New York: Random House, 1976.

The Free-Lance Pallbearers: An Irreverent Novel. New York: Atheneum, 1989.

Japanese by Spring. New York: Atheneum, 1993.

The Last Days of Louisiana Red. New York: Atheneum, 1989.

Mumbo Jumbo. Garden City: Doubleday, 1972.

New and Collected Poems. New York: Atheneum, 1989.

Reckless Eyeballing. New York: Atheneum, 1988.

The Reed Reader. New York: Basic Books, 2000.

Shrovetide in Old New Orleans. New York: Atheneum, 1978.

The Terrible Threes. New York: Atheneum, 1990.

The Terrible Twos. New York: Atheneum, 1988.

Writin' Is Fightin': Thirty-Seven Years of Boxing on Paper. 1988; New York: Atheneum, 1990.

Yellow Back Radio Broke-Down. New York: Atheneum, 1988.

"The Neo-HooDoo Aesthetic." *New and Collected Poems*. New York: Atheneum, 1989. Initially published as part of Ishmael Reed's collection *Conjure: Selected Poems, 1963–1970*. Amherst: University of Massachusetts Press, 1972.

Reed, Ishmael, ed. *19 Necromancers from Now*. New York: Doubleday, 1970.

Rogers, J. A. *From Superman to Man*. 1917; Freeport, NY: Books for Libraries Press, 1972.

Sanda (pseudonym of W. H. Stowers and W. H. Anderson). *Appointed: An American Novel*. Detroit: Detroit Law Printing Co., 1894; New York: AMS, 1977.

Sanders, Dori. *Clover*. New York: Fawcett Columbine, 1990.

Sapphire, *Push*. New York: Alfred A. Knopf, 1996.

Schuyler, George S. *Black Empire*. Boston: Northeastern University Press, 1991.

Black No More: Being an Account of the Strange and Wonderful Workings of Science in the Land of the Free, A.D. 1933–1940. New York: Macauley, 1931.

Scott, Walter. *Ivanhoe*. 1819; London: Dent, 1970.

Shange, Ntozake. *Betsey Brown*. New York: Picador, 1985.

Steinbeck, John. *The Grapes of Wrath*. 1939; Ed. Peter Lisca. New York: Viking Press, 1972.

Stowe, Harriet Beecher. *Uncle Tom's Cabin: or, the History of a Christian Slave*. London: Partridge & Oakey, 1852.

Styron, William. *Confessions of Nat Turner*. 1967; New York: Vantage International Editions, 1992.

Thurman, Wallace. *The Blacker the Berry* . . . New York: Macauley, 1929.

    Fire!! Devoted to Younger Negro Artists. 1926; Westport: Negro Universities Press, 1970.

    Infants in the Spring. New York: Macauley, 1932.

Tillman, K. D. C. *Beryl Weston's Ambition: The Story of an Afro-American Girl's Life*. 1893; in *The Works of Katherine Davis Chapman Tillman*. New York: Oxford University Press, 1991.

    Clancy Street. 1898–1899; in *The Works of Katherine Davis Chapman Tillman*. New York: Oxford University Press, 1991.

Toomer, Jean. *Cane*. New York: Boni & Liveright, 1923.

Van Vechten, Carl. *Nigger Heaven*. New York: Alfred A. Knopf, 1926.

Walker, Alice. *Anything We Love Can Be Saved: A Writer's Activism*. New York: Random House, 1997.

    By the Light of My Father's Smile. New York: Random House, 1998.

    The Color Purple. New York: Harcourt Brace & Company, 1982.

    In Search of Our Mothers' Gardens: Womanist Prose. New York: Harcourt Brace & Company, 1983.

    Meridian. New York: Harcourt Brace Jovanovich, 1976.

    Possessing the Secret of Joy. New York: Harcourt Brace Jovanovich, 1992.

    The Same River Twice. New York: Scribner, 1996.

    The Temple of My Familiar. New York: Harcourt Brace Jovanovich, 1989.

    The Third Life of Grange Copeland. With Afterword. 1970; New York: Simon & Schuster/Pocket Books, 1988.

    "Anything We Love Can Be Saved: The Resurrection of Zora Neale Hurston and Her Work." *Anything We Love Can Be Saved*. New York: Random House, 1997. 45–50.

    "Everyday Use." *Love and Trouble*. New York: Harcourt Brace Jovanovich, 1973.

Walker, Margaret. *For My People*. New Haven: Yale University Press, 1942.

    How I Wrote Jubilee *and Other Essays on Life and Literature*. Ed. Maryemma Graham. New York: The Feminist Press, 1990.

    Jubilee. Boston: Houghton Mifflin, 1966.

Waring, R. L. *As We See It*. 1910; College Park: McGrath Pub. Co., 1969.

Washington, Booker T. *Up From Slavery, An Autobiography*. New York: Doubleday, 1951.

Webb, Frank J. *The Garies and Their Friends*. With an Introductory Preface by Harriet B. Stowe. London: Routledge, 1857.

West, Dorothy. *The Living Is Easy*. 1948; Old Westbury: The Feminist Press, 1982.

West, Nathanael. "The Dreame Life of Balso Snell." *Novels and Other Writings*. New York: Library of America, 1997.

White, Walter. *The Fire in the Flint*. New York: Alfred A. Knopf, 1924.

Whitehead, Colson. *John Henry Days*. New York: Doubleday, 2001.

Wideman, John Edgar. *A Glance Away*. New York: Harcourt, Brace & World, 1967.

    All Stories Are True. New York: Vintage, 1992.

    The Cattle Killing. Boston: Houghton Mifflin, 1996.

    Damballah. New York: Avon, 1981.

    Fatheralong: A Meditation on Fathers and Sons, Race and Society. New York: Pantheon, 1994.

    Fever. New York: Holt, 1989.

    Hiding Place. New York: Avon, 1981.

    The Homewood Books: Damballah, Hiding Place, Sent for You Yesterday. Pittsburgh: University of Pittsburgh Press, 1992.

    Hurry Home. New York: Harcourt, Brace & World, 1969.

    The Lynchers. New York: Harcourt, Brace & Jovanovich, 1973.

    Philadelphia Fire. New York: Holt, 1990.

    Reuben. New York: Holt, 1987.

    Sent for You Yesterday. New York: Avon, 1983.

    Two Cities. Boston: Houghton Mifflin, 1998.

Williams, James. *Narrative of James Williams, An American Slave*. New York: American Anti-Slavery Society, 1838.

Williams, John A. *Clifford's Blues*. Minneapolis: Coffee House Press, 1999.

    Sissie. New York: Farrar Strauss and Cudahy, 1963.

Williams, Sherley Anne. *Dessa Rose*. New York: William Morrow, 1986.

Wilson, Harriet E. *Our Nig or, Sketches from the Life of a Free Black, In a Two-Story White House, North. Showing that Slavery's Shadows Fall Even There. By "Our Nig."* 1859. Ed. R. J. Ellis. Nottingham: Trent, 1998.

Wright, Charles. *The Wig, A Mirror Image*. New York: Farrar, Straus, and Giroux, 1966.

Wright, Richard. *Black Boy*. 1945; New York: Harper and Row, 1966.

    Eight Men. Cleveland: World, 1961.

    Lawd Today! New York: Walkers and Co., 1963.

    The Long Dream. New York: Doubleday, 1958.

    Native Son. New York: Harper and Brothers, 1940.

    The Outsider. New York: Harper and Brothers, 1953.

    Rite of Passage. New York: HarperCollins, 1994.

    Savage Holiday. New York: Avon Books, 1954.

    Uncle Tom's Children. New York: Harper and Brothers, 1938.

Wright, Richard. *How "Bigger" Was Born*. New York: Harper, 1940 (pamphlet).

    "Blueprint for Negro Writing." *New Challenge II* (Fall 1937): 53–65.

    "Rascoe-Baiting." *The American Mercury* 50 (July 1940): 376–377.

X, Malcolm with Alex Haley. *The Autobiography of Malcolm X*. London: Hutchinson, 1966.

Yerby, Frank. *Foxes of Harrow*. 1946; New York: Dial, 1947.

    "How and Why I Write the Costume Novel." *Harper's Magazine* (October 1959): 145–150.

Young, Al. *Snakes*. New York: Holt Rinehart and Winston, 1970.

Secondary works

Aaron, Daniel. *Writers on the Left*. New York: Avon, 1965.

Abbandonato, Linda. "Rewriting the Heroine's Story in The Color Purple." *Alice Walker: Critical Perspectives Past and Present*. Ed. Henry Louis Gates and K. Anthony Appiah. New York: Amistad, 1993. 296–308.

Adeleke, Joseph Ajibola. "Feminism, Black Feminism and the Dialectics of Womanism." *Critical Essays on the Novel in Francophone Africa*. Ed. Aduke Adebayo. Ibadan: AMD Publishers, 1996. 21–36.

Albert, Richard N., ed. *From Blues to Bop: A Collection of Jazz Fiction*. Baton Rouge: Louisiana State University Press, 1990.

Allan, Tuzyline Jita. "*The Color Purple*: A Study of Walker's Womanist Gospel." *Womanist and Feminist Aesthetics: A Comparative Review*. Athens: Ohio University Press, 1995. 69–94.

"Introduction: Decoding Womanist Grammar of Difference." *Womanist and Feminist Aesthetics: A Comparative Review*. Athens: Ohio University Press, 1995. 1–17.

"Womanism Revisited: Women and the (Ab)use of Power in *The Color Purple*." *Feminist Nightmares: Women at Odds*. Ed. Susan Ostrov Weisser and Jennifer Fleischner. New York: New York University Press, 1994. 88–105.

Amritjit Singh, ed. *Postcolonial Theory and the United States: Race, Ethnicity, and Literature*. Jackson: University Press of Mississippi, 2000.

Anatol, Giselle Liza. "'I Going Away, I Going Home': Mothers and Motherlands in Paule Marshall's *Brown Girl, Brownstones*" in *Mango Season: Caribbean Women's Writing* 13.1 (Spring 2000): 43–53.

Andrews, William L. "The 1850s: The First Afro-American Literary Renaissance." *Literary Romanticism in America*, ed. William L. Andrews. Baton Rouge: Louisiana State University Press, 1981. 38–60.

"Toward a Poetics of Afro-American Autobiography." *Afro-American Literary Study in the 1990s*. Eds. Houston A. Baker, Jr. and Patricia Redmond. Chicago: University of Chicago Press, 1989. 78–90.

To Tell a Free Story: The First Century of Afro-American Autobiography, 1760–1865. Urbana: University of Illinois Press, 1986.

Antin, David. "Modernism and Postmodernism." *Boundary* 2 1 (1972). Qtd. *The New Princeton Encyclopedia of Poetry and Poetics*. Ed. Alex Preminger and T. V. F. Brogan, Princeton: Princeton University Press, 1993.

Aptheker, Herbert, ed. *Book Reviews by W. E. B. Du Bois*. Millwood, NY: Kraus-Thompson, 1977.

Arnett, Paul and Arnett, William, eds. *Souls Grown Deep: African American Vernacular Art of the South, Volume 1: The Tree Gave the Dove a Leaf*. Atlanta: Tinwood Books, 2000.

Arnold, Martin. "Books by Blacks in Top 5 Sellers." *The New York Times*, July 26, 2001.

"Coming Soon: Paperbacks That Sound like Hip-Hop." *The New York Times*, Sept. 21, 2000.

Ashcroft, Bill, Gareth Griffiths, and Helen Tiffin. *The Empire Writes Back: Theory and Practice in Post-Colonial Literatures*. New York: Routledge, 1989.

Babb, Valerie M. "William Melvin Kelley." *Afro-American Fiction Writers after 1955.* Ed. Thadious M. Davis and Trudier Harris. Detroit: Gale, 1984. 135–143.

Bailey, Guy. "Speech, Black." *Encyclopedia of Southern Culture.* Ed. Charles Reagan Witson and William Ferris. Chapel Hill: University of North Carolina Press, 1989. 194–195.

Baker, Houston Jr. *Blues, Ideology, and Afro-American Literature.* Chicago: University of Chicago Press, 1984.

Modernism and the Harlem Renaissance. Chicago: University of Chicago Press, 1987.

Bakhtin, Mikhail M. *The Dialogic Imagination: Four Essays by M. M. Bakhtin.* Ed. Michael Holquist Austin, TX: The University of Texas Press, 1981.

Speech Genres and Other Late Essays. Ed. Caryl Emerson and Michael Holquist. Austin: University of Texas Press, 1986. 10–59.

Bancaud-Maënen, Florence. *Le Roman de formation au XVIIIème siècle en Europe.* Paris: Nathan, 1998.

Barlow, William. *Looking Up at Down: The Emergence of Blues Culture.* Philadelphia: Temple University Press, 1989.

Barrett, Leonard E. Sr. *The Rastafarians: Sounds of Cultural Dissonance.* Boston: Beacon Press, 1988.

Barthes, Roland. *La Chambre claire: Note sur la photographie.* Paris: Seuil, Gallimard Cahiers du Cinéma, 1980.

Baym, Nina. *Woman's Fiction: A Guide to Novels by and about Women in America, 1820–1870.* Ithaca: Cornell University Press, 1978.

Bell, Bernard W. *The Afro-American Novel and Its Tradition.* Amherst: University of Massachusetts Press, 1987.

Bennett, Tony, ed. *Popular Fiction: Technology, Ideology, Production, Reading.* London and New York: Routledge, 1990.

Benston, Kimberly W. "Architectural Imagery and Unity in Paule Marshall's *Brown Girl, Brownstones.*" *Negro American Literature Forum.* 9:3 (Fall 1975): 67–70.

Bergman, Peter M. *The Chronological History of the Negro in America.* New York: Harper & Row, 1969.

Bernard, Emily. "What He Did for the Race." *Soundings* 80 (1997): 531–542.

Blair, Sara. "Modernism and the Politics of Culture." *The Cambridge Companion to Modernism.* Ed. Michael Levinson. Cambridge: Cambridge University Press, 1999.

Blassingame, John W. *The Slave Community: Plantation Life in the Ante-Bellum South.* New York: Oxford University Press, 1979.

Bloom, Harold. *Toni Morrison: Modern Views.* New York: Chelsea House Publishers, 1990.

Bone, Robert A. *The Negro Novel in America.* New Haven: Yale University Press, 1965.

Bontemps, Arna. Review of *The Outsider. Saturday Review* 36 (March 28, 1953): 15–16.

Boyer, Jay. *Ishmael Reed.* Boise: Boise State University Press, 1993.

Braxton, Joanne M. and Andrée Nicola McLaughlin, eds. *Wild Women in the Whirlwind: Afra-American Culture and the Contemporary Literary Renaissance.* New Brunswick: Rutgers University Press, 1990.

Brignano, Russell C. *Richard Wright: An Introduction to the Man and His Works.* Pittsburgh: University of Pittsburgh Press, 1970.

Bröck, Sabine. "Transcending the 'Loophole of Retreat': Paule Marshall's Placing of Female Generations." *Callaloo.* 10:1 (Winter 1987): 79–90.

Brooker, Peter. "Modernism Deferred: Langston Hughes, Harlem and Jazz Montage." *Locations of Literary Modernism: Region and Nation in British and American Modernist Poetry.* Ed. Alex Davis and Lee M. Jenkins. Cambridge: Cambridge University Press, 2000.

Brown, Sterling A. "Review of *God Sends Sunday.*" *Opportunity* 9 (1931): 181.

The Negro in American Fiction. 1937; Port Washington, NY: Kennikat Press, 1968.

Brown, William Wells. "A True Story of Slave Life." London *Anti-Slavery Advocate* 1.3. 1852: 23.

Bruce, D. D. *Black American Writing from the Nadir: The Evolution of a Literary Tradition, 1877–1915.* Baton Rouge: Louisiana State University Press, 1989.

Bryant, Jacqueline K. *The Foremother Figure in Early Black Women's Literature: Clothed in My Right Mind.* New York: Garland Publishing, 1999.

Bryant, J. H. *Victims and Heroes: Racial Violence in the African American Novel.* Amherst: University of Massachusetts Press, 1997.

Buff, Rachel. *Immigration and the Political Economy of Home: West Indian Brooklyn and American Indian Minneapolis, 1945–1992.* Berkeley: University of California Press, 2001.

Burt, Nancy V. and Fred L. Standley. *Critical Essays on James Baldwin.* Boston: G.K. Hall, 1988.

Byerman, Keith. *Fingering the Jagged Grain. Tradition and Form in Recent Black Fiction.* Athens: University of Georgia Press, 1985.

"Angularity: An Interview with Leon Forrest." *African American Review* 33.3 (1999). 440–442.

Campbell, Jane. *Mythic Black Fiction: The Transformation of History.* Knoxville: University of Tennessee Press, 1986.

Canaday, Nicholas. "The Antislavery Novel prior to 1852 and Hildreth's *The Slave* (1836)." *CLA Journal* 17 (1973): 175–191.

Cannon, Katie Geneva. *Katie's Canon: Womanism and the Soul of the Black Community.* New York: Continuum, 1995.

Cannon, Steve, *et al.* "A Gathering of the Tribe: A Conversation with Ishmael Reed." *Conversations with Ishmael Reed.* Ed. Bruce Dick and Amritjit Singh. Jackson: University Press of Mississippi, 1995. 361–381.

Carby, Hazel. *Reconstructing Black Womanhood: The Emergence of the Afro-American Woman Novelist.* New York: Oxford University Press, 1987.

Carroll, Rebecca. *Sugar in the Raw: Voices of Young Black Girls in America.* New York: Three Rivers Press, 1997.

Carson, Warren. "Manhood, Masculinity, and Male Bonding in *Just Above My Head.*" *Re-viewing James Baldwin: Things Not Seen.* Ed. Quentin D. Miller. Philadelphia: Temple University Press, 2000, p. 215–232.

Chernow, Barbara A., ed. *Columbia Encyclopedia.* New York: Columbia University Press, 1993.

Christian, Barbara. *Black Feminist Criticism: Perspectives on African American Women Writers.* New York: Pergamon Press, 1985.

"Alice Walker: The Black Woman Artist as Wayward." *Black Women Novelists (1950–1980).* Ed. Mari Evans. New York: Anchor Books, 1982. 457–477.

"But What Do We Think We're Doing Anyway: The State of Black Feminist Criticism(s) or My Version of a Little Bit of History." 1989. *Within the Circle: An Anthology of African American Literary Criticism from the Harlem Renaissance to the Present.* Ed. Angelyn Mitchell. Durham: Duke University Press, 1994. 499–514.

"The Race for Theory." 1987. *Within the Circle: An Anthology of African American Literary Criticism from the Harlem Renaissance to the Present.* Ed. Angelyn Mitchell. Durham: Duke University Press, 1994. 348–359.

Cohn, David L. "Review of *Native Son.*" *Atlantic Monthly* 165 (May 1940): 659–661.

Coleman, James W. *Blackness and Modernism: The Literary Career of John Edgar Wideman.* Jackson: University Press of Mississippi, 1989.

Conner, Marc. *The Asethetics of Toni Morrison: Speaking the Unspeakable.* Jackson: University Press of Mississippi, 2000.

Cooper, Wayne F. *Claude McKay: Rebel Sojouner in the Harlem Renaissance.* Baton Rouge: Louisiana State University Press, 1987.

Crouch, Stanley. "Kinships and Aginships." *The Critical Response to Ishmael Reed.* Ed. Bruce Dick. Westport: Greenwood Press, 1999. 152–155.

Cruse, Harold. *The Crisis of the Negro Intellectual.* New York: William Morrow, 1967.

Crystal, David. *The Cambridge Encyclopedia of the English Language.* New York: Cambridge University Press, 1995.

Davies, Carole Boyce. *Black Women, Writing, and Identity: Migrations of the Subject.* New York: Routledge, 1994.

Davies, Carole Boyce and Elaine Savory Fido., eds., *Out of the Kumbla: Caribbean Women and Literature.* Trenton: Africa World Press, 1994.

Davis, Allison. *Leadership, Love & Aggression.* New York: Harcourt Brace Javanovich, 1983.

Davis, Thadious. "Foreword to the 1989 Edition." *There is Confusion* by Jessie Fauset. Boston: Northeastern University Press, 1989. v–xxvi.

Davison, Carol Margaret. "'Love 'em and Lynch 'em': The Castration Motif in Gayl Jones's *Eva's Man.*" *African American Review* 29.3 (Fall 1995): 393–410.

De Lancey, Frenzella E. "Squaring the Afrocentric Circle: Womanism and Humanism in Alice Walker's *Meridian.*" *The Literary Griot* 5:1 (Spring 1993): 1–16.

Dick, Bruce. *The Critical Response to Ishmael Reed.* New York: St. Martin's Press, 1997.

Dick, Bruce and Amritjit Singh. *Conversations with Ishmael Reed.* Jackson: University Press of Mississippi, 1995.

Diedrich, Maria, Henry Louis Gates Jr., and Carl Pedersen, eds. *Black Imagination and the Middle Passage.* New York: Oxford University Press, 1999.

Diedrich, Maria, Carl Pedersen, and Justine Tally, eds. *Mapping African America. History, Narrative Formation, and the Production of Knowledge.* Hamburg: LIT Verlag, 1999.

Diedrich, Maria, and Werner Sollors. eds. *The Black Columbiad. Defining Moments in African American Literature and Culture.* Cambridge: Harvard University Press: 1994.

Dieke, Ikenna, ed. *Critical Essays on Alice Walker*. Westport: Greenwood Press, 1999.

Dixon, Chris. *African America and Haiti: Emigration and Black Nationalism in the Nineteenth Century*. Westport: Greenwood Press, 2000.

Dodson, Jualynne E. "Jarena Lee." *African American Women in America: An Historical Encyclopedia*. Vol. I. Ed. Darlene Clark Hine. Brooklyn: Carlson Publishing, Inc., 1993. 707.

Dominguez, Virginia R. *From Neighbor to Stranger: The Dilemma of Caribbean Peoples in the United States*. New Haven: Yale University Antilles Research Program, 1975.

Dubey, Madhu. *Black Women Novelists and the Nationalist Aesthetic*. Bloomington: Indiana University Press, 1994.

"'To Survive Whole': The Integrative Aims of Womanism in the *Third Life of Grange Copeland*." *African American Women Novelists and the Nationalist Aesthetic*. Bloomington: Indiana University Press, 1994. 106–125.

Du Bois, W. E. B. "Criteria of Negro Art." *Crisis* 32 (1926): 292.

"The Negro in Literature and Art." *Annals of the American Academy of Political and Social Science* (September 1913). Rpt. in *Writings*, ed. Nathan Huggins. New York: The Library of America, 1986. 862–867.

DuCille, Ann. *The Coupling Convention: Sex, Text, and Tradition in Black Women's Fiction*. New York: Oxford University Press, 1993.

Dunlea, William. "Wright's Continuing Protest." *Commonweal* 69 (October 31, 1958): 131.

Eckley, Grace. "The Awakening of Mr. Afrinnegan: Kelley's *Dunfords Travels Everywheres* and Joyce's *Finnegan's Wake*." *Obsidian* 12 (Summer 1975): 27–41.

Edwards, Brent Hayes. "Three Ways to Translate the Harlem Renaissance." *Temples for Tomorrow: Looking Back at the Harlem Renaissance*. Ed. Genevieve Fabre and Michel Feith. Bloomington: Indiana University Press, 2001. 288–313.

Fabi, M. G. *Passing and the Rise of the African American Novel*. Urbana: University of Illinois Press, 2001.

Fabre, Geneviève, and Michel Feith, eds. *Temples for Tomorrow: Looking Back at the Harlem Renaissance*. Bloomington: Indiana University Press, 2001.

Fabre, Geneviève, and Robert O'Meally, eds. *History and Memory in African American Culture*. New York: Oxford University Press, 1994.

Fabre, Michel. "Ishmael Reed's *Free-Lance Pallbearers* or the Dialectics of Shit." *Obsidian* 3.3 (Winter 1977): 5–19.

"Postmodernist Rhetoric in Ishmael Reed's *Yellow Back Radio Broke-Down*." *The Afro-American Novel Since 1960*. Ed. Peter Bruck and Wolfgang Karrer. Amsterdam: Grüner, 1982. 167–189.

Richard Wright: Books and Writers. Jackson: University Press of Mississippi, 1990.

The Unfinished Quest of Richard Wright. New York: William Morrow, 1973; Urbana: University of Illinois Press, 1993.

The World of Richard Wright. Jackson: University Press of Mississippi, 1985.

Farrison, William Edward. *William Wells Brown: Author and Reformer*. Chicago: University of Chicago Press, 1969.

"If Baldwin's Train Has Not Gone." *James Baldwin: A Critical Evaluation*. 69–81.

Favor, J. Martin. *Authentic Blackness: The Folk in the New Negro Renaissance.* Durham: Duke University Press, 1999.

Fisher, Dexter and Robert Stepto, eds. *Afro-American Literature: The Reconstruction of Instruction.* 1979; New York: PMLA, 1990.

Fleming, Cynthia Griggs. "Ruby Doris Robinson-Smith." *African American Women in America: An Historical Encyclopedia.* Vol. II. Ed. Darlene Clark Hine. Brooklyn: Carlson Publishing, Inc., 1993. 1,085–1,086.

Foster, F. S. *Written by Herself: Literary Production by African American Women, 1746–1892.* Bloomington: Indiana University Press, 1993.

Fox, Robert Elliot. *Conscientious Sorcerers: The Black Postmodernist Fiction of LeRoi Jones/Amiri Baraka, Ishmael Reed, and Samuel R. Delany.* Westport: Greenwood Press, 1987.

"Blacking the Zero: Toward a Semiotic of Neo-HooDoo." *Masters of the Drum: Black Lit/oratures across the Continuum.* Westport: Greenwood Press, 1995. 49–62.

Fraile-Marcos, Ana Maria. "'As Purple to Lavender': Alice Walker's Womanist Representation of Lesbianism." *Literature and Homosexuality.* Ed. Michael J. Meyer, Amsterdam: Rodolpi, 2000. 111–134.

Gaines, Ernest. "Miss Jane and I." *Callaloo* 1.3 (May 1978): 37–38.

Gates, Henry Louis Jr. *Figures in Black: Words, Signs and the "Racial" Self.* New York: Oxford University Press, 1987.

The Signifying Monkey: A Theory of Afro-American Literary Criticism. New York: Oxford University Press, 1988.

Introduction and Notes. Hannah Crafts, *The Bondwoman's Narrative. 1850s. Unpublished Manuscript.* Ed. Henry Louis Gates Jr. New York: Warner Books, 2002.

Introduction. *Our Nig: or, sketches from the life of a free black, in a two-story white house, North.* By Harriet E. Wilson. New York: Random House, 1983. xi–lix.

Gates, Henry Louis Jr., and K. Anthony Appiah, eds. *Toni Morrison: Critical Perspectives Past and Present.* New York: Amistad, 1993.

Richard Wright: Critical Perspectives Past and Present. New York: Amistad, 1993.

Alice Walker: Critical Perspectives Past and Present. Amistad Literary Series. New York: Amistad, 1993.

Gayle, Addison Jr. *Richard Wright: Ordeal of a Native Son.* New York: Doubleday, 1990.

The Way of the New World: The Black Novel in America. Garden City: Anchor Press/Doubleday, 1975.

Gayle, Addison Jr., ed. *The Black Aesthetic.* Garden City: Doubleday, 1971.

Geismar, Maxwell. "Growing Up in Fear's Grip." *New York Herald Tribune Book Review* (November 16, 1958): 10.

Gibson, Donald B. *The Politics of Literary Expression.* Westport, CT: Greenwood Press, 1981.

Gibson, Donald. "The Political Anatomy of Space." *James Baldwin: A Critical Evaluation.* Ed. Therman B. O'Daniel. Washington: Howard University Press, 1977. 3–18.

Gilroy, Paul. *The Black Atlantic: Modernity and Double Consciousness.* Cambridge: Harvard University Press, 1994.

Glasrud, Bruce A., and Laurie Champion. "'The Fishes and the Poet's Hands': Frank Yerby, A Black Author in White America." *Journal of American and Comparative Cultures* 23 (Winter 2000): 15–21.

Glissant, Edouard. *Caribbean Discourse: Selected Essays*. Trans. J. Michael Dash. Charlottesville: University Press of Virginia, 1989.

Gloster, Hugh M. *Negro Voices in American Fiction*. Chapel Hill: University of North Carolina Press, 1948.

Gold, Ivan. "The Spirit of Christmas Future." *The New York Times Book Review* (July 18, 1982): 9 & 21.

Goldberg, David Theo. *Racist Culture: Philosophy and the Politics of Meaning*. Cambridge: Blackwell, 1993.

Goode, Greg. "Donald Goines." *Dictionary of Literary Biography*, vol. XXXIII: *Afro-American Fiction Writers after 1955*. Detroit: Gale Research, 1984.

Govan, Sandra Y. "Speculative Fiction." *The Oxford Companion to African American Literature*. Ed. William L. Andrews, Frances Smith Foster, and Trudier Harris. New York: Oxford University Press, 1997.

Gover, Robert. "Interview with Ishamael Reed." *Black Literature Forum* 12.1 (Spring 1978): 12–19.

Graham, Maryemma. "Bearing Witness in Black Chicago: A View of Selected Fiction by Richard Wright, Frank London Brown, and Ronald Fair." *CLA Journal* 33.3 (March 1990): 291–292.

Green, Charles, and Basil Wilson. *The Struggle for Black Empowerment in New York City: Beyond the Politics of Pigmentation*. New York: Praeger, 1989.

Greene, J. Lee. *Blacks in Eden: The African American Novel's First Century*. Charlottesville: University Press of Virginia, 1996.

Grewal, Gurleen. *Circles of Sorrow, Lines of Struggle: The Novels of Toni Morrison*. Baton Rouge: Louisiana State University Press, 1998.

Griffin, Farah Jasmine. "*Who Set You Flowin'?*" *The African-American Migration Narrative*. New York: Oxford University Press, 1995.

Grimes, Dorothy. "Mariama Bâ's *So Long a Letter* and Alice Walker's *In Search of Our Mothers' Gardens*: A Senegalese and an African American Perspective on 'Womanism.'" *Global Perspectives on Teaching Literature: Shared Visions and Distinctive Visions*. Ed. Sandra Ward Lott, *et al*. Urbana: National Council of Teachers, 1993. 65–76.

Gysin, Fritz. "Centralizing the Marginal. Prologomena to a Study of Boundaries in Contemporary African American Fiction." *Race and the Modern Artist*. Ed. Heather Hathaway, Josef Jařab, and Jeffery Melnick. New York: Oxford University Press, 2003. 209–239.

——. "'Do Not Fall Asleep in Your Enemy's Dream.' John Edgar Wideman and the Predicaments of Prophecy." *Callaloo* 22.3 (Summer 1999): 623–628.

——. "From 'Liberating Voices' to 'Metathetic Ventriloquism.' Boundaries in Recent African American Jazz Fiction." *Callaloo* 25.1 (Winter 2002): 274–287.

——. "Predicaments of Skin: Boundaries in Recent African American Fiction." *The Black Columbiad. Defining Moments in African American Literature and Culture*. Ed. Maria Diedrich and Werner Sollors. Cambridge: Harvard University Press, 1994. 286–297.

Gysin, Fritz, and Christopher Mulvey, eds. *Black Liberation in the Americas*. Hamburg: LIT Verlag, 2001.

Hakutani, Yoshinobu. *Richard Wright and Racial Discourse*. Columbia: University of Missouri Press, 1996.

Haley, Alex. "Black History, Oral History, and Genealogy." *Oral History: An Interdisciplinary Anthology*. Ed. David K. Dunaway and Willa K. Baum. Nashville: American Association for State and Local History, 1984.

Hall, Stuart, "Notes on Deconstructing 'the Popular.'" *People's History and Socialist Theory*. Ed. Raphael Samuel. London: Routledge, 1981.

Hamilton, Thomas. "Apology," *Anglo-African Magazine. Volume 1 – 1859*. New York: Arno Press and the New York Times, 1968.

Hansberry, Lorraine. "Review of *The Outsider*." Freedom 14 (April 1953): 7.

Harper, Philip Brian. *Framing the Margins. The Social Logic of Postmodern Culture*. New York: Oxford University Press, 1994.

Harris, Trudier. *Black Women in the Fiction of James Baldwin*. Knoxville: University of Tennessee Press, 1985.

Fiction and Folklore: The Novels of Toni Morrison. Knoxville: The University of Tennessee Press, 1994.

"From Victimization to Free Enterprise: Alice Walker's *The Color Purple*." *Studies in American Fiction* 14 Spring 1986: 1–17.

"On *The Color Purple*, Stereotypes and Silence." *Black American Literature Forum* 18 (Winter 1984): 155–61.

Hassan, Ihab. *The Dismemberment of Orpheus: Toward a Postmodern Literature*. Madison: University of Wisconsin Press, 1971.

Paracriticisms: Seven Speculations on the Times. Urbana: Indiana University Press, 1975.

The Postmodern Turn: Essays in Postmodern Theory and Culture. Columbus: Ohio State University Press, 1987.

Henke, Holger. *The New Americans: The West Indian Americans*. Westport, CT: Greenwood Press, 2001.

Henry, Joseph. "A MELUS Interview: Ishmael Reed." *Conversations with Ishmael Reed*. Ed. Bruce Dick and Amritjit Singh. Jackson: University Press of Mississippi, 1995: 205–218.

Hernton, Calvin C. *The Sexual Mountain and Black Women Writers: Adventures in Sex, Literature and Real Life*. New York: Anchor Press, 1987.

Herzog, Kristin. *Women, Ethnics, and Exotics*. Knoxville: University of Tennessee Press, 1983.

Hicks, Granville. "The Portrait of a Man Searching." *New York Times Book Review* (March 22, 1953): 1, 35.

"The Power of Richard Wright." *Saturday Review* 41 (October 18, 1958): 13, 65.

Hite, Molly. "Romance, Marginality, Matrilineage: *The Color Purple*." *The Color Purple*. Model Critical Interpretations Series. Ed. Harold Bloom. Philadelphia: Chelsea House Publishers, 2000. 89–105.

hooks, bell. *Black Looks: Race and Representation*. Boston: South End Press, c. 1992.

Yearning: Race, Gender, and Cultural Politics. Boston: South End Press, 1990.

"Writing the Subject: Reading *The Color Purple*." *The Color Purple*. Model Critical Interpretations Series. Ed. Harold Bloom. Philadelphia: Chelsea House Publishers, 2000. 53–66.

Hoover, Paul. "Pair of Figure for Eshu: Doubling of Consciousness in the Work of Kerry James Marshall and Nathaniel Mackey." *Callaloo* 23.2 (Spring 2000): 728–748.

Howard, Lillie P., ed. *Alice Walker and Zora Neale Hurston: The Common Bond*. Westport, CN: Greenwood Press, 1993.

Howe, Irving. "Realities and Fictions." *Partisan Review* 26 (Winter 1959): 133–134.

Huggins, Nathan Irvin. *Harlem Renaissance*. New York: Oxford University Press, 1971.

Hughes, Langston. Review of *Blues: An Anthology*. By W. C. Handy. *Opportunity* (August 1926).

Hull, Akasha Gloria. *Soul Talk: The New Spirituality of African American Women*. Rochester, VT: Inner Traditions, 2001.

Humez, Jean. *Gifts of Power: The Writings of Rebecca Cox Jackson, Black Visionary, Shaker Eldress*. Amherst: University of Massachusetts Press, 1981.

"Rebecca Cox Jackson." *African American Women in America: A Historical Encyclopedia*. Vol. I. Ed. Darlene Clark Hine. Brooklyn: Carlson Publishing, Inc., 1993. 626–627.

Hutcheon, Linda. *A Poetics of Postmodernism*. New York: Routledge, 1988.

Hutchinson, George. *The Harlem Renaissance in Black and White*. Cambridge: Harvard University Press, 1995.

"Subject to Disappearance: Interracial Identity in Nella Larsen's *Quicksand*." *Temples for Tomorrow: Looking Back at the Harlem Renaissance*. Ed. Genevieve Fabre and Michel Feith. Bloomington: Indiana University Press, 2001. 177–192.

Jablon, Madelyn. *Black Metafiction. Self-Consciousness in African American Literature*. Iowa City: University of Iowa Press, 1997.

Jahn, Janheinz. *A History of Neo-African Literature*. New York: Grove, 1968.

James, Rotimi. "In the Market for Romance." *Black Enterprise* (Dec 1996): 62.

"Womanism and Feminism in African Letters: A Theoretic Perspective. *The Literary Criterion* 25:2 (1990): 25–35.

James, Stanlie M., and Abena P. A. Busia, eds. *Theorizing Black Feminisms: The Visionary Pragmatism of African American Women*. New York: Routledge, 1993.

James, Winston. *Holding Aloft the Banner of Ethiopia: Caribbean Radicalism in Early Twentieth-Century America*. New York: Verso, 1998.

Jameson, Fredric R. *Postmodernism, or, the Cultural Logic of Late Capitalism*. Durham: Duke University Press, 1991.

Jones, Gayl. *Liberating Voices. Oral Tradition in African American Literature*. Cambridge: Harvard University Press, 1991.

Joyce, Joyce Ann. *Richard Wright's Art of Tragedy*. Iowa City: University of Iowa Press, 1986.

Juncker, Clara. "Womanizing Theory." *American Studies in Scandinavia* 30.2 (1998: 43–49.

Katz, William Loren, ed. *Flight From the Devil: Six Slave Narratives*. Trenton: Africa World Press, 1996.

Kent, George. *Blackness and the Adventure of Western Culture*. Chicago: Third World Press, 1972.

King, Deborah K. "Multiple Jeopardy, Multiple Consciousness: The Context of a Black Feminist Ideology." *Words of Fire: An Anthology of African American*

Feminist Thought. Ed. Beverly Guy-Sheftall. New York: The New Press, 1995. 294–317.

Kinnamon, Keneth. *The Emergence of Richard Wright: A Study in Literature and Society.* Urbana: University of Illinois Press, 1973.

"James Baldwin." *American Writers.* Ed. Leonard Unger. New York: Scribner, 1974. 47–71.

Klevan, Miriam. *The West Indian Americans.* New York: Chelsea House Publishers, 1990.

Köhler, Michael. "Postmodernismus': Ein begriffsgeschichtlicher Überblick." *Postmodernism in American Literature: A Critical Anthology.* Ed. Manfred Pütz and Peter Freese. Darmstadt: Thesen Verlag, 1984. 3–5.

Korda, Michael. *Making the List: A Cultural History of the American Bestseller.* New York: Barnes & Noble, 2001.

Krasny, Michael. "Pyrotechnic Amulets: 'The Terrible Twos.'" *San Franciso Review of Books* (January–February, 1983): 10 & 14.

Kubitschek, Missy Dehn. *Claiming the Heritage: African-American Women Novelists and History.* Jackson and London: University Press of Mississippi, 1991.

Kuenz, Jane. "The Face of America: Performing Race and Nation in Jessie Fauset's *There Is Confusion.*" *Yale Journal of Criticism* 12 (1999): 89–111.

Labbe, Theola. "Black Books in the House." *Publishers Weekly.* Dec. 11, 2000.

Lange, Art, and Nathaniel Mackey, eds. *Moment's Notice: Jazz in Poetry and Prose.* Minneapolis: Coffee House Press, 1993.

Lauret, Maria. *Alice Walker.* New York: St. Martin's Press, 2000.

Lee, A. Robert. *Designs of Blackness. Mappings in the Literature and Culture of Afro-America.* London: Pluto Press, 1998.

LeSeur, Geta. *Ten is the Age of Darkness: The Black Bildungsroman.* Columbia and London: University of Missouri Press, 1995.

Levinson, Michael, ed. *The Cambridge Companion to Modernism.* Cambridge: Cambridge University Press, 1999.

Lewis, David Levering. *When Harlem Was in Vogue.* New York: Vintage/Random House, 1982.

Lewis, Jan Ellen, and Peter S. Onuf, eds. *Sally Hemings and Thomas Jefferson: History, Memory, and Civic Culture.* Charlottesville: University Press of Virginia, 1999.

Lidell, Janice Lee, and Yakini Belinda Kemp, eds. *Arms Akimbo: Africana Women in Contemporary Literature.* Gainesville: University Press of Florida, 1999.

Lock, Helen. "'A Man's Story is his Gris-gris': Ishmael Reed's Neo-HooDoo Aesthetic and the African-American Tradition." *South Central Review* 10.1 (Spring 1993): 67–77.

Lodge, David. *The Modes of Modern Writing: Metaphor, Metonymy, and the Typology of Modern Literature.* London: Edward Arnold, 1977.

Logan, R. W. *The Negro in American Life and Thought: The Nadir, 1877–1901.* New York: Dial, 1954.

Loggins, Vernon. *The Negro Author: His Development In America.* New York: Columbia University Press, 1931.

Lorde, Audre. "Uses of the Erotic: The Erotic as Power." *Sister Outsider: Essays & Speeches.* Freedom, CA: Crossing Press, 1984. 53–59.

Lowe, John. *Jump At the Sun: Zora Neale Hurston's Cosmic Comedy.* Urbana: University of Illinois Press, 1994.

Ludwig, Sämi. *Concrete Language: Intercultural Communication in Maxine Hong Kingston's The Woman Warrior and Ishmael Reed's Mumbo Jumbo.* New York: Peter Lang, 1996.

Lyotard, Jean-François. *La Condition postmoderne.* Paris: Minuit, 1979. *The Postmodern Condition.* Trans. Geoffrey Bennington and Brian Massumi. Minneapolis: University of Minnesota Press, 1984.

McCabe, Tracy. "The Multifaceted Politics of Primitivism in Harlem Renaissance Writing." *Soundings* 80 (1997): 475–497.

McDowell, Deborah E. "Introduction: Regulating Midwives." *Plum Bun: A Novel Without a Moral.* Ed. Jessie Redmon Fauset. Boston: Beacon Press, 1990. x–xxxiii.

"New Directions for Black Feminist Criticism." *Within the Circle: An Anthology of African American Literary Criticism from the Harlem Renaissance to the Present.* Ed. Angelyn Mitchell. Durham: Duke University Press, 1994. 429–441.

"A Novel with a Moral." *New York Age* (September 4, 1926): 1.

McDowell, Deborah E., and Arnold Rampersad, eds. *Slavery and the Literary Imagination.* Baltimore: Johns Hopkins University Press, 1987.

McGee, Patrick. *Ishmael Reed and the Ends of Race.* New York: St. Martin's Press, 1997.

"From Legba to PaPa LaBas: New World Metaphysical Self/Re-Fashioning in Ishmael Reed's *Mumbo Jumbo.*" *The African Diaspora: African Origins and New World Identities.* Ed. Isidore Okpewho, *et al.* Bloomington: Indiana University Press, 1999. 350–366.

McHale, Brian. *Constructing Postmodernism.* London: Routledge, 1992. *Postmodernist Fiction.* London: Methuen, 1987.

McKay, Nellie. *Critical Essays on Toni Morrison.* Boston: G. K. Hall, 1989.

Mackey, Nathaniel. *Discrepant Engagement. Dissonance, Cross-Culturality, and Experimental Writing.* New York: Cambridge University Press, 1993.

Madden, David, ed. *Proletarian Writers of the Thirties.* Carbondale: Southern Illinois University Press, 1968.

Major, Clarence. *Juba to Jive: A Dictionary of African-American Slang.* New York: Penguin Books, 1994.

Maretti, Franco. *The Way of the World: The Bildungsroman in European Culture.* London: Verso, 1987.

Margolies, Edward. *Native Sons: A Critical Study of Twentieth-Century Negro American Authors.* New York: Lippincott, 1968.

Marshal, Brenda K. *Teaching the Postmodern. Fiction and Theory.* New York: Routledge, 1992.

Marshall, Paule. "From the Poets in the Kitchen." *Callaloo.* 6:2 (Spring-Summer (1983): 22–30.

Martin, Reginald. *Ishmael Reed and the New Black Aesthetic Critics.* New York: St. Martin's Press, 1988.

Matus, Jill. *Toni Morrison: Contemporary World Writers.* Manchester: Manchester University Press, 1998.

Maxwell, William. *New Negro / Old Left: African-American Writing and Communism Between the Wars.* New York: Columbia University Press, 1999.

Mayer, Henry. *All on Fire: William Lloyd Garrison and the Abolition of Slavery.* New York: St. Martin's Press, 1998.

Middleton, Davis. *Toni Morrison: Contemporary Criticism.* New York: Garland, 1997.

Miller, Floyd J. Introduction. *Blake; or the Huts of America.* By Martin R. Delany. Boston: Beacon Press, 1970. xi–xxv.

Miller, Quentin D., ed. *Reviewing James Baldwin: Things Not Seen.* Philadelphia: Temple University Press, 2000.

Mills, Charles W. *The Racial Contract.* Ithaca: Cornell University Press, 1997.

Minzeheimer, Bob. "Slave's Novel Sparks Historic Search for Its Author." *USA Today* Mar. 26, 2002: 9B.

Morrison, Toni. "Rootedness: The Ancestor as Foundation." *Black Women Writers 1950–1980: A Critical Evaluation.* Ed. Mari Evans. New York: Anchor Books, 1984.

"Unspeakable Things Unspoken: The Afro-American Presence in American Literature." *Michigan Quarterly Review* (Winter 1989): 1–34.

Mvuyekure, Pierre-Damien. "Ishmael Reed." *Contemporary African American Novelists: A Bio-Bibliographical Critical Sourcebook.* Ed. Emanuel Nelson. Westport: Greenwood Press, 1999. 391–400.

Myrdal, Gunnar. *An American Dilemma: The Negro Problem and Modern Democracy.* New York: Harper & Row, 1944.

Naylor, Paul, ed. *Nathaniel Mackey: A Special Issue. Callaloo.* 23.2 (Spring 2000).

Nazareth, Peter. *In the Trickster Tradition: The Novels of Andrew Salkey, Francis Ebejar, and Ishmael Reed.* London: Bogle L'Ouverture Press, 1994.

"An Interview with Ishmael Reed." *Conversations with Ishmael Reed.* Ed. Bruce Dick and Amritjit Singh. Jackson: University Press of Mississippi, 1995. 181–195.

Nelson, Anne. "Rock-A-Bye Niño: Confessions of a White Mother with a Brown Caregiver." *Mother Jones* 16.3 (May/June 1991): 40–42, 72–74.

Nelson, Emanuel S., ed. *Contemporary African American Novelists. A Bio-Bibliographical Sourcebook.* Westport, CT: Greenwood Press, 1999.

Nielsen, Aldon Lynn. *Black Chant: Languages of African-American Postmodernism.* New York: Cambridge University Press, 1997.

Nicholls, David G. *Conjuring the Folk: Forms of Modernity in African America.* Ann Arbor: University of Michigan Press, 2000.

O'Brien, John. "Alice Walker: An Interview." *Alice Walker: Critical Perspectives Past and Present.* Ed. Henry Louis Gates and Kwame Anthony Appiah. Amistad Literary Series. New York: Amistad, 1993. 326–346.

O'Brien Hokanson, Robert. "Jazzing It Up: The Be-Bop Modernism of Langston Hughes." *Mosaic* 31.4 (1998): 61–82.

O'Daniel, Thurman. *James Baldwin: A Critical Evaluation.* Washington, DC: Howard University Press, 1977.

Oates, Joyce Carol. "A Quite Moving and Very Traditional Celebration of Love." *Critical Essays on James Baldwin.* Ed. Fred L. Standley and Nancy V. Burt. Boston: G.K. Hall, 1988. 158–61.

Ogunyemi, Chikwenye Okonjo. "Womanism: The Dynamics of the Contemporary Black Female Novel in English." *Signs* 11:1 (Autumn 1985): 63–80.

Olney, James. "'I Was Born': Slave Narratives, Their Status as Autobiography and as Literature." *The Slave's Narrative.* Ed. Charles Davis and Henry Louis Gates. New York: Oxford University Press, 1985.

Osborne, Gwendolyn. "The Legacy of Ghetto Pulp Fiction." *Black Issues Book Review*, Sept. 2001.

Osofsky, Gilbert. *Puttin' On Ole Massa: Slave Narratives of Henry Bibb, William Wells Brown, and Solomon Northup*. New York: Harper and Row, 1969.

Otten, Terry. *The Crime of Innocence in Toni Morrison's Fiction*. Columbia: University of Missouri Press, 1989.

Pack, Robert, and Jay Parini, eds. *American Identities: Contemporary Multicultural Voices*. Hanover, NH: Middlebury College Press, 1994.

Page, Philip. *Dangerous Freedom: Fusion and Fragmentation in Toni Morrison's Novels*. Jackson: University Press of Mississippi, 1995.

Painter, Nell Irvin. "Martin R. Delany: Elitism and Black Nationalism." *Black Leaders of The Nineteenth Century*. Ed. Leon Litwack and August Meier. Urbana: University of Illinois Press, 1988. 149–171.

"Sojourner Truth." *African American Women in America: An Historical Encyclopedia*. Vol. II. Ed. Darlene Clark Hine. Brooklyn: Carlson Publishing, Inc., 1993. 1,172–1,176.

Palmer, Ransford W. *Pilgrims from the Sun: West Indian Migration to America*. New York: Twayne Publishers, 1995.

Patterson, Anita. "Jazz, Realism, and the Modernist Lyric: The Poetry of Langston Hughes." *Modern Language Quarterly* 61.4 (2000): 651–682.

Patton, Venetria K. *Women in Chains: The Legacy of Slavery in Black Women's Fiction*. Albany: State University of New York Press, 2000.

Payant, Katherine B., ed. *Immigrant Experience in North American Literature: Carving Out a Niche*. Westport, CT: Greenwood Press, 1999.

Peterson, Nancy. *Toni Morrison: Critical and Theoretical Approaches*. Baltimore: The John Hopkins University Press, 1997.

Petry, Ann. "The Novel as Social Criticism." *Call and Response: The Riverside Anthology of the African American Literary Tradition*. Ed. Patricia Liggins Hill, et al. Boston: Houghton Mifflin Company, 1998. 1,114–1,119.

Pfeiffer, Kathleen. Introduction. *Nigger Heaven*. By Carl Van Vechten. Urbana: University of Illinois Press, 2000. ix–xxxix.

Pinckney, Darryl. "Blues for Mr. Baldwin." *Critical Essays on James Baldwin*. Ed. Fred L. Standley and Nancy V. Burt. Boston: G.K. Hall, 1988. 161–166.

Plasa, Carl, and Betty J. Ring, eds. *The Discourse of Slavery: Aphra Behn to Toni Morrison*. London and New York: Routledge, 1994.

Porter, Horace. *Stealing the Fire: The Art and Protest of James Baldwin*. Middletown, CT: Wesleyan University Press, 1990.

Potts, Howard E. *A Comprehensive Name Index for the American Slave*. Westport, CT: Greenwood Press, 1997.

Powell J., Richard "Art History and Black Memory: Toward a Blues Aesthetic." *The Jazz Cadence of American Culture*. Ed. Robert G. O'Meally. New York: Columbia University Press, 1998. 182–195.

Powell J., Richard, ed. *The Blues Aesthetic and Modernism*. Washington, DC: Washington Project for the Arts, 1989.

Pratt, Louis. *James Baldwin*. Boston: Twayne Publishers, 1978.

Preminger, Alex, and T. V. F. Brogan, eds. *The New Princeton Encyclopedia of Poetry and Poetics*. Princeton: Princeton University Press, 1993.

Prescott, Orville. Review of *The Outsider. New York Times* (March 18, 1953): 29.

Rampasad, Arnold. "Langston Hughes and Approaches to Modernism in the Harlem Renaissance." *The Harlem Renaissance: Revaluations.* Ed. Amritjit Singh, William S. Shiver, and Stanley Brodwin. New York: Garland, 1989. 49–71.

Rascoe, Burto. "Negro Novel and White Reviewers." *The American Mercury* 50 (May 1940): 113–116.

Raynaud, Claudine. *Toni Morrison: L'Esthétique de la survie.* Paris: Belin, 1996.

Redding, Saunders. "The Way It Was." *New York Times Book Review* (October 26, 1958): 4, 38.

Redding, J. Saunders. *To Make a Poet Black.* Chapel Hill: University of North Carolina Press, 1939.

Reed, Linda. "Fannie Lou Hamer." *African American Women in America: An Historical Encyclopedia.* Vol. I. Ed. Darlene Clark Hine. Brooklyn: Carlson Publishing, Inc., 1993. 518–520.

Rhodes, Jewell Parker. *Free Within Ourselves: Fiction Lessons for Black Authors.* New York: Main Street Books, 1999.

Richardson, Marilyn. "Preface." *Maria W. Stewart: America's First Black Woman Political Writer, Essays and Speeches.* Bloomington: Indiana University Press, 1987. xiii–xvii.

Rigney, Barbara. *The Voices of Toni Morrison.* Columbus: Ohio State University Press, 1991.

Roberts, John W. "James Baldwin," *Dictionary of Literary Biography*, Vol. 33, Detroit: Gale Group Publishing, 1989. 3–16.

Robinson, Cedric. *Black Marxism: The Making of the Black Radical Tradition.* London: Zed, 1983.

Rodgers, Lawrence R. *Canaan Bound: The African-American Great Migration Novel.* Urbana: University of Illinois Press, 1997.

Rowley, Hazel. *Richard Wright: The Life and Times.* New York: Henry Holt, 2001.

Rushdy, Ashraf H. A. *Neo-Slave Narratives: Studies in the Social Logic of a Literary Form.* New York: Oxford University Press, 1999.

  Remembering Generations: Race and Family in Contemporary African American Fiction. Chapel Hill and London: University of North Carolina Press, 2001.

  "Ishmael Reed's Neo-HooDoo Slave Narrative." *Narrative* 2.2 (May 1994): 112–139.

  "Neo-Slave Narratives." *The Oxford Companion to African American Literature.* Ed. William L. Andrews, Trudier Harris, and Frances Smith Foster. New York: Oxford University Press, 1997.

  "Reading Black, White, and Gray in 1968: The Origins of the Contemporary Narrative of Slavery." *Criticism on the Color Line: Desegregating American Literary Studies.* Ed. Henry B. Wonham. New Brunswick: Rutgers University Press, 1996.

  "'Relate Sexual to Historical': Race, Resistance, and Desire in Gayl Jones's *Corregidora.*" *African American Review* 34.2 (Summer 2000): 273–297.

Rutledge, Gregory E. "Futurist Fiction & Fantasy: The *Racial* Establishment." *Callaloo* 24.1 (2001): 236–252.

Sallis, James. *Ash of Stars: On the Writings of Samuel R. Delany.* Jackson, MS: University Press of Mississippi, 1996.

Saunders, James Robert. "Womanism as the Key to Understanding Zora Neale Hurston's *Their Eyes Were Watching God* and Alice Walker's *The Color Purple*." *The Hollins Critic* 25:4 (Oct. 1988): 1–11.

Scanlon, Larry. "'Death is a Drum': Rhythm, Modernity, and the Negro Poet Laureate." *Music and the Racial Imagination*. Ed. Ronald Radano and Philip V. Bohlman. Chicago: University of Chicago Press, 2000.

Schmitz, Neil. "Neo-HooDoo: The Experimental Fiction of Ishmael Reed." *Twentieth-Century Literature*. (April 1974): 126–140.

Schöpp, Joseph C. "'Riding Bareback, Backwards Through a Wood of Words': Ishmael Reed's Revision of the Slave Narrative." *Historiographic Metafiction in Modern American and Canadian Literature*. Ed. Bernd Engler and Kurt Miller. Germany: Ferdinand Schöningh, 1994. 267–278.

Scruggs, Charles. *Sweet Home: Invisible Cities in the Afro-American Novel*. Baltimore: John Hopkins University Press, 1993.

Silet, Charles L. P. *The Critical Response to Chester Himes*. Westport, CT: Greenwood Press, 1999.

Simmons, Philip E. *Deep Surfaces. Mass Culture and History in Postmodern American Fiction*. Athens: University of Georgia Press, 1997.

Simson, Rennie. "Christianity: Hypocrisy and Honesty in the Afro-American Novel of the Mid-19th Century." *University of Dayton Review* 15.3 (1982): 11–16.

Singh, Amritjit. *The Novels of the Harlem Renaissance: Twelve Black Writers, 1923–33*. University Park: Pennsylvania State University Press, 1976.

Smith, Barbara. "Toward a Black Feminist Criticism." 1977. *African American Literary Theory: A Reader*. Ed. Winston Rapier. New York: New York University Press, 2000. 132–146.

Smith, V. *Self-Discovery and Authority in Afro-American Narrative*. Cambridge: Harvard University Press, 1987.

Smith, Valerie. "Gender and Afro-Americanist Literary Theory and Criticism." 1988. *Within the Circle: An Anthology of African American Literary Criticism from the Harlem Renaissance to the Present*. Ed. Angelyn Mitchell. Durham: Duke University Press, 1994. 482–498.

Soitos, Stephen. *The Blues Detective: A Study of African American Detective Fiction*. Amherst: University of Massachusetts Press, 1996.

Sollors, Werner. *Neither Black Nor White Yet Both: Thematic Explorations of Interracial Literature*. New York: Oxford University Press, 1997.

Starling, Marion Wilson. *The Slave Narrative: Its Place in American History*. Washington, DC: Howard University Press, 1988.

Stepto, Robert B. *From Behind the Veil: A Study of Afro-American Narrative*. Urbana: University of Illinois Press, 1979.

Stone, Albert E. *The Return of Nat Turner: History, Literature and Cultural Politics in Sixties America*. Athens and London: University of Georgia Press, 1992.

Stowe, Harriet Beecher. *Uncle Tom's Cabin; or, Life among the Lowly*. Boston: John P. Jewett and Company; Cleveland: Jewett, Proctor & Worthington, 1852.

Sundquist, Eric J. *The Hammers of Creation: Folk Culture in Modern African-American Fiction*. Athens: University of Georgia Press, 1992.

"The Literature of the Literature of Slavery and African American Culture." *The Cambridge History of American Literature*. Vol. 2: 1820–1865. Ed. Sacvan

Bercovitch and Cyrus R. K. Patell. Cambridge: Cambridge University Press, 1995. 239–328.

Sy, Marieme. "Dream and Language in *Dunfords Travels Everywheres*." *CLA Journal* 25, 4 (June 1982): 458–467.

Sylvander, Carolyn Wedin. *Jessie Redmon Fauset, Black American Writer*. New York: Whitston, 1981.

Tate, Claudia. *Black Women Writers at Work*. New York: Continuum, 1983.

    Domestic Allegories of Political Desire: The Black Heroine's Text at the Turn of the Century. New York: Oxford University Press, 1992.

    Psychoanalysis and Black Novels: Desire and the Protocols of Race. New York: Oxford University Press, 1998.

    "Reshuffling the Deck; Or, (Re)Reading Race and Gender in Black Women's Writing." *Tulsa Studies in Women's Literature* 7:1 (Spring 1988): 128.

Tate, Gayle T. "Zilpha Elaw." *African American Women in America: A Historical Encyclopedia*. Vol. I. Ed. Darlene Clark Hine. Brooklyn: Carlson Publishing, Inc., 1993. 388–389.

Taylor, Yuval. *An Anthology of Classic Slave Narratives. Volume One 1770–1849. Volume Two. 1849–1866*. Edinburgh: Payback Press, 1999.

Taylor-Guthrie, Danielle. *Conversations with Toni Morrison*. Jackson: University Press of Mississippi, 1994.

Towers, Robert. "Good Men Are Hard to Find." *The New York Times Book Review* 29.13 (August 12, 1982): 35–36.

Tracy, Steven C. *Langston Hughes and the Blues*. Urbana: University of Illinois Press, 1988.

    "The Devil's Son-In-Law and *Invisible Man*." *MELUS* 15.3 (Fall 1988): 47–64.

Tracy, Steven C., ed. *Write Me a Few of Your Lines: A Blues Reader*. Amherst: University of Massachusetts Press, 1999.

Trotter, David. "The Modernist Novel." *The Cambridge Companion to Modernism*. Ed. M. Levinson. Cambridge: Cambridge University Press, 1999.

Trouillot, Michel-Rolph. *Silencing the Past: Power and the Production of History*. Boston: Beacon Press, 1995.

Van Deburg, Williams L. *Slavery and Race in American Popular Culture*. Madison: University of Wisconsin Press, 1984.

    "No Mere Mortals: Black Slaves and Black Power in American Literature, 1967–80." *South Atlantic Quarterly* 83 (1984): 297–311.

Viswanathan, Meera, and Evangelina Mancikam. "Is Black Woman to White as Female is to Male? Restoring Alice Walker's Womanist Prose to the Heart of Feminist Literary Criticism." *Indian Journal of American Studies* 28:1–2 (1998): 15–20.

Walker, Alice, ed. *I Love Myself When I Am Laughing . . . and Then Again When I Am Looking Mean and Impressive: A Zora Neale Hurston Reader*. New York: The Feminist Press, 1979.

Wall, Cheryl. *Women of the Harlem Renaissance*. Bloomington: Indiana University Press, 1995.

Wallace, Michele. "Female Troubles: Ishmael Reed's Tunnel Vision." *The Critical Response to Ishmael Reed*. Ed. Bruce Allen Dick. Westport, CT: Greenwood Press, 1999. 183–191.

"Ishmael Reed's Female Troubles." *Invisibility Blues: From Pop to Theory*. New York: Verso, 1990. 146–154.

Washington, Mary Helen. "'The Darkened Eye Restored:' Notes Toward a Literary History of African American Women. 1987. *Within the Circle: An Anthology of African American Literary Criticism from the Harlem Renaissance to the Present*. Ed. Angelyn Mitchell. Durham: Duke University Press, 1994. 442–453.

Weems, Robert. *Desegregating the Dollar: African American Consumerism in the Twentieth Century*. New York: New York University Press, 1998.

Weisenburger, Steven. *Fables of Subversions: Satire and the American Novel, 1030–1980*. Athens: University of Georgia Press, 1995.

Werner, Craig Hansen. *Playing the Changes: From Afro-Modernism to the Jazz Impulse*. Urbana: University of Illinois Press, 1994.

West, Cornel. "Black Critics and the Pitfalls of Canon Formation," in Cornel West, *Keeping Faith: Philosophy and Race in America*. New York and London: Routledge, 1993.

Williams, Kemp. "The Metaphorical Contruction of Sexuality in *Giovanni's Room*." *Literature and Homosexuality*. Ed. Michael J. Meyer. Amsterdam: Rodolpi: 2000.

Williams, Sherley Anne. "The Lion's History: The Ghetto Writes B[l]ack." *Soundings* 76.2–3 (1993): 248.

"Some Implications of Womanist Theory." 1990. *Within the Circle: An Anthology of African American Literary Criticism from the Harlem Renaissance to the Present*. Ed. Angelyn Mitchell. Durham: Duke University Press, 1994. 515–521.

Wilson, Sharon. "A Conversation with Alice Walker." *Alice Walker: Critical Perspectives Past and Present*. Ed. Henry Louis Gates and Kwame Anthony Appiah. Amistad Literary Series. New York: Amistad, 1993. 319–325.

Winchell, Donna Haisty. *Alice Walker*. New York: Twayne Publishers, 1992.

Winslow, Henry F. "Forces of Fear." *The Crisis* 60 (June–July 1953): 381–383.

Yaffe, David. "Ellison Unbound." *The Nation*. March 4, 2002.

Yarborough, Richard. "The First-Person in Afro-American Fiction." *Afro-American Literary Study in the 1990s*. Ed. Houston A. Baker Jr. and Patricia Redmond. Chicago: University of Chicago Press, 1989. 105–121.

Yellin, Jean Fagan. "Written by Herself: Harriet Jacob's Slave Narrative," *American Literature* 53 (1981): 479–486.

Young, Mary E. *Mules and Dragons: Popular Culture Images in the Selected Writings of African-American and Chinese-American Women Writers*. Westport, CT: Greenwood Press, 1993.

Zamir, Shamoon. "The Artist as Prophet, Priest and Gunslinger: Ishmael Reed's 'Cowboy in the Boat of Ra.'" *Callaloo* 17.4 (1994). 1205–1235.

Zéphir, Flore. *Trends in Ethnic Identification Among Second-Generation Haitian Immigrants in New York City*. Westport, CT: Bergin & Garvey, 2001.

Internet sources

African American Book Club Summit.http://www.pageturner.net/Cruise/index.htm.

African American Literature Book Club. "Demographics"; http://aalbc.com/aalbcdemographics.htm.

Andrews, William L. *North American Slave Narratives, Beginnings to 1920*. Nov. 2001. http://docsouth.dsi.internet2.edu/neh/neh.html.

Blenkinsopp, Alexander J. "Gates Acquires Slave's Novel." *Harvard Crimson OnLine Edition*. Nov. 14, 2001. http://www.thecrimson.com/article.aspx?ref=160652.

Eastman, Dick "The Bondwoman's Narrative." *Ancestry.com*. Jan. 15, 2002. http://www.ancestry.com/library/view/columns/eastman/4911.asp.

Hall, Ken. *Ken' s Korner: News and Views from the World of Antiquing and Collecting*. www.go-star.com/antiquing/kens1201.htm.

Henry, Tanu T. "Rediscovery of a Lost Manuscript Rewrites Literary History." *Africana.com: Gateway to the Black World*. Jan. 15, 2002. http://www.africana.com/DailyArticles/index_20011119.htm.

Kirkpatrick, David. "Slave Woman's Life Story Unearthed After 140 Years." London *Observer*, November 11, 2001. http://www.guardian.co.uk/Archive/Article/0,4273,4296756,00.html.

Project on the History of Black Writing, University of Kansas. http://www.ku.edu/~phbw.

Theis, Ann Chambers. *Fiction Hot List 2002 – The Biggies*. http://www.overbooked.org/biggies2002.html.

INDEX

Be-Bop music/language, 206, 207, 208
Beck, Robert, 161
Bedouin Hornbook (Mackey), 150
Behn, Aphra, 25
Bell, Bernard, 1, 4
Bell, Derrick, 165
Bellamy, Edward, 40
Beloved (Morrison), 100, 101, 102, 158, 228–229
Betsey Brown (Shange), 108, 116
Beyond the Limbo Silence (Nuñez), 77
Bildungsroman, 41, 60, 108–109. *See also* coming of age novel
Bildungsroman, anti-, 114
Bildungsroman, female, 59. *See also* coming of age novel, female
The Black Aesthetic (Gayle), 30
black artist. *See also* art; writers
  artistic creation as form of call-and-response, 260
  choices available to legitimized, 257
  model for the, 58
  Neo-HooDooism and the, 205, 206, 210
  process *vs.* product focus of, 262
  role in contemporary society, 199–200
  self-perception in postmodern novel, 149–151
Black Arts/Black Aesthetic Movement, 6, 186
Black Boy (Wright), 2, 132, 158
The Blacker the Berry . . . (Thurman), 62
black feminist. *See* feminist
black folk
  blues music used to reflect, 128
  culture of, celebrated in the post-slavery novel, 46
  Renaissance era, interest in, 56
black girls. *See* black women
black identity. *See* identity, black
black inferiority, 36, 39, 65. *See also* racial equality
black men. *See also* African Americans
  bisexual used for protagonist, 199–200
  choices available to legitimized, 256
  dark-skinned, 40
  double standard for sexually active, 80
  emasculation, issues of, 56
  heroic slave model for, 25
  male bonding and liberation, 201
  masculinity issues, 201
  models of behavior for, 196
  noble African model for, 25
  relationships, bonds and barriers in, 56, 201

  self-knowledge barriers, 55
  sexuality and freedom issues of, 56
  Uncle Tom characterization, 26, 257, 259
  working-class life of, 55, 57–58
  in work of Reed, 212
black middle class. *See also* black men; black women
  blues music used to reflect, 128
  classism in, 131
  class-lines crossed in coming of age, 116
  growth effect on African American fiction, 50
  limitations accepted by women in, 128
  New Negro Renaissance, novel of the, 51
  popular fiction of the, 167
Black Nationalist approach *vs.* Neo-HooDooism, 204
blackness, 44. *See also* identity, black
Black No More (Schuyler), 62–63
"The Black Novelists: Our Turn," 89
Black Power Movement, 30, 89, 90
Blackson, Lorenzo D., 41
Black Studies programs, 3, 30, 89, 90
Black Thunder (Bontemps), 66–67
Black Woman's Era, 42
black women. *See also* African Americans; feminist; womanist
  appropriation of the body of, 93, 101
  in blues novels, 137
  blues woman as symbol, 107
  dark-skinned, 40
  as detectives, 40, 158
  of domestic novels, 42
  double standard for, 80
  female blues tradition, 130, 137
  field blacks model, 26
  friendships between, 225–226
  limitations accepted by, 128, 130
  marginalization consequences for girls, 222–223
  as professionals, 40, 42
  publishing industry and, 167
  rape as legacy, 81, 93, 94
  rape in coming of age process, 109, 115
  Reed, Ishmael, writing on, 216
  in science fiction, as protagonist, 164
  voice emergent in, 131
Black Women Novelists (Christian), 1
black women's fiction
  of the New Negro Renaissance, 54
  signifyin(g) revisions of, in works by Reed, 215

CAMBRIDGE COMPANIONS TO LITERATURE

CAMBRIDGE COMPANIONS TO CULTURE